READING
Sociology
Canadian
Perspectives

READING Sociology

Canadian Perspectives

Edited by

Lorne Tepperman
Harley Dickinson

Published in partnership with

THE CANADIAN SOCIOLOGICAL ASSOCIATION
LA SOCIÉTÉ CANADIENNE DE SOCIOLOGIE

OXFORD
UNIVERSITY PRESS

OXFORD
UNIVERSITY PRESS

70 Wynford Drive, Don Mills, Ontario M3C 1J9

www.oupcanada.com

Oxford University Press is a department of the University of Oxford.
It furthers the University's objective of excellence in research, scholarship,
and education by publishing worldwide in

Oxford   New York

Auckland   Cape Town   Dar es Salaam   Hong Kong   Karachi
Kuala Lumpur   Madrid   Melbourne   Mexico City   Nairobi
New Delhi   Shanghai   Taipei   Toronto

Oxford is a trade mark of Oxford University Press
in the UK and in certain other countries

Published in Canada
by Oxford University Press

Library and Archives Canada Cataloguing in Publication Data

Reading sociology : Canadian perspectives / edited by Lorne Tepperman and Harley Dickinson.

Includes bibliographical references.
ISBN-13: 978-0-19-542292-4
ISBN-10: 0-19-542292-9

1. Sociology—Textbooks.   I. Dickinson, Harley D., 1951– .   II. Tepperman, Lorne, 1943– .

HM586.R43 2007   301   C2006-906319-2

Cover Design: Joan Dempsey
Cover Image: Thomas Barwick/Getty Images

4 5 6 – 11 10 09

This book is printed on Forest Stewardship Council
certified paper which contains 99% post-consumer waste.
Printed in Canada

Mixed Sources
Product group from well-managed
forests, and other controlled sources
www.fsc.org Cert no. SW-COC-002358
© 1996 Forest Stewardship Council

Contents

Introduction   xiii

Contributors   xv

PART I   **What is Sociology? Theories and Research Methods   1**

Chapter 1   What Can I Do With a Sociology Degree?   3
John Goyder, Corinne Carter, Jaime Robinson, and Marina Korotkikh

Chapter 2   Reading Reflexively   7
Bruce Curtis

Chapter 3   The Value of Anecdotal Evidence   11
Stephen Harold Riggins

Chapter 4   Moral Panic and the Nasty Girl   14
Christie Barron and Dany Lacombe

Questions for Critical Thought   17

PART II   **Culture   19**

Chapter 5   The Hacker Spirit: An Interactionist Analysis of the Hacker Ideology   21
Steven Kleinknecht

Chapter 6   Short-Changed: Media Representations of Squeegeeing and Panhandling   24
Tara Carnochan

Chapter 7   Politicizing Aboriginal Cultural Tourism: The Discourse of Primitivism
in the Tourist Encounter   28
Siegrid Deutschlander and Leslie J. Miller

Chapter 8   Tattooing and Civilizing Processes: Body Modification as Self-control   31
Michael Atkinson

Chapter 9   Buddhism in the Multicultural Context of Toronto, Canada:
Local Communities, Global Networks   35
Janet McLellan

Questions for Critical Thought   38

PART III   **Socialization   41**

Chapter 10   'Even if I don't know what I'm doing, I can make it look like I know what
I'm doing': Becoming a Doctor in the 1990s   43
Brenda L. Beagan

Chapter 11   On the Assimilation of Racial Stereotypes among Black Canadian Young
              Offenders   47
              John F. Manzo and Monetta M. Bailey

Chapter 12   The Pendulum of Family Change: Comparative Life Course Transitions of
              Young Adults   51
              Barbara A. Mitchell

Chapter 13   Searching, Working, and Shopping: Is This Prolonged Youth?   55
              Rebecca Raby

Chapter 14   Duality and Diversity in the Lives of Immigrant Children: Rethinking the
              'Problem of the Second Generation' in Light of Immigrant Autobiographies   58
              Nedim Karakayali

              Questions for Critical Thought   62

PART IV   Deviance   65

Chapter 15   Resistance to Education: Self-Control and Resistance to School   67
              M. Reza Nakhaie, Robert A Silverman, and Teresa C. LaGrange

Chapter 16   Gender, Crime, and Community: An Analysis of Youth Crime in Canada   71
              Joanna C. Jacob

Chapter 17   Keeping an Eye on Crime Control Culture: The Rise of Open-street
              Closed-circuit Television Surveillance in Canada   75
              Kevin Walby

Chapter 18   Mega-security: Concepts and Context for Olympic-sized Security Networks   78
              Philip Boyle

              Questions for Critical Thought   85

PART V   Families   87

Chapter 19   Love- and Arranged-Marriage in India Today: Negotiating Adulthood   89
              Nancy S. Netting

Chapter 20   Life Cycle Events and the Creation of Transnational Ties among Second Generation
              South Indians   92
              Kara Somerville

Chapter 21   Balancing Ethnicity and Sexuality: Gay Jewish Men Seek the Same   95
              Randal F. Schnoor and Morton Weinfeld

Chapter 22   Earning and Caring   98
              Roderic Beaujot

Chapter 23   Quebec's $7/day Childcare: Some Preliminary Findings   102
              Patrizia Albanese

Chapter 24   Self-Employment as a Response to the Double Day for Women and Men
              in Canada   105
              A. Bruce Arai

              Questions for Critical Thought   108

PART VI   **Education   111**

Chapter 25   Activities and Interdependencies in the Educational Process: An Interactionist
              Approach to Student Ventures in Learning   113
              Robert Prus

Chapter 26   Polite, Well-dressed, and On Time: Secondary School Conduct Codes and the
              Production of Docile Citizens   116
              Rebecca Raby

Chapter 27   Crafting Legitimation Projects: An Institutional Analysis of Private
              Education Businesses   119
              Janice Aurini

Chapter 28   University Restructuring and the Female Liberal Arts Undergraduate: Does She
              Get 'Value for the Money' at Corporate U?   123
              Marilee Reimer and Adele Mueller

Chapter 29   Academic Paths, Aging, and the Living Conditions of Students in the
              Late Twentieth Century   126
              Arnaud Sales, Réjean Drolet, and Isabelle Bonneau

              Questions for Critical Thought   129

PART VII   **Work   131**

Chapter 30   What is Work? Looking at All Work through the Lens of Unpaid Housework   133
              Margrit Eichler and Ann Matthews

Chapter 31   How Job Information Enters and Flows through Social Networks: The Role
              of Labour Market Characteristics and Tie Strength   136
              Alexandra Marin

Chapter 32   The Use of Communication Media: A Case Study of a High-Tech Organization   139
              Anabel Quan-Haase

Chapter 33   'Knowledge Workers' and the 'New Economy': A Critical Assessment   143
              Antonie Scholtz and David W. Livingstone

              Questions for Critical Thought   147

PART VIII   **Aging   149**

Chapter 34   The Great Purge: Forced Retirement and the 'Succession Question' in
                  Canadian Sociology   151
                  David MacGregor and Thomas R. Klassen

Chapter 35   Older Women's Bodies and the Self: The Construction of Identity in Later Life   154
                  Laura Hurd Clarke

Chapter 36   Aging among Chinese Canadian Immigrants—Reflections   159
                  Neena L. Chappell

                  Questions for Critical Thought   162

PART IX   **Health   163**

Chapter 37   An Epidemic in Search of a Disease: The Construction of Sexual Dysfunction
                  as a Social Problem   165
                  Barbara L. Marshall

Chapter 38   Citizenship and Health: The Governance of 'Imported Malaria' and the Safety of
                  Anti-Malarial Drugs   168
                  Kimberly-Anne Ford

Chapter 39   The Impact of Financial Compensation on Treatment Outcomes for Chronic Pain:
                  A Test of the 'Money Matters' Thesis   172
                  David Lewis, Kevin Brazil, and Paul Krueger

Chapter 40   Where Will the Jurisdiction Fall? The Possible Regulation of Traditional Chinese
                  Medicine/Acupuncturists in Ontario   175
                  Sandy Welsh, Heather Boon, Merrijoy Kelner, and Beverley Wellman

Chapter 41   Disability: A Rose By Any Other Name? 'People-first' Language in
                  Canadian Society   178
                  Tanya Titchkosky

                  Questions for Critical Thought   182

PART X   **Inequality and Stratification   185**

Chapter 42   'Canada's Most Notorious Bad Mother': The Newspaper Coverage of the
                  Jordan Heikamp Inquest   187
                  Krista Robson

Chapter 43   Street Youth Labour Market Experiences and Crime   190
                  Stephen W. Baron

Chapter 44   Building Hope: Confronting Social Exclusion and Violence in Toronto's Black
                  Community, 2001   194
                  Grace-Edward Galabuzi

Chapter 45   Workplace Accommodation for the Disabled in the Federal Public Service:
             An Institutional Ethnography   197
             J.L. Deveau

Chapter 46   Women's Inequality in the Workplace as Framed in News Discourse:
             Refracting from Gender Ideology   200
             Amber Gazso

Chapter 47   Dispersion and Polarization of Income among Aboriginal and Non-Aboriginal
             Canadians   205
             Paul S. Maxim, Jerry P. White, Paul C. Whitehead, and Dan Beavon

             Questions for Critical Thought   209

PART XI   Sex and Gender   211

Chapter 48   'They should make it more normal': Young People's Critical Standpoints and
             the Social Organization of Sexuality Education   212
             Libby Alexander

Chapter 49   Preserving Domesticity: Reading Tupperware in Women's Changing Domestic,
             Social, and Economic Roles   215
             Susan Vincent

Chapter 50   Analyzing Women's Situated Knowledge for Menopause Construction   218
             Mary Patton

Chapter 51   Balancing Work and Caring: Midlife Women Assess their Accommodations   222
             Ann Duffy, Nancy Mandell, and Sue Wilson

             Questions for Critical Thought   225

PART XII   Immigration, Race, and Ethnicity   227

Chapter 52   Immigrant–Native Boundaries in North America and Western Europe   228
             Richard Alba

Chapter 53   What Colour is Your English?   231
             Gillian Creese and Edith Ngene Kambere

Chapter 54   Rising Low-Income Rates and the Adaptation of Canadian Immigrant Youth   234
             Paul Anisef and Kelli Phythian

Chapter 55   Poverty, Social Exclusion, and Racialized Girls and Young Women   238
             Jo-Anne Lee

Chapter 56   The Sentiment of Settlement among Some Chinese Immigrants in
             Small Towns   241
             Ho Hon Leung

             Questions for Critical Thought   244

PART XIII   Globalization   247

Chapter 57   Social Solidarity, Democracy, and Global Capitalism   249
Gordon Laxer

Chapter 58   Post-Socialist Transition and Globalization: Academic Debates in Political Surroundings   252
Ivanka Knezevic

Chapter 59   A World of Emergencies: Fear, Intervention, and the Limits of Cosmopolitan Order   256
Craig Calhoun

Chapter 60   Should I Stay or Should I Go? Investigating Resilience in British Columbia's Coastal Communities   260
Justin Page, Sandra Enns, Todd E. Malinick, and Ralph Matthews

Chapter 61   Globalization and 'Repositioning' in Coastal British Columbia   264
Ralph Matthews and Nathan Young

Questions for Critical Thought   266

PART XIV   States and Government   269

Chapter 62   Thirty Thousand Calls for Justice: The Human Rights Movement, Political Graffiti, and the Struggles over Collective Memory in Argentina   270
Erin E. Armi Kaipainen

Chapter 63   The Emerging Role of Information in Canada's Security Environment   273
Erin Kruger

Chapter 64   Feminist Representations of Women Living on Welfare: The Case of Workfare and the Erosion of Volunteer Time   277
Jacinthe Michaud

Chapter 65   The Distrustful Citizen: Theories and Observations from Small-group Settings   280
John R. Parkins

Chapter 66   Framing and Temporality in Political Cartoons: A Critical Analysis of Visual News Discourse   283
Josh Greenberg

Questions for Critical Thought   287

PART XV   **Environment   289**

Chapter 67   Automobilization and Traffic Safety   290
Arlene Tigar McLaren

Chapter 68   Dealing with Toxicity in the Risk Society: The Case of the Hamilton,
Ontario Plastic Recycling Fire   293
S. Harris Ali

Chapter 69   Constructing Environmental Identity: The Constraints of Power and
Common Sense   296
Justin Page

Chapter 70   Collective Identity in the Sustainable Consumption Movement: The Case
of *Cool Communities*   299
Miriam Padolsky

Questions for Critical Thought   302

Glossary   305

Acknowledgements   315

Introduction

This book started to take shape at a June 2004 discussion in Winnipeg between Lisa Meschino (Acquisitions Editor of Oxford University Press) and the Executive Committee of the (then) Canadian Sociological and Anthropological Association (CSAA)—now, the Canadian Sociological Association (CSA). The idea was to work together to publish a book, roughly 250 pages in length, intended for use in one- and two-term introductory sociology courses—whether at universities or community colleges—to supplement the main textbook.

The imagined book was to be organized around the major topic areas of sociology. It would include pieces selected from among the best papers submitted and chosen for presentation at the 2005 CSA Conference. Authors of the papers selected would be asked to submit a brief, readable précis of their paper (of 1000–1500 words).

The book editors would check them for quality and readability, and request speedy revisions where needed. They would assemble the revised papers into a manuscript that would be provided to the publisher in a timely fashion.

We believed then (and still believe) that many instructors of introductory sociology at Canadian colleges and universities would ask their students to read such a book, if the selection and editing were good. Such a book would introduce new Canadian sociology to undergraduate students in small, manageable pieces; and it would let professional sociologists know about some of the newer work emerging at Canadian colleges and universities. Ideally, this book would be revised every few years, to reflect new developments in Canadian sociology. All royalties would go to the CSA.

Here we are, roughly two years later, and here is the book we had imagined. The book in your hands is the result of a lengthy collaboration between the book editors and the authors of the 70 pieces it contains; and between CSA and Oxford

University Press. The book departs in only a few ways from what we originally imagined. Specifically, we have included shortened versions of papers recently published in CRS (formerly, CRSA)—the journal of the CSA—to round out some of the sections. As well, we have included five shortened versions of the honorary Porter Lectures given by winners of the CSA's annual prize for best sociological book of the year.

In preparing this book we have received wonderful co-operation from the authors of the pieces included: thank you, authors, for your patient help. More important, thank you for your insight and creativity—as revealed in the pages of this book. The reader will note that many of the included pieces are by new scholars—doctoral candidates and junior faculty members throughout Canada. The energy and imagination of our youngest sociologists gives us a great deal to look forward to in years to come.

We also received great assistance from Lorne Tepperman's Work–Study Group of 2005–6, which included Monica Beron, Maygan Jorge, Weeda Mehran, Mauve Patrontasch, Cheryl Pe, Ingrid Seo, Amy Umpleby, and Hannah Yang. They gave us undergraduate assessments of all the pieces and helped us find additional interesting journal articles in CRS. A subset of undergraduate assistants—Dana Gore, Jing Jing Zeng, Joanna Dafoe, Jessica Kuredjian, Miranda Ng, Wen Xiao, and William Boateng—one of Harley Dickinson's doctoral students and graduate student assistant—also helped by editing the published journal articles, making up discussion questions, contributing to the glossary, and drafting section introductions. Stuart Leard, another of Harley Dickinson's doctoral students and research assistants, worked closely with him and William Boateng on the final proofreading of the manuscript. Work–Study alumnus, Erik Landriault, assisted with the correspondence and administration of the project, ensuring that everything we received was reviewed and revised and nothing got lost. Special thanks are extended to Jenny Pui Shan Wong at the University of Toronto, who so carefully read and suggested improvements to the first half of the text. Anonymous professional sociologists helped by reviewing the articles we had collected and suggested what to keep and what to cut.

At Oxford University Press, Lisa Meschino stayed with us from beginning to end, making sure that we were on track. However, our greatest help at Oxford came from Developmental Editor Roberta Osborne who, with great imagination and good humour, helped us find, choose, and organize articles for the book. Roberta has been a constant source of support and encouragement; more than that, she has pitched in and helped with the hard work. Like Lisa, Roberta came out to our monthly Work–Study meetings, ate Cora's Pizza with the undergraduates, and gently prodded us all to do the right things. Finally, Jessie Coffey at Oxford University Press copy-edited the huge amount of material generated by this project, made many improvements to the content, and brought the book elegantly under control. Thank you, Roberta and Jessie. You made the birth of this book easier, and were fun to work with.

This was the first collaboration between editors Lorne Tepperman and Harley Dickinson, and like all collaborations at a distance, this one had to overcome practical difficulties. Overall, the collaboration went smoothly and pleasantly—proving that Toronto and Saskatoon are only far apart on a map.

We want to dedicate this book first, to the Canadian Sociological Association—for over forty years the CSA has been the voice of professional sociology in Canada, helping sociological researchers tell the story of Canadian society to new generations of students. In addition, we dedicate this book to our friend and colleague Jim Curtis, who passed away in May 2005. Jim was to have co-edited this book. In that way, and in countless others over his thirty-five-year career, Jim was an exemplary member of Canada's sociological community as a teacher, researcher, administrator, colleague, and friend. No one contributed more to the development of Canadian sociology. We will miss him.

Lorne Tepperman
University of Toronto

Harley Dickinson
University of Saskatchewan

Contributors

RICHARD ALBA Department of Sociology, State University of New York at Albany

PATRIZIA ALBANESE Department of Sociology, Ryerson University

LIBBY ALEXANDER Laurentian University

S. HARRIS ALI Faculty of Environmental Studies, York University

PAUL ANISEF Department of Sociology, York University

A. BRUCE ARAI Wilfrid Laurier University

MICHAEL ATKINSON Department of Sociology, McMaster University

JANICE AURINI Department of Sociology, McMaster University

MONETTA M. BAILEY Department of Sociology, University of Calgary

STEPHEN BARON Queen's University

CHRISTIE BARRON Department of Sociology, University of Calgary

BRENDA L. BEAGAN School of Occupational Therapy, Dalhousie University

RODERIC BEAUJOT Department of Sociology, University of Western Ontario

DAN BEAVON Indian and Northern Affairs, Ottawa, ON

ISABELLE BONNEAU Department of Sociology, Université de Montréal

HEATHER BOON Faculty of Pharmacy, University of Toronto

PHILIP BOYLE Department of Sociology, University of Alberta

KEVIN BRAZIL St Joseph's Health System Research Network, Hamilton, ON

CRAIG CALHOUN Social Science Research Council

TARA CARNOCHAN Department of Sociology, Queen's University

CORINNE CARTER Department of Psychology, University of Waterloo

NEENA L. CHAPPELL Centre on Aging, University of Victoria

LAURA HURD CLARKE Department of Human Kinetics, University of British Columbia

GILLIAN CREESE Department of Sociology, University of British Columbia

BRUCE CURTIS Department of Sociology and Anthropology, Carleton University

SIEGRID DEUTSCHLANDER Department of Sociology, University of Calgary

J.L. DEVEAU School of Graduate Studies, University of New Brunswick

RÉJEAN DROLET Williams School of Business, Bishop's University

ANN DUFFY Department of Sociology, Brock University

MARGRIT EICHLER Ontario Institute for Studies in Education, University of Toronto

SANDRA ENNS Department of Sociology, University of British Columbia

KIMBERLY-ANNE FORD PhD (Sociology) from Carleton University

GRACE-EDWARD GALABUZI Department of Politics, Ryerson University

AMBER GAZSO Department of Sociology, University of Alberta

JOHN GOYDER Department of Sociology, University of Waterloo

JOSH GREENBERG Department of Sociology and Anthropology, Carleton University

JOANNA C. JACOB Department of Sociology, University of Waterloo

ERIN E. ARMI KAIPAINEN Department of Sociology, Brock University

EDITH NGENE KAMBERE University of British Columbia

NEDIM KARAKAYALI Department of Sociology, University of Toronto

MERRIJOY KELNER Professor Emeritus, University of Toronto

THOMAS R. KLASSEN Department of Political Science, York University

STEVEN KLEINKNECHT Department of Sociology, McMaster University

IVANKA KNEZEVIC Department of Sociology, University of Toronto

MARINA KOROTKIKH Department of Sociology, University of Waterloo

ERIN KRUGER Department of Sociology, University of Alberta

PAUL KRUEGER St Joseph's Lifecare Centre, Brantford, ON

DANY LACOMBE Department of Sociology and Anthropology, Simon Fraser University

TERESA C. LAGRANGE Department of Sociology, Cleveland State University

GORDON LAXER Department of Sociology, University of Alberta

JO-ANNE LEE Department of Women's Studies, University of Victoria

HO HON LEUNG Department of Sociology, State University of New York at Oneonta

DAVID LEWIS Departments of Medicine and Family Medicine, McMaster University

DAVID W. LIVINGSTONE Ontario Institute for Studies in Education, University of Toronto

DAVID MACGREGOR Department of Sociology, King's University College, University of Western Ontario

ARLENE TIGAR MCLAREN Department of Sociology and Anthropology, Simon Fraser University

JANET MCLELLAN Department of Religion and Culture, Wilfrid Laurier University

TODD E. MALINICK Department of Anthropology and Sociology, University of British Columbia

NANCY MANDELL Department of Sociology, York University

JOHN F. MANZO Department of Sociology, University of Calgary

ALEXANDRA MARIN Department of Sociology, University of Toronto

BARBARA L. MARSHALL Department of Sociology, Trent University

ANN MATTHEWS Ontario Institute for Studies in Education, University of Toronto

RALPH MATTHEWS Department of Sociology, University of British Columbia

PAUL S. MAXIM Department of Sociology, University of Western Ontario

JACINTHE MICHAUD School of Women's Studies, York University

LESLIE J. MILLER Department of Sociology, University of Calgary

BARBARA A. MITCHELL Department of Sociology and Anthropology, Simon Fraser University

ADELE MUELLER Departments of Sociology and Women's Studies, St. Thomas University

M. REZA NAKHAIE Department of Sociology and Anthropology, University of Windsor

NANCY S. NETTING Sociology Unit, Irving K. Barber School of Arts and Sciences, University of British Columbia Okanagan

MIRIAM PADOLSKY Department of Sociology, University of California, San Diego

JUSTIN PAGE Department of Anthropology and Sociology, University of British Columbia

JOHN R. PARKINS Canadian Forest Service, Edmonton, AB

MARY PATTON Ontario Institute for Studies in Education, University of Toronto

KELLI PHYTHIAN Department of Sociology, University of Western Ontario

ROBERT PRUS Department of Sociology, University of Waterloo

ANABEL QUAN-HAASE Faculty of Information and Media Studies, University of Western Ontario

REBECCA RABY Department of Child and Youth Studies, Brock University

MARILEE REIMER Departments of Sociology and Women's Studies, St Thomas University

STEPHEN HAROLD RIGGINS Department of Sociology, Memorial University

JAIME ROBINSON University of Waterloo

KRISTA ROBSON Department of Sociology, Queen's University

ARNAUD SALES Department of Sociology, Université de Montréal

RANDAL F. SCHNOOR Department of Sociology, York University

ANTONIE SCHOLTZ Ontario Institute for Studies in Education, University of Toronto

ROBERT A SILVERMAN Department of Sociology, Queen's University

KARA SOMERVILLE Department of Sociology, University of Toronto

TANYA TITCHKOSKY Department of Sociology, St. Francis Xavier University

SUSAN VINCENT Department of Anthropology, St. Francis Xavier University

KEVIN WALBY Department of Sociology and Anthropology, Carleton University

MORTON WEINFELD Department of Sociology, McGill University

BEVERLEY WELLMAN Institute for Human Development, Life Course and Aging, University of Toronto

SANDY WELSH Department of Sociology, University of Toronto

JERRY P. WHITE Department of Sociology, University of Western Ontario

PAUL C. WHITEHEAD Department of Sociology, University of Western Ontario

SUE WILSON Department of Nutrition, Ryerson University

NATHAN YOUNG Department of Cell Biology and Anatomy, University of Calgary

Part I

What is Sociology?
Theories and Research Methods

Sociology is an intriguing discipline because it studies the forces that affect every aspect of our lives. On a macro scale, human interaction creates the social institutions such as economy, government, and culture, which shape our most important activities. Ironically, although individuals create these institutions, these institutions constrain individuals in their behaviour and life choices. Take, for example, the effect of popular culture's influence on the way people dress, speak, and act—the importance of fashions, fads, television personalities, and so on. Sociologists work to understand the individual's creation of and influence on society, and in turn society's impact on the individual.

Sociologists study social life in two main ways, using both a micro perspective and a macro perspective. Microsociologists examine social interaction on a small scale to discover patterns of interaction. Macrosociologists, by contrast, explore large, lasting social institutions, such as the educational system. These approaches, although sometimes at odds, are mostly complementary and help form a rounded view of society and social life. Within sociology, we find at least four major approaches. Structural functionalism, based on the work of Émile Durkheim, sees society as a self-regulating organism. Every unit of society has a role that contributes towards its smooth operation as a whole. Conflict theory, with its roots in the work of Karl Marx, stresses inequality and the struggle of different groups for power as the basis of societal operation. Symbolic interactionism works on a micro scale and concentrates on the use of symbols by individuals to interact with each other. These flexible interactions result in larger social structures, including society as a whole. Finally, the feminist perspective focuses on the different experiences and treatment of men and women in society.

Each approach can be used to analyze any given aspect of society but none alone can present the whole story. Bruce Curtis's essay in Part 1 stresses the importance of narrative and its impact on historical data. Even censuses, which people assume contain hard data, are influenced by the social conditions of the time as well as the people who took the census. Similarly, Stephen Harold Riggins examines anecdotes as a valuable clue to social attitudes and patterns of interaction. In addition, Christie Barron and her co-author analyze today's panic about female violence, arguing that it is a socially constructed backlash against feminism.

Although the essays in this section vary widely in topic, they all reflect how social structures are created and how they affect—that is, help to create—us. The impact of social structures may be on a large scale, such as a new public attitude towards female youth, or on as small a scale as the decisions of people in a poker game. Given the generality of the subject matter, people sometimes imagine that sociology is too vague, obvious, or abstract. One misconception about sociology is that it is not useful in every day life. Goyder and his co-authors dispel this myth in the opening chapter, 'What Can I Do With a Sociology Degree?'. This chapter shows that undergraduates with a sociology degree go on to work in fields as diverse as education, law, social work, and in a surprisingly high number of managerial positions.

CHAPTER 1

What Can I Do With a Sociology Degree?

John Goyder, Corinne Carter, Jaime Robinson, and Marina Korotkikh

How many sociology department chairs and undergraduate directors across the country have invested time into staffing a booth at a recruiting fair, only to experience the following: A fresh-faced young man or woman about to complete high school approaches and says: 'I am really interested in majoring in sociology!' And a step or two behind treads a hovering mother or father, who adds in a glum voice, 'What kind of job can he/she do with a degree in sociology?' 'Ah, um, all kinds of things really,' the professor replies. 'Sociologists are found in lots of different jobs. It's a great preparation for many things. Critical thinking is valued by all employers.' Buzz, next contestant please. It is not enough; the answer was too vague and the prospect is already picking up brochures over at the accounting or the commerce booth.

The first author, John Goyder, began a term as a sociology department chair hoping to find a more definitive answer to the what-do-I-do-with-it question. There is some information out there, to be sure. Davis and Davis (1986) focused on under-employment issues from a 1983 Ontario survey of 1982 graduates. Some of Novek's material became part of the booklet *Opportunities in Sociology* distributed by the CSA in 1988. McMaster University has examined the matter of post-graduation employment within its Faculty of Social Sciences (McMaster University, 2000), and Drewes (2002) examined the 1993–7 *Survey of Labour and Income Dynamics* in order to study a national comparison of social science graduates versus others.

It was the Drewes (2002) study that most inspired this research. 'The school-to-work transition is clearly more difficult for the humanities and social sciences,' he began, then added: 'The picture changes considerably, however, if one looks

beyond the several years following graduation.' For wages too, 'hourly wage rates for both genders with humanities and social science degrees catch up and then overtake those of their applied counterparts in the over 45 year old age group.' Thus a long view is needed before making conclusions about what sociology graduates do with their degrees.

In the course of our research, we discovered that our alumni office at the University of Waterloo was sitting on historical data well worth exploring. The UW alumni data set is cumulative and stretches back to the origins of the university in the late 1950s. Survey data, such as the NGS, do not reach nearly that far back. Indeed, there was scarcely any survey data in Canada at that time (Pineo, 1981). The earliest record in our UW alumni data set of sociology graduates dates from 1963, the year of the Kennedy assassination; the set, at the time of writing, graduated in 2004. The occupation descriptions were coded into the **National Occupational Classification** (NOC) (Human Resources Development Canada, 2001), recording both the unit groups (four digit scores) and the 26-category set of major groups. The major groups form a convenient mapping of the labour force, within a fold-out chart accompanying the NOC coding manuals, in which nine 'skill types' are cross-classified by four 'skill levels'. Managerial occupations have their own skill level in the matrix that separates them from the other skills. Of 2,358 UW sociology graduates since 1963, 806 gave replies codeable as unit groups and 834 at the major group level. Some of the missing occupation information would be due to those never in the labour force, but many working alumni simply do not report information despite the considerable effort the University puts into

Table 1.1 The Top 20 Occupations held by UW Sociology Graduates, 1963–2004

NOC Unit Group	Description	%
4141/2	School teacher	23.0
4121	University professor	4.8
4152	Social workers	4.0
4212	Community and social service workers	2.2
4112	Lawyers and Quebec notaries	2.1
0621	Retail trade managers	2.0
6261	Police offers (except commissioned)	2.0
4153	Family, marriage and other related counsellors	1.9
0611	Sales, marketing and advertising managers	1.8
1121	Specialists in human resources	1.8
0112	Human resources managers	1.7
0014	Senior managers health, education, social and community services and membership organizations	1.4
0313	School principals and administrators of elementary and secondary education	1.4
4163	Business development officers and marketing researchers and consultants	1.1
0013	Senior managers financial, communications and other business services	1.0
4143	Educational counsellors	1.0
4155	Probation and parole officers and related occupations	1.0
4164	Social policy researchers, consultants and program officers	1.0
4165	Health policy researchers, consultants and program officers	1.0
1411	General office clerks	0.9
Total		57.1

(111 other occupations, comprising the remaining 42.9 per cent of cases)

mailings and telephone solicitations. Those most likely to disclose occupations were from Ontario rather than another province or out of country, honours co-op students rather than four-year general students, and, to a slight degree, female rather than male.

Table 1.1 shows the 20 most frequent occupations reported within the alumni sample. In all, 131 unit groups of occupations are represented, but the first 20 represent about 57 per cent of the cases. At a careers night held in our department recently, an alumnus told the audience, 'when I was a student in the 1970s, people with sociology degrees either went into teaching, law school, or driving taxi's!' The teaching part is correct; it accounted for nearly a quarter of the labour force captured within this sample. Law ranked number five, but a number of other possibilities also turn up. The relatively large number of university professors (4.8 per cent) was something of a surprise, the incidence of social workers (4 per cent) and community service workers (2.2 per cent) less so. One of the payoffs from this long view of employment among sociology alumni comes from the incidence of senior managers. NOC codes 0014-health and 0013-financial both end up in the top 20 occupations. Other managerial skill types are represented in the data set, but in lesser frequencies.

A cross-classification by NOC skill type and skill level appears in Table 1.2. These reproduce the major groups structure of the NOC. Note that not every combination of skill type and skill level

Table 1.2 Skill Level by Skill Type

	Skill Level					
	Managerial Skills	Highest Schooling Level	Second Schooling Level	Third Schooling Level	Lowest Schooling Level	Total
Senior managers of all skill types	3.8					3.8
Skill Type						
Business, finance and administrative occupations	4.2	4.6	4.7	2.8		16.2
Natural and applied sciences and related occupations	0.2	1.6	0.4			2.2
Health occupations	3.1	1.3	0.2	0.1		4.8
Occupations in social science, education, government service and religion	1.1	51.7	4.2			57.0
Occupations in art, culture, recreation and sport	0.4	2.3	0.2			2.9
Sales and service occupations	5.4		3.6	2.6	0.1	11.8
Trades, transport and equipment operators and related occupations	0.4		0.1	0.1	0.0	0.6
Occupations unique to primary industry			0.1		0.0	0.1
Occupations unique to processing, manufacturing and utilities	0.4		0.2	0.1	0.0	0.7
Total	18.9	61.4	13.8	5.8	0.1	100.0

exists within the NOC major groups, and in Table 1.2 these appear as blank cells rather than as zero entries. The success of sociology graduates in managerial positions becomes clear in this tabulation of major groups. Just over 15 per cent of the respondents hold middle management positions. This would make them the second most frequent occupation in Table 1.1, if the major group were entered as a unit group. The six subcategories of senior managers together comprise 3.8 per cent of the sample. A further cluster outside the traditional sociological outlets of teaching, social work, and law appears in the business, finance, and administrative occupations all part of skill levels one and two. As the NOC coding manual notes, skill level one 'occupations usually require university education' and level two 'occupations usually require college education or apprenticeship training.' In the major group, combining business skill type with second skill level, we may be encountering those who take a sociology BA then more specialized vocational training at a college. In all, 21 of the 26 NOC major groups are represented in the database, supporting the truism that 'sociologists are found in lots of different jobs.'

The alumni database records the type of degree, present place of residence, gender, and year of completion. Some models based on this information are shown in Table 1.3. Here the NOC unit groups have been coded into their major groups, and then scored for the **occupational prestige** for

Table 1.3 Prediction of Prestige of Occupation, Sociology Graduates

	Prestige Rating	Prestige, Residualized for Income
Gender (female)	.228	.828*
Years since graduation	.102***	.020
Type of degree (reference category= three year general)		
Four year general	−.839	−.555
Four year honours	1.152*	.308
Co-op program	2.108**	−.340
Teacher	6.679***	5.318***
Constant	67.857***	−.625
R	.287	.466

N = 782. Graduates in Sociology with UW undergraduate degrees.
Range for prestige = 52.3 to 80.9, with standard deviation of 6.5.

* p <.05
**p <.01
***p <.001

each major group. The prestige scale is an unpublished development from a similar scale in Goyder et al. (2003), using a national sample collected in 2005. Some 14 per cent of the alumni had graduate degrees, and these are excluded from the **regression analysis**. Many of those with Waterloo undergraduate degrees would have gone on to some further post-secondary program, whether graduate work, a professional program such as law, or courses at a community college. It would bias results to include those who come to Waterloo's graduate school with a bachelor's degree from elsewhere, but it would not create bias to track UW BA's who take further study at another institution. The mean prestige score for these UW BA's is 72.5 points, just above the national average of 71 for the university-educated population from the 2005 survey from which the prestige scale is derived.

Two models are computed, with identical predictors, but first with prestige rating as the dependent variable (referred to henceforth as 'raw prestige') and then with prestige **residualized** for mean income. In this latter model, the mean income for each NOC unit group was computed

from Statistics Canada tabulations for the 2001 Canada census (table 97F0019XCB2001050). The **mean** of these means was then taken for each major group, logged, and prestige for the group then regressed on mean income. The two relate at the level of r = 0.7. The residual is the amount of over- or under-rewarding people given to occupation groups in terms of prestige points in relation to the mean income of the group. It is a scale of occupational prestige net of income rewards.

The two concepts of occupational prestige perform slightly differently. Women have no statistically significant advantage over men in raw prestige, but they have 0.08 of a point more residualized prestige on the 100-point scale. This means that female sociology graduates are showing up in the less well paid but more respected jobs, often in the social service area. The number of years in the labour force since graduation enhances raw prestige at the rate of 1 point per decade. This may echo the Drewes effect noted above: Sociology graduates do not take the job market by storm at the entry level, but they achieve steady career gains over time. The three-year general BA degree is the reference category for the set of degree type indicators. Four-year general BAs confer no advantage over the three-year general; the **coefficient** is in fact negative, albeit non-significant, and therefore best read as zero. Four-year general programs subtract one year from the graduate's time in the labour force, compared to three-year general programs, with no credential differential. As expected, four-year honours does give a measurable occupational prestige increment over three year general. This is primarily a raw prestige premium. Co-operative education, the program around which Waterloo has built its reputation, adds 2.1 raw prestige points.

Although the data reported here describe just one university they may have some generalizeability to other Canadian sociology departments. The descriptive results are in line with the studies from the 1980s noted earlier. So, after all that number crunching, the correct answer to 'What can you do with a sociology degree' is: 'Well, the predicted occupational prestige in ten years time will be $0.228 + .102$ times $10 = 1.02$ plus 1.152 if one does an honours degree, plus 2.108 for co-op, plus the constant of 67.857. Add about seven points if the student wants to become a teacher. And don't forget about the residualized prestige!'

References

Davis, C., and C.K. Davis. 1986. 'The Employment Status of 1982 Ontario Sociology Graduates', *Society/Société* 10, 2 (May): 9–11.

Drewes, T. 2002. 'Value Added: Humanities and Social Sciences Degrees', *Ontario Confederation of University Faculty Associations Forum* Spring Issue: 10–12.

Goyder, J., M.E. Thompson, and S. Dixon. 2003. 'Scaling the Major Groups of the National Occupational Classification'. Paper presented at the 2003 Meetings of the Canadian Sociology and Anthropology Association. 4 June 2003, Halifax, Nova Scotia.

Human Resources Development Canada (HRDC). 2001. *National Occupational Classification*. Catalogue No. MP53-25-1/2-2001E. Ottawa: Ministry of Public Works and Government Services.

McMaster University. 2000. 'Spoiled for Choice?', *Socialights* 4, 2 (Winter): 1.

Novek, J. 1986. 'Sociology and Anthropology Graduates and Jobs: Some Preliminary Observations', *Society/Société* 10, 2 (May): 5–8.

Pineo, P.C. 1981. 'Prestige and Mobility: The Two National Surveys', *Canadian Review of Sociology and Anthropology* 18, 5 (December): 615–26.

CHAPTER 2

Reading Reflexively

Bruce Curtis

This discussion begins with **narratives** because one of the most interesting developments in sociology and the other social sciences over the last two decades—the recognition of the inescapably narrative quality of our accounts of the social (for

instance White, 1987; Somers, 1994). I propose that this awareness extends to that seemingly least narrative of objects: numerical census returns. A great many developments both in and outside the academy have undermined the credibility of sociology's earlier attempts at **master narratives**, as in **systems theory** or **Marxism**. The growing awareness of the existence of a multiplicity of narratives has increased interest in the ways in which narratives are constructed, work, become hegemonic, and are discredited.

From the sociology side, the use of new data sources and the multiplication of historical voices encouraged critical interrogation of the dominant accounts of social development. For instance, in the historical sociology of education, the reigning account of the origins of public education, until the late 1960s, was one in which progressive bourgeois, or middle class, intellectuals fought against the dark forces of oligarchy and privilege to bring the light of learning into the humble homes of the people. Any opposition to public education or to the school was a defense of ignorance or, as Talcott Parsons put it, simply sour grapes on the part of those unable to adapt to the needs of modern society (Parsons, 1964).

Some critics at the time did point out that the claims about popular literacy levels depended on dubious assumptions about the meaning of entries on census forms (Mays and Manzl, 1974). There was, and continues to be, concern among many sociologists, economic historians, and historical demographers about the internal coherence of the Canadian manuscript censuses that many researchers embraced enthusiastically. As the so-called quantitative history took off, a few people, such as Marvin McInnis from Queen's, were warning that some of the censuses were suspect, and were calling for a systematic investigation of census execution. But such cautions tended not to be heard and the census returns themselves were assimilated into scholarly practice, with generations of history graduate students and junior faculty now joining their sociological counterparts and finding themselves constrained to use the census or to deal with others who did.

Remarkably, while there have been literally hundreds of studies in Canadian social history and historical sociology that have drawn on manuscript and aggregate census data, until *Politics of Population*, no one attempted to give a systematic account of 'how the census was done', nor to investigate the effects of practices of census knowledge production on the substance of the returns.

We can identify reasons for such neglect, but without a working understanding of the organization of **knowledge production**, one cannot locate the traces of it. And one typically has to read through, over, and around the official documentary system to construct defensible inferences about what actually was done, especially since government departments often destroy their guilty secrets. There is a kind of craft knowledge involved here that entails learning about how official documentary systems are constructed and mobilized for purposes other than the ones that might interest us, and then patching surviving pieces together to construct a credible narrative. And this is often monk's work: too slow for a dissertation, too big for anyone without secure employment, and unlikely to captivate most researchers.

There are other good reasons for the failure to scrutinize census-making. Aggregate returns carry the sanction of the state. Sovereign authority commonly works to construct and enforce truths, and census returns are made into truths practically, in that people's life chances are often determined by policies that draw on census information. As Bourdieu pointed out (1999, 2001), sociologists are dependent on the state in order to be critical of the state and so, without **epistemological** vigilance, concepts and practices of state tend to colonize our thinking. As well, of course, aggregate returns are largely expressed in numbers, seemingly the furthest possible from narrative, and the closest possible to objective truth. My recent work shows that the numbers are indeed narratives, and it has been revealing to me to see how shocking it is to some researchers when first they notice that census numbers were in fact reports of reports of reports with oral history accounts at the bottom, given the denigration of popular memory by those who want to privilege the numerical form as 'hard data'.

One might respond to variations in a population data set by investigating the circumstances and the mechanics of the process of enumeration and revision; one might deal with provenance. Of course, this would demand a collective research project for world population data. Keilman instead turns inwards towards the data set and proposes that data quality can be evaluated by 'measuring the extent to which historical estimates have been revised in later years' at the national level. He proposes that 'a large spread' in estimates contained at different moments within the data source 'indicates large problems with data quality, and, by hypothesis, low accuracy' (2001: 152). So Keilman seeks to validate the data by using criteria internal to the data set—his main criterion is internal consistency. The best national census data sets are those without wildly fluctuating revisions, those whose population reports remain relatively constant: these are the ones we should most trust. And I think that the invocation of the notion of 'accuracy', although Keilman does not elaborate on it, is an implicit theory of reference. That is, smooth data sets that repeat a story consistently without wild fluctuations best capture the nature of the reality to which they refer; they are the most accurate. Because Keilman invokes no empirical evidence to sustain his position, I believe his is an aesthetic choice.

Phrased in this way, the claim cannot sustain critical scrutiny. A strong refutation comes from Peter Uvin's (2002) essay, 'On Counting, Categorizing, and Violence in Burundi and Rwanda'. In Rwanda, there were mass killings of Tutsi in 1962 and 1963, with about 10,000 people being murdered, and with somewhere between 140,000–250,000 fleeing to neighbouring countries. In late 1972, the Tutsi army in Burundi killed between 100,000 and 150,000 Hutu, with as many more fleeing that country. Uvin shows that 'both Rwandan and Burundian **population statistics** manage to hide these instances of mass violence,' which should have been clearly evident in countries where annual increments were about 60,000. Instead, 'all sets of Rwandan population data indicate that population increases continued exactly on trend.' In the Burundian case, the census scheduled for 1972 was dropped. No census was conducted for 7 years and then the returns showed a gradual decline. 'In order to make [the census total] compatible with older data, a ten-year-long decline in population growth was invented (and then reproduced by the United Nations)—and the selective genocide had disappeared with a statistical sleight of hand' (2002: 153–4). Smoothness in data sets, a constant theme with limited variations, then, is by no means a criterion for a reliable portrayal of violently uneven events.

An additional level of complexity lies in the fact that those who actually do the work of census enumeration cannot possibly ever see everyone, even if we wanted to privilege the vision of an enumerator as the measure of reality. In practice, enumeration takes place—in the periods before mail-in self-enumeration—by some kinds of people going around asking some other kinds of people about a third category of people. In fact, the census is not simply a discovery project. Who is to count as a person, where they are to be found, and who is to provide information about them are modelled, more or less coherently, conceptually before the enumeration begins and census managers then translate the model, more or less efficiently, into field measures. Yet census returns also result from negotiated understandings between enumerators and informants mediated by the text of enumeration schedule and other documents, and by the physical, environmental, and cultural aspects of the encounter. Informants may not cooperate. Informants may not command the information sought. Enumerators may not be able to write outdoors in winter and may copy more or less vaguely remembered information onto schedules later. The categories mobilized by the census may clash with the categories used by informants. The conceptual model drives observational practice, which is not to say that observed objects or relations fit with it.

I have been referring repeatedly and positively to **reflexive sociology**. In keeping with many others who are interested in the 'practice turn' in sociology, (among others, Bryant, 1995; Flyvbjerg, 2001) I am an advocate for a version of it about which I want to say a few words in conclusion. In Bourdieu's terms, the inherently controversial nature of our discipline compels us to exercise a particular form of epistemological vigilance. For him that meant we need to operate our categories and interrogate them at the same time, and we need also to be able to relate the strategies of knowledge production that we adopt as individuals and as members of specialties to our own positions and investments in the sociological field (Bourdieu, 2001). Practically, from my point of view, such vigilance must also involve alertness to the areas in which we are invited to suspend disbelief so that our narratives will work, attention to the aesthetic qualities of practices and relations, and cognizance of the dependence of knowledge claims on contextual elements. The refusal to suspend disbelief is relatively easy; often we need only to be alert to foundational assumptions and narrative devices.

The issue of aesthetics invites us to be alert to our reactions and to those of others to research questions and research materials. I do not have a therapeutic agenda in this matter, even if I do think that the capacity to adopt a stance of moral and political agnosticism is one dimension of reflexivity. Rather, we don't want any guilty secrets; we need to know about what strikes us as the startling, the monstrous, the gripping, because such things define the contours of our conceptual postulates, and point to powerful zones of **normativity**. At the same time, for many of us, what doesn't fit, what is out of place, what won't work in the ways we're accustomed to things working can be instructive if we're prepared to notice. Category slippage, Bourdieu reminds us, is our bread and butter. And I am also thinking of things as simple as strange idioms: One enumerator describing his work in Canada in 1861 claimed that 'many of the heads of families, when comeatable, did not know how to answer my questions about acres of land, quantities of crops, etc.' Where does 'comeatable' fit? In a world where polling, questionnaires, forms, and surveys have not made it commonplace for just anyone to walk up to just anyone else and start asking questions? A world that has not yet been remade in the image of sociology (see Osborne and Rose 1999)?

I'm not interested in saying we should jettison the numerical and statistical in favour of the literary. Sociology, in my view, needs to identify regularities and to analyze effects of structure. It depends on systematic social observation. Yet a reflexive sociology has to be cognizant of the ways in which the numerical and statistical decontextualize local particulars and enlist them in attempts to recontextualize. These practices are selective, disciplinary, and potentially violent. We need to be aware of the ways in which the local and particular are worked up into the general and abstract; and we need to be aware of the degrees of fit present when the abstract and general returns to confront the local and particular. We need to know things because what we don't know is when next it may blow up a gale.

References

Bourdieu, P. 2001. *Science de la science et réflexivité. Cours du Collège de France. 2000–2001.* Paris: Éditions Raisons d'Agir.

Bryant, C.G.A. 1995. *Practical Sociology. Post-empiricism and the Reconstruction of Theory and Application.* Oxford: Basil Blackwell.

Curtis, B. 2001. *The Politics of Population: Statistics, State Formation, and the Census of Canada, 1840–1875.* Toronto: University of Toronto Press.

Flyvbjerg, B. 2001. *Making Social Science Matter: Why Social Inquiry Fails and How it Can Succeed Again.* Cambridge: Cambridge University Press.

Keilman, N. 2001. 'Data Quality and the Accuracy of United Nations *Population Projections, 1950–95'*, *Population Studies* 55: 149–64.

Mays, H.J., and H.F. Manzl. 1974. 'Literacy and Social Structure in Nineteenth Century Ontario: An Exercise in Historical Methodology', *Histoire sociale/ Social History*: 33–45.

Parsons, T. 1964. 'The School Class as a Social System: Some of its Functions in American Society', in *Social Structure and Personality*, pp. 129–54. New York: Free Press.

Uvin, P. 2002. 'On Counting, Categorizing, and Violence in Burundi and Rwanda', in *Census and Identity*, pp. 148–75, D.I. Kertzer and D. Arel, eds. Cambridge: Cambridge University Press.

CHAPTER 3

The Value of Anecdotal Evidence

Stephen Harold Riggins

Scientists tend to view anecdotes as the opposite of sound data and theory. However, the fact that anecdotes are memorable and spread quickly may indicate that a minor form of narrative and a social ritual are more significant for sociologists than one might think. Anecdotes are found in all types of social occasions and societies. They may be windows into the dynamics of broad social phenomena and should not be so easily dismissed as unreliable and irrelevant or associated only with gossip and trivia. Anecdotes can be conceptualized as (1) a type of micro-narrative, (2) a mode of interaction, and (3) a trigger for inferences.

Anecdotal evidence is common in sociological studies utilizing participant observation or personal documents that record an individual's experiences in his or her own words, such as letters, diaries, biographies, and life-histories. For example, members of the Chicago School of Sociology, influential from about 1900 to 1940, did not shy away from including anecdotal information in their publications because they preferred these methods to learn about the subjective side of social experiences. Clifford Shaw's (1930) book *The Jack-Roller: A Delinquent Boy's Own Story* is a classic example. A jack-roller is an old slang word for a mugger who specialized in robbing publicly intoxicated poor men, such as hobos, and gay men because both were relatively safe targets. *The Jack-Roller* is a collection of stories which 'Stanley' (1909–82), the son of working-class Polish immigrants to Chicago, wrote about his delinquent experiences at Shaw's request. Stanley was about 21 years old at the time; he had first come to the attention of the police when he was 6-and-a-half years old and he had spent much of his childhood in institutions. Like most sociologists, Shaw took anecdotes at face value and did not have a theory to explain them or a methodology to exploit them. He ignored the way story telling is an interactive event in which the listener or reader plays an important role.

A Type of Micro-Narrative

Anecdotes are a type of brief story or narrative, usually set in one location and involving a single episode. Characters and reported dialogue are normally reduced to a functional minimum as a preparation for the more or less surprising point the storyteller makes and which carries the load of explicit information. Humour is often foregrounded but anecdotes need not to be funny. Anecdotes are supposed to be factual, or at least plausible, stories of events that happened to the storyteller or to some other real person. They are exemplary statements in that they reveal what is perceived as essential about a person, situation, or group and thus imply a broader story. Anecdotes can be related to many other short forms of oral communication, such as jokes, gossip, proverbs, and parables. Anecdotes tend to contain proverb-like statements that convey some perceived universal truths.

The story in an anecdote consists of at least one agent, who is specified by some qualities, and who is confronted by a crisis usually involving (an)other agent(s). Many things can qualify as a crisis: a hurdle to clear, a puzzle to solve, confusion to be cleared up, tension to be resolved, etc. An investigation of anecdotes told or written by ordinary people cannot be restricted to the literary prototypes of the genre because their qualities are so rare. In particular, 'everyday anecdotes' may lack the clever word play of written examples collected in anthologies. But the speaker or writer must make some sweeping generalization.

Anecdotes can be construed as a 'granular medium' in the sense that they are small packages of information that are transferable, recyclable, and an inexpensive tool for communication which does not require any technology except a population of human brains. They are micro-narratives that come full circle. You always know when one is finished.

A Mode of Interaction

Although anecdotes are told in a social context, they also help to create a context. They are produced in a developing relationship between an addressor and addressee, both of whom are pursuing some kind of immediate practical goals. The implications of anecdotes may depend on whether they appear in situations of long acquaintanceship or first encounters. Anecdotes can be used to start a relationship by assigning a level of trust, understanding, or status to the addressee and at the same time disclosing some qualities of the addressor. If you do not want to tell the story of your life to a stranger of interest, telling an anecdote or two is an economical way of conveying enough information to illustrate your attitude to the interaction, place yourself in a hierarchical order, establish a

basis for communication and mutual assessment, capture someone's attention, or throw a challenge to an addressee. You may also hear back from another person the anecdote you told, sometimes in a modified form. They circulate among networks of people.

Telling anecdotes requires co-operation and trust between an addressor and addressee because the storyteller claims to be speaking the truth. Some kind of valuable information is entrusted to the addressee. Without this co-operation, the story will not be credible. It will be perceived as a lie, fiction, exaggeration, or joke rather than an anecdote worthy of attention. The telling of an anecdote may also be a claim for status. It implies that the speaker has insider knowledge, although either speaker or listener may be gullible or perceived as such. In a social context anecdotes can bring interaction to a close or initiate a cycle of further anecdotes and commentaries. Although the story is very condensed, given the right circumstances it can be expanded.

A Trigger for Inferences

If anecdotes dramatize sociological consciousness, they should yield general information about social conditions. A contemporary sociologist would not concentrate on the 'facts' reported in anecdotes but on the information they imply about attitudes, social representations, societal forces, and the anticipation of the future. Part of the difficulty in studying anecdotes is that the arguments they make tend to be implicit and experiential rather than formal and explicit. Unfortunately, it is easier to investigate what is represented in a text than what is implied but the challenge can be met with an appropriate method.

An ideal methodology for studying the implications of anecdotes is critical discourse analysis. The methodology was developed by linguists in order to investigate the subtle way meanings are conveyed through words. It is based on the idea that the relationship between truth and words is tenuous or weak. The methodology encourages its practitioners to radically question to what extent statements are 'fact' or 'interpretation'. In reality, much of what interests sociologists would be classified as interpretations.

A discourse is a socially accepted way of thinking and using language. It is thus a type of knowledge. Discourses may differ in terms of their vocabulary, form, values, beliefs, and emotions. Feminism and patriarchy are examples of discourses. Discourses do not faithfully reflect reality, like mirrors. Instead, they are artifacts of language through which the very reality they purport to reflect is constructed.

Discourse analysis acquires a critical dimension when the focus is on the relation of language to power and privilege. The goal of the analysis is to provide a detailed description, explanation, and critique of the textual strategies writers use to naturalize discourses, that is, to make them appear to be commonsense, apolitical statements (Gee, 1999; Fairclough, 2005). Most critical discourse analysts take an explicit political stance, identifying with those who lack the institutional levers to produce counter-discourses. Their ultimate motivation appears to be the hope that their work will contribute to social emancipation.

Critical discourse analysts would argue that *The Jack-Roller* combines collaborative autobiography, adventure stories, and therapeutic stories. In a collaborative autobiography it is often not clear who speaks. Is it the storyteller or the collector/editor/contextualizer? Stanley told adventure stories at the expense of the self-reflection, which is a characteristic of therapeutic stories. Exaggeration and invention are expected in adventure stories, factuality in therapeutic literature.

Why Stanley never became an adult criminal has puzzled readers. However, if Stanley's stories are seen in the context of an interactional strategy of story telling, it would be evident that he needed to establish status as a credible delinquent without compromising Shaw. Since the boy's parents were deceased and he had a poor relationship with his stepmother, Shaw became a father figure. There was mutual dependence between the sociologist and the street kid. Shaw could not produce a book without a co-operative delinquent; Stanley needed money, assistance in finding jobs, a home, and counselling. Stanley had to establish a credible level of delinquency in order to ensure the continuing interest of Shaw. Telling anecdotes was a cheap way of accomplishing this because the addressor did not have to give real evidence.

In his commentary to *The Jack-Roller,* Ernest Burgess (1930) made some generalizations about how Stanley's personality was typical of delinquents. This gives us some insight into the way anecdotes function to trigger inferences. According to Burgess, Stanley was given to moralizing. He had a hypercritical attitude towards others, an excessive need for attention, lacked insight into his motives, and made decisions too quickly. In modern critical discourse analysis these qualities would not be attributed so easily to the personality of a storyteller. Instead, they would be considered to reflect anecdotes as a form of literature as well as the social relationship between addressor and addressee.

Stanley conveys to readers the impression that he is an unreliable storyteller in part because he fails to express the pleasures of recreational deviance and the fun of being on the road as a hobo. Why? Readers are forced to imagine the reasons. In his adventure stories Stanley tells without showing—but conciseness is an inherent characteristic of anecdotes. Perhaps he could have provided longer explanations for his actions, and thus have shown more insight, but it would have implied that he was less dependent on the sociologist.

The anecdotes and longer stories which sociologists frequently hear are often about emotionally difficult experiences. Since many interviewees prefer not to dwell on these events, critical discourse analysis is an essential tool for investigating their silences and omissions.

References

Burgess, E. 1930. 'Discussion', in *The Jack-Roller: A Delinquent Boy's Own Story*, pp. 184–97, C.R. Shaw, ed. Chicago: University of Chicago Press.

Fairclough, N. 2005. 'Critical Discourse Analysis', *Marges Linguistiques* 9 (May). Available at http://www.marges-linguistiques.com.

Gee, J.P. 1999. *An Introduction to Discourse Analysis: Theory and Method*. London: Routledge.

Shaw, C.R. 1930. *The Jack-Roller: A Delinquent Boy's Own Story*. Chicago: University of Chicago Press.

CHAPTER 4

Moral Panic and the Nasty Girl

Christie Barron and Dany Lacombe

This paper examines why, despite evidence to the contrary, recent incidents of female violence have been interpreted as a sign that today's girls are increasingly nasty. We argue that the Nasty Girl phenomenon is the product of a **moral panic**. While girl violence has always existed, today's discussion is dominated by the concept of risk. Reform initiatives resulting from the panic consist of disciplinary mechanisms acting on the body of the individual delinquent, and techniques that regulate individuals through the fostering of **risk society** and a culture of risk management and security consciousness. Finally, we situate the panic in the current backlash against feminism.

Female violence became a topic of much discussion in the mid-1990s in the wake of the gruesome sexual murders of teenagers by the infamous Ontario couple Paul Bernardo and Karla Homolka. But it was the murder of Reena Virk by a group of mostly female teens, in a suburb of Victoria in November 1997, which led Canadians to believe that something had gone terribly wrong with teenage girls. However, the belief that girl violence is rampant is a social construction. According to Statistics Canada, the annual youth charge rate for

violent crime dropped 5 per cent in 1999, signalling a decline for the fourth year in a row (Statistics Canada, 2000). Moreover, Doob and Sprott (1998) have shown that the severity of youth violence did not change in the first half of the 1990s. Questioning the federal government's concern about the increase in girls' participation in violent and gang-related activities, Reitsma-Street (1999) indicates that the number of girls charged for murder and attempted murder has been constant for the past 20 years and that such charges are infrequent. Although statistics indicate a phenomenal increase in the number of young women charged with minor or moderate assault over the past 10 years (from 710 charged under the Juvenile Delinquents Act in 1980 to 4,434 under the Young Offenders Act in 1995–6), several researchers indicate that the increase is more a reflection of the youth justice system's change in policy and charging practices than a 'real' change in behaviour (Doob and Sprott, 1998; Reitsma-Street, 1999). Yet the public continues to believe that youth violence, particularly girl violence, is increasing at an alarming rate and necessitates immediate attention (Chesney-Lind and Brown,

1999). This perception begs the important question: Why, despite evidence to the contrary, are recent isolated incidents of female violence interpreted as a sign that today's girls have become increasingly 'nasty'?

We argue that the recent alarm over girl violence is the product of a moral panic that has had a significant impact on social, educational, and legal policy making. All moral panics identify and denounce a personal agent responsible for the condition that is generating widespread public concern. As Schissel explains, 'folk devils are inherently deviant and are presumed to be self-seeking, out of control and in danger of undermining the stability of society . . .' (1997: 30). Hence, during the 'warning phase' of a panic there are, as shown in the documentary *Nasty Girls*, predictions of impending doom, sensitization to cues of danger, frequent overreactions, and rumours speculating about what is happening or what will happen (Cohen, 1980: 144–8). Subsequently, a large part of the public becomes sensitized to the threat, and, as in the case of the Nasty Girl, when confronted with an actual act of girl violence their perception of danger and risk solidifies.

It is not surprising; therefore, that the beating and murder of 14-year-old Reena Virk by a group of seven girls and one boy would become the event that provided evidence that girl violence had become a significant problem in Canada.

As is often the case in a moral panic, the media distorted and exaggerated the extent of isolated acts of girl violence following Virk's death. For example, newspaper and magazine headlines associated the case with a larger trend in girl violence: 'Bad Girls: A Brutal BC Murder Sounds an Alarm about Teenage Violence' (Chisholm, 1997), 'Spare the Rod and Run for Cover: When Students Hold the Cards, School Violence Grows, Especially among the Girls' (McLean, 1999), 'When She Was Bad: Violent Women and the Myth of Innocence' (Chesney-Lind, 1999), 'Virk's Death Triggers Painful Questions: Girls' Involvement "Exacerbates Rage"' (Mitchell, 1997), and 'In Reena's World, being a "Slut" Can Get You Killed' (Anon., 1997).

Also central to the creation of a climate of fear is statistical manipulation of crime data to establish the amplitude of girl violence. As journalist Nolan astutely recognizes in her analysis of the media reporting of the Virk case: ' "experts" and authors were appearing on TV and radio talk shows trumpeting—with the solemn self-importance that always accompanies adult laments about the various wickedness of youth—the shocking fact that, according to the Canadian Centre for Justice Statistics, crime by young girls had increased 200 per cent since 1986' (1998: 32). However, most articles failed to recognize that the increase was in reference to minor assaults, such as pushing or slapping, which did not cause serious injury.

The panic over the Nasty Girl has had a significant impact on legal, educational, and social policy in Canada. The result has been an increase in both formal and informal mechanisms of control. While proposals for legal reform mostly consist of repressive measures targeted at delinquent youths, social and educational programs contain informal mechanisms of control targeting society more generally. Proposals for reform are not only disciplinary mechanisms of power acting on the body of the individual delinquent, but they are also part of the more recent governmental techniques of power which regulate and manage free individuals through the fostering of a culture of risk management, public safety and security consciousness (Foucault, 1982; Cohen, 1985; O'Malley, 1996; Garland, 1997).

Following the Virk case and other high-profile youth crimes, state policies on violent youth have become punitive. The Youth Criminal Justice Act (YCJA) came into effect on 1 April 2003 and, although it offers positive measures to reduce the number of youths being incarcerated, its clear distinction between 'non-violent', 'violent', and 'seriously violent' offences reflects public desire to deal harshly with violent youth.

Of even more concern for girls specifically is the passage of the Secure Care Act (Bill 25) in British Columbia. Following the lead of Alberta's Protection of Children Involved In Prostitution Act (PCHIP), the

Secure Care Act is intended 'to provide, when other less intrusive means are unavailable or inadequate, a means of assessing and assisting children who have an emotional or behavioural condition that presents a high risk of serious harm or injury to themselves and are unable to reduce the risk. . . . These conditions may [include] severe substance misuse or addiction or the sexual exploitation of a child' (Section 2 [1], cited in Busby, 2001). In essence, this legislation, meant to protect children, ultimately blames victims of sexual exploitation and permits the apprehension and incarceration of girls—who will be targeted more than boys due to their differential involvement in prostitution.

While harsh legal policy is aimed at incapacitating both violent boys and girls, informal mechanisms of control targeting young girls in particular have also resulted from the panic over girl violence. This groundwork has produced new definitions of violence and new methods of controlling both young females and society in general.

The expansion in definitions of violence is most obvious in relation to what goes on at school, a site where the threat of the violent girl is most apparent. Pepler, who was commissioned by the Ontario and Canadian Governments to prepare strategies for aggressive girls, helped foster a new rationality of bullying—teasing, gossiping, and quarrelling—as an intolerable act of aggression.

The new rationality and concern over bullying is not only targeting the aggressive girl. It also actively seeks the participation of school authorities in the informal control of girls. For example, Pepler and Sedighdeilami's caution that '[g]irls in families with violence, ineffective parenting, and high levels of conflict should be identified for supportive interventions' encourages school staff to observe and detect signs of risk in girls.

Why did the reaction to girl violence take the particular form and intensity it did during the late 1990s? The moral panic literature emphasizes that, during a panic, the anxieties the public experiences are real, but their reaction is often misplaced. Hence, the object of the panic—the violent girl— is not always the source of people's anxiety.

We start our attempt at contextualizing the moral panic over the violent girl by examining the larger structural forces characterizing our present. According to Young (1999), the transition from modernity (the 'Golden Age' of the postwar period) to the present late modernity (late 1960s and onwards) resulted in significant structural and psychological changes that produced social anxieties. The shift primarily entailed a movement from an inclusive to an exclusive society: from a society that incorporated its members and enjoyed full (male) employment, rising affluence, stable families, and conformity, to an exclusive society arising from changes in the labour force. These changes included a shift from a more social-based, communitarian labour force to one of individualism stemming from the new knowledge-based, technology society. As late-modern society became increasingly characterized by a plurality of values, self-reflexivity, multiculturalism, and scientific and political relativism, the solid foundation of modernity began to melt. Material certainty and shared values shattered, leaving us with a heightened sense of risk and uncertainties. In such a precarious climate, crime acquires a powerful symbolic value. If we could only control crime better, we would bring safety into one aspect of our disrupted lives. It is not surprising that our quest for security often translates into a projection of our fears onto specific scapegoats, who are made responsible for our feelings of insecurity.

Although the moral panic framework has much utility in understanding the recent concerns about girl violence, it also has the potential to dismiss them. The framework can be used simply to deconstruct the sources of fear for the purpose of demonstrating that the societal concern is unfounded. We think, however, it should be used to uncover how the configuration of ideas surrounding a phenomenon has come into being and has moulded our life, customs, and science (Doyle and Lacombe, 2000). In this way, we would be in a better position to resist the insidious effects of a moral panic.

References

Anon. 1997. 'In Reena's World, Being a "Slut" Can Get You Killed', *Toronto Star*, 6 December: E1, E4.

Busby, K. 2001. 'Protective Confinement of Children Involved in Prostitution: Compassionate Response or Neo-criminalization?' Notes for a presentation at the Women Behind Bars Conference. University of New Brunswick, Fredericton, New Brunswick, 9 February.

Chesney-Lind, M. 1999. 'When She Was Bad: Violent Women and the Myth of Innocence', *Women and Criminal Justice* 10, 4: 113–18.

Chesney-Lind, M., and M. Brown. 1999. 'Girls and Violence: An Overview', in *Youth Violence: Prevention, Intervention and Social Policy*, D. Flannery and C.R. Huff, eds. Washington, DC: American Psychiatric Press.

Chisholm, R. 1997. 'Bad Girls: A Brutal BC Murder Sounds an Alarm about Teenage Violence', *Maclean's* 8 December: 12.

Cohen, S. 1980. *Folk Devils and Moral Panics: The Creation of the Mods and Rockers*. New York: St Martin's Press.

———. 1985. *Visions of Social Control*. New York: Oxford University Press.

Doob, A., and J.B. Sprott. 1998. 'Is the "Quality" of Youth Violence Becoming More Serious?', *Canadian Journal of Criminology and Criminal Justice* 40, 2: 185–94.

Doyle, K., and D. Lacombe. 2000. 'Scapegoat in Risk Society: The Case of Pedophile/Child Pornographer Robin Sharpe', *Studies in Law, Politics and Society* 20: 183–206.

Foucault, M. 1982. *The Subject and Power*, 2nd ed., H.L. Dreyfus and R. Rabinow, eds. Chicago: Chicago University Press.

Garland, D. 1997. '"Governmentality" and the Problem of Crime: Foucault, Criminology, Sociology', *Theoretical Criminology* 1, 2: 173–214.

Justice for Girls. 2001. 'Statement of Opposition to the Secure Care Act'. Available at http://www.moib.com/jfg/publications/p_sca.htm.

McLean, C. 1999. 'Spare the Rod and Run for Cover: When Students Hold the Cards, School Violence Grows, Especially among the Girls', *British Columbia Report* 10, 9: 52–4.

Mitchell, A. 1997. 'Virk's Death Triggers Painful Questions: Girls' Involvement "Exacerbates Rage",' *Globe and Mail*, 28 November: A1, A8.

Nolan, N. 1998. 'Girl Crazy: After the Brutal Murder of Reena Virk, the Media Whipped the Country into a Frenzy over a Supposed "Girl Crime Wave"', *This Magazine* 31, 5 (March/April): 30–5.

O'Malley, R. 1996. 'Risk and Responsibility', in *Foucault and Political Reason*, pp. 189–208, A. Barry, T. Osborne, and N. Rose, eds. Chicago: University of Chicago Press.

Pepler, D. 1998. 'Girls' Aggression in Schools: Scenarios and Strategies'. Unpublished paper. Ministry of Training and Education, Government of Ontario.

Pepler, D.J., and F. Sedighdeilami. 1998. *Aggressive Girls in Canada*. Working papers. Hull, QC: Applied Research Branch, Strategic Policy, Human Resources Development Canada.

Reitsma-Street, M. 1999. 'Justice for Canadian Girls: A 1990s Update', *Canadian Journal of Criminology and Criminal Justice* 41, 3: 335–64.

Schissel, B. 1997. *Blaming Children: Youth Crime, Moral Panics and the Politics of Hate*. Halifax, NS: Fernwood Publishing.

Statistics Canada. 2000. 'Crime Statistics', *The Daily* 18 July. Available at http://www.statcan/Daily/English/000718/d00718a.htm.

Questions for Critical Thought

What Can I Do With a Sociology Degree?

1. Why do you think sociology graduates hold so many positions that aren't in the field of sociology? Specifically, why are so many graduates in managerial positions?
2. Explain the difference between raw prestige and occupational prestige.
3. Explain why the income trend for humanities and social science graduates goes up gradually with age.

4. For whichever discipline you are interested in as a career, think about and explain how sociology might be of use in that field.
5. What evidence is there in the results of this study of gender inequality?

READING REFLEXIVELY

1. Explain how the ways in which a census was taken may affect numerical values.
2. Can you think of a historical document generally believed to be true that has been revised and/or affected by narrative?
3. Explain why it may be hard to retrieve information concerning the accuracy of censuses.
4. Are you convinced by the author's argument that censuses are affected by narrative? Why or why not?
5. Do you think it is possible for any written document to be unaffected by narrative? Explain your answer.

THE VALUE OF ANECDOTAL EVIDENCE

1. After reading the author's arguments, do you believe that anecdotes are valuable and should be examined by sociologists? Why or why not?
2. Explain how an anecdote conveys a mode of interaction.
3. Think of an anecdote you told or were told by someone. Can you think of any inferences that were triggered by this anecdote?
4. Explain how critical discourse analysis is used to evaluate anecdotes.
5. Based on the author's description of how an anecdote is a micro-narrative, write an anecdote of your own.

MORAL PANIC AND THE NASTY GIRL

1. Think of everyday examples in your own life that illustrate that we live in a risk society.
2. Do you believe that the Nasty Girl phenomenon is a backlash against feminism? Why or why not?
3. Think of an example of a moral panic that has occurred within your lifetime and explain how it was constructed.
4. Describe an example of an informal measure of controlling youth that you have witnessed or experienced.
5. Think back over your lifetime: have you seen evidence of the Nasty Girl phenomenon, or only more media coverage of it?

Part II Culture

Culture varies from one place to another and even within the same physical locale and culture changes from one period to another. Within each society a culture preserves the norms, values, beliefs, and artifacts that inhabitants live by. They pass the culture onto the next generation by means of language, socialization, and other symbolic means. Yet within the larger culture we find distinct groups of subcultures consisting of people who share particular attitudes, values, and behaviours that differ from those of the mainstream culture. Also, for every culture, a counterculture may exist that opposes it.

Culture carries different meanings under the different sociological approaches. According to functionalists, the different types (for example, pop culture versus high culture), and ingredients of culture work together. They create a mosaic that serves both the mainstream and marginal populations, as well as society's various subgroups. Conflict theorists, for their part, hold the view that some subcultures are favoured over others, producing class inequalities in cultural as well as in material realms. Symbolic interactionists examine culture in day-to-day personal interactions where people constantly interpret the meanings of symbols and words. The feminist perspective considers culture in the light of gender inequality that, in a patriarchal society, justifies major roadblocks to equal opportunities and outcomes for women.

In this section, we will examine five articles that reflect various aspects of culture. As a participant observer in an interactionist study that examines the hacker ideology, Steven Kleinknecht devises a list of seven fundamental principles that characterize and justify the hacking behaviour. These principles are consistent with hackers' overarching values of 'knowledge and an unorthodox approach to learning', that form the basis for hacker's counterculture ideology and activities. Also from a symbolic interactionist approach, Tara Carnochan shows that when taken out of the context of deprivation and homelessness, squeegiers and panhandlers are portrayed as criminal offenders who are responsible for their actions. The transformation from a war on poverty to a war against the poor prompts the government to take actions against the have-nots instead of helping them to climb out of their misery.

In a discourse analysis, Siegrid Deutschlander and Leslie J. Miller show the meanings contained in cultural tourism are neither static nor obvious; they remain to be interpreted during meetings between the host and the visitor. Contrary to the traditional social psychological approach that views tattooing as irrational and self-destructive, Michael Atkinson adopts a figurational approach that reveals tattooing has pro-social and confidence-boosting qualities. Finally, Janet McLellan presents the complexities of reestablishing Buddhist identities in a multicultural city such as Toronto and the roles the Buddhist temples play at the local, national, and global levels.

As the articles in Part 2 show, each subculture within a main culture contains a unique set of ideologies and behaviours. For example, the reestablished Buddhist communities in Toronto provide job networks and simplify the settlement of immigrants and refugees while the Native Canadians display their history and rituals in the context of cultural tourism. Alongside the subcultures are counter-cultures the mainstream culture disapproves of and excludes, often for their 'risky' behaviour or threatening appearance. Examples include illegal computer hackers as well as squeegiers and pan-handlers. An example of how culture varies over time is the changing opinion of tattoo projects in Canada. Although people used to consider tattooing deviant and irrational, now people often admire tattoos as wonderful pieces of moving art that provide a refined expression of personal identity. In short, people pass on both material and ideological cultures from one generation to another. Simultaneously, global movement of people, goods, and services promotes the diffusion of cultures between countries.

CHAPTER 5

The Hacker Spirit: An Interactionist Analysis of the Hacker Ideology

Steven Kleinknecht

Introduction

A major characteristic distinguishing a particular **subculture** from the broader community is its **ideology** or group perspective (Shibutani, 1955; Fine and Kleinman, 1979; Prus, 1997). An ideology represents a unique way of understanding the world, which tends to justify what the subculture is all about. Within the hacker subculture this ideology is referred to as the 'hacker ethic' or 'hacker spirit'. By engaging self-defined hackers in **participant observation** and in-depth interviews, the goal of this essay is to offer an ethnographic examination and analysis of the hacker ideology.

While the term 'hacker' once served as a positive label for someone who was a 'technological wizard', the term over the course of the last 50 years has come to carry a negative connotation. The public image of what *actually* constitutes a hacker has shifted, and now, hackers are more likely to be defined as 'computer criminals' or 'electronic vandals' than as being 'technological aficionados'. However, as hackers indicate, public perception is at odds with their own perspectives on what actually constitutes a hacker. Hackers are more apt to classify themselves as individuals *who passionately and creatively work towards finding a solution to any given problem*. Quite often this desire to understand is applied specifically to computers and thus, a desire to learn and improve computers is frequently at the heart of hackers' definition of what it is they do.

This article explores the hacker perspective in an in-depth fashion and offers an insider look at the hacker ideology and its applications. To evaluate and move beyond often-stereotypical outsider representations of the hacker subculture, I adopt the symbolic interactionist stance that it is essential to gain intimate familiarity with our subject matter (Blumer, 1969). The data for this project are based on two years of on- and off-line fieldwork. During this time, I attended hacker meetings in the central and southwestern Ontario area and engaged in online participant observation with five different groups of hackers from Canada and the United States. Along with several informal conversations, 15 qualitative interviews were also conducted.

What follows is an overview of the central tenets of the hacker perspective, which updates Levy's (1984) original treatise on the hacker ethic. Analyses of how hackers draw social boundaries between different subgroups of hackers and invoke their ideology as a way of rationalizing their behaviour are also presented.

The Hacker Spirit and the Pursuit of Knowledge

Representing the ideology of the first generation of hackers, Levy (1984) argued that the following elements made up key components of the hacker ethic:

- Access to computers—and anything that might teach you something about the way the world works—should be unlimited and total. Always yield to the Hands-On Imperative!
- All information should be free.
- Mistrust Authority—Promote Decentralization.
- Hackers should be judged by their hacking, not bogus criteria such as degrees, age, race, or position.

- You can create art and beauty on a computer.
- Computers can change your life for the better (40–5).

Similar to Levy's (1984) *Hacker Ethic*, seven fundamental and interrelated elements of the hacker spirit were observed in analyzing the data for this project. Each of these elements is premised on the overarching goal that one should strive to acquire an ever greater understanding of how things work. To hackers, knowledge and an unorthodox approach to learning are valued above all else. Consistent with this goal, the following principles represent the essence of the hacker perspective.

Principle #1: Higher understanding requires an unorthodox approach. In order to reach a level of higher understanding, hackers maintain that it is essential to take a creative approach to problem-solving. As such, it is not uncommon for hackers to define the term hacker as 'Someone who thinks outside of the box' (interview).

Principle #2: Hacking involves hard work. Along with taking a creative approach to problem-solving, hackers point out that to be a hacker one must realize that solving problems can be, and often is, hard work. As Raymond (2001) argues, 'Being a hacker is lots of fun, but it's a kind of fun that takes lots of effort.' Therefore, long hours of dedication to one's project(s) are essential. It was suggested that younger generations of hackers often lack this sort of concerted focus and thus, are critized for their laziness and misappropriating the hacker label.

Principle #3: Hacking requires a 'learn for yourself' approach—learn by doing. Problem-solving not only requires a great deal of ingenuity and hard work, but a hacker must also be self-motivated and seek to understand by taking a hands-on approach. Hackers suggest that you do not learn how to be a hacker, rather hacking is a way of thinking about and approaching a problem that cannot be taught; it is self-directed and something that 'comes from within'. Matthew maintains that '[To be a hacker] I had to learn how to learn. . .There is no amount of knowledge that can qualify you as a hacker, or a

newbie, or what have you. It all comes down to a willingness to learn new things' (interview).

Principle #4: Share your knowledge and information with others. In striving for ever greater levels of understanding, hackers argue that it is imperative that people share their solutions to problems so that other hackers can devote their time to new problems and build upon one another's findings. However, hacker groups have different informal protocols that one should follow when asking for information. Knowing 'who does what' within the hacker community, developing informal networks across the community, and knowing what information the different groups covet, as well as the value (e.g., monetary, reputational, 'pure' knowledge) they place on their knowledge, for hackers, are important factors to recognize when seeking out information.

Principle #5: You're evaluated based on what you know and your desire to learn. Hackers indicate that physical appearance, educational degrees, and style are inconsequential in the subculture. Instead, a hacker's status and reputation are based upon his or her level of knowledge, creative self-directed problem-solving, and display of skill. Consequently, ignorance is highly disparaged. The following hacker quote is poignant in this regard: 'In grade school, I was teased for my lack of style and grace, but this is a new era, and in my world, you'll be taunted endlessly for your lack of intelligence' (interview). However, some hackers suggest that this principle does not appear to be as important to the latest generation of 'hackers'.

Principle #6: Mistrust authority. Hackers believe that people who hold positions of power within society value and impose conformity, which hackers see as stifling creativity. Authority figures are also seen as not always acting in society's best interests. Therefore, hackers argue that these people are to be mistrusted and their attitudes challenged. Kris's comments capture this sentiment well: 'I think the hacker mindset is to challenge everything. Always push the button that says "do not push", always try the door to see if it's locked, always challenge authority, especially when it claims to be acting in your best interests' (interview).

Principle #7: All information should be free. Hackers believe that information that is of any worth to society should be made available to everyone. In order to safeguard against abuses of information and assist in the furthering of knowledge, hackers maintain that ownership of information should be opposed. As an alternative, they advocate a model based on the free-flow and sharing of knowledge. A pertinent example of information sharing is the development of open source software, to which a community of hackers contribute their programming efforts. Some hackers suggest that the *all information should be free* aspect of their ideology can be taken too far and that certain 'so-called hackers' (e.g., script kiddies, crackers) misuse the principle to justify inappropriate behaviour.

Many aspects of the hacker ethic first described by Levy in 1984, still hold a great deal of relevance to the current generation of hackers. One significant difference, however, is the way in which the ideology is now being applied in light of 'new' hacker activities.

It is important to note how the various 'subcategories' of hackers use the ideology. For instance, hackers draw boundaries between the different subgroups within the community in terms of how they apply their ideology. When used to justify illegal behaviours within a subculture, such as copying proprietary software, the person is more appropriately identified as a 'cracker', not a hacker. So while an outsider may identify hackers in terms of their endorsement of the subculture's ideological principles, hackers further distinguish between members of their community in terms of how fully they subscribe to the hacker spirit and how the ideology is applied to rationalize their activities.

The tenets of the ideology are used to counter prevailing perspectives and rationalize certain behaviours. In this sense, we can also see how the hacker ideology becomes used as a **vocabulary of motive** (Mills, 1940) for the different subgroups—

that is, as a way of talking about hacking that justifies the behaviour. Although hackers incorporate aspects of the hacker spirit into their vocabulary, the different activities that their ideology is used to justify vary. For instance, while one group might draw upon the *all information should be free* tenet to rationalize defacing a 'corrupt' government's website, another group employs it to rationalize the communal development of open source software. For acts interpreted as deviant or criminal by outsiders, the use of the hacker ideology to rationalize these behaviours becomes a technique of neutralization—that is, as a way of neutralizing guilt and possible delinquent self-images associated with 'deviant' acts. Thus, their ideology also functions as a way of managing the stigma—a discrediting social attribute—that both outsiders and certain insiders associate with particular types of hackers and their behaviours.

Conclusion

Hackers present a picture of their ideology, and subculture more generally, that is very much at odds with outsider characterizations. Taking a symbolic interactionist approach to the study of hackers allows us to move beyond such portrayals. While most hackers disagree with being labelled as criminals, they very much agree with the counterculture overtones of their ideology and activities. Although recognizing that outsiders see their subculture as deviant, hackers feel that their ideology and activities are normal and often admirable. Like the jazz musicians described by Becker (1963) and the mystics in Simmons's (1973) study, hackers see their perspective as being elite, as their approach represents a better way of doing things and seeing the world than other outsider belief systems. Freedom of information over ownership of information, creativity over conventionality, hard work and self-direction over indolence, intellectualism over looks and style, and unorthodoxy over conformity are highly valued, noble pursuits within the hacker subculture.

References

Becker, H. 1963. *Outsiders*. New York: Free Press.

Blumer, H. 1969. *Symbolic Interactionism*. Berkeley, CA: University of California Press.

Fine, G.A., and S. Kleinman. 1979. 'Rethinking Subculture: An Interactionist Analysis', *American Journal of Sociology* 85, 1: 1–20.

Levy, S. 1984. *Hackers: Heroes of the Computer Revolution*. New York: Bantam Doubleday Dell.

Mills, C.W. 1940. 'Situated Actions and Vocabularies of Motive', *American Sociological Review* 5: 904–13.

Prus, R. 1997. *Subcultural Mosaics and Intersubjective Realities: An Ethnographic Research Agenda for Pragmatizing the Social Sciences*. Albany: SUNY Press.

Raymond, E.S. 2001. 'How to Become a Hacker'. Available at http://www.catb.org/~esr/faqs/hacker-howto.html.

Shibutani, T. 1955. 'Reference Groups as Perspectives', *American Journal of Sociology* 60: 562–9.

Simmons, J.L. 1973. 'Maintaining Deviant Beliefs', in *Deviance: The Interactionist Perspective*, pp. 308–14, E. Rubington and M.S. Weinberg, eds. New York: Macmillan Company.

CHAPTER 6

Short-Changed: Media Representations of Squeegeeing and Panhandling

Tara Carnochan

Beginning in the mid-1990s, squeegeeing and panhandling—income generation activities commonly engaged in by the homeless population—have received attention from both the media and the law as new social problems in Canada. Perhaps the most palpable example of this trend is Ontario's Safe Streets Act (2000)—enacted on 31 January 2000—which criminalizes squeegeeing and aggressive panhandling throughout the entire province. The Ontario Safe Streets Act was primarily in response to pleas from politicians, business people, and tourists claiming that squeegiers and panhandlers were keeping business away from local shops, making people fearful and uncomfortable, and otherwise interfering with the lives of those who live, work, and travel in downtown urban areas. This essay reports the results of an in-depth qualitative content analysis of the media coverage from 31 January 2000 through 31 January 2001, describing the public discussion of squeegeeing and panhandling and the correspondent legislation.

On a broad scale, globalization, corporate downsizing, and a restructuring of the welfare state have contributed to increasing class inequalities in Canada (Comack, 1999; Schrecker, 2000; Brooks, 2002). According to the market-basket measure of poverty, more than 15 per cent of Canadians are unable to afford sufficient food, shelter, clothing, and transportation required for a healthy lifestyle and 13.1 per cent of Canadians, nearly four million people, are considered to be poor (CBC News Online, 2003). While the average income for low-income earners increased by only $80 from 1990–2000, the income of the richest ten per cent of Canadians increased 14.6 per cent in the same time period (NAPO, 2003). Furthermore, 770,000 Canadians now use food banks every month

(Howlett, 2005). With growing inequalities, homelessness has become increasingly common, visible, and problematic in many Canadian cities. Moreover, some anti-homelessness activists estimate that, in Toronto, one homeless citizen dies every six days (Layton, 2000). In 1998, the mayors and councils of Canada's 10 largest cities declared homelessness a national disaster (Layton, 2000; Murphy, 2000). That same year, Canada received the strongest rebuke ever from the UN's Committee on Economic, Social, and Cultural Rights for its inaction on homelessness and other poverty issues (Murphy, 2000: 15).

Research indicates that when compared to the Canadian public, homeless young people report much higher levels of criminal victimization (Baron, 1997, 2003; Fitzpatrick, LaGory, and Ritchey, 1999; Gaetz, 2004). Stephen Gaetz (2004) notes that while the General Social Survey (GSS) reports that approximately 25 per cent of Canadians are victims of crime in any given year, 81.9 per cent of the street youth he surveyed reported having been victims of crime in the last year; additionally, 79.4 per cent reported two or more incidents. Street youth are also five times more likely than domiciled youth to report being victims of childhood sexual abuse (Rotheram-Borus et al., 1996). Homelessness, Fitzpatrick, et al. (1999: 439) argue, is 'a stress-filled, dehumanizing, dangerous circumstance in which individuals are at high risk of being witness to or victims of a wide range of violent acts'. With specific regard to homeless youth, Baron notes (2003: 37) that 'dangerousness and vulnerability can be viewed as "two sides of the same coin" as the factors that contribute to dangerousness also enhance vulnerability.' Therefore, it is clear that homeless youth are a population particularly vulnerable to criminal victimization.

However, rather than focusing on the unique vulnerability of the homeless population, the coverage studied contained a significant theme discussing squeegiers and panhandlers as *criminal offenders* suffering only from individual pathology, or poor choices. For example, Attorney General Jim

Flaherty referred to a 'small industry' of aggressive panhandlers (Freed, 2000) and two Toronto police officers referred to squeegiers as 'real terrorists' (Taylor, 2000). Toronto Mayor Mel Lastman echoed these concerns: 'They're not kids, by the way, they're squeegee troublemakers, they're squeegee pests. They're people who, if you don't give them money, will swear at you, they'll intimidate you, they'll damage your car, they'll throw dirty water on your car' (Gollom, 2000). Moreover, panhandlers were described as 'drunk' (Hall, 2000; McNairn, 2000; Johnson, 2000) and 'disorderly' (Sibley, 2000; McNairn, 2000; Tonner, 2000). The public discussion surrounding squeegiers and panhandlers often focused on personal vilification through an emphasis on individual choices, as illustrated by the words of Attorney General Jim Flaherty: 'squeegeeing isn't a career option. It's a dead end' (Bourette, 2000). This media focus created a narrow typification of squeegiers and panhandlers that removed them from the broader context of poverty and homelessness. With respect to such ideology, Gusfield (1985) notes that *troubled* people are commonly recast as *troublesome*—correspondingly, social control replaces social welfare as the organizing principle of state policy (Reinarman, 1998). This personal vilification framed squeegeeing and panhandling as public issues that have developed out of private troubles, rather than as a result of structural forces, such as poverty, unemployment, homelessness, and inequality.

The usage of melodramatic imagery by politicians, police officials, and journalists, transformed squeegiers and panhandlers from unintended victims of unequal class relations into threatening victimizers that should be held accountable for their behaviour. This sentiment was most poignantly expressed by then-Attorney General Jim Flaherty: 'all people in Ontario have the right to drive on the roads, walk down the street, or go to public places without being or feeling intimidated. When they are unable to do so, it is time for the government to act' (McCarten, 2000). In this way, forces of legal control were constructed as heroes with altruistic intentions: protecting victims from villains. Squeegeeing and panhandling, behaviours commonly associated with the conditions of poverty and homelessness, have been targeted by lawmakers as a form of victimization. In this manner, the **hegemonic ideology** was supported: squeegeeing and panhandling were decontextualized from poverty and homelessness and discussed within a law and order policy solution frame.

With regards to the homeless population, this individualized framing is particularly interesting. Much of the literature on homeless youth indicates that a large percentage of the population is homeless as a result of their experiences of victimization (Baron, 1997, 2003; Tyler and Johnson, 2004). Researchers (Baron, 1997, 2003; Tyler et al., 2001; Tyler and Johnson, 2004) note that prior abuse contributes to the likelihood of victimization among homeless youth by placing them on trajectories for early independence, which in turn increases their vulnerability to offenders and exposure to deviant activities. Although much of the literature regarding the homeless population has focused on the offending behaviours of homeless youth, some researchers have contended that 'victims' and 'offenders' are not mutually exclusive categories but, rather, represent a dynamic group in which victims offend and offenders are victimized (Kennedy and Baron, 1993; Tyler and Johnson, 2004). Similarly, Hagan and McCarthy (1997) argue that homeless young people generally have

high rates of offending and are vulnerable to crime given their street exposure. Accordingly, homelessness simultaneously increases one's vulnerability to victimization and propensity towards offending.

With regard to this particular study, the actions of squeegiers and panhandlers were removed from the conditions of deprivation and exclusion in which they occur. The introduction of criminal law as a means of regulating the poor exemplifies a shift from conceiving of the homeless as villains rather than victims. This shift in discourse illustrates that the war on poverty so vehemently declared in the 1960s has quickly become a war against the poor (Katz, 1990; Gavigan, 1999; Mitchell, 2003). As noted by Wright (1997: 1), 'visible homeless bodies, their comportment and appearance, have replaced invisible abstract notions of "poverty" as a key social concern.' This artificial differentiation between homelessness and poverty has significant implications for public policy and those living on the streets. Specifically, this study indicates that public policies regarding the homeless appear to be paradoxical: while policy debates of crime commonly include homeless youth with reference to their role as offenders, they often overlook the real possibility that homeless youth may disproportionately be victims of crime. The most tangible example of this paradox is a plethora of legal and public scrutiny devoted to the survival tactics of the homeless.

References

Baron, S. 1997. 'Risky Lifestyles and the Link Between Offending and Victimization', *Studies on Crime and Crime Prevention* 6: 53–72.

———. 2003. 'Street Youth, Violence, and Victimization', *Trauma, Violence, and Abuse: A Review Journal* 4, 1: 22–44.

Bourette, S. 2000. 'Critics, Panhandlers Plan Next Move as Province's Squeegee Law Takes Effect', *Globe and Mail*, A19.

Brooks, C. 2002. 'Globalization and a New Underclass of "Disposable" People', in *Marginality and Condemnation: An Introduction to Critical Criminology*, B. Schissel and C. Brooks, eds. Halifax, NS: Fernwood Publishing.

CBC News Online. 2003. 'New Poverty Indicator shows 1 in 8 Canadians are Poor', 27 May 2003. Available at http://www.cbc.ca/stories/2003/05/27/canada/poverty_basket030527 (accessed 3 April 2005).

Comack, E. 1999. 'Theoretical Excursions', in *Locating Law Race/Class/Gender Connections*, pp. 19–68, E. Comack, ed. Halifax, NS: Fernwood.

Fitzpatrick, K., M. LaGory, and F. Ritchey. 1999. 'Dangerous Places: Exposure to Violence and its Mental Health Consequences for the Homeless', *American Journal of Orthopsychiatry* 69: 438–47.

Freed, D.A. 2000. 'Squeegee to Challenge New Safe Streets Act', *Toronto Star*, 9 February: A1.

Gaetz, S. 2004. 'Safe Streets for Whom? Street Youth, Social Exclusion, and Criminal Victimization', *Canadian Journal of Criminology and Criminal Justice* 46, 4: 423–55.

Gavigan, S. 1999. 'Poverty Law, Theory, and Practice: The Place of Class and Gender in Access to Justice', in *Locating Law: Race/Class/Gender Connections*, E. Comack, ed. Halifax, NS: Fernwood Press.

Gollom, M. 2000. 'Law In Effect Today to Wipe Away Squeegee Kids', *National Post*, 31 January 31: A19.

Gusfield, J.R. 1985. 'Theories and Hobgoblins', *SSSP Newsletter* 17 (Fall): 16–18.

Hagan, J., and B. McCarthy. 1997. *Mean Streets: Youth Crime and Homelessness*. New York: Cambridge University Press.

Hall, V. 2000. 'Mayor Wants Patrols to Empty Sidewalks of Panhandlers, Drunks', *Edmonton Journal*, 16 September: A1.

Howlett, D. 2005. *We Can Make Child Poverty History in Canada*. Available at http://www.napo-onap.ca/en/news/makechildpovertyhistory.htm (accessed 3 April 2005).

Johnston, B. 2000. 'Mayor: Begging Only for Drunks, Mentally Ill', *Halifax Daily News*, 7 September: 4.

Katz, M.B. 1990. *The Undeserving Poor: From the War on Poverty to the War on Welfare*. New York: Pantheon Books.

Kennedy, L.W., and S.W. Baron. 1993. 'Routine Activities and a Subculture of Violence: A Study of Violence on the Street', *Journal of Research in Crime and Delinquency* 30, 1: 88–112.

Layton, J. 2000. Homelessness. *The Making and Unmaking of a Crisis*. Toronto: Penguin Books.

McCarten, J. 2000. 'Squeegee Kids, Begging Banned', *Kingston Whig Standard*, 31 January: 10.

McNairn, K. 2000. 'Group Urges Panhandling Crackdown: Downtown Businesses Plead for Stricter Enforcement of Bylaw', *Saskatoon Star Phoenix*, 9 December: A6.

Mitchell, D. 2003. *The Right to the City: Social Justice and the Fight for Public Space*. New York: The Guilford Press.

Murphy, B. 2000. *On the Streets: How We Created the Homeless*. Canada: J. Gordon Shillingford Publishing Inc.

National Anti-Poverty Organization (NAPO). 1999. *Short-Changed on Human Rights: A NAPO Position Paper on Anti-Panhandling By-Laws*. Ottawa.

Reinarman, C. 1998. 'The Social Construction of an Alcohol Problem: The Case of Mothers Against Drunk Drivers and Social Control in the 1980s', in *Constructing Crime: Perspectives on Making News and Social Problems*, G.W. Potter and V.E. Kappeler, eds. Illinois: Waveland Press Inc.

Rotheram-Borus, M.J., K.A. Mahler, C. Koopman, and K. Langabeer. 1996. 'Sexual Abuse History and Associated Multiple Risk Behaviour in Adolescent Runaways', *American Journal of Orthopsychiatry* 66: 390–400.

Schrecker, T. 2000. 'Crime, Property, and Poverty in the 1990s: Learning from the 1790s', in *New Perspectives on Deviance: The Construction of Deviance in Everyday Life*, pp. 163–79, L. Beaman, ed. Toronto: Prentice Hall Inc.

Sibley, R. 2000. 'Please Do Not Feed the Panhandlers', *Ottawa Citizen*, 17 July: A12.

Taylor, B. 2000. 'Squeegee Kids All Washed Up', *Toronto Star*, 31 January: A1.

Tonner, M. 2001. 'If You Want Safer Streets, Do What New York Did and Add More Cops', *Vancouver Province*, 26 January: A32.

Tyler, K., and K. Johnson. 2004. 'Victims and Offenders: Accounts of Paybacks, Invulnerability, and Financial Gain and Homeless Youth', *Deviant Behavior* 25: 427–49.

Tyler, K., D. Hoyt, L. Whitbeck, and A. Mari Cauce. 2001. 'The Impact of Childhood Sexual Abuse on Later Sexual Victimization Among Runaway Youth', *Journal of Research on Adolescence* 11: 151–76.

Wright, T. 1997. *Out of Place: Homeless Mobilizations, Subcities, and Contested Landscapes*. Albany: SUNY Press.

CHAPTER 7

Politicizing Aboriginal Cultural Tourism: The Discourse of Primitivism in the Tourist Encounter

Siegrid Deutschlander and Leslie J. Miller

Aboriginal cultural tourism is a potentially high-growth segment of the Canadian tourism industry that is currently enjoying widespread demand among Europeans, especially German visitors. This paper uses a discourse analysis approach to examine the tourist encounter at various Aboriginal tourist sites in southern Alberta. It analyzes the negotiation of 'Indianness' and Indian culture by both Native interpreters and foreign visitors. These negotiations are shown to be informed by the primitivist discourse that, ironically, reinforces the Enlightenment notion of the 'noble savage'. We argue that, despite its colonialist and essentialist aspects, the primitive discourse can nevertheless function as a strategy of resistance to a social system viewed by many First Nations as politically oppressive.

A **discourse** that is central to Aboriginal **cultural tourism** (and to this study) is the 'primitivist discourse' (Thomas, 1994), also called the 'antimodernist discourse' (Smith, 2000). A legacy of Enlightenment thought, primitivism attributes 'an exemplary status to simple or archaic ways of life, and thus frequently shares the progressivist understanding of tribal society as an original and antecedent form, but revalues its rudimentary character as something to be upheld' (Thomas, 1994: 174). The primitivist discourse flourished in the nineteenth century in the image of the 'Noble Savage' and inspired painters, photographers, and writers 'to save the memory of a vanishing race' (Goetzmann and Goetzmann, 1986: 15). For German-speaking Europeans, no one exerted more influence on the popular imagination than the writer Karl May (1842–1912), whose *Winnetou* trilogy remains in circulation today. As reflected in the term 'Noble Savage', the primitivist discourse

carries both negative and positive meanings. On the one hand, it promotes Native society as superior to white society for its spirituality and purity; on the other, it demotes Native society to inferior status for being primitive and uncivilized. Cultural tourism sites provide an occasion to explore the ways in which the two sides of the primitivist discourse are taken up.

Spirituality

Native ceremonies that include prayers and sweats have become popular features at tourist sites and native interpreters make ongoing efforts to cast these events as spiritual practices, not commercial enterprises. Visitors to the camp may be welcomed with pipe ceremonies, sweet grass smudges (the smoke from the sweet grass is scooped up in the hands and fanned over the body), and prayers. At powwows, elders pray for the blessing and the protection of all people. When used as welcome and farewell greetings at culture camps, prayers may symbolize the boundary between non-native and native society. They tell visitors that they are entering a numinous world. By constructing these events as spiritual, rather than commercial, Native interpreters implicitly invoke and reaffirm the positive side of the primitivist discourse ('we are spiritual, not heathen/corrupt'). We can identify several ways, in addition to prayers, through which the visitor is enlisted in this version of events.

We found that challenges to the spirituality of the ceremonies were quite rare. Still, visitors are occasionally suspicious that their hosts are only 'playing Indian' (see Peers, 1999)—that the sweat is being put on just for them, or altered out of all recognition because of tourist demands. This worry particularly surfaces when ceremonies are discovered to have been adjusted to suit the needs of visitors. Sweats for visitors may be less hot, for example; there may be fewer rounds (three instead of four) and they may take less time. On one occasion a visitor wondered to the researcher: 'Is this how they proceed among themselves as well?' (field notes). For him, the issue was whether this adjustment rendered the sweat inauthentic, or, in other words, whether this was merely a commodified performance given to tourists. After a short explanation to outline that there are different types of sweats, that some native sweats are very long, and so forth, no further concerns were raised. Thus, this explanation preserved the spirituality of the ceremony by defining some of its aspects—in this case, the duration, the number of rounds, and the temperature—as non-essential to its authentically spiritual nature. Moreover, the sweat remained 'spiritual' because the ceremonialist was Native and claimed to have obtained the transferred right to conduct it.

Respect for Nature and Animals

The presentations at Head-Smashed-In Buffalo Jump (HSIBJ) attempt to pre-empt the charge of cruelty to animals in three major ways. First, guides repeatedly emphasize the respect of the Blackfoot people for nature and animals. The introductory comment to the main video reaffirms this: 'A few of the scenes in this movie might appear cruel to some people. Please feel assured that no animals were harmed in any way during the production of this movie.' The guides add that only animals that had died of natural causes prior to making the film were used. One guide conceded that 'some of the things we did at HSIBJ sound cruel,' only to add, 'but we had to do this to survive' (field notes). These comments define killing as a necessary part of a traditional lifestyle to prevent starvation.

Secondly, Native people are said to have the spiritual right to hunt buffalo. The presentation notes that the actual hunt proceeded only after the buffalo-hunting ceremony was performed. According to one guide, buffalo used to eat humans, but the Creator changed this order of things because it was wrong (field notes).

Linked to the killing of the buffalo is the emphasis on its efficient utilization by the Blackfoot people. Approximately 300 animals were killed every year in the fall hunt to feed the people who gathered for this undertaking. The implication is that the killing of 300 animals once a year was not much, given that they were the complete food supply for several bands for the whole winter. Out of 60 million, 300 animals seem insignificant. A second aspect of efficiency is the assertion that nothing was wasted. Mary, a Native guide, states: 'The Blackfoot people were very dependent on the buffalo and got everything they needed from [them]: tools, clothing, food, shelter.' The displays also show some of the 150 items that were obtained from these animals.

Then, the visitor is introduced to the hunting of buffalo en masse by white sport hunters during the second half of the nineteenth century. Visitors are surrounded by stacked-up buffalo skulls and display cases containing mounds of buffalo bones (used for fertilizer and ammunition), and life-sized photomurals and paintings of the shooting of buffalo from trains. All this visual evidence documents the destruction of thousands of years of Native life. These displays clearly suggest that the members of white society showed no respect for the animals and, by extension, for Native culture. Instead, they destroyed the balance with nature by invading a territory in which they had no right to be. The effect is the construction of a sharp moral contrast between Native peoples, whose hunt is represented as being 'in harmony with nature' and the white people, whose hunt is represented as 'senseless slaughter'. The conclusion is that white—not Native—society is destructive and cannot live in harmony with nature. Moreover, some Native visitors are prepared to extend this indictment of corrupt white attitudes into the present day; says Richard: 'North America is candy for the white man. They don't save anything and that's what's killing Mother Earth.'

Politicizing Cultural Performances

Critics of cultural tourism generally argue that community identity, history, and traditions are diminished when they are performed for others in the tourist setting. MacCannell (1989) argued that the '**staged authenticity**' of heritage sites and performances is ineluctably alienating. By tearing the practice out of its natural setting, he contended, performance interrupts the flow and integrity of everyday life. Moreover, staging culture represents it in a standardized (and thus commodifiable) format (but see counterarguments about the inalienable character of tradition, in Macdonald, 1997: 172–4): it lifts cultural events from their local and particular settings, and endows them with a universalizing 'semantic reach'—that is, with a broader, global significance for the visitor—they never had in everyday life. Thus, MacCannell might argue, the HSIBJ site makes the European slaughter of the buffalo and its effects on the indigenous peoples around HSIBJ into just one more instance of the general category of 'oppression', and its particularity is thereby erased.

We have already noted how guides at HSIBJ, according to their own various convictions, attempt to orchestrate the meaning of the buffalo hunt for the visitor by the way they lead them toward or away from the contentious 'white-blaming' exhibit at the interpretive centre. While some interpreters feel constrained by the etiquette of host–guest relations, others are ready to 'set the record straight' and tell things 'as they really are' in the present: 'People need to know that we don't live on reserves

by choice,' says Mary. Moreover, by forging tight connections between the past, as represented at a historic site like HSIBJ or a Sun Dance, and the present, the Native staff politicize the sites not just for the visitors, but for themselves, and thus manage, Peers notes, to offset the alienating effect that 'playing Indian' allegedly has in the eyes of critics like MacCannell. Peers notes that the interpreters do not see themselves as playing dead people in a distant era; instead, they say: '[W]e're playing ourselves, the real First Nations people' (Peers, 1999: 47).

In this paper we have attempted to show how cultural performances can be opened up and their historical and traditional meanings renegotiated to the benefit of Native communities. We have highlighted the specific representational strategies employed at selected tourist sites, and especially the interpretive practices of Native guides, which are aimed at enlisting visitors in this positive version of Native culture and history. By focusing on the context of interaction, we intend to emphasize that the meaning of these performances and displays is never final, nor can agreement be imposed. As analysts, therefore, we cannot simply assert that positive or favourable readings will prevail over negative ones (as Macdonald seems to when she argues that the Aros Centre in Skye is able to counter commercialism by 'putting it [commercialization] in the service of culture', rather than the other way around [Macdonald, 1997: 159]). This will finally, inevitably, be an empirical matter. In short, the 'real meaning' of a museum display or a ceremony is never secured. It must constantly be worked up anew.

References

Goetzmann, W.H., and W.N. Goetzmann. 1986. *The West of the Imagination*. New York: W.W. Norton & Company.

Government of Alberta. n.d. *Head-Smashed-In Buffalo Jump*. Calgary: Community Development.

MacCannell, D. 1989. *The Tourist: A New Theory of the Leisure Class*. New York: Random House.

Macdonald, S. 1997. 'A People's Story: Heritage, Identity and Authenticity', in *Touring Cultures: Transformation of Travel and Theory*, pp. 155–75, C. Rojek and J. Urry, eds. London: Routledge.

May, K. 1951. *Winnetou*. Bamberg: Karl-May-Verlag.

Peers, L. 1999. 'Playing Ourselves: First Nations and Native American Interpreters at Living History Sites', *The Public Historian* 21, 4: 39–61.

Smith, S.L. 2000. *Reimagining Indians: Native Americans through Anglo Eyes, 1880–1940*. Oxford: Oxford University Press.

Thomas, N. 1994. *Colonialism's Culture: Anthropology, Travel and Government*. Princeton, NJ: Princeton University Press.

CHAPTER 8

Tattooing and Civilizing Processes: Body Modification as Self-control

Michael Atkinson

Theoretical Underpinnings

Mainstay social-psychological interpretations of tattooing revolve around a construction of tattoo enthusiasm as inherently pathological (Howell et al., 1971; Gittleson and Wallfn, 1973; Newman, 1982; Grumet, 1983; Houghton et al., 1996). Social psychologists typically contend that a tattooed body is the manifestation of a mind fraught with disorder. Furthermore, they suggest wearers cannot conform to dominant social **norms**, values, and beliefs as a result of developmental or cognitive defect (see Williams, 1998). If we accept classic social psychological interpretations of tattooing offered by Gittleson et al. (1969), Goldstein (1979), Lombroso-Ferrero (1972), Measey (1972), and Pollak and McKenna (1945), tattooing predicts more serious deviance; as individuals who brutally mutilate their bodies in such a barbaric way cannot contain other 'primitive' or contra-normative impulses.

In related medical and epidemiological research, tattooing is attributed to youthful impetuousness and irrationality (Armstrong, 1994, 1995; Armstrong and McConnell, 1994; Houghton et al., 1996; Armstrong and Pace-Murphy, 1997; Gurke and Armstrong, 1997; Martin, 1997; Grief and Hewitt, 1998; Armstrong et al, 2000). Tattooing indicates immaturity among 'at-risk youth' and is correlated with other forms of self-harm such as physical aggressiveness, promiscuity, substance abuse, and suicide (Kom, 1996; Braithwaite et al., 2001; Roberts and Ryan, 2002).

The nature of tattooing as a normative practice is rarely considered, because both the pathology of the act and actor is assumed. Reflective of this ongoing tradition of interpretation, there presently exists a giant schism between social scientific interpretations of tattooing and contemporary sensibilities about the act circulated by Canadian practitioners. The dominant manner of analyzing tattoos in academic research may, however, be challenged by exploring several of the sensitizing principles of figurational sociology (Elias, 1994, 1996).

Tattooing and the 'Civilized' Habitus

Figurational sociologists argue that body projects like tattooing cannot be understood outside of the 'figurations' within which they are produced (Atkinson, 2003a). A 'figuration' is a complex matrix of social relationships based on far-ranging individual and group interdependences that interconnect family, school, workplace, leisure, religious, and political spheres. Elias's concept of the figuration is based upon a rather simple idea that individuals are mutually bound to one another through extended networks or 'chains' of action:

> The network of interdependences among human beings is what binds them together. Such interdependences are the nexus of what is

here called the figuration, a structure of mutually oriented and dependent people. Since people are more or less dependent on each other, first by nature and then by social learning, through education, socialization, and socially generated reciprocal needs, they exist, one might venture to say, only as pluralities, only in figurations (1994: 214).

Through social interaction processes within figurations, common cultural ways of thinking, or 'habituses', are formed (Elias, 1996). A habitus is internalized through socialization processes and becomes a socially learned 'second nature' of behaviour (Elias, 1983, 1996).

By attending to enthusiasts' tattooing narratives we realize how the practice is a *learned cultural habit* that is dialogical with, and not irreverent to, diffuse body norms within a figuration. As tattoo enthusiast Matthew (22) suggests, 'I never thought about getting tattooed until I started hanging around with a lot of people who had them, you know.' Modifying the body as a normative act is learned through and reinforced by one's interdependencies with others. As such, we must examine the conditions of social interdependence giving rise to tattooing habits and the character of broader body modification norms 'framing' (Goffman, 1974) cultural understandings of tattooing.

Rational identity expression

At a very basic level, tattooing projects reinforce and reflect 'I–WE' figurational relationships (Elias, 1978, 1991). Tattooing the body represents one's sense of 'I' within social circles; starting with quite intimate and mutually identified 'WE' groups (e.g., family, friends, peers, or social club members) and extending to WE groups bound by lengthy chains of interdependency (e.g., social classes, religious groups, or fellow lifestyle participants).

Conformity to established WE ideals about the body beautiful often involves commodifying the flesh (Falk, 1994; Featherstone, 2000; Miles et al., 1998). Canadians flock in droves to professional 'body modificationists' to rework their bodies/

selves in a multitude of non-invasive or invasive ways. Fitness experts, dieticians, physical therapists, cosmetic surgeons, aestheticians, and personal stylists collectively instruct people to redesign, rehabilitate, reconstruct, and extend their bodies through the aid of commercial products and services. Their services allow us to achieve preferred cultural body shapes through precise techniques, and understand the body as something to be individually 'worked'. The flesh is subjected to a series of rationalized services and products in the burgeoning body industries, and becomes more structured by specific 'technologies of the self' (Foucault, 1977).

In fact, many enthusiasts describe tattooing as a calculated effort to 'fit in with other people and look appealing' (Jill, age 34). Tattoos are clearly forms of 'social capital' (Bourdieu, 1984) in this respect, and document the social power, accolade, and acceptance garnered by manipulating the 'natural' body to comply with diffuse figurational norms. Tattooing narratives speak of a cultural pressure to do 'something' with the body and make it more physically attractive.

In sum, tattoo enthusiasts' projects of self-redesign are 'customized' forms of compliance to established body norms and practices in Western figurations like Canada. Tattoos reflect one's position in **social networks** of identification and illustrate one's identities and statuses held therein. The marks do not ring with irreverence to others, as they are interpreted by wearers as rational gestures of identity given to be 'read' as cultural signs. Tattooing projects also reverberate with a cultural preference to beautify the body through highly individualized bodywork, especially via the help of service professionals. Enthusiasts ultimately contend that their predilections for tattooing are congruent with established cultural habituses detailing appropriate body use and display.

Affect Management and Conformity

Among some women tattoo enthusiasts body markings are replete with strong feelings of sexual desire. Tattoos draw wanted sexual attention to the body and heighten erotic sensations in certain contexts of exchange (i.e., in a night club, on a date, within a leisure scenario, or during intimate sexual interaction). Since Canadian women have been, at least historically, dissuaded from participating in tattooing in light of its hypermasculinist image (Wroblewski, 1992; Cohen, 2000; Atkinson, 2002), marking the body in this manner may signify sexual independence, freedom, and self-determination; qualities recently popularized by 'girl power' attitudes in Canada.

Where certain tattoo enthusiasts intextuate symbols of social anxiety onto the body, others symbolize 'positive' emotions like joy and exuberance through tattoos. Tattooing the body can be a gesture of love, happiness, excitement, and belonging for those seeking to display the satisfaction gleaned from involvement in valued WE-groups. Individuals denote the value placed on emotional attachments and publicly announce the importance of such bonds by indelibly inscribing the skin.

For a small group of the enthusiasts, however, tattooing projects express 'negative' feelings of anger, resentment, or aggression. These enthusiasts pursue tattooing projects as mutually identifiable and personally controlled coping mechanisms. Instead of attacking the source of frustration through a physically threatening or malicious act, they design corporeal projects to illustrate their learned capacities for self-restraint. Even though substantial portions of the social-psychological literature depict tattooing as symptomatic of an inability to cope with aggression (i.e., the tattoo is a quintessential mark of aggression or an anger-based lifestyle), enthusiasts articulate how tattooing the body releases anger in a restrained fashion.

Discussion

Preferred academic interpretations of the body project hold firmly to a conceptualization of tattoo enthusiasts as impulsive and non-reflexive social misfits who express disdain for conventional body practices (see Armstrong, 1992; Loimer and Werner, 1992; Armstrong and Pace-Murphy, 1997). Despite recent estimates that anywhere from 10–20 per cent of Canadians have tattoos (Atkinson, 2003a), academics generally deconstruct tattooing as atypical and isolated risk-taking behaviour. However, by letting go of heretofore preferred theoretical constructions of tattooing and actually conversing with tattoo enthusiasts, we begin to appreciate 'alternative' empirical lessons about this brand of body modification.

Figurational sociology may help rebuild the decaying analytical bridge between social-psychological constructions of tattooing and everyday interpretations of tattoos that wearers make. Akin to Copes and Forsyth's (1993) analysis of the body project, figurational sociologists point out how popular uses of tattooing reflect a collective sensitivity to the social importance of publicly performed inner restraint and acceptance of established cultural body habits (Atkinson 2003a, 2003b). Enthusiasts' narratives suggest how social interdependencies influence both the desire to become tattooed and the character of tattooing projects. Furthermore, individuals either explicitly or implicitly manage affective expression through their tattoos, thereby transforming the skin into a social billboard of normative emotion work.

Contemporary tattooing in Canada is, then, a social paradox and strange amalgam of cultural values about the body and its display. The tattooed body both marks long-term 'civilized' cultural preferences to alter the flesh as part of 'doing' social identity, and signifies more recent social influences on body modification preferences arising from corporeal commodification, risk processes and technological innovation. In reading the tattooed body as a marker of figurational ebbs and flows, the 'micrological' and 'macrological' influences on our cultural attitudes regarding tattooed flesh are highlighted. Future social-psychological research on tattooing in Canada and abroad should challenge overly simplistic, ahistorical and stereotypical constructions of the tattooing process, and pursue empirical explanations of the practice grounded in the lived experience of being tattooed.

References

Armstrong, M. 1994. 'Tattoos: A Risk-taking Art', *Texas Nursing* 68, 2: 8–9.

———. 1995. 'Adolescent Tattoos: Educating vs. Pontificating', *Pediatric Nursing* 21, 6: 561–4.

Armstrong, M., and C. McConnell. 1994. 'Tattooing in Adolescence, More Common Than You Think: The Phenomenon and Risks', *Journal of School Nursing* 10, 1: 22–9.

Armstrong, M., and K. Pace-Murphy. 1997. 'Tattooing: Another Adolescent Risk Behavior Warranting Health Education', *Applied Nursing Research* 10, 4: 181–9.

Armstrong, M., Y. Masten, and R. Martin. 2000. 'Adolescent Pregnancy, Tattooing, and Risk Taking', *American Journal of Maternal/Child Nursing* 25, 5: 258–61.

Armstrong, R. 1992. 'Tattooing should be Regulated', *New England Journal of Medicine* 326, 3: 207.

Atkinson, M. 2002. 'Pretty in Ink: Conformity, Resistance, and Negotiation in Women's Tattooing', *Sex Roles* 47, 5/6: 219–35.

———. 2003a. *Tattooed: The Sociogenesis of a Body Art*. Toronto: University of Toronto Press.

———. 2003b. 'The Civilizing of Resistance: Straightedge Tattooing', *Deviant Behavior* 24, 3: 197–220.

Bourdieu, E. 1984. *Distinction: A Social Critique of Judgement of Taste*. Cambridge: Harvard University Press.

Braithwaite, R., A. Robillard, T. Woodring, T. Stephens, and K. Arriola. 2001. 'Tattooing and Body Piercing among Adolescent Detainees: Relationship to Alcohol and Other Drug Use', *Journal of Substance Abuse* 13, 1/2: 5–16.

Cohen, T. 2000. *The Tattoo*. London: Greenwich Editions.

Copes, J., and C. Forsyth. 1993. 'The Tattoo: A Social Psychological Explanation', *International Review of Modern Sociology* 23: 83–9.

Elias, N. 1978. *What is Sociology?* London: Hutchinson.

———. 1983. *The Court Society*. Oxford: Basil Blackwell.

———. 1991. *The Society of Individuals*. Oxford: Basil Blackwell.

———. 1994. *The Civilising Process*. Oxford: Basil Blackwell.

———. 1996. *The Germans: Studies of Power Struggles and the Development of Habitus in the Nineteenth and Twentieth Centuries*. Oxford: Polity Press.

Falk, E. 1994. *The Consuming Body*. London: Sage.

Featherstone, M. 2000. *Body Modification*. London: Sage.

Foucault, M. 1977. *Discipline and Punish: The Birth of the Prison*. London: Penguin Books.

Gittleson, N., and G. Wallfn. 1973. 'The Tattooed Male Patient', *British Journal of Psychiatry* 122, 568: 295–300.

Gittleson, N., G. Wallfn, and K. Dawson-Butterworth. 1969. 'The Tattooed Psychiatric Patient', *British Journal of Psychiatry* 115: 1249–53.

Goffman, E. 1974. *Frame Analysis*. Cambridge. Harvard University Press.

Goldstein, N. 1979. 'Laws and Regulations Relating to Tattoos', *Journal of Dermatologic Surgery and Oncology* 5: 913–15.

Grief, J., and W. Hewitt. 1998. 'The Living Canvass: Health Issues in Tattooing, Body Piercing and Branding', *Advances for Nurse Practitioners* 12: 26–31.

Grumet, G. 1983. 'Psychodynamic Implications of Tattoos', *American Journal of Orthopsychiatry* 3: 482–92.

Gurke, B., and M. Armstrong. 1997. 'D-tag: Erasing the Tag of Gang Membership', *Journal of School Nursing* 13, 2: 13–17.

Houghton, S., K. Durkin, E. Parry, Y. Turbett, and R. Odgers. 1996. 'Amateur Tattooing Practices and Beliefs among High School Adolescents', *Journal of Adolescent Health* 19, 6: 420–5.

Howell, R., R. Payne, and A. Roe. 1971. 'Differences among Behavioral Variables, Personal Characteristics, and Personality Scores of Tattooed and Non-tattooed Prison Inmates', *Journal of Research in Crime and Delinquency* 8: 32–7.

Kom, K. 1996. 'Body Adornment and Tattooing: Clinical Issues and State Regulations', *Physician Assistant* 20, 5: 85–100.

Loimer, N., and E. Werner. 1992. 'Tattooing and High-risk Behaviour among Drug Addicts', *Medicine and Law* 11, 3/4: 167–74.

Lombroso-Ferrero, G. 1972. *Criminal Man: According to the Classification of Cesare Lombroso*. Montclair, NJ: Patterson Smith.

Martin, A. 1997. 'On Teenagers and Tattoos', *Journal of the American Academy of Child and Adolescent Psychiatry* 36, 6: 860–1.

Measey, L. 1972. 'The Psychiatric and Social Relevance of Tattoos in Royal Navy Detainees', *British Journal of Criminology* 12: 182–6.

Miles, S., D. Cliff, and V. Burr. 1998. 'Fitting In and Sticking Out: Consumption, Consumer Meanings and the Construction of Young People's Identities', *Journal of Youth Studies* 1, 1: 81–120.

Newman, G. 1982. 'The Implication of Tattooing in Prisoners', *Journal of Clinical Psychiatry* 43: 231–4.

Pollak, O., and E. McKenna. 1945. 'Tattooed Psychotic Patients', *American Journal of Psychiatry* 101: 673–4.

Roberts, T., and S. Ryan. 2002. 'Tattooing and High-Risk Behavior in Adolescents', *Pediatrics* 110, 6: 1058–83.

Williams, K. 1998. 'Tattoos, Scars, Body Adornment and Dishevelment in an Acute Psychiatric Population', *Psychiatric Bulletin* 22: 94–6.

Wroblewski, C. 1992. *Tattooed Women*. London: Virgin Publishing.

CHAPTER 9

Buddhism in the Multicultural Context of Toronto, Canada: Local Communities, Global Networks

Janet McLellan

Since 1967, approximately 500,000 Asian immigrants and refugees have settled in the Greater Toronto area. Similar to other ethnic groups, they have turned to religious institutions for support in their adjustment and adaptation to Canadian life. In 1965, the Toronto Buddhist Church was the only Buddhist group in Toronto. Within 30 years, over 65 new temples and Buddhist associations became established, with several undergoing expansion or developing sister branches within the city. The dramatic growth of Buddhism reflects sociocultural dynamics of ethnic, national, and linguistic diversity as well as disparate immigration patterns.

The re-creation of Buddhist identities reflects the interplay of local, national, and global contexts. From a local perspective, similar to the religious adaptation of other minority ethnoreligious groups in Canada, adherence to traditional beliefs and practices has played a dynamic role in the adjustment process of Buddhist immigrants and refugees. Buddhist identities have been significantly altered and redefined within the various communities, most notably in innovative forms of worship and ritual services, in new models of

social interaction and affiliation, and in transformed authority patterns and gender roles for both Sangha and laity. Consequently, there is enormous differentiation among Buddhist groups, even those that share ethnic and linguistic backgrounds, raising issues of authenticity and representation. Some Toronto Buddhist groups are part of Canadian national organizations while others engage in transnational/global religious networks that reinforce ethnic and nationalist commitments across borders. These linkages influence inter-Buddhist relations within Toronto and concepts of national and religious identities.

For most Asian Buddhists, Buddhism has been the religion into which they were born, and this comprises their religious identity. Religious identity, along with ethnicity, however, often takes on new meaning and significance for newcomers to Canada, especially as community bonds and **networks** are recognized and expanded. For the last thirty years, multicultural policies and the Charter of Rights and Freedoms have transformed the conditions of settlement for Asian and other immigrants. The re-creation of Asian Buddhism today is dramatically different from the social context of racism and discrimination that shaped patterns and practices of Japanese Canadian Jodo Shinshu for over 60 years. In 1965, Porter described the vertical mosaic as a system of ethnic stratification in which those of British origin were at the top in terms of wealth, income, professional, and managerial status. Today, this is no longer the case and there is as much variation within ethnic groups as between them, distinguished along ethnic, economic, regional, political, and class identities. A different kind of vertical mosaic can be found in the class and power structures of Canadian Buddhists and among the many distinct yet unequal national and ethnic groups.

Relationships between ethnicity, social class, and migration experiences reflect themes of inequality in the ability of Asian Buddhists to re-create and sustain meaningful religious identities and communities. The extent of social and economic capital creates conditions not only affecting social, political, and economic adaptation and integration, but also ethnic resiliency and the capacity for accommodation and compromise. A vertical mosaic is evident in how Buddhist groups and institutions identify and use opportunities; take advantage of social resources and recognition; gain social, political, or local acceptance; and participate fully in Canadian society. Ethnic stratification among Buddhists is clearly seen in cultural capital and global networks—both influencing linguistic and community maintenance—as well as enhancing strength and strategies for expression and organization of Buddhist identities, especially resistance and challenge to forms of social subordination. Two areas will be highlighted in this paper—the resources and opportunity structures within different Toronto-based Buddhist groups, and their association and participation with globalized transnational networks.

Social and Economic Wealth

Immigrants and refugees significantly differ in the process through which they have come to Canada.

For immigrants, migrating to a new country may be the result of several years of preparation and extensive financial planning or family support. The recent Hong Kong and Taiwanese immigrants, many of whom came within the Business Class and Investment category, epitomize the well-planned migration. Chinese Buddhists in Toronto have the largest number of ordained clergy, temples, and practice centres (over 23), several of which depict traditional architecture, have undergone massive expansion, or developed sister branches within the city.

In contrast, refugees are forced to flee their homes, frequently in haste, with little time to plan or secure their belongings or savings. Families are often separated due to situations of social chaos, violence, or random killings. Refugees may find asylum in another country, only to face further discrimination or to languish for years in unsanitary, overcrowded camps until they are repatriated or resettled. For those small numbers who arrive in Canada, there is little money and shattered social networks are difficult to mend and re-establish. Refugees with extensive psychological trauma and physiological weakness and whose social and community bonds have been undermined, suffer long term effects, leading to chronic poverty, poor adaptation, and communal fragility. The Cambodian Buddhist community epitomizes these facets of refugee resettlement.

In comparison, although Tibetan refugees also arrived poor and in weakened health, the extensive support and encouragement from the Dalai Lama and the Tibetan government-in-exile facilitated strong community bonds and successful integration. The small Tibetan Buddhist community not only maintains traditional religious customs and ceremonies, but also sustains homeland nationalism and a committed political activism, focusing on social justice concerns and human rights violations in Tibet. Similarly, the strong social capital among Vietnamese refugees has influenced the degree to which their religious identities, beliefs, and practices are re-created. As traditional religious beliefs and practices respond to spiritual needs of the community, the Vietnamese Buddhist temple also provides a culturally appropriate venue for a variety of secular programs and services.

Among both immigrants and refugees, Buddhist organizations facilitate resettlement needs by providing family counselling, job networks, emotional support, or senior citizen programs. These organizations often become the focal point of social interaction and the centre for community life. Adherence to linguistic and cultural traditions encourages strong ethnic ties as worship and other religious programs are conducted in the home language, and cultural traditions including food, dress, and artistic activities—such as dance, songs, lotus lantern festivals, dharma painting, or calligraphy—are promoted. Ethnically identified social norms, values, and attitudes concerning gender roles, hierarchical relationships, and culturally established ideals of harmony, non-aggression, and compassion are also reinforced. In an effort to address and respond to communal and individual mental health concerns, one large Vietnamese Buddhist temple transformed individual memorial practices (Ky Sieu) into a weekly practice, enabling community members to share their loss and commemorate the death of loved ones together. As Asians in general are hesitant to address mental health concerns outside the family, the Buddhist monk or nun is a culturally appropriate intermediary.

Globalization

Networks and relationships that comprise many Asian Buddhist identities in Toronto are positioned between membership in the Canadian nation-state and large transnational communities of faith dispersed across the globe. Many Asian Buddhist groups retain a primary reference to these overseas, transnational communities and remain dependent on them for religious and cultural leadership, doctrinal authority and legitimacy, extended social relations, and ethnic identity. Belonging to larger transnational and global religious communities further influence attitudes toward resettlement issues and to the degree of identification with Canadian life, including nationalist sentiments, authority or gender patterns, and ideological values such as Canadian democracy and human rights. Transnational networks provide a variety of strategies which Toronto Asian Buddhist communities may draw upon to identify and resolve particular issues of accommodation and adaptation, for example, detailing how to respond to encounters with co-religionists of different ethnic and national backgrounds; responses to inter-faith forums or other demands of multicultural social climates; mediating social hostility, discrimination, or ignorance; providing guidelines for inter-faith activities, ethnic retention, or maintaining connections with homeland or **diaspora** institutions and leaders through newsletters, magazines, and other forms of communication. The combination of external transnational forces with those arising from internal local conditions often provides the impetus to suppress or accentuate selected aspects of distinctiveness or identity.

Summary

Buddhist immigrants and refugees bring with them familiar ritual practices, culturally constructed ideas about Dharma, personalized versions of karma, various images of Buddha (including all the accompanying embodiments), lay interpretations and terms for explicit doctrine, differential attitudes towards the Sangha (monks, nuns, priests, gurus, and teachers), and a variety of roles and restrictions toward the active participation of women. As such, each Buddhist group in Toronto illustrates a distinct example of the continuities and transformation of their respective traditions. Which particular parts of religious practice are emphasized, the role and choice of symbols, the focus on renunciation or worldly affirmation, and the transformed structural arrangements within religious organizations reflect the determinants of coming to Canada, systemic changes made after arrival, and the national and global networks in which they are embedded. The diversity of

Asian Buddhism in Toronto can be seen as a direct consequence of contemporary globalization.

Ethnic stratification is a global phenomenon and the world system itself is a 'vertical mosaic' in which global labour markets and exploitation give rise to ethnic conflict and refugee movements on the one hand, and the transilient (Richmond, 1969) migration of the business and investment class on the other. Religious and ethnic identities are continually unfolding within global conditions, while particularistic characteristics of these identities are being developed and asserted within the Canadian context. The construction of Buddhist identities in Toronto can thereby be viewed as shifting and complex, reflecting multiple voices asserted within identifiable spheres of power, history, and culture, which respond to changing local, national, and global realities.

In conclusion, although Buddhists in Toronto remain theoretically significant from an academic perspective, they tend to be 'relatively invisible'. Their style of dress, social mannerisms, dietary practices, integration of their children in school, or expectation of social recognition do not set them apart. Buddhists are not targeted with anti-Buddhist pamphlets or other messages of aversion, nor are they associated with social controversy, whether that involves advocating for separate religious schools or distinct rights based on religious practices. Instead, Buddhists quietly contribute to Canadian society through their aspirations for social tolerance and good citizenship (for example one group, the Tzu Chi foundation gave a Vancouver hospital $6 million), through their influence on psychological counselling and stress reduction treatments (especially the incorporation of mediation and visual imagery), and through their social and political activism. The effects of the Dalai Lama's Nobel Peace Prize in 1990, films such as *Little Buddha*, *Kundun*, or *The Cup*, as well as the high profiles of other well known Buddhist monks such as Thich Nhat Hanh or Maha Ghosananda, continue to stimulate growing interest in Buddhism. Unlike other minority religious traditions, Buddhism has attracted large numbers of non-Asian practitioners. The conversion of North Americans to Buddhism represents a reversal of traditional ideas about 'assimilation' or 'integration' of immigrants, thereby further increasing the complexity and diversity of Canadian society. Multicultural Canada in the twenty-first century is directly linked to the **world system** through transnational networks, of which the Buddhist links are a small but significant part.

References

Richmond, A.H. 1969. 'Sociology of Migration in Industrial and Postindustrial Societies', in *Sociological Studies, Volume 2*, J. Jackson, ed. Cambridge: Cambridge University Press.

Questions for Critical Thought

THE HACKER SPIRIT: AN INTERACTIONIST ANALYSIS OF THE HACKER IDEOLOGY

1. Discuss how the popular definition of computer hacker differs from the ways in which hackers define themselves. How might you account for these differing definitions?
2. Kleinknecht took a participant observer role to gather information on computer hackers, which involved hanging out with hackers to watch what they do and say on a first-hand basis. If you were to conduct a study on hackers, how might you approach your research differently? What benefits do you see to the author's approach versus your approach and vice versa?

3. By taking a participant observer role to collect his data on computer hackers, what types of obstacles do you think the author might have faced?

4. What are the seven key attributes that make up the hacker spirit, and how do these attributes differ from those first identified by Levy (1984) in his book the *Hacker Ethic*? How might you account for these differences?

5. What does Kleinknecht mean when he states that hackers use their ideology as a *vocabulary of motive*? Identify another group that is commonly thought of as 'deviant', and discuss how members of this group might apply their ideology as a vocabulary of motive.

Short-Changed: Media Representations of Squeegeeing and Panhandling

1. Which factors led to the enactment of the Ontario Safe Streets Act in 2000? Which factors contributed to increasing class inequalities in Canada? How can these situations affect the lives of the poor and homeless citizens?

2. Which past experience separates street youth from domiciled youth? How might you account for any relationship between this experience and the increased vulnerability of street youth?

3. How do politicians, police officials, and the media portray squeegiers and panhandlers? Do you think squeegiers and panhandlers can choose their behaviour? Why or why not?

4. Discuss how squeegiers and panhandlers are both victims and perpetrators of crime. By transforming the war on poverty to a war against the poor, have the city officials and the media lost their focus and vilified innocent have-nots?

5. Imagine that you are invited to attend a conference with the Mayor of Toronto to discuss possible ways to reduce street youth victimization and homelessness. What are your five key suggestions?

Politicizing Aboriginal Cultural Tourism: The Discourse of Primitivism in the Tourist Encounter

1. In primitivist discourse, how does the term 'Noble Savage' carry both positive and negative connotations? Do you think the Canadian society as a whole values the 'noble savage'? If so, in which ways? If not, why not?

2. Do you think spiritual ceremonies should be adjusted to suit the needs of visitors, for example by providing less hot and fewer rounds of sweats? Why or why not?

3. How do we, or can we, prove to foreigners that the ceremonies they observe and partake in are truly authentic and are not merely shows that 'play Indian'?

4. Discuss the pros and cons of cultural tourism. Is it simply a commodity or is it a means for indigenous people to share their history and culture with non-Natives?

5. According to Native interpreters, the decimation of the buffalos was largely due to the wasteful killing by whites, which disrupted the balance with nature. Can white man live in harmony with nature? Why or why not?

Tattooing and Civilizing Processes: Body Modification as Self-control

1. Social psychologists and medical researchers have traditionally associated tattooing with deviant behaviour. Describe their views and conclusions.

2. Considering that many tattoo enthusiasts get tattoos to 'fit in with other people and look appealing', is tattooing a product of peer pressure and another expression of consumerism in the form of 'customized' individuality?

3. Compare the benefits and meanings that tattoos confer to different enthusiasts.

4. How does tattooing reinforce and reflect the 'I–WE' figurational relationships? Give an example.
5. If you already have at least one tattoo, what is the symbol (pick one tattoo) that you have chosen and why? If you plan to get another or to get your first tattoo, what will it be and what does it symbolize? How do you think it will change your lifestyle and/or personality, if at all?

BUDDHISM IN THE MULTICULTURAL CONTEXT OF TORONTO, CANADA: LOCAL COMMUNITIES, GLOBAL NETWORKS

1. What are some background circumstances that bring Asian Buddhists to Canada? How do you think the social and economic wealth of these newcomers will affect their integration and settlement into Canada?
2. Compare and contrast the roles that Buddhist temples and services provide to their respective target ethnic groups.
3. Do you think there should be more communication between the different Asian Buddhist communities in Canada in order to share their social and economic wealth? Or should the groups be more or less independent to maintain their cultural and ethnic identity?
4. Give examples of programs and cultural activities that are promoted by Buddhist organizations. Do you think they should also actively engage the non-Buddhist community in these special events? Why or why not?
5. What are some benefits that transnational networks are able to offer to Asian Buddhist communities? Do you think the local Buddhist groups can offer the same or better benefits than those offered by the transnational networks? Why or why not?

Part III

Socialization

Every society has beliefs, values, and norms that it passes on from one generation to the next. Beginning at an early age, we teach children to distinguish behaviours that are socially acceptable from those that are condemned and disapproved. As children learn to internalize society's norms and values, they are actively engaging in the process of socialization. They learn to associate good behaviours with rewards and praise, and bad behaviours with punishments and rejection. These early moral lessons and social values will influence the actions they take later as adult members of society. In addition, children will use these internalized views of behaviours later in life when they take on different roles and identities. Socialization, therefore, helps to ease the transitions of youth as they move from one stage of life to another.

This section on socialization is about present-day youth and the challenges that they may face growing up in fast-paced Canadian society. The way in which society perceives youth affects their self-concept or, as Charles H. Cooley coined the term, their 'looking-glass self'. For example, John F. Manzo and Monetta M. Bailey show that the way in which media presents stereotypes of black youth affects their own identity formation, which in turn affects the possibility of committing criminal activities.

Rebecca Raby notes that today's young people are increasingly obliged to map out their own futures, which leaves them feeling anxious, anomic, and passive. Though some see a chance for self-direction and freedom, others fear the potential misdirection and self-absorption of an early adulthood will prevent proper integration into society. However, the pursuit of higher education prolongs youth for those who remain dependent on family for support. In brief, there are subtle differences between adolescence and adulthood that explain both the prolonged and narrowed nature of youth. Accordingly, Barbara A. Mitchell compares the family transitions to adulthood of present-youths to historical data. Examining the reccuring trends, family behaviours are affected by the social realm in which families are situated. However, Mitchell also notes how an individual's actions affect existing social patterns, for example, how the decisions of thousands of young adults are transforming the experience of later adulthood and family life.

Socialization is a lifelong process and it does not end with youth. Professional identity is fostered in the workplace. Brenda L. Beagan examines how medical students of different backgrounds identity themselves as future physicians. The process of identity formation is also difficult for children of immigrants as they experience a clash of many cultures—those of their parents and those of the new country. Nedim Karakayali investigates the tension experienced by immigrant children through autobiographies as their socialization experience is a new social phenomena stirred from recent global movements.

In conclusion, socialization at home, school, or in another setting passes on certain values and beliefs to children. Because of underlying social inequalities based on factors such as gender, religion, and class, children will learn to evaluate people's identities in a socially unequal context. Therefore, in the interests of a more egalitarian society, it is important that we limit the unconscious planting of prejudices in children by teaching them to be more open-minded towards differences. In addition, the lack of a clear demarcation between adolescence and adulthood confirms the challenge that youth face as they mature. On the one hand, youth are portrayed as dependent and immature; on the other hand, they are independent producers and consumers. To avoid misdirection, frustration, and self-absorption, it is necessary to provide youth with resources that will enable them to develop into responsible and confident adults who can one day contribute significantly to society.

CHAPTER 10

'Even if I don't know what I'm doing I can make it look like I know what I'm doing': Becoming a Doctor in the 1990s

Brenda L. Beagan

Introduction

When students enter medical school they are nothing more than normal lay people with some science background. When they leave four years later they have become physicians; they have acquired specialized knowledge and taken on a new identity of medical professional. What happens in those four years? What processes of **socialization** go into the making of a doctor?

Most of what we know about how students come to identify as future physicians derives from research conducted when students were almost exclusively male, white, middle- or upper-class, young, and single—for example, the classics *Boys in White* (Becker, Geer, Strauss, and Hughes, 1961) and *Student Physician* (Merton, Reader, and Kendall, 1957). When women and students of colour were present in this research it was in token numbers. Even when women and non-traditional students were present, as in Sinclair's (1997) recent ethnography, their impact on processes of professional identity formation and the potentially distinct impact of professional socialization on these students have been largely unanalyzed. What does becoming a doctor look like now, when many students are female, are of diverse backgrounds, are working-class, gay, and/or parents?

This study draws on survey and interview data from students and faculty at one Canadian medical school to examine the processes of professional identity formation and how diverse undergraduate medical students in the late 1990s experience these processes. As the results will show, the processes are remarkably unchanged from those documented 40 years ago.

Research Methods and Participants

This research employed three complementary research strategies: a survey of a third-year class (123 students) at one medical school, interviews with 25 students from that class, and interviews with 23 faculty members from the same school. Third-year students were chosen because in a traditional medical curriculum the third year is a key point for students; it is an important transition as they move out of the classroom to spend the majority of their time working with patients—patients who may or may not call them 'doctor', treat them as doctors, and reflect them back to themselves as doctors (cf., Coombs, 1978; Haas and Shaffir, 1987).

Survey respondents also identified faculty members who they believed were 'especially interested in medical education'. Twenty-three faculty interviews were conducted. All interviews took 60–90 minutes following a semi-structured interview guide, and were tape-recorded and transcribed.

Processes of Identity Formation

FIRST EXPERIENCES BECOME COMMONPLACE

When identifying how they came to think of themselves as medical students, participants described a process whereby what feels artificial and unnatural initially comes to feel natural, simply through repetition. For many students, a series of 'first times' were transformative moments.

CONSTRUCTING A PROFESSIONAL APPEARANCE

Students are quite explicitly socialized to adopt a professional appearance: 'When people started to relax the dress code a letter was sent to everybody's mailbox, commenting that we were not to show up in jeans, and a tie is appropriate for men.' Most students, however, do not require such reminders; they have internalized the requisite standards. Dressing neatly and appropriately is important in order to convey respect to patients, other medical staff, and the profession. It probably also helps the patients consider the students seriously (survey comment). When asked whether or not they ever worry about their appearance or dress at the hospital, 41 per cent of the survey respondents said they do not, while 59 per cent said they do.

CHANGES IN LANGUAGE, THINKING, AND COMMUNICATION SKILLS

Acquiring a huge vocabulary of both new words and old words with new meanings—what one student called 'medical-ese'—is one of the central tasks facing medical students, and one of the major bases for examining them (Sinclair, 1997). Students were well aware of the importance of adopting the formal language of medicine.

The language of medicine is the basis for constructing a new social reality. Even as it allows for communication, language constructs 'zones of meaning that are linguistically circumscribed' (Berger and Luckmann, 1966: 39). Medical language encapsulates and constructs a worldview wherein reducing a person to body parts, tissues, organs, and systems becomes normal, natural, and 'the only reasonable way to think' (Good and Good, 1993: 98–9). Students described this as learning to pare away 'extraneous' information about a patient's life to focus on what is clinically relevant.

Not surprisingly, students may simultaneously lose the communication abilities they had upon entering medical school.

LEARNING THE HIERARCHY

Key to becoming a medical student is learning to negotiate the complex hierarchy within medicine, with students positioned at the bottom. A few faculty saw this hierarchy as a fine and important tradition facilitating students' learning. Students,

and most faculty members, were far less accepting of this traditional hierarchy—particularly of students' place in it. Both faculty and students pointed out the compliance the hierarchical structure inculcates in students, discouraging them from questioning those above them. For students, being a 'good medical student' means not challenging clinicians. Although virtually every student described seeing things on the wards they disagreed with, as long as there was no direct harm to a patient they stayed silent and simply filed away the incident in their collection of 'things not to do when I am a doctor'. These students had developed a sense of alliance with other members of the profession rather than with lay people and patients—a key to professional socialization.

RELATIONSHIP TO PATIENTS

As students are learning their place in the hierarchy within medicine, they are simultaneously learning an appropriate relationship to patients. Within the medical hierarchy students feel powerless at the bottom. Yet, in relation to patients, even students hold a certain amount of power. In the interviews there were widely diverging views on the degree of professional authority physicians and student-physicians should display.

Some faculty drew a very clear connection between professionalism and the 'emotional distancing' Fox documented in medicine in 1957, describing students developing a 'hard shell' as a 'way of dealing with feelings' to prevent over-identifying with patients. Emotional involvement and over-identification are seen as dangerous. Students must strike a balance between empathy and objectivity, learning to overcome or master their emotions (Haas and Shaft, 1987; Conrad, 1988): 'I only become of use if I can create some distance so that I can function.' In contrast, several faculty members rejected the 'emotional distancing' approach to medicine in favour of one based in egalitarian connection.

PLAYING A ROLE GRADUALLY BECOMES REAL

Along with emotional distancing, Fox (1957) identified 'training for uncertainty' as key to medical socialization, including the uncertainty arising from not knowing everything, and not knowing enough. Alongside gathering the knowledge and experience that gradually reduces feelings of uncertainty, students also grow to simply tolerate high levels of uncertainty. At the same time, they face routine expectations of certainty—from patients who expect them 'to know it all' and faculty who often expect them to know far more than they do and who evaluate the students' competence (Haas and Shaffir, 1987). Students quickly learn that it is risky to display lack of certainty; impression management becomes a central feature of clinical learning (Conrad, 1988). Haas and Shaffir (1987: 110) conclude that the process of professionalization involves, above all, the successful adoption of a cloak of competence such that audiences are convinced of the legitimacy of claims to competence.

RESPONSES FROM OTHERS

The more others treat students as if they really were doctors, the more the students feel like doctors (cf., Coombs, 1978). In particular, the response from other hospital personnel and patients can help confirm the student's emerging medical professional identity.

For many students, patients were the single most important source of confirmation for their emerging identity as physicians. Simply being called 'doctor' by others, especially by patients, is one response that has a tremendous impact (Konner, 1987; Shapiro, 1987). Survey results show 68 per cent (n = 48) of students had been called 'doctor' at least occasionally by people other than family or friends. All but two fully recalled the first time they were called 'doctor' and how they felt about it. Not being referred to as a doctor—especially when your peers are—can be equally significant. In previous accounts, being white and being male have greatly improved a medical student's chances of being identified as a doctor (Gamble, 1990; Dickstein, 1993; Lenhart, 1993; Kirk, 1994). In this study, although social class background, minority status, and first language made no difference, significantly more

men than women were regularly called doctor and significantly more women had never been called doctor.

Secondary Socialization: Subsuming the Former Self?

The fact that **roles** carry with them established expectations heightens the potential for clashes with the identity characteristics of new incumbents. Education processes, which are inevitably processes of secondary socialization, must always contend with individuals' already formed and persistent selves, selves established through primary socialization. In this research, most students indicated that medicine had largely taken over the rest of their lives, diminishing their performance of other responsibilities. While 55 per cent of survey respondents thought they were doing a good job of being a medical student, many thought they were doing a poor to very poor job of being a spouse (26 per cent) or family member (37 per cent); 46 per cent gave themselves failing grades as friends. Fewer than a quarter of respondents thought they were doing a good job of being an informed citizen (18 per cent) or a member of their religion, if they had one (17 per cent). What emerged from most interviews and from the survey was a picture of medical school dominating all other aspects of daily life. Overwhelmingly, students talked about sacrifice.

Thus, some students do not or cannot integrate their medical student identities with their former sense of self; rather they let go of parts of themselves, bury them, abandon them, or put them aside, at least for a while. Another option for students who experience incongruities between their medical student identities and other aspects of themselves is to segregate their lives. Because human beings have the ability to reflect on our own actions, it becomes possible to experience a segment of the self as distinct, to 'detach a part of the self and its concomitant reality as relevant only to the role-specific situation in question' (Berger and Luckmann, 1966: 131). In this research 31 per cent of survey respondents felt they are one person at school and another with friends and family.

Difference as a Basis for Resistance

Elsewhere I have argued that intentional and unintentional homogenizing influences in medical education neutralize the impact of social differences students bring into medicine (Beagan, 2000). Students come to believe that the social class, 'race', ethnicity, gender, and sexual orientation of a physician are not—and should not be—relevant during physician–patient interactions. Nonetheless, at the same time those social differences can provide a basis for critique of and resistance to aspects of medical professional socialization. A study of medical residents found that those most able to resist socialization pressures minimized contact and interaction with others in medicine, maintained outside relationships that supported an alternative orientation to the program, and entered their programs with a 'relatively strong and well-defined orientation' (Shapiro and Jones, 1979: 243). Complete resocialization requires 'an intense concentration of all significant interaction within the [new social] group' (Berger and Luckmann, 1966: 145); it is also facilitated by minimal contradictions between the previous social world and the new world.

Conclusion

What is perhaps most remarkable about these findings is how little has changed since the publication of *Boys in White* (Becker et al., 1961) and *Student Physician* (Merton et al., 1957), despite the passage of 40 years and the influx of a very different student population. The basic processes of socializing new members into the profession of medicine remain remarkably similar, as students encounter new social norms, a new language, new thought processes, and a new world view that will eventually enable them to become full-fledged members of 'the team' taking the expected role in the medical hierarchy

Finally, this research shows that the same sources of differentiation that mark some students as not quite fitting in also serve as sources of resistance against medical socialization. Older students, gay students who refuse to be closeted, and students who come from poverty or from working-class backgrounds, may be more likely than others to 'do medical student' differently. Whether that translates into 'doing doctor' differently is a matter for further empirical research. Future research needs to examine how these 'different' students, these resisting students, experience residency and professional practice, and whether and how they remain in medical practice.

References

Beagan, B.L. 2000. 'Neutralizing Differences: Producing Neutral Doctors for (almost) Neutral Patients', *Social Science of Medicine* 51, 8: 1253–65.

Becker, H.S., B. Geer, A.L. Strauss, and E.C. Hughes. 1961. *Boys in White: Student Culture in Medical School*. Chicago: University of Chicago Press.

Berger, P.L., and T. Luckmann. 1966. *The Social Construction of Reality: A Treatise in the Sociology of Knowledge*. New York: Doubleday.

Conrad, P. 1988. 'Learning to Doctor: Reflections on Recent Accounts of the Medical School Years', *Journal of Health and Social Behavior* 29: 323–32.

Cooley, C.H. 1964. *Human Nature and the Social Order*. New York: Schocken.

Coombs, R.R. 1978. *Mastering Medicine*. New York: Free Press.

Dickstein, L.A. 1993. 'Gender Bias in Medical Education: Twenty Vignettes and Recommended Responses', *Journal of the American Medical Women's Association* 48, 5: 152–62.

Fox, R.C. 1957. 'Training for Uncertainty', in *The Student-Physician: Introductory Studies in the Sociology of Medical Education*, pp. 207–44, R.K. Merton, G.G. Reader, and P.L. Kendall, eds. Cambridge: Harvard University Press.

Gamble, V.N. 1990. 'On Becoming a Physician: A Dream not Deferred', in *The Black Women's Health Book: Speaking for Ourselves*, pp. 52–64, E.C. White, ed. Seattle: Seal Press

Goffman, E. 1959. *The Presentation of Self in Everyday Life*. New York: Doubleday

Good, B.J. and M.J. DelVecchio Good. 1993. ' "Learning medicine": The Constructing of Medical Knowledge at Harvard Medical School', in *Knowledge, Power, and Practice: The Anthropology of Medicine and Everyday Life*, pp. 81–107, S. Lindbaum and M. Lock, eds. Berkeley: University of California Press.

Haas, J., and W. Shaffir. 1987. *Becoming Doctors: The Adoption of a Cloak of Competence*. Greenwich, CN: JAI Press.

Kirk, J. 1994. 'A Feminist Analysis of Women in Medical Schools', in *Health, Illness, and Health Care in Canada*, 2nd ed., pp. 158–82, B.S. Bolaria and H.D. Dickenson, eds. Toronto: Harcourt Brace.

Konner, M. 1987. *Becoming a Doctor: A Journey of Initiation in Medical School*. New York: Viking.

Lenhart, S. 1993. 'Gender Discrimination: A Health and Career Development Problem for Women Physicians', *Journal of the American Medical Women's Association* 48, 5: 155–9.

Mead, G.H. 1934. *Mind, Self, and Society: From the Standpoint of a Social Behaviorist*. Chicago: University of Chicago Press.

Merton, R.K., G.G. Reader, and P.L. Kendall. 1957. *The Student Physician: Introductory Studies in the Sociology of Medical Education*. Cambridge: Harvard University Press.

Shapiro, M. 1987. *Getting Doctored: Critical Reflections on Becoming a Physician*. Toronto: Between the Lines.

Shapiro, E.C., and A.B. Jones. 1979. 'Women Physicians and the Exercise of Power and Authority in Health Care', in *Becoming a Physician: Development of Values and Attitudes in Medicine*, pp. 237–45, E. Shapiro and L. Lowenstein, eds. Cambridge: Bellinger.

Sinclair, S. 1997. *Making Doctors: An Institutional Apprenticeship*. New York: Berg.

CHAPTER 11

On the Assimilation of Racial Stereotypes among Black Canadian Young Offenders

John F. Manzo and Monetta M. Bailey

Introduction

An association between race and criminal justice processing in Canada has been documented, particularly with respect to Black and Native persons. Wortley (1999) notes that, in 1997, Native persons represented about four per cent of the population but constituted fourteen per cent of federal prison inmates. Black persons accounted for roughly two per cent of the population while representing over six per cent of those in federal correctional institutions. Native persons had an incarceration rate of 184.85 per 100,000 persons, while that of Black Canadians was 146.37; non-Native, non-Black Canadians were incarcerated at a rate of about 100 per 100,000 (Wortley, 1999).

This evident association between race and crime (or incarceration), among other factors, has led many in society to develop negative stereotypes based on racial identities. In Canada, these negative impressions stem not only from actual experiences of prisoners in the criminal justice system, but also from images in North American culture and media. Despite the relatively small Black population in Canada, Canadians are almost certainly familiar with the image of the Black 'gangsta' from media imagery imported from the US, a nation with more than six times the population of Black persons, per capita, and embracing a Black population with a history, culture, and level of social segregation different from that in Canada.

The focus of this paper is on the responses given by interview respondents with regard to the social depiction of their race, the possible impact of this depiction in their racial identity formation, and the relationship between this depiction and their criminal actions. We will also investigate whether and how this portrayal has been internalized by these youth to inform or influence their criminal actions.

Theoretical Perspectives

We consider 'race' to be a socially constructed, malleable, interpersonally relevant, and thus a 'micro'-level phenomenon; we also recognize that 'race' has an historical and otherwise 'macro' social resonance and meaning that exists over and above individuals' perception of and claims to it. For these reasons, the theoretical perspectives of this paper adopt views that partake of both historical and social-interactional construal of race. This paper deploys social construction perspectives as developed by Berger and Luckmann (1966) with notions of the historically embedded construction of race derived from post-colonial theory (Fanon, 1967; Said, 1978), and, at the level of lived and lively social experience, we rely on the notion of cultural transmission that is based on the contributions of C. Wright Mills (1963) with respect to what he termed 'vocabularies of motive'. The first two of these theories account for 'race' as socially and historically defined and embedded, as aspects of a cultural endowment that is given, and more clearly for post-colonial theory, imposed, on persons; the last theoretical theme considers how, through what concrete discursive means, the content of racial typifications is 'taught' to occupants of those historically and socially constructed racial categories.

Social construction theory (cf., Berger and Luckmann, 1966) maintains that individuals define themselves based on social conceptions of the group to which they claim membership. Social construction theory holds that the basis for 'subjective' reality is, in fact, the social world: the self is created through a dialectical, reflexive relationship between the individuals and their social milieux. Social construction theory thus argues that persons see themselves in the same terms that society views them.

Colonial theory adds to social-construction approaches by accounting for social conceptualizations of race based on historical relations among different racial and ethnic groups. In his seminal *Black Skin, White Masks*, Fanon (1967) proposes that, in a former colonial society, socially accepted modes of thought are based on the views of the dominant, 'colonizing' group. The culture, language, and customs of the colonizers come to be normative and to be considered superior to both local indigenous cultures and to those who were part of subsequent non-white diasporas to post-colonial societies.

Methodology

THE SAMPLE

This paper examines interviews with respondents from a study entailing interviews of eight Black or mulatto young offenders between 14–18 years old in Alberta, Canada. Three were in open-custody residential 'group homes', and five were in secure custody at a youth detention facility. The ages and placements for each interviewee are indicated the first time each is cited in this report.

The second author, who is herself a Black Canadian originally from Barbados, conducted the interviews. As part of our protocol for the protection of human subjects and following the insistence of our gate-keeping agencies, she was not permitted to inquire about our subjects' crimes (although they were, of course, permitted to discuss or allude to them themselves); additionally, aside from knowing that subjects had committed crimes that were sufficiently serious to warrant their placements in these facilities, she was not apprised of what those crimes were for any case.

Respondents who were of 'mixed' (mulatto) racial heritage were included if they identified as Black.

INTERVIEWS AND ANALYSIS

Our research questions were:

1. How do Black young offenders define their racial category? Do they associate criminality with that identity?
2. Do respondents perceive their identities to have been influenced by popular cultural discourse, such as rap music?
3. What attitudes do the youth hold toward the police, and what do they believe the police think of them?
4. Have these influences been mediated through social support systems or networks, as Tatum (2000) proposes?

These topics were addressed in open-ended interview format. The focus of this report is the first two of these questions.

ETHICAL CONSIDERATIONS AND COMPLICATIONS

The study was conducted to ensure confidentiality, anonymity, and informed consent of the interviewees, including, where necessary, consent of parents or guardians. Although interviewees are sometimes identified by name in interview excerpts, these names are pseudonyms and are only included here for clarity in exposition. An additional ethical issue that arose concerned the possibility that respondents would mention crimes for which they had not yet been charged. Our precaution against this was to avoid questions about specific crimes. We did not, in any case, see these special ethical precautions as compromising this research.

Findings

RESPONDENTS' PERSPECTIVES ON SOCIETAL VIEWS OF BLACK PERSONS

Overall, and unsurprisingly, respondents expressed the view that stereotypical ideas of Black persons did exist socially, and that these images owed largely to what the youths construed as representations depicted in media and in the larger culture. The respondents seemed, moreover, to identify with these stereotypes, some more than others.

STEREOTYPES OF BLACKS

Respondents suggested that stereotypes of Blacks were of two categories. First, people saw Blacks as being 'dangerous', as possessing at best defiant attitudes and at worst criminal tendencies, in line with what might be called a 'gangsta' image. Although the respondents demonstrated a partial acceptance of this stereotype in that they also stated that style of dress influences how they judge other Black persons, they expressed some anger that non-Blacks did this. They were quite vocal in their objection to others placing Blacks into categories, and determining membership in a category according to style of dress. This objection was largely founded on the fact that the respondents believed that when others viewed them, based on their style of dress, as in the 'gangsta' category, they associated criminal behaviour with it.

The second stereotype that respondents noted saw Black persons as entertainers, that is, as athletes, actors, musical performers, and so on. This view of Blacks is not mutually exclusive with respect to the 'gangsta' image; indeed, the essence of 'gangsta' is demonstrated by a look adopted by rap stars and other Black celebrities, including some athletes. Consequently, respondents stated that they believe that many people in society assumed that they were criminals.

Portrayals of Blacks in the Media

The respondents saw the overall portrayal of Blacks in the media as mixed with respect to the relative amount of positive and negative imagery that are portrayed, but saw these images as conforming to stereotypes regardless. For example, respondents reflected on how Black persons are shown possessing special talents, as athletes in particular sports or as entertainers in a very delimited range of arts (as rappers or comedians, for example).

The other way they are seen in the media, from our respondents' experiences, was as criminals. The interesting thing about the criminal portrayal was that the judgment associated with it depended on the media outlet. Some respondents noted that the criminal image often portrayed by the news and mainstream media could also have positive connotations.

Respondents' Perspectives on the 'Gangsta' Image

It became clear that the majority of respondents felt some connection to a 'gangsta' image. The respondents defined this image as specific to Blacks, and as opposed to the 'normal' social depiction of whites as not 'gangsta'. While the youths under study here allowed that some Blacks were 'normal', respondents also saw 'gangstas' or 'thugs' as uniquely Black constructs. Moreover, respondents expressed no desire to assume a conventional, socially acceptable image. These respondents all suggested that their refusal to conform to 'normal' social types, to which some outrightly referred to as 'looking and acting white', meant that they were seen as that particular other known as 'gangstas'. They chose to embrace this image.

The youths deployed the word 'nigga' recurrently. Several respondents, explicitly or implicitly, made the distinction between a 'nigga' and a 'gangsta'. Ricky suggested that a 'gangsta' just 'goes around and causes trouble, or jacks somebody for no reason', on the other hand, a 'nigga' 'beats up somebody, but there is a reason'. For these youth, there was more pride and, one may conclude, social acceptability in being a 'nigga' than in a being a 'gangsta'. Thus, it is fair to say that some of the youth identified more closely with the image of a 'nigga' rather than that of a 'gangsta'. It should also be noted that most of the youth did not make this distinction, and that it is fair to say that most respondents could be said to identify with both typologies.

Respondents' Views on 'Oppression'

Most respondents suggested that there were disadvantages associated with being Black in Canada, but they expressed pride in being Black. The interviewees suggested, in general, that while there was racism in society, they did not believe themselves to be seriously affected by it, even while admitting to being influenced by and sometimes judged unfairly due to the currency of a 'gangsta' image of blacks. The reason behind this may be that black respondents seemed to take pride in some of the stereotypes of their race, both positive and negative. These depictions included stereotypes that blacks are especially talented in certain sports, and as entertainers, but some also took pride in evincing images such as 'gangstas' and 'thugs'. Many also claimed that they simply did not care what others' views of them were in the first place; indeed, we note that respondents even deployed a fatalistic view of societal opinions of them as a variety of vocabulary of motive, one that said, to paraphrase, 'if this is how society sees me, I might as well act in this way.'

Conclusions

The participants in this study articulate a view of themselves and of Black persons in general that is consistent with certain stereotypes. This finding supports the claims of social construction and postcolonial theories, both of which anticipate that a member of any racial minority—particularly one whose history entailed overt oppression, discrimination or slavery—would adopt self-images in line with those prescribed and maintained by the larger society. However, it is vital that we emphasize that our findings do not support these theories tout court; in particular, the implication of victimization tacit in social construction and, especially, post-colonial theory is not clearly present in our respondents' discourses. Yes, their self-concepts appear riddled, in one sense, with the typifications of 'Black' provided them in their cultures. Paradoxically, in accepting, to varying degrees, the existence of these social stereotypes, our respondents were also distancing themselves from mainstream (especially 'white') society by embracing them. Not only do the interviewees admire, and in some cases aspire to, 'gangsta', but they also take pride in certain other stereotypes, for example that Blacks are good athletes, actors, rappers, and singers. While these youth sometimes expressed frustration with the stereotypes, they also supported them in their responses.

References

Berger, P., and T. Luckmann. 1966. *The Social Construction of Reality: A Treatise in the Sociology of Knowledge.* New York: Anchor Books.

Fanon, F. 1967. *Black Skin, White Masks.* New York: Grove Weidenfeld.

Mills, C.W. 1963. 'Situated Actions and Vocabularies of Motive', In *Power, Politics and People*, pp. 439–52, I.L. Horowitz, ed. New York: Oxford University Press.

Said, E. 1978. *Orientalism*. Harmondsworth, UK: Penguin.

Tatum, B. 2000. *Crime, Violence and Minority Groups.* Aldershot, UK: Ashgate Publishing.

Wortley, S. 1999. 'A Northern Taboo: Research on Race, Crime and Criminal Justice in Canada', *Canadian Journal of Criminology* 41, 1: 261–74.

CHAPTER 12

The Pendulum of Family Change: Comparative Life Course Transitions of Young Adults

Barbara A. Mitchell

Introduction

This paper highlights changing and emergent patterns of family-related transitions to adulthood over the past century. Particular attention will be paid to contextualizing contemporary transitions to adulthood using historical data, particularly from the 1950s until the turn of the twenty-first century. Although primary emphasis is on Canadian patterns, international comparisons will also be made with the United States and several selected European countries. In light of the significant socio-demographic, economic, and political transformations facing families, implications relevant to the fluctuating life course patterns of young men, young women, and their mid-life parents will be highlighted.

Striking changes are taking place in the family lives of young adults in Western, industrialized societies. Notably, the 'complete' transition to adulthood has been extended as young people depart parental homes and begin their own families at increasingly older ages. Family behaviours such as homeleaving and union formation are also subject to relatively high rates of impermanence and reversibility. As a result, many commentators characterize the transition to adulthood as 'on hold' and fraught with uncertainty, indecision, chaos, and complexity (e.g., see Beck, 1992; Côté and Allahar, 1994; Mortimer and Larson, 2002; Zinn, 2004; Draut, 2006).

Yet, while there may be some support for these allegations, Coontz (1992: 1) argues that, 'the actual complexity of our history—even of our own personal experience—gets buried under the weight of an idealized image.' Indeed, some researchers argue that there was never a 'golden age' of family stability and that there has always been diversity and fluctuations in family patterns (e.g., see Gee, 2000). In response to this ongoing controversy, this paper will highlight changing family transitions (leaving home, cohabitation, marriage, parenthood, and divorce) in Canada from a historical, life-course perspective.

International comparisons are also made with the US and several Western European countries (Britain, France, Germany, Italy, Netherlands, and Sweden). The primary historical benchmark that is used to compare contemporary transitions will be the prototypical 1950s nuclear *Leave it to Beaver*-type family structure. However, fluctuations over the past century will also be noted to elucidate underlying trends of continuity, diversity, and social change. The paper concludes with a brief exploration of implications for modern-day family transitions to adulthood and intergenerational relationships.

Theoretical Perspective

A **life course** theoretical approach (e.g., Elder, 1995, 1998; Hareven, 1996; Giele and Elder, 1998; Mitchell, 2003; 2006) provides a dynamic and flexible model of family behaviour and lifelong age-related social processes. This framework encompasses socio-historical and geographic variability, structural constraints and human agency, and diversity in resources. Variability in the timing of transitional events occurs across time, geographic locales, and within families. Within families, diversity is due to multiple bases of inequality (e.g., age, gender, ethnicity, immigration status, and socio-economic status). Moreover, unlike previous life cycle depictions of family life, the life course perspective does not assume a linear course of family development. Transitions to adulthood, for instance, can become reversed, such as in the case of home returning or divorce.

Another central theme is the notion of '**linked lives**'. Societal and individual experiences are linked through the family and its network of shared relationships (Elder, 1998). Thus, transitions to adulthood and transition reversals are deemed to affect others, such as parent–child relations in the family of origin. For example, when a young adult marries and has a child, this creates counter transitions of in-laws and grandparenthood. Or, when a child returns home as a '**boomerang kid**', the empty nest phase of the middle generation reverts to a 'refilled nest'. Thus, changes in the role status and living arrangement of one family member can bring significant repercussions for the daily lived experiences of other family members.

Key Findings

The timing and prevalence of family transitions are found to have fluctuated and transformed over time. For example, Canadian young adults typically left home, married, and became parents at relatively late ages during the 1930s and 1940s compared to the 1950s to 1970s, at which time these ages began to increase again. Moreover, the trend toward early timing of family transitions occurred later in Canada and in Western Europe than in the United States. Yet, behaviours such as home returning, cohabitation, and divorce exhibit a general rise in their prevalence over time, although divorce rates have generally stabilized or declined in recent times.

Moreover, despite a general '**rise of the primary individual**' (Kobrin, 1976), there remains continuity in much family behaviour alongside dramatic alterations. Specifically, the formation of intimate partnerships and parenthood are still popular, and young adults typically live with their parents until they are able to establish their own work and family lives. Considerable diversity both across countries (e.g., in comparing Sweden and Italy) and within countries is also found. For example, it is very common for Italian young adults (especially men) to live at home past the age 30, whereas this is quite rare in Sweden. Further, regardless of country of origin, transitions are socially structured by factors including: gender, socio-economic status, race/ethnicity, religiosity, family structure, region, and the quality of intergenerational support.

Discussion and Implications

These patterns establish that family transitions in Canada and other Western societies do not reflect a simple linear pattern of change as a result of industrialization, modernization, and the 'rise of the primary individual.' Instead, a more accurate depiction is that of a pendulum of family change that conceives of family behaviours as 'swinging back and forth.' This metaphor also illustrates how the timing of family behaviours is dynamic, fluid, and elastic in response to changing economic and socio-cultural environments.

Moreover, while there is value in comparing today's transitions to a mid-century benchmark such as the stereotypical *Leave it to Beaver*-type family, this nuclear family structure is based primarily on the American experience. Also, it was only for a short period of history—the post-Second World War 'baby boom years' (circa 1946–62) that Canada, and most of the European countries, begin to approach any degree of family stability, characterized by early ages of homeleaving, marriage, and parenthood, and low rates of divorce and home returning. Thus, while baby boomer parents may have experienced a predictable 'package of transitions' to adulthood, this experience was not the norm from a historical perspective.

Moreover, it appears that these behaviours have occurred in response to adaptations to both public realms (e.g., economic, educational, work, and technological) and private spheres (e.g., emergence of new family forms and structures, gender roles). It is also well established that demographic change (e.g., increased life expectancy and reduced fertility), and cultural contexts affect family transitions. Emergent behaviours, when routinized, can also create or alter pre-existing trends. This highlights how social forces not only 'trickle down' from social structures to individual's lives but also 'percolate up' from individuals'

actions to modify existing social patterns and institutions and perhaps create new ones (Mayer and Tuma, 1990: 5).

In this way, the life course evolves in a dynamic interplay between young people and society. It is an element of social structure that is a product of historical and institutional forces, individual action, and organizational processes, including state regulations (Mayer and Miller, 1986; Mayer and Tuma, 1990; Heinz, 1991). Moreover, individual's lives are intimately connected to those of others, and an individual's development is bound to, and shaped by, those ties (Settersten, 1999: 15). As Elder and Caspi (1990) observe, 'all lives are lived interdependently, and this connectedness defines a medium through which historical change plays out its influence over time.'

Cognizant of this point, there are several implications that can be identified. Social change, coupled with demographic aging of kinship structures, has restructured family socialization and intergenerational roles and responsibilities over the life course. While high rates of intergenerational co-residence were witnessed in the 1930s and 1940s, the timing of the transition to the empty nest is once again occurring later in the family life cycle. However, unlike previous times, it is now more likely to refill as many young people flock home as 'boomerang kids' to meet their economic and social needs (Mitchell, 2000; 2006; Mitchell et al., 2004). With respect to cohabitation, many researchers argue that this phenomenon further delays the transition to marriage and has played a role in the declining marriage rate (e.g., see Harper, 2003). It can also affect **intergenerational relations**. For example, in Canada, we are experiencing high rates of immigration from Asian countries. However, in many of these cultures, cohabitation is not as socially acceptable; generational conflict may arise when young people from traditional, familistic backgrounds choose this type of partnership (Mitchell, 2001).

Furthermore, similar to the early decades of the twentieth century, increasingly, parents must wait until older ages to experience their children's marital and parenthood transitions. This increases the average age of grandparenthood; although they now have the opportunity to watch their grandchildren grow up. Finally, although marital unions have the potential to last far longer than was historically possible, some argue that this has placed additional strains on family relationships and has contributed to more divorce, ambiguity, and stress in intergenerational relations (Harper, 2003).

Summary, Limitations and Directions for Future Research

This research is limited in a number of ways and highlights areas in need of further investigation. For example, additional detail on gender differences in the life courses of men and women in relation to social change, cultural context, shifting gender roles, and patterns of convergence would be valuable (e.g., see Ravenera et al., 2004). Moreover, we lack historical and contemporary data on micro-sociological processes, such as young people's perceptions of risk, uncertainty, and chaos during the transition to adulthood.

The general aging of family transitions coupled with ever lengthening life spans suggests that today's young people have been provided the ability to make a wider range of decisions with respect to their living arrangements and types of partnerships. Yet, it is recognized that the possibilities for an expansion of choices and innovation may be more limited for those who lack financial power, education, and supportive social networks (Giele, 1998). Thus, future research on this topic can shed additional light on how the pendulum of family change impacts the everyday lives of young people from diverse backgrounds. In this way, we can garner a more complete understanding of how young adults navigate their way to adulthood in relation to themes of continuity, diversity, and social inequality, amidst an ever-shifting landscape of challenge and opportunity.

References

Beck, U. 1992. *Risk Society: Towards a New Modernity*. Thousand Oaks, CA: Sage Publications.

Coontz, S. 1992. *The Way We Never Were: American Families and the Nostalgia Trap*. New York: Basic Books.

Côté, J., and A. Allahar. 1994. *Generation on Hold: Coming of Age in the Late Twentieth Century*. Toronto: Stoddart.

Draut, T. 2006. *Strapped: Why America's 20- and 30-Somethings Can't Get Ahead*. New York: Doubleday.

Elder, G.H., Jr. 1995. 'The Life Course Paradigm: Social Change and Individual Development', in *Examining Lives in Context: Perspectives on the Ecology of Human Development*, pp. 101–39, P. Moen, G.H. Elder, Jr., and K. Luscher, eds. Washington, DC: American Psychological Association.

———. 1998. 'The Life Course as Developmental Theory', *Child Development* 69: 1–12.

Elder, G.H., Jr., and A. Caspi. 1990. 'Studying Lives in a Changing Society: Sociological and Personological Explorations', in *Studying Persons and Lives*, pp. 201–47, A.I. Rabin, R.A. Zucker, and S. Frank, eds. New York: Springer.

Gee, E.M. 2000. 'Contemporary Diversities', in *Canadian Families: Diversity, Conflict and Change*, pp. 78–111, N. Mandell and A. Duffy, eds. Toronto: Harcourt Canada.

Giele, J.Z. 1998. 'Innovation in the Typical Life Course', in *Methods of Life Course Research: Qualitative and Quantitative Aproaches*, pp. 231–63, J.Z. Giele and J.H. Elder, Jr., eds. Thousand Oaks, CA: Sage Publications.

Giele, J.Z., and G.H. Elder, Jr. 1998. *Methods of Life Course Research: Qualitative and Quantitative Approaches*. Thousand Oaks, CA: Sage Publications.

Hareven, T.K., ed. 1996. *Aging and Generational Relations: Life-course and Cross-cultural Perspectives*. New York: Aldine de Gruyter.

Harper, S. 2003. 'Changing Families as European Societies Age', *Archives Européennes de Sociologie* 44: 155–84.

Heinz, W.R., ed. 1991. *The Life Course and Social Change: Comparative Perspectives*. Weinheim: Deutscher Studien Verlag.

Kobrin, F.E. 1976. 'The Primary Individual and the Family: Changes in Living Arrangements in the

United States since 1940', *Journal of Marriage and the Family* May: 233–9.

Mayer, K.U., and N.B. Tuma. 1990. *Event History Analysis in Life Course Research*. Madison, WI: University of Wisconsin Press.

Mayer, K.U., and W. Müller. 1986. 'The State and the Structure of the Life Course', in *Human Development and the Life Course: Multidisciplinary Perspectives*, pp. 217–45, P. Moen, G.H. Elder, Jr., and K. Luscher, eds.Washington, DC: American Psychological Association.

Mitchell, B.A. 2000. 'The Refilled Nest: Debunking the Myth of Families in Crisis', in *The Overselling of Population Aging: Apocalyptic Demography, Intergenerational Challenges and Social Policy*, pp. 80–99, E.M. Gee and G. Gutman, eds. Toronto: Oxford University Press.

———. 2001. 'Ethnocultural Reproduction and Attitudes towards Cohabiting Relationships', *Canadian Review of Sociology and Anthropology* 38: 391–413.

———. 2003. 'Life Course Theory', in *The International Encyclopedia of Marriage and Family Relationships*, 2nd ed, pp. 1051–5, J.J. Ponzetti, ed. New York: Macmillan Reference.

———. 2006. *The Boomerang Age: Transitions to Adulthood in Families*. New Jersey: Aldine-Transaction Publishers.

Mitchell, B.A., A.V. Wister, and E.M. Gee. 2004. 'The Family and Ethnic Nexus of Home Leaving and Returning among Canadian Young Adults', *Canadian Journal of Sociology* 29: 543–75.

Mortimer, J.T., and R.W. Larson. 2002. 'Macrostructural Trends and the Reshaping of Adolescence', in *The Changing Adolescent Experience: Societal Trends and the Transition to Adulthood*, pp. 1–17, J.T. Mortimer and R.W. Larson, eds. New York: Cambridge University Press.

Ravenera, Z.R., F. Rajulton, and T.K. Burch. 2004. 'Patterns of Age Variability in Life Course Transitions', *Canadian Journal of Sociology* 29: 527–42.

Settersten, R.A., Jr. 1999. *Lives in Time and Place. The Problems and Promises of Developmental Science*. Amityville, NY: Baywood.

Zinn, J.O. 2004. 'Health, Risk and Uncertainty in the Life Course: A Typology of Biographical Certainty Constructions', *Social Theory and Health* 3: 199–221.

CHAPTER 13

Searching, Working, and Shopping: Is This Prolonged Youth?

Rebecca Raby

Diverse views on current transitions from youth to adulthood emphasize either a prolonged or a shrunken youth. Nonetheless these views share assumptions about youth and adulthood as **life stages**. There is a gap between our assumptions about such life stages and our experiences of them, however, making it possible to both disrupt such assumptions and to recognize the influence of social structure on people's lives. This paper suggests that youth is both prolonged and narrowed—a logical position if we recognize contradictions, elasticity, and marginality in the construction of youth, as well as diversity in young people's lives.

Individualization theories stress the effects of growing up in the globalized, late modern society of the late twentieth and early twenty-first centuries (Beck, 1992). Faced with loosened class and gender structures, people must increasingly shape their own life paths and inequality is individualized

(Wyn and Dwyer, 1999; Beck and Beck-Gernsheim, 2002). Working from this perspective, some youth scholars investigate how the weakening of such structural 'anchors' prolongs youth, as young people are faced with a wide range of options and challenges to explore (Baethge, 1985; Côté, 2000). Several see promise in these individualization processes, with options for freedom, self-exploration, and the formation of temporary communities based on choice (Heitmeyer and Olk, 1995; Arnett, 2004), yet others are concerned that such promise will not be embraced by young people. Rather, people's self-absorption, misdirection, and passive mass consumption will prevent maturation into adulthood and thus prolong their youth (Côté, 2002).

While these theorists recognize that the intensity of individualization depends on factors such as class, region, and gender, they downplay structural inequality. Political economists such as Furlong and Cartmel (1997) emphasize the ongoing relevance of such inequality, however. They argue that we currently live within an **'ecological fallacy'**: there is a *perception* that the effects of social structure have dramatically weakened, yet structural inequalities like class remain prominent and distribute social risks unequally. One consequence is that those young people who fail to thrive in this 'new' social climate are more likely than in the past to blame themselves, or be blamed by others, for their lack of success. To Furlong and Cartmel, while youth is prolonged today, structural determinants remain relevant to our personal life paths. For instance, a prolonged youth may be more accessible to those in the middle class (Thompson et al., 2004).

Yet, do most young people really have a prolonged period of time in which to reflect on their individualized identities and life paths? Anita Harris (2004) contends that young people, specifically young women, have learned early in life to govern, groom, and 'self-invent' themselves to be skilled, flexible workers who catapult themselves into adulthood as they become workers and consumers early in life. Young people must also consciously make educational choices that they feel significantly shape their futures. Again, however, this 'can-do' girl is individualized, holding herself responsible for her own success or failure as the effects of structurally-based life chances are overlooked (Harris, 2004). Buchmann (1989) similarly argues that as young people have gained political rights and protection through social legislation, they have become independent, responsible decision-makers who demand autonomy at an earlier age. Here individualization speeds young people towards adulthood, despite the economic dependence and extended years of education that many young people experience at the same time. More popularly, this perceived shrinking of childhood, adolescence, and youth is echoed in anxieties about young people's early sexual activity, teenage pregnancy, agency as consumers, media influences, and newfound cyber-freedoms (e.g. through internet usage).

The above perspectives reflect common, yet unstable, distinctions between youth and adulthood. Life course transitions are institutionalized through formal rules regarding rights and roles, including legal indicators of 'coming of age' such as voting or drinking alcohol. Youth has lengthened through prolonged education, yet lowering the penal age and increasing access to childhood rights suggest movement towards earlier adulthood at the same time (Buchmann, 1989). Also, the line between 'child' and adult may be clear locally, but variations in jurisdiction—for example, between provinces or context (e.g. criminal responsibility versus voting age)—illustrates the lack of social consensus on such markers (Thompson et al., 2004).

Plug et al. (2003) find that in the Netherlands, lower-class youth assume a job and family to bring forward adulthood, and middle class youth focus more on independence gained through career, family, and personal interests. Thompson et al. (2004) observe that many young people themselves see adulthood in terms of personal competence, autonomy, and independence, a position Plug et al. associate more with higher class youth.

These findings suggest that conceptions of adulthood also vary by context.

Apart from legal age markers, many define adulthood in terms of the development of psychological traits, such as a coherent value structure and a sense of self (e.g. Côté, 2000). In this approach, modern youth is a time of becoming, with adulthood as the ultimate end-goal or destination (Lesko, 1996). Such distinctions between youth and adulthood are undermined by more post-modern arguments that suggest one's identity and sense of self changes *throughout* one's life.

Sociologists have commonly measured transition to adulthood in terms of certain forms of production and consumption, especially full employment and independent housing. This position is also destabilized, however, as youth have become a dominant consumer market and as youth (such as 'can-do' girls) are fully engaged in processes of production through working in both full and part-time jobs, volunteering, and skill-based schooling. A blurring of work and school is now common (Wyn and Dwyer, 1999). Adults, at the same time, are frequently disenfranchised from these very markers of adulthood through unemployment, shifting employment, retraining, and unattainable housing.

Finally, adolescence and youth have traditionally been distinguished from adulthood in terms of social relations, specifically marriage and child-bearing (Furlong and Cartmel, 1997). Such assumptions are complicated by social forces that include late marriage, common-law relationships, gay relationships, high divorce rates, early parenthood, delayed parenthood, intentional childlessness, and intentional singleness—forces that may be much more common today than in the post-war years, but that have always been present to some extent. Marriage and child-bearing, as markers of maturity, have the added flaw of marginalizing those who do not (or cannot) marry and those who do not (or cannot) have children. Yet while young people are not focusing on marriage as a clear transition point, they do currently see relational responsibility as an indicator of adulthood.

Several of these potential markers clearly indicate that how we define adulthood is, in part, 'related to processes of social inclusion and exclusion' (Thompson et al., 2004: 220). Ultimately, recognizing variations in life courses (Thompson et al., 2004) and the dissolution of clear lines between youth and adulthood (Plug et al., 2003) dismantles an over-arching, normative life stage narrative, including any solid category of youth or adulthood. Individualization theorists examine this dissolution to some extent but many continue to discuss youth in terms of 'becoming', and adulthood as 'having arrived'. They also frequently downplay the on-going and pivotal role of social structural features: age norms persist, social inequalities persist, and individualization masks social patterns of inequality (Harris, 2004; Furlong and Cartmel, 1997).

This brief paper thus highlights gaps between conceptions and experience: between individualization and structural inequalities, and between common assumptions about life stages or transitions and our lived life courses. Ironically, individualization suggests a fluidity to our life courses that is a myth while normative stage and transition-based positions suggest a predictability to our life courses that is also a myth. Thus we can see that youth is both prolonged and narrowed within the Western social context. Youth are dependent, attending school, infantilized, prevented from acquiring traditional markers of adulthood, criticized, and idealized—all prolonged within the current social-structural context. At the same time, however, youth are fully engaged producers and consumers, occupy an age of majority, are 'self-making', sexual, individualized, unanchored, independent, and celebrated. Ultimately, it is the instability of life stages that in part allows for these contradictions to coincide.

References

Arnett, J.J. 2004. *Emerging Adulthood*. New York: Oxford University Press.

Baethge, M. 1985. 'Individualization as Hope and Disaster: Contradictions and Paradoxes of Adolescence in Western Societies', *International Social Science Journal* 106: 441–54.

Beck, U. 1992. *Risk Society: Towards a New Modernity*. London: Sage Publications.

Beck, U., E. Beck-Gernsheim. 2002. *Individualization: Institutionalized Individualism and its Social and Political Consequences*. London: Sage Publications.

Buchmann, M. 1989. *The Script of Life in Modern Society: Entry into Adulthood in a Changing World*. Chicago: University of Chicago Press.

Côté, J.E. 2000. *Arrested Adulthood: The Changing Nature of Maturity and Identity*. New York: New York University Press.

———. 2002. 'The Role of Identity Capital in the Transition to Adulthood: The Individualization Thesis Examined', *Journal of Youth Studies* 5, 2: 117–34.

Furlong, A., and F. Cartmel. 1997. *Young People and Social Change: Individualization and Risk in Late Modernity*. Buckingham: Open University Press.

Harris, A. 2004. *Future Girl: Young Women in the Twenty-First Century*. New York: Routledge.

Heitmeyer, W., and T. Olk. 1995. 'The Role of Individualization Theory in Adolescent Socialization', in *Individualization in Childhood and Adolescence*, G. Neubauer and K. Hurrelmann, eds. Berlin: Walter de Gruyter.

Lesko, N. 1996. 'Past, Present and Future Conceptions of Adolescence', *Educational Theory* 46, 4: 453–72.

Plug, W., E. Zeijl, and M. Du Bois-Reymond. 2003. 'Young People's Perceptions on Youth and Adulthood: A Longitudinal Study from the Netherlands', *Journal of Youth Studies* 6, 2: 127–44.

Thompson, R., J. Holland, S. McGrellis, R. Bell, S. Henderson, and S. Sharpe. 2004. 'Inventing Adulthoods: A Bibliographical Approach to Understanding Youth Citizenship', *The Sociological Review*: 218–39.

Wyn, J., and P. Dwyer. 1999. 'New Directions in Research on Youth in Transition', *Journal of Youth Studies* 2, 1: 5–21.

CHAPTER 14

Duality and Diversity in the Lives of Immigrant Children: Rethinking the 'Problem of the Second Generation' in Light of Immigrant Autobiographies

Nedim Karakayali

Introduction

In an article published at the dawn of the twentieth century, the renowned social statistician Richmond Mayo-Smith (1894) identified three major groups among what he called 'the whites' in America. First, there were 'the native-born of native parentage', the 'true Americans' who constituted 'a homogeneous body, and to this body the others of more recent arrival tend to be assimilated'. Then, there were 'the whites of foreign birth, the immigrants . . . the real element to be assimilated'. Finally, there was the 'the native-born of foreign parents . . . the second generation of immigrants, so to speak'. Second-generation immigrants, Mayo-Smith wrote, 'stand half-way . . . between the native and the foreign element. . . . They represent the process of assimilation in the act' (437–8).

Although few researchers today, if any, would proceed with such a simplistic scheme, Mayo-Smith's remarks are far from being obsolete. In fact, most social research on children of immigrants in the twentieth century has unfolded in the broader context of the integration of immigrant groups. More specifically, the idea that children of immigrants are caught between the 'worlds' or 'cultures' of their parents and the host society remains relevant.

This paper is an examination of the **two-worlds** thesis in light of autobiographies written by children of immigrants in twentieth-century North America. The major issues addressed will focus on **duality**. First, although the experience of duality is expressed in almost all the autobiographies, once we begin to zoom into the 'worlds' of immigrant children, we also observe an immense diversity. Children of immigrants 'live' in many—not just two—worlds. In this respect, my findings concur with recent ethnographic studies in multiethnic contexts in Western Europe (Ålund, 1995; Back, 1995; Qureshi and Moores, 1999; Soysal, 2001). By focusing on the experience of duality, the two-worlds thesis depicts an existence shaped by uncertainty and ambivalence. It is this condition that constitutes 'the problem of the second generation' (Hansen, 1952). Autobiographies, however, also reveal the presence of dreams and a desire for a different kind of life. The second argument of this paper is that the realization of these dreams is an equally important aspect of the 'problem'. I will also therefore suggest that the so-called 'problem of the second generation' should be located in the tension between diversity and duality, rather than in being caught between two worlds.

Data Sources and Limitations of the Study

AUTOBIOGRAPHIES AS A DATA SOURCE

Children of immigrants can neither be defined as a class, an ethnic group, or an age group. The classic proponents of the two-worlds thesis justify this categorization on the grounds that children of immigrants share a common subjective experience (Stonequist, 1937; Hansen, 1952).

That 'immigrant autobiographies' can provide a key for understanding the 'experience' of immigrants was first stressed in the pioneering work of Boelhower (1982). We should nevertheless note that not all immigrant autobiographies deal with the experience of migration, nor do they always focus on children. In fact, it might be quite misleading to treat them as a unified genre. We have no reason to assume that there is a unified 'experience' associated with being a second-generation migrant.

METHODOLOGICAL LIMITATIONS

Since the main objective in the limited space of this study is to show in what ways the accounts given in the autobiographies diverge from the two-worlds thesis, there is little emphasis on the ways in which the autobiographies differ from each other. I try to reveal the multiplicity of relationships and potentials that often remain invisible from the point of view of the two-worlds thesis. It is nevertheless important to note immigrant children—depending on race, ethnicity, and gender—articulate these relationships and potentials in different ways.

DATA SOURCES AND THE HISTORICAL PERIOD

In this study I have consulted some thirty autobiographical sources from North America (Canada and the United States), though only about half of them are cited/quoted here. Most of these sources are published autobiographies written almost exclusively by children of immigrants. The publication dates of the autobiographies analyzed range from 1925 to 1998.

A Brief History of the Two-Worlds Thesis

The two-worlds thesis states that immigrants will bring with them 'the principles of the governments they leave. . . . These principles, with their language, they will transmit to their children. In proportion to their numbers, they will share legislation with us. They will infuse into it their spirit, warp or bias its direction, and render it a heterogeneous, incoherent, distracted mass' (Jefferson, 1964: 152).

In How Many Worlds Do Children of Immigrants Live?

In autobiographies written by children of immigrants, individuation begins with the immediate family. For the immigrant child the relation between his or her mother and father is at least as important as how the two together relate to the society at large. In certain cases, the mother and father, as two different personalities, complement each other (Maynard, 1972; Antin, 1997: 155). In others, they develop deep conflicts. Sometimes the lot of the immigrant child consists of a despotic father and a helpless mother who 'did not count for much . . . except to take the beatings when things went wrong in the home' (Ruddy, 1975: 11). In other cases, one of the parents might be completely missing and the focus shifts to the relations between the single parent and his or her partners (Santiago, 1998). Parents also differ from each other in terms of their attitudes towards the host society. Horn (1997: 47) notes that, while his father considered the decision to immigrate to Canada from the Netherlands as the 'greatest blunder of his life', his mother was comfortable in her position as an immigrant since, having been raised in Java, she was 'less rooted in the Netherlands'. Similar observations can be made about brothers, sisters, and grandparents.

Not only do autobiographies shatter the image of the 'immigrant family' as an undifferentiated entity, but they also reveal that there is no uniform, 'typical' relationship between the immigrant child and his or her family. Furthermore, the composition of the 'immigrant family' changes over time and, especially for poor families, harsh living conditions often entail death and remarriage, and hence the need to form new relations—a typical theme in many autobiographies (Kohut, 1925; Adamic, 1969; Covello, 1970).

Finally, while the children might be highly conscious of the barriers between their ethnic community and host society, these two domains cannot be understood in terms of a simple opposition. Indeed, the desire to take part in the society at large is often induced by encounters in the ethnic community itself.

Becoming 'Someone Else': Diversity, Desire, and the Secret Life of Immigrant Children

Almost invariably, autobiographic sources indicate that an immigrant child, especially in his or her adolescent years, is likely to develop a myriad of relationships and participate in many different 'lives'. It is worth noting here that researchers identify a positive potential—'projects' and 'dreams'— emerging out of this complexity. In this sense the autobiographies of immigrant children can be seen as the stories of a new person—if not a new people—in the making. Autobiographies are not mere inventories of a myriad of encounters and disjointed worlds; in them these separate parts are woven into a narrative and become elements of a singular life. As Deleuze and Guattari (1986: 17) insist, 'marginality' does not have to be a completely crippling condition: 'If the writer is in the margins or completely outside of his or her fragile community, this situation allows the writer all the more possibility to express another possible community and to forge the means for another consciousness and another sensibility.'

Why Do Children of Immigrants Feel That They Live in Two Worlds?

Why, then, do children of immigrants themselves often feel that they are caught between two worlds? On the basis of the autobiographies analyzed, we propose one straightforward answer. If the theme of two worlds is omnipresent in them, this is mainly because it is omnipresent in the everyday life of immigrant children. Almost from the day they are born, the distinction between a 'homeland' and a 'new land' permeates their lives, even seeping through the tales they hear, for example when grandparents would tell stories of their homelands to grandchildren.

Some of the proponents of the two-worlds thesis come very close to observing the division that cuts through the everyday life of immigrant children and how such divisions become a source of tension. 'The sons and the daughters of immigrants,' writes Hansen (1952: 494), 'were subjected to the criticism and taunts of the native [sic] Americans and to the criticism and taunts of their elders as well. . . . The source of all their woes . . . lay in the strange dualism into which they had been born.'

Concluding Remarks

The real problem with the two-worlds thesis is not its argument that immigrant children feel caught between two worlds, but its failure to note that this experience follows from the condition of living in a world where most people believe that there are only two worlds. By depicting this belief—this constructed reality—as the only reality of immigrant children, the two-worlds thesis unwittingly contributes to its reproduction. Moreover, to state, as Hansen does, that all the 'woes' of immigrant children can be located in the 'duality into which they were born' is to miss the point that there is also a desire to escape this duality—a desire for a new identity. The actualization of this desire is no less a 'problem' than the experience of being caught up between two worlds.

References

Adamic, L. 1969. *Laughing in the Jungle*. New York: Arno Press.

Ålund, A. 1995. 'Alterity in Modernity', *Acta Sociologica* 38, 4: 311–22.

Antin, M. 1997. *The Promised Land*. New York: Penguin Books.

Back, L. 1995. 'X Amount of Sat Siri Akal!: Apache Indian, Reggae Music and Intermezzo Culture', in *Negotiating Identities*, A. Ålund and R. Granqvist, eds. Amsterdam: Rodopi.

Boelhower, W. 1982. *Immigrant Autobiography in the United States*. Verona, Italy: Essedue edizioni.

Covello, L. 1970. *The Teacher in the Urban Community, or The Heart Is the Teacher*. Totowa, NJ: Littlefield, Adams and Co.

Deleuze, G., and E. Guattari. 1986. *Kafka: Toward a Minor Literature*. Minneapolis: University of Minnesota Press.

Hansen, M.L. 1952. 'The Problem of the Third Generation Immigrant', *Commentary* 14, 4: 492–500.

Horn, M. 1997. *Becoming Canadian*. Toronto: University of Toronto Press.

Jefferson, T. 1964. *Notes on the State of Virginia*. New York: Harper & Row.

Kohut, R. 1925. *My Portion: An Autobiography*. New York: T. Seltzer.

Maynard, F.B. 1972. *Raisins and Almonds*. Toronto: Doubleday Canada.

Mayo-Smith, R. 1894. 'Assimilation of Nationalities in the United States', *Political Science Quarterly* 9, 3: 426–44.

Qureshi, K., and S. Moores. 1999. 'Identity Remix: Tradition and Translation in the Lives of Young Pakistani Scots', *European Journal of Cultural Studies* 2, 3: 311–30.

Ruddy, A.C. 1975. *The Heart of the Stranger*. New York: Arno Press.

Santiago, E. 1998. *Almost a Woman*. Reading, MA: Perseus Books.

Soysal, L. 2001. 'Diversity of Experience, Experience of Diversity: Turkish Migrant Youth Culture in Berlin', *Cultural Dynamics* 13, 1: 5–28.

Stonequist, E., ed. 1937. *The Marginal Man*. New York: Charles Scribner's Sons.

Questions for Critical Thought

'Even if I don't know what I'm doing I can make it look like I know what I'm doing': Becoming a Doctor in the 1990s

1. Account for some possible reasons why many medical school students suffer from an 'imposter syndrome' and feel they are unqualified for their current role.
2. Many students claim that they try to maintain professional relationships with patients to avoid 'human' feelings. Do you believe that a good doctor is an impersonal one or a compassionate one? Include personal experiences in your answer.
3. 'For many students, patients were the single most important source of confirmation for their emerging identity as physicians.' Explain this statement.
4. When surveyed, many medical school students said that their physical appearance was very important in maintaining a professional image. Why do you think appearance is so important in maintaining a professional image?
5. Although women have made progress professionally and personally in the past century, the majority of doctors are still white and male. Is it possible that the medical profession is simply not suited for women?

On the Assimilation of Racial Stereotypes among Black Canadian Young Offenders

1. When interviewed, an astounding number of respondents blamed the media for its portrayal of blacks as an influence on society's views. To what extent do you believe this is true and how does the media portray black people?
2. Respondents who were of 'mixed' (mulatto) racial heritage were included in this study if they identified as black. What do you believe it takes to identify as being 'black'?
3. Many of the black respondents said that society either views them as entertainers or criminals. Do you agree with this view? Explain.
4. Black and Native Canadians do have significantly higher rates of incarceration than white Canadians. Do you believe that this is because blacks and natives are more deviant or that white people are just less likely to get caught?
5. Many attempts to study deviance pose ethical and other dilemmas. What precautions do you believe that the authors of this study had to take when conducting their research?

The Pendulum of Family Change: Comparative Life Course Transitions of Young Adults

1. How has the increasing need for post-secondary education and other economic change contributed to delays in the transition to adulthood and the 'boomerang kid' phenomenon?
2. To what extent does social structure play a role in the timing and nature of key life course transitions to adulthood? Relate your answer to family background factors (e.g., social class, regional locale, ethnicity, intergenerational relations) and gendered processes.
3. Provide specific examples of how parent–child relations may be affected when a young adult experiences a transition 'reversal' (e.g., returning home, divorce), both in the short and long-term.
4. From a global perspective, discuss how the transition to adulthood might vary across cultures, for example, between developing and developed nations.

5. Is it possible that we could return to some form of the stereotypical 'traditional' 1950s family structure in the future, given cyclical patterns and fluctuations over time in family-related behaviour? Also, consider the role of factors such as immigration trends, patterns of religious involvement, gender roles, and political transformations.

SEARCHING, WORKING, AND SHOPPING: IS THIS PROLONGED YOUTH?

1. How are youth and adulthood commonly distinguished from one another? What social patterns complicate such distinctions?
2. What does adulthood mean to you? How will you know when you have attained adulthood?
3. Based on your definition of adulthood, what types of social inequality might either prolong or narrow a person's youth?
4. What kinds of work do young people engage in and with what kinds of pay? Does this work speed them towards adulthood or does it prolong their youth?
5. 'Credentialism' is the process through which people need increasing academic credentials for the same occupations. What is the role of credentialism in either shrinking or lengthening youth?

DUALITY AND DIVERSITY IN THE LIVES OF IMMIGRANT CHILDREN: RETHINKING THE 'PROBLEM OF THE SECOND GENERATION' IN LIGHT OF IMMIGRANT AUTOBIOGRAPHIES

1. Should duality among immigrants be seen as a positive or negative attribute?
2. In Canadian society, the duality of immigrants is seen positively and is perpetuated through policies of multiculturalism and bilingualism. Do you believe that these policies impede the smooth integration of immigrants into Canadian society or ease it?
3. Although autobiographies are provided as the main source of information in this article, they provide a very micro view of immigrants. What macro scale factors can also provide insight into the duality of immigrants?
4. Do you believe that the 'two-worlds thesis' applies to most immigrants or is that an unwarranted generalization?
5. Richmond Mayo-Smith (1894) identified three major groups among what he called 'the whites' in America. First, there were 'the native-born of native parentage', the 'true Americans' who tend to be assimilated. Then, there were 'the whites of foreign birth, the immigrants . . . the real element to be assimilated'. Finally, there was the 'the native-born of foreign parents . . . the second generation of immigrants, so to speak'. Second-generation immigrants, Mayo-Smith wrote, 'stand half-way . . . between the native and the foreign element. . . . They represent the process of assimilation in the act'. Is Mayo's theory of groups too broad or is there truth in it?

Part IV

Deviance

We have all engaged in acts of deviance. At times, all of us have done things we should not have, things that have made us ashamed, anxious, or which gave us a secret thrill. Though our actions did not seem deviant at the time, the stigma surrounding them makes our actions deviant. We may even admire people—say, political rebels or environmental activists—who break the law and risk serious penalties to act on their principles. What is most likely to interest a sociologist is not the deviant behaviour itself, but how deviance and conformity are related to each other. Deviance, as we shall see, is another aspect of social order. *Society creates deviance* by expecting, insisting on, and enforcing social order.

Deviance, then, is not a special topic of study but a measure of how strictly a society is organized. Every area of social life provides a chance to deviate. Deviance occurs in all the tiny activities of daily life. Whenever we lie, cheat, seduce, disgust, or simply annoy one another, we are deviating from *someone's norms*. Deviant acts occur in many subcultural groups, such as juvenile gangs. The dominant view is that these acts are deviant and, often, they are seen as harmful.

Most of us think of crime when we think of deviance and, specifically, the major crimes such as murder, armed robbery, or rape. However, 'deviance' covers a much wider variety of actions. It includes criminal organizations such as the Mafia and those 'legitimate' organizations that engage in criminal acts by bribing officials, cheating customers, or selling dangerous and defective products. Deviance ranges from murder at one extreme to pushing to the head of a line of people waiting for a bus at the other. Deviance also includes keeping a dog off-leash in restricted areas, taking one's clothes off in the lobby of a doctor's office, bargaining at Eaton's, and eating poached worms in Regina.

Behaviours termed 'deviant' all threaten what members of one group or another feel are their cherished values or their security. To sociologists, then, deviance is a general term referring to any behaviour that leads to a negative reaction by some part of the community. When no one feels threatened by an uncommon behaviour—for example, by wearing a polka-dot bow tie—people are likely to see it as simply an expression of individuality. Such behaviour may be considered eccentric, even charming, but not deviant. There is much room in North American popular culture for the acceptance, even admiration, of people who are eccentric (like Mother Theresa) or who rebel in fashionable ways (like kd lang).

Reactions to uncommon behaviour depend largely on how the behaviour is seen. Still, perception by itself is not enough; for an act to be deviant, perception must be turned into action. How much weight that action carries will depend on how much power people have to *enforce* their own views of acceptable behaviour.

In Part 3 we see how deviance takes on many forms and expressions. For example, in the article by M. Reza Nakhaie and colleagues, we will explore the many factors surrounding a student's resistance to learning. Joanna C. Jacob discusses social disorganization theory and the effects of community structure on the prevalence of crime, both for men and women. Kevin Walby's chapter is especially interesting because it provides insight into the issues surrounding surveillance as a method of crime control. Walby's discussion raises the question of what sort of activities individuals would participate in if they thought no one was watching. Finally, in Philip Boyle's article, we take an in-depth look at mega-security and the hidden rationale for its existence, other than its preventative effects on terrorist activity.

CHAPTER 15

Resistance to Education: Self Control and Resistance to School

M. Reza Nakhaie, Roberta A. Silverman, and Teresa C. LaGrange

Introduction

Some students regularly resist school and the educational experience it offers. Research often explains this resistance by factors such as **class** and class-based socialization. The argument goes something like this: Schools generally favour middle-class values such as ambition, deference for authority, individual responsibility, deferred gratification, future and goal orientations, and the control of physical aggression and violence. Values such as present orientation, spontaneity, risk and thrill seeking, and physical prowess are said to be incongruent with the curricula of school, though consistent with working/ lower-class culture. It is therefore not surprising that working-class children do not do as well as middle-class children in school. These observations are made, in one way or another, by both **criminologists** and cultural theorists (Cohen, 1955; Miller, 1958; Bowles and Gintis, 1976; Bourdieu, 1977; Bourdieu and Boltanski, 1978; Giroux, 1983).

Data for this research were generated by the University of Alberta Study of Juvenile and Adolescent Behaviour, a **cross-sectional survey** of secondary school students completed in Edmonton, Alberta in 1994 (N = 2495).

According to Gottfredson and Hirschi (1990: 89), criminal acts provide immediate, easy, or simple gratification; are exciting, risky, and thrilling; require little skill or planning; result in pain and discomfort for the victim; and provide few long-term benefits. The study contained 25 questions that correspond to these traits (see Grasmick et al., 1993; Arneklev et al., 1993). For each of the questions, respondents were given the options of agreeing or disagreeing. For this analysis, lack of

self-control received a score of 1, while self-control received a score of 2. Those who did not provide an answer (a very small percentage of the survey) were excluded. Principal components analysis showed that these 25 questions load on six factiors.

The survey includes 19 questions that measure parental control and attachment to friends. For these questions, higher scores mean more **social control**.

The dependent variables include 19 questions representing different aspects of resistance to school. These variables are factor analyzed and summed to create five general resistance indices. First, we used the educational aspiration of students as an indication of students' perception of the relevance of school for their perceived future. Second, students were asked to state their feelings of belonging and/or loneliness in school. Schools are said to represent middle-class curricula and values, and thus lower-class students should feel lonely and/or isolated. Third, lower-class students are expected to view school as boring and homework as a waste of time. Fourth, it is expected that lower-class students would develop an inversion of the middle-class values for which they get punished in school. Finally, and consequently, it is expected that lower-class students will fail courses and skip classes. Overall, these traits are intended to capture individuals who buck the system by establishing a counter-school culture that resists the **norms** and behavioural expectations of the school. These indices correspond to what Richer (1990: 96) calls informal-passive resistance. This construct is coded so that a higher score means more resistance to school.

We used information from both parents' occupations by assigning the occupation of the most advantaged parent as the class of respondent. Thus, if the father had a managerial position and the mother a clerical occupation, the father's occupation is used determine the respondent's class. The resulting classification includes: (a) managerial and professional; (b) lower white-collar; (c) skilled workers; (d) semi-skilled workers; and (e) unskilled workers. As well, two other class categories are included.

Finally, we include three variables that have proved to be important predictors of crime and resistance: Gender (males = 1, females = 0), age (under 15, 15 and over), and ethnicity (Aboriginal people = 1, other visible minorities = 2, others = 0). Aboriginal people (Inuit, Native Indian. and Métis) constitute 6.3 per cent of the respondents. Other visible minorities (Chinese/Asians, Blacks, and Indo-Pakistanis) constitute 21.9 per cent of the respondents and the remaining 71.8 per cent are non-Aboriginal, non-visible minority.

Results showed that males and older students reported significantly lower self- and social control, and were more likely to resist school than females and younger students. Aboriginal people showed significantly lower self- and social control and higher resistance than the rest of the sample. Other visible minorities, in contrast, exhibited higher self- (but not social) control and lower resistance than the reference category. There was little evidence of class differences in self-control. Finally, self-control was about twice as strong as social control in explaining resistance.

Table 15.1 shows the individual effects of the self- and social control dimensions on attributes of resistance. We note that social class is generally not a good predictor of resistance. The only exception is that children of unskilled workers and **surplus population** families had low scholastic aspiration compared with children of managerial and professional parents. Moreover, neither age nor gender is related to low scholastic aspiration. Resistance is differentially affected by ethnicity. Aboriginal students express low scholastic aspiration and high truancy, results that are diametrically opposed to those for other visible minorities.

Generally, these findings are supportive of research on the relationship between gender, ethnicity, and resistance (see Fine, 1991; Anisef and Andres, 1996; Davies, 1994).

Among the self- control traits, temper and present orientation are poorer predictors of various aspects of resistance than are other traits. Temper is related only to lack of belonging and present orientation is related only to misbehaviour. Third, risk seeking seems to be a better predictor of resistance than the other five components of self-control. Fourth, each aspect of resistance has a tendency to be better explained by a specific self-control trait. For example, estrangement from school is best explained by carelessness; misbehaviour by impulsivity; lack of belonging by both impulsivity and restlessness; truancy and low aspiration by risk seeking. Fifth, taken together, the predictors are better able to explain truancy, followed by misbehaviour and estrangement, than other measures of resistance.

Finally, not all of these indicators are equally important in predicting resistance. In fact, risk seeking is the only consistent predictor of all measures of resistance. Impulsiveness, carelessness, and temper are related to four indicators, restlessness to three indicators, and present orientation to only one indicator of resistance.

Discussion and Conclusion

Most research on youth resistance has focused on the role of class origin. **Deviance** is portrayed as a political expression of position in the working class. This is found most notably in the work of British cultural theorists (Murdock, 1974; Willis, 1977), who presented working-class deviance in school as challenging the 'hegemonic domination'. We found some support for this assertion in that students from among the surplus population are significantly more likely to resist school than students from managerial or professional categories (as measured by parents' occupational status in both cases).

Contemporary criminological theory focuses on external and internal social controls. When these

Table 15.1 Unstandardized and Standardized Regression Coefficients of Resistance of Independent Variables

	Model 1		Model 2	
	B	Beta (s.e.)	B	Beta (s.e.)
Age	.48	.20 (.05)**	.32	.13 (.34)**
Males	1.53	.16 (.19)**	.86	.09 (.16)**
Ethnicity, others = reference				
Aboriginal	1.77	.09 (.40)**	.55	.03 (.34)
Other visible	−1.77	−.10 (.40)**	−.95	.09 (.19)**
Household class, Professional/ managerial = reference				
Low white collars	−.14	−.01 (.29)	−.39	.03 (.24)
Skilled workers	.27	−.02 (.31)	−.12	.01 (.25)
Semi-skilled workers	.37	.02 (.33)	.17	.01 (.21)
Unskilled workers	−.23	−.02 (.28)	−.05	−.01 (.23)
Surplus population	1.55	−.07 (.50)**	.66	.02 (.43)
Parentless	.68	−.03 (.46)	−.91	−.04 (.40)*
Self-control			−.40	−.46 (.02)**
Social Control			−.24	−.25 (.02)**
Constant	1.64*		14.01**	
Adjusted R2	.097		.445	
N	2121		1921	

* p < .01.

are introduced into the equation, the class relationship disappears. The only persistent class effects are in the significantly lower scholastic aspirations of the most disadvantaged, in comparison with the managerial and professional categories. This finding is understandable and consistent with previous research that pointed to the economic disadvantages of these strata with a consequent low expectation of future opportunities (see Porter et al., 1973; Bourdieu, 1977: 495; Nakhaie, 1996). It seems that conservative criminological theory offers a more powerful explanation for resistance than does class-based theory. We should caution, however, that our measures of class are based on a technical division of labour (occupation), reported

by students' evaluation of what their parents do, as well as on mean neighbourhood income. Our class measures are not based on the social relations of production (i.e., ownership).

Further, this study demonstrates that social class is not a strong predictor of the other four dimensions of resistance to school. This is perhaps also understandable, given that at least one view of compulsory schooling is that it was designed as a mechanism of social control. Although students are recruited from different classes, they participate in a common educational milieu and, therefore, their class differences in resistance tend to be suppressed. Furthermore, the lack of class effects shown here could be an artifact of a cohort needing minimum education to find employment in a postindustrial service economy. Even the most menial jobs now require some level of educational attainment, which means that lower- (and middle) class youths may not conceptualize elementary and secondary education as irrelevant for future employment. This requirement is fundamentally different from the cultural setting of industrial Britain in the 1970s, where cultural theory originated (see Tanner 1990; Davies, 1994: 440). Finally, it could be that the weak class-based school **counterculture** is a function of a higher mobility opportunity perception in Canada than in Britain (see Frith, 1985: 376; Brake, 1985).

Our study has showed that the introduction of self- and social control into the equations containing class, gender, ethnicity, and age reduces the effect of these variables on resistance. However, these variables maintain their independent effects, as well. On the one hand, we can conclude that if the link between social class (or gender and ethnicity) and resistance is low (at least in Canada), it may be because the self- and social control differences that produce or reject resistance are not strongly linked to social class (and/or ethnicity and gender). If we conceptualize self-control as a type of **cultural capital**, then its link to social class, gender, and ethnicity is weak. On the other hand, self- and social control are not able to account fully for gender and/or ethnic differences in resistance. That is, one cannot wash away gender and ethnic/racial differences in resistance or crime by a pattern of early socialization and failure of child-rearing practices.

Although self-control is found to be significantly and strongly related to all types of resistance, some of its dimensions are better and more consistent predictors (e.g., risk taking) of resistance than others. This finding is inconsistent with the unidimensionality of the self-control concept proposed by the authors of the **General Theory**. In fact, the finding that, among the self-control traits, risk taking is the best predictor of crime diminishes the novelty of the General Theory, as earlier criminological theories also pointed to the importance of risk taking in explaining crime. For example, **power-control theory** (Hagan, Gillis, and Simpson, 1985) uses risk taking as the main predictor, accounting for gender differences in delinquency. This is understandable, since risk taking is a more proximate determinant of crime and thus should produce a stronger effect than other personality traits (see Arneklev et al., 1993: 243).

Certainly this study is not definitive, but does add to the growing literature that, on the one hand, offers support for some of the General Theory's precepts while, on the other hand, suggests that the theory needs some modifications to take into account findings that diverge from its predictions.

References

Anisef, P., and L. Andres. 1996. 'Dropping out in Canada: The Construction of a Crisis?', in *Debating Dropouts: Critical Policy Research Perspectives on School Leaving*, pp. 84–100, D. Kelly and J. Gaskell, eds. New York: Columbia University, Teacher's College Press.

Arneklev, B.J., H.G. Grasmick, and C.R. Tittle. 1993. 'Low Self-control and Imprudent Behavior', *Journal of Quantitative Criminology* 9, 3: 225–47.

Bowles, S., and H. Gintis. 1976. *Schooling in Capitalist America: Educational Reform and the Construction of Economic Life*. New York: Basic Books.

Bourdieu, P. 1977. 'Cultural Reproduction and Social Reproduction', in *Power and Ideology in Education*, pp. 487–511, J. Karabel and A.H. Halsey, eds. New York: Oxford University Press.

Bourdieu, P., and L. Boltanski. 1978. 'Changes in Social Structure and Changes in Demand for Education', in *Contemporary Europe: Structural Change and Cultural Patterns*, pp. 197–227, S. Giner and M. Archer, eds. London: Routledge and Kegan Paul.

Brake, M. 1985. *Comparative Youth Culture: The Sociology of Youth Subcultures in America, Britain and Canada*. London: Routledge and Kegan Paul.

Cohen, A.X. 1955. *Delinquent Boys*. New York: Free Press.

Davies, S. 1994. 'Class Dismissed? Student Opposition in Ontario', *The Canadian Review of Sociology and Anthropology* 31, 4: 422–45.

Fine, M. 1991. *Framing Dropouts: Notes on the Politics of an Urban High School*. Albany: SUNY Press.

Frith, S. 1985. 'The Sociology of Youth', in *Sociology: New Directions*, M. Haralamas, ed. Ormskirk: Causeway.

Giroux, H.A. 1983. *Theory and Resistance in Education: A Pedagogy for the Opposition*. London: Heinemann.

Gottfredson, M.R., and T. Hirschi. 1990. *A General Theory of Crime*. Stanford, CA: Stanford University Press.

Grasmick, H.G., C.R. Tittle, R.J. Bursik, Jr, and B. Arneklev. 1993. 'Testing the Core Empirical Implications of Gottfredson and Hirschi's General Theory of Crime', *Journal of Research in Crime and Delinquency* 30, 1: 5–29.

Hagan, J., and B. McCarthy. 1997. *Mean Streets: Youth Crime and Homelessness*. London: Cambridge University Press.

Hagan, J., A.R. Gillis, and J. Simpson. 1985. 'The Class Structure of Gender and Delinquency: Toward a Power-control Theory of Common Delinquent Behavior', *American Journal of Sociology* 90: 1151–78.

Miller, W. 1958. 'Lower-class Culture as a Generating Milieu of Gang Delinquency', *Journal of Social Issues* 14: 5–19.

Murdock, G. 1974. 'Mass Communications and the Construction of Meaning', in *Reconstructing Social Psychology*, pp. 205–20, N. Armistead, ed. London: Penguin.

Nakhaie, R. 1996. 'The Reproduction of Class Relations by Gender in Canada', *Canadian Journal of Sociology* 21, 4: 523–8.

Nielsen, M., and R.A. Silverman, eds. *Native Americans, Crime, and Justice*. Boulder, CO: Westview.

Porter, J., B. Blishen, and M. Porter. 1973. *Does Money Matter?* Toronto: Institute of Behavioural Research, York University.

Richer, S. 1988. 'Equality to Benefit from Schooling: The Issue of Educational Opportunity', in *Social Issues: Sociological Views of Canada*, 2nd ed., pp. 262–88, D. Forcese and S. Richer, eds. Scarborough, ON: Prentice-Hall Canada Inc.

Tanner, J. 1990. 'Reluctant Rebels: A Case Study of Edmonton High School Drop-outs', *Canadian Review of Sociology and Anthropology* 27, 1: 74–94.

Willis, P. 1977. *Learning to Labour: How Working-Class Kids Get Working-Class Jobs*. England: Saxon House.

CHAPTER 16

Gender, Crime, and Community: An Analysis of Youth Crime in Canada

Joanna C. Jacob

Introduction

Official crime statistics consistently show a large disparity in the rates of offending by male and female youths. Despite an increasing awareness of female youths' involvement in crime, few criminological theories and empirical studies account for their actions. One area, among many others, of criminological research that has not explicitly considered the causes of female delinquency is the eco-logical study of crime. Traditionally applied to males and predominantly studied using American data, these studies contribute to the understanding of the social conditions associated with variations in crime rates.

This paper examines whether and to what degree social disorganization theory is applicable to male and female youth crime in Canada. The findings may provide insight for formulating community crime prevention policies, and in turn, suggest ways to mobilize communities to actively engage in crime prevention.

Theoretical Perspective

Clifford Shaw and Henry McKay, scholars at the University of Chicago, believe that to understand crime one has to examine the characteristics of neighbourhoods rather than characteristics of individual delinquents. In the 1940s and the 1960s, they developed **social disorganization theory**, which links socially disorganized communities with variations in delinquency rates. Social disorganization refers to 'the inability of a community structure to realize the common values of its residents [such as living in a crime free area], and maintain effective social controls' (Sampson and Groves, 1989). Thus, disorganized communities are unable to supervise and control youth crime. Shaw and McKay (1969) argued that areas of Chicago with low rates of delinquency are characterized more or less by 'uniformity, conformity, and universality of conventional values and attitudes with respect to child care, conformity to law and related matters; whereas in the high-rate areas, systems of competing and conflicting morals have developed' (88). In the absence of social order, delinquency may arise.

Five community characteristics based on early and current studies are thought to impede the ability of residents to form the **social networks** necessary for social organization: socioeconomic status, residential instability, racial and ethnic heterogeneity, urbanization, and supervision (Wirth, 1938; Shaw and McKay, 1969; Sampson and Groves, 1989; Hartnagel and Lee, 1990; Bursik and Grasmick, 1993; Hartnagel, 1997; Schulenberg, 2003; Jacob, 2006). Findings concerning the impact of these community characteristics on crime rates are quite diverse, and in some cases, contradictory (Fein, 2002).

Methods

The expectation, based on previous theory and research, is that community characteristics, which represent the community's **social cohesion** and informal social control, will be related to male youth crime rates; however whether these characteristics will also able to account for female youth crime is unclear.

VARIABLES

The indicator of official *youth crime* in the Canadian Uniform Crime Reporting Survey (UCR) is the rate of male and female youths apprehended by police (per 100,000 youth population). This includes youths (aged 12–17 years) that are charged and youths that are apprehended by police but not charged (i.e. dealt with informally by police).

In order to capture the level of social disorganization in a community, four community characteristics were studied: *socioeconomic status* (percentage of individuals with income of at least $40,000; percentage of the community with high educational attainment; percentage of the community in professional and managerial positions); *residential instability* (percentage of residential movers over a five-year period); *urbanization* (population size and population density); and *supervision* (percentage of lone-parent families).

DATA AND UNIT OF ANALYSIS

Several sources of data including the 1996 Canadian Census, the 1996 Canadian Uniform Crime Reporting Survey (UCR), and custom tabulations from the Canadian Centre for Justice Statistics were integrated for this study (for details see Fein, 2002). The unit of analysis in the present study is the municipal police jurisdiction (i.e., the area under the jurisdiction of an individual police service, detachment of the provincial police, or RCMP).

Analysis and Results

The statistical analysis of community characteristics and male and female youth crime rates used **multivariate analysis**. The **partial regression coefficients** (ß) presented in Table 16.1 allows us to compare the relative impact of each of the independent variables (community characteristics) on

Table 16.1 Regression Results of Youth Apprehension Rates, by Gender[a]

Dependent Variables	Female youth apprehension rates (N = 533)		Male youth apprehension rates (N = 532)	
Independent Variables	B	s.e	B	s.e
Managers & supervisors (%)	−0.314**	0.047	−0.293**	0.047
Highly educated (%)	−0.268**	0.043	−0.221**	0.042
High income (%)	0.308**	0.053	0.232**	0.057
Movers (%)	0.284**	0.044	0.339**	0.041
Population size (log)	0.112*	0.048	...[b]	
Population density (square root)	0.115*	0.043	...[b]	
Lone parent families (%)	0.174**	0.016	0.263**	0.043
Adjusted R^2	0.270	0.240		

[a] Table includes standardized partial slopes (,) and their standard errors
[b] Omitted from regression model because of skewness and non-significance
**Significant at the 0.01 level; *Significant at the .05 level

the dependent variable (youth crime rates). For example, looking at Table 16.1, in the 'Female youth apprehension rates' column, the results show that the percentage of the community working as managers and supervisors has the strongest relationship with female youth crime rates, relative to the other community variables (ß = -0.314); population size appears to have the weakest impact on female youth crime rates relative to the other variables (ß = 0.112).

The multivariate analysis of community characteristics and youth crime rates produces many interesting results. For both genders, socioeconomic status and residential instability are the most important predictors for rates of youth crime (Table 16.1). With the exception of high income, increased community socioeconomic status and residential stability are related to lower rates of youth crime for both genders. The percentage of the community with a high income is positively associated with the rates of both male and female youth crime, which was not expected. Gender similarities continue when looking at the percentage of the community who are lone-parents.

Other community characteristics had less clear relationships based on gender, and relatively weak relationships with youth crime. Population size

and population density of the community show only very weak associations with female youth crime, and no associations with male youth crime (Table 16.1).

Discussion

Social disorganization theory suggests that communities characterized by high socioeconomic status will have residents who are in a position to establish and maintain strong social ties. In this study, the findings for the occupational status and educational attainment of the community show that communities with these high socioeconomic status characteristics are associated with low rates of youth crime for both genders. These communities appear to have strong social cohesion and more informal social control of community youths. Unexpectedly, this study found that higher income is associated with higher youth crime rates for males and females. It is not clear why high income is the only socioeconomic status indicator to be positively related to youth crime. A study by Smith and Jarjoura (1988) suggests income needs to be understood as an interaction with stability, while Wright et al. (1999), suggest high socioeconomic status indirectly works to both increase and decrease delinquency because youths in higher socioeconomic status communities have an increased taste for risk taking, including delinquent activities.

Residential instability was expected to weaken the ability of a community to informally control youth crime because in areas with higher levels of residents moving in and out, it is more difficult for residents to form and maintain strong social networks within a community (Sampson and Groves, 1989; Hartnagel, 1997; South and Messner, 2000). Thus, communities with higher rates of instability, have weaker social ties, poor community integration, and higher rates youth crime. In relation to the control of male and female youth crime, the present study finds support for this theory in Canadian communities for both genders.

Unexpectedly, in this analysis the impact of urbanization (population size and population density) appears to be mediated by socioeconomic status and residential instability. This well known theory has been contested by many researchers (Gans, 1968; Harries, 1974) and in Canada has had little support (Hartnagel and Lee, 1990; Schulenberg, 2003; Jacob, 2006). The present study finds only partial support for urbanization; it appears that increasing population size and population

density weaken informal control enough to allow female youth crime to increase slightly, but not enough to impact male youth crime.

Supervision (or family disruption) research has had more recent attention by social disorganization scholars. Communities characterized mainly by two-parent households are thought to have a greater number of resources and a larger network of people to monitor the properties and activities of the youths in the neighbourhood (Sampson, 1995). Thus regardless of their own family situation, male and female youths in predominantly two-parent communities are more highly supervised. The present study finds support for the relationship between supervision and rates of youth crime for both genders.

Conclusion

The findings lend some support for the application of social disorganization theory at the community level in Canada. They also suggest that there are many similarities, rather than differences, in the community characteristics that are related to rates of youth crime for both males and females, despite the gap in official crime rates by teenage boys and girls.

References

Bursik, R.J., Jr, and H.G. Grasmick. 1993. *Neighborhoods and Crime: The Dimensions of Effective Community Control.* Toronto: Maxwell Macmillan Canada and Lexington Books.

Fein, J.C. 2002. Does Gender Matter? Structural Correlates of Male and Female Youth Crime in Canada. MA Thesis. University of Waterloo.

Hartnagel, T.J. 1997. 'Crime among the Provinces: The Effect of Geographic Mobility', *Canadian Journal of Criminology* 35, 4: 387–402.

Hartnagel, T.J., and G. Won Lee. 1990. 'Urban Crime in Canada', *Canadian Journal of Criminology* 32: 591–606.

Jacob, J.C. 2006. 'Male and Female Youth Crime in Canadian Communities: Assessing the Applicability

of Social Disorganization Theory', *Canadian Journal of Criminology and Criminal Justice* 48, 1: 31–60.

Sampson, R.J. 1995. 'The Community', in *Crime*, J.Q. Wilson and J. Petersilia, eds. San Francisco: ICS.

Sampson, R.J., and B.W. Groves. 1989. 'Community Social Structure and Crime: Testing Social Disorganization Theory', *American Journal of Sociology* 94, 4: 774–802.

Schulenberg, J.L. 2003. 'The Social Context of Police Discretion with Young Offenders: An Ecological Analysis', *Canadian Journal of Criminology and Criminal Justice* 45, 2: 127–57.

Shaw, C.R., and H.D. McKay. [1942] 1969. *Juvenile Delinquency and Urban Areas: A Study of Rates of Delinquency in Relation to Differential Characteristics of*

Local Communities in American Cities, Rev. ed. Chicago: University of Chicago Press..

Smith, D.A., and G.R. Jarjoura. 1988. 'Social Structure and Criminal Victimization', *Journal of Research in Crime and Delinquency* 25: 27–52.

South, S.J., and S.F. Messner. 2000. 'Crime and Demography: Multiple Linkages, Reciprocal Relations', *Annual Review of Sociology* 26: 83–106.

Wirth, L. 1938. 'Urbanism as a Way of Life', in *Urbanism in World Perspective: A Reader*, pp. 3–24, S.F. Flava, ed. New York: Thomas Y. Crowell.

Wright, B.R.E., A. Caspi, T.E. Moffitt, R.A. Miech, and P.A. Silva. 1999. 'Reconsidering the Relationship between SES and Delinquency: Causation but not Correlation', *Criminology* 37, 1: 175–94.

CHAPTER 17

Keeping an Eye on Crime Control Culture: The Rise of Open-street Closed-circuit Television Surveillance in Canada

Kevin Walby

In its simplest form, open-street closed-circuit television (CCTV) surveillance consists of people, places, and technologies. An operator or officer watches, on TV, an area observed by a video camera. The video camera could be mounted on a wall, a street lamp, a fence or the roof of a building. The difference between open-street CCTV and private camera surveillance (in a mall, for instance) is that open-street CCTV monitors public places and is operated by people representing public institutions. Even though the crime rate in Canada has been falling since the 1970s, open-street CCTV is becoming a popular crime control tool.

Surveillance theorists and criminologists have not been able to fully explain the rise of open-street CCTV surveillance. Dominant metaphors in surveillance studies conceive of power as a top-down exercise performed by state apparatuses. Consider Orwell's (1949) notion of Big Brother, Giddens's (1985) focus on totalitarianism, and, to a lesser extent, Foucault's **Panopticon**. Made fashionable by Foucault's (1979) *Discipline and Punish*, the Panopticon (see Figure 17.1) was originally an architectural design proposed by Jeremy Bentham as a means to reform the eighteenth century English prison system. Prison guards standing behind semi-closed blinds could watch inmates constantly (or not at all) from a centralized observation deck surrounded by a circular housing of prison cells. That prisoners did not know if they were being gazed upon induced in them a state of conscious and permanent visibility that assured the automatic functioning of power through self-regulation. Foucault's notion of the Panopticon has dominated studies of surveillance for several decades. The problem is that the many different practices we call 'surveillance' have changed in ways Orwell, Giddens, and even Foucault cannot comment on. In the case of Orwell and Giddens, the state is not the only institution that desires to use surveillance (Lyon, 2001). Nor have we seen the closure of agency implied in Foucault's version of the Panopticon.

Recent research on open-street CCTV argues that camera surveillance is imposed from above by the powerful to control deviants in the neo-liberal city (Coleman, 2003, 2004). From this perspective, open-street CCTV serves the interests of elite partnerships, bolstering a new techno-logical form of crime control, which is extended out of the prison and into city space. Attempting to displace the dominant panoptic paradigm by substituting the elites of neoliberalism for the role traditionally occupied by state apparatuses in top-down approaches, the rise of open-street CCTV is explained in terms of **responsibilization** (where the state activates non-state actors to perform crime control activities). This approach is insuffi-cient because, despite claims to 'partnerships,' in the end it sees the rise of CCTV as state-driven and thus reproduces the top-down determinisms already mentioned.

An important analytic which serves the inverse function of the Panopticon is the **Synopticon** (see Mathiesen, 1997). Inverse to the Panopticon, where a single agent observes a total social body, synoptic processes refer to media communication situations where 'the many watch the few'. In the Synopticon, 'the many' are a viewing/reading pub-lic who actively consume various media pertaining to crime, injustice, etc. 'The few' are those depicted as deviant folk devils, perhaps caught on a CCTV camera, written about in a newspaper, or imagined as the embodiment of urban disorder. Media influ-ence enculturation, actively filtering and shaping the information that citizens consume, and the intensification of surveillance measures has always been intimately linked with forms of media com-munication. The concept of the Synopticon allows researchers to better understand the role of media communication in shaping forms of subjectivity, which ultimately work to legitimate the implemen-tation of regulatory projects like open-street CCTV, and suggests possible analytical avenues for exam-ining where regulatory projects like open-street CCTV are generated.

Acknowledging the role media plays in the social construction of what is considered risky or immoral behaviour in the city, I propose an alter-native method for conceptualizing the rise of open-street CCTV surveillance in Canada. In terms of social positioning, projects that seek to regulate perceptions of deviance can emerge from above, from the middle, and from below (also see Hunt, 1999). State or police-driven surveillance is the most pertinent example of regulation from above. Business or other non-state organizations com-prise the position of the middle. Regulation aris-ing from public hostility characterizes projects from below.

How is it that agents from different social posi-tions mobilize to participate in governance projects? As a regulatory tool, open-street CCTV gains its legitimacy from purported levels of crime and fear of crime, and in the process vulnerable populations are moralized and constructed as imagined communities of risk. These anxieties are fostered by **problematization** (when some people contest the conduct, values, or culture of others) in the media. Local press are key for communicating beliefs, but are not, however, an elite instrument. Local media outlets have autonomy, make their own political decisions, and are sometimes as directly involved with funding open-street CCTV. The television and newspaper press *are* businesses, and can therefore be conceptualized as a regula-tory agency that fits in the middle of our analytic framework whilst serving to communicate know-ledge about crime implicated in top-down and bottom-up processes. Of course, in everyday life an agent or agency could at the same time occupy more than one social position or change positions over time. A member of a downtown business association could at one time exert pressure for CCTV from the middle but at the same time be involved in a community-based drive for regula-tory intervention. TV and newspaper media are implicated in each position. My fundamental point is that pace outdated the metaphors conceiving of social monitoring in terms of top-down processes. Community initiatives can precede and inspire state policing strategies.

Governance from below as it concerns open-street CCTV is best exemplified by the example from London, ON. The sixteen-camera opera-tive—which went operational on 9 November 2001—is a citizens' initiative. The violent murder of Michael Goldie-Ryder resulted in the formation of 'Friends Against Senseless Endings', a moral entrepreneurial group against violence. The group, headed by Goldie-Ryder's mother and others, was organized in response to the grievance against Goldie-Ryder and its aim was to voice the public's concerns about safety in the local media. Nearly 800 Londoners staged a walkathon, 'walking against violence' in memory of Goldie-Ryder, raising $10,000 for the cause (Miner, 2001). The media fuelled the grief brought on by this isolated incident. In this instance, the citizen initiative preceded police policy. In other instances, the configuration of agents, agencies, and problematization is completely different. In early May 2001, Centurion Security Services installed four CCTV cameras on the roof of a building in downtown Yellowknife as part of a marketing demonstration. As a regulatory project, the urban CCTV operative in Yellowknife can be conceptualized as being generated from the middle, as the operative was controlled and maintained solely by a business interest in separation from police or citizens' interests.

At other times police and non-state agencies implement open-street CCTV operatives before public consultation. The Hamilton Police Service joined forces with the Downtown Hamilton Business Improvement Area in 2001 to purchase five cameras, intending to monitor the King Street East core of Hamilton, ON. In the Hamilton case, the risky community was again imagined, but also de-personified, such that an entire geo-spatial area in the city was problematized in the media as unmanageable. Public consultations were not held until a year after the purchase of the cameras. In Kelowna, BC, a single open-street CCTV camera jointly funded by the City and the Downtown Kelowna Business Association but operated by RCMP was implemented on 23 February 2001, above the Queensway bus loop near City Hall. The camera was implemented for the purposes of monitoring the sex

and drug trade in a downtown park. In December 1996, Sudbury, ON, became the first Ontario city to implement an open-street CCTV camera. Plans for a video monitoring program in Sudbury began in 1994 when Chief of Police Alex McCauley learned of the CityWatch Program in Glasgow, Scotland: a monitoring system consisting of thirty-two cameras modelled on apparent success rates realized in Airdrie and Birmingham, UK. McCauley then visited Scotland in 1995, and worked out the plans for CCTV in Sudbury (see KPMG, 2000). The Sudbury project is aptly named 'Lion's Eye in the Sky,' as the Lion's Club was a major funding partner, although Northern Voice and Video (who donated the first camera), Sudbury Hydro, CP Rail, Sudbury Metro Centre, and Ontario Works have also been contributors. While these economic enterprises committed capital to the 'Eye in the Sky,' Sudbury's CCTV system was initially generated through police interest. Many other municipalities in Canada plan to pursue open-street CCTV in the future.

Seeing surveillance projects as generated from numerous social positions displaces top-down approaches to power. Diverse non-state agents and agencies advance their own strategies of governance in particular geo-spatial areas. People are not passive receptacles of ideological manipulation, but actually constitute the zones on which they act and the entities upon which they act (Rose, 2000: 145). This analysis points to how, in response to the growing sense of insecurity in the city, the liberal dichotomy between regulation and emancipation is obliterated. As Roger Matthews (2002: 222) puts it, 'emancipation collapses into regulation with the consequence that regulation is seen. . .as one of the main routes through which emancipation might be achieved.' Ultimately, the foregoing investigation suggests the need to rethink future strategies for resisting the intensification of surveillance.

References

Coleman, R. 2003. 'Images from a Neoliberal City: The State, Surveillance and Social Control', *Critical Criminology* 12: 21–42.

Foucault, M. 1979. *Discipline and Punish: The Birth of the Prison*. New York: Vintage Books.

Giddens, A. 1985. *The Nation-State and Violence: Volume Two of a Contemporary Critique of Historical Materialism*. Cambridge: Polity Press.

Hunt, A. 1999. *Governing Morals: A Social History of Moral Regulation*. Cambridge: Cambridge University Press.

KPMG. 2000. 'Evaluation of the Lion's Eye in the Sky Video Monitoring Project.'

Miner, J. 2001. 'Walk Against Violence Raises $10,000', *London Free Press* 17 May.

Lyon, D. 2001. *Surveillance Society: Monitoring Everyday Life*. Buckingham, UK: Open University Press.

Mathiesen, T. 1997. 'The Viewer Society: Michel Foucault's "Panopticon" Revisited', *Theoretical Criminology* 1, 2: 215–34.

Matthews, R. 2002. ' "Crime and Control in Late Modernity", Book review of David Garland's *The Culture of Control: Crime and Social Order in Contemporary Society'*, *Theoretical Criminology* 6, 2: 217–26.

Rose, N. 2000. 'Governing Liberty', in *In Governing Modern Societies*, R.V. Ericson and N. Stehr, eds. Toronto: University of Toronto Press.

CHAPTER 18

Mega-security: Concepts and Context for Olympic-sized Security Networks

Philip Boyle

Introduction

The massive display of security at the 2004 Athens Summer Olympic Games is the clearest example of **mega-security** networks that have been increasingly popping up in cities across the world to secure urban **mega-events**. Treating terrorism as the singular reason for mega-security efforts, however, obscures the complex of underlying economic anxieties regarding the place and function of cities within a post-industrial context that mega-events intensify. Using the 2004 Athens Summer Olympics as a case study, this paper argues that terrorism becomes a focal point for these latent anxieties and that mega-security efforts serve the double function of guarding against terrorism as well as shoring up urban representations.

Mega-security

The massive display of security strength at the 2004 Athens Summer Olympic Games set a new benchmark for mega-event security efforts. At a total cost of approximately $1.5 billion (USD), security provision at the Games consisted of around 45,000 security personnel drawn from the local police (25,000 personnel), the Greek military (7,000), trained civilian volunteers (5,000), contract private security officers (3,500), the Greek Coast Guard (3,000), and firefighters from across the region (1,500). Numerous surveillance technologies were integrated with this array of human actors such as CCTV cameras with face recognition and biometric identification cards. NATO air and sea crafts surveyed the city and cruise ships in nearby ports doubled as floating hotels while a surveillance blimp floated directly over the major venues for almost the entire duration of the Games. Connecting all these actors and technologies was an extensive digital communications infrastructure that connected all discrete security elements and arranged them into a fairly cohesive network. Provided by Science Applications International Corporation (SAIC)—an American research, technology, and engineering corporation under contract by the Greek and Athens governments to coordinate security efforts—the system, known as C4I—an alpha-numeric acronym for Command, Control, Communications, Coordination, and Integration—is

> composed of 29 subsystems integrated into a unified command and control system linking the Greek police and firefighters, Greek Coast Guard and Greek Army security forces through 130 fixed and five mobile command centers. Subsystems also include a communication and information system, a digital trunk radio system with 23,000 terminals, security infrastructure for nine main ports, 1,300 closed circuit television surveillance cameras, and an airborne video system for two helicopters and an airship (SAIC, n.d.).

The C4I system acted as the digital nervous system for the entire security apparatus of the Games, an effort that John Pike, a defence analyst of Virginia's Global Security think tank, called 'the single biggest security detail in history' (in Knight, 2004).

This massive security network is the clearest expression of something I will refer to as 'mega-security'—security efforts at short-term, high-profile urban mega-events (such as the Olympics and World's Fair, see Hiller [2000] on mega-events) where the intensive security needs generated by the event far outstrip that which can be provided locally and which thus require additional security resources drawn from outside sources. My discussion here is limited largely to the Olympic Games,

and to the Athens Games in particular, but the dynamics I outline are easily observable at both other mega-events and at smaller events such as the Superbowl or G8 and World Trade Organization meetings.

The spectre of terrorism is one obvious reason for the 'securitization' of a wide range of business, leisure, and cultural sectors, particularly those where large crowds gather and especially those under intense media scrutiny. For the Olympics, terrorism has been a concern since at least the 1972 Munich Games when Palestinian militants assassinated 11 Israeli competitors. Every host city since 1972 has reinforced their security detail with outside resources. The events of 9/11 have, for good reason, radically intensified these concerns across the spectrum of all events that draw together a large number of people, including the Olympics. However, to simply draw a causal link between 9/11 and mega-security efforts over simplifies a more subtle factors that come together to make mega-security efforts acceptable, desirable, and even indispensable when planning mega-events.

Certainly, terrorism is a concern and the loss of human lives is an important reason for increased security, but deeper dynamics are also involved. My argument is that the threat of terrorism touches a nerve with local boosters and officials eager to capitalize on the regenerative potential of hosting the Olympics, and that focusing on terrorism serves as a useful intellectual shorthand to encapsulate a host of underlying, pre-existing economic anxieties regarding urban revitalization and urban representation. The concern of terrorism is about the destructive potential of unforeseen attacks and it is about the loss of human lives, but it is *also* about terrorism derailing these revitalization projects and about long-term, potential devastating economic consequences that such derailment can have. The Olympics thus serve to hyper-intensify a cluster of latent concerns regarding municipal rejuvenation, economic prosperity, urban images, branding, and marketing in such a way that terrorism then becomes a focal point through which they can be addressed. To fully support this argument, the economic background of cities in global economies must first be briefly outlined.

Cities in a Global Context

A number of commentators (David Harvey, 1989a; Scott Lash and John Urry, 1994; Manuel Castells, 2000; and Saskia Sassen, 2001) argue that since the late 1960s and early 1970s the economies of many European and North American countries have undergone dramatic changes. While these authors differ from one another in the specifics of their arguments and use a range of different terms, in a general way they all speak to what Daniel Bell (1976) initially referred to as *post-industrial society*. As a dominant form of social organization since the 1970s, **post-industrialism** refers to economic arrangements where the primary economic driving forces are no longer in areas such as primary resource extraction and processing, mass manufacturing, or industrial production. Instead, the forces are centred in information, services, leisure, and cultural industries. The primary industries that characterized early periods of capitalism in Western countries and produced the urban landscapes now referred to as the 'rust belt' are, it is argued, being squeezed-out by sectors less reliant on the production of tangible goods and more on knowledge-heavy services such as legal counselling, advertising, publishing, accounting/financial services, and software and information technologies—in short, all the 'command and control' functions needed to command today's vast multinational corporations—or which deal in the creative and cultural industries such as tourism and leisure. To the extent that these corporations and, collectively, economies, rely less upon the industrial production of goods (such as automobiles) while specializing in intangible or informational services (such as legal consulting), or the creation and marketing of images (advertising for Nike or Coca-Cola), they can be considered post-industrial. These changes are, of course, highly geographically contingent and specific, but they

reflect attempts of social theory to come to grips with the vast economic changes that have occurred in Western countries over the last three decades.

The importance of these arguments is found within the changes they hold for the place and function of cities within post-industrial economics. As economies shift from primarily industrial to post-industrial bases, many cities across North America and throughout much of Europe have been forced to find new, non-industrial sources of capital in order to replace industrial foundations (for the European situation, see Van den Berg, Pol, Van Winden, and Woets, 2005; Van Kempen, Vermeulen, and Bann, 2005; for the North American situation see Gibson, 2004). Transformations in state regulatory regimes that expose cities to the fluctuations of global markets because of the scaling back of the welfare state and the corresponding dominance of global markets and neo-liberal thought compound the situation (Brenner, 2004). Cities are thus, in a sense, caught in a pincer between economic transformations that have removed the sources of capital that gave them life and political transformations that are hesitant to offer substantial support when it is needed most. The result is an urban 'entrepreneurialism' where cities compete against one another as economic units to secure new sources of capital to fill the void left by the evacuation of industry within the global division of labour (Harvey, 1989b). As Harvey summarizes,

> given the grim history of deindustrialization and restructuring that left most major cities in the advanced capitalist world with few options except to compete with each other, mainly as financial, consumption, and entertainment centers, imaging a city through the organization of spectacular urban spaces became a means to attract capital and people (of the right sort) in a period (since 1973) of intensified inter-urban competition and urban entrepreneurialism (1989a: 92).

The competitive and entrepreneurial strategy turned to by many cities has been to brand themselves as a particular *kind* of city with a particular 'skill set' that will attract a targeted audience, such as being known as a high-tech city region (Seattle), a financial center (New York), or a tourist destination (Las Vegas) (Brenner, 2004; Gibson, 2004). The goal of attracting the right sort of people, as Harvey states, often relies on attracting the twin pillars of urban revitalization: knowledge- and information-based companies on one hand and the culture and tourism industries on the other. These urban revitalization goals don't just 'happen' of course; significant financial investments must be sunk into the corresponding infrastructures and amenities needed to attract new, post-industrial sources of capital. On one hand, building knowledge-based infrastructures means significant investments into digital telecommunications infrastructures, higher education facilities, and high technology centres. On the other hand, becoming a cultural centre means fostering museums, galleries, and all sorts of quality-of-life amenities such as upscale dining and shopping districts that cater to the desires of world-savvy tourists. In conjunction with these physical interventions, the image of the city must also be established, and hence the aggressive marketing campaigns (such as Toronto's recent unveiling of its *Toronto Unlimited* campaign) designed to create a particular image of the city in the eyes of desired visitors (Greenberg, 2000). While the complexity of the dynamics described above have been greatly simplified here, these transformations can be witnessed in cities across the Western world as they attempt to refashion themselves within a new economic context. Every city wants to be perceived as a desirable, fun, and 'smart' destination with all of today's super-modern amenities amassed in one place (Hannigan, 1998; Brenner, 2004; Gibson, 2004).

Post-Industrial Urbanism and the Olympics

It is within this post-industrial context that the impact of terrorism at the Olympics Games can more fully be appreciated. There is considerable desire on the part of a number of cities to host the Olympics, a desire created not only by the highly symbolic nature of the event but in the promise it holds for urban revitalization along the lines described above. Urban festivals and special events have a long history of fostering urban and national identities, particularly in the late nineteenth and and early twentieth centuries when modern industrial nation-states were consolidating their economic positions within early industrial capitalism (Gold and Gold, 2005). Today, the Olympics contribute to the consolidation of post-industrial positions. For cities looking for a catalyst to energize its place and role within a post-industrial, tourism- and knowledge-heavy, and highly competitive economic background, the Olympics is viewed enviously by local boosters and politicians as an enormously powerful opportunity—indeed, the opportunity—to establish or consolidate a city's position as a global post-industrial city.

The opportunity to do so is two-fold. Municipal infrastructure projects that have been long needed but for which there has been insufficient funding may suddenly by fast-tracked to completion and large venues constructed specifically for the Olympics can find themselves the centrepiece of long-term revitalization plans and major investments in key urban assets—such as stadiums and airports—are all potential outcomes of hosting the Olympics. In other words, the Olympics can justify major infrastructural investments that will have long-term use. Second, the global audience attracted by the Olympics is a significant opportunity to establish a particular image of the city in the eyes of the world. Although some previous Olympic Games such as Montreal (Winter 1976) and, to a lesser extent, Atlanta (Summer 1996) were in some ways debacles for the cities which hosted them, the Barcelona (Summer 1992) and Sydney (Summer 2000) Games are good models of how the Olympics can be used as a springboard to establish an image of cultural vibrancy and historical significance to the world. These images are not without their political differences and silenced voices (see Degen, 2004; Lenskyi, 2002), but they show how the Olympics can be mobilized as part of long-term urban revitalization plans, in these examples revolving around the promotion of culture and tourism (Fox Gotham, 2002, 2005).

These revitalization agendas are not necessarily hidden; indeed, they are often explicitly formulated. Pasqual Maragall, Barcelona mayor for the Summer 1992 Games, is quoted as saying 'we used the Games as a pretext' for improving the city's quality of life, generating economic returns, and establishing Barcelona as a major European cultural centre (Degen, 2004: 134). Similar comments were made by Turin mayor Sergio Chiamparion about the Winter 2006 Games: 'It would be mistaken to confine the discussion of Turin's transformation to construction projects. We are distancing ourselves from the old stereotype of a grey, industrial city, and showing instead that we are a European, multicultural, eclectic and dynamic place where tradition and innovation work together" (CNNTraveller, n.d.). To summarize, local officials and corporate boosters hope that hosting the Olympics will be a powerful economic catalyst to jumpstart municipal ambitions of becoming a revitalized and rejuvenated post-industrial economic centre for culture- and knowledge-based forms of capital. The Olympics are, therefore, not an isolated punctuation in the otherwise unimpeded course of a city's identity and history, but critical junctures where urban identities can be refashioned, future directions forged, and past lineages overwritten in an age of intensive inter-urban competition.

What makes the Games attractive for host cities, however, also makes them attractive terrorist targets. If terrorist acts seek to send a message of protest to the greatest possible audience there is perhaps no better platform and no greater audience than the Olympic Games. As mentioned above, terrorism has been a concern for the Games for some time, but what makes this long-standing threat a greater concern now is that terrorism exacerbates the background factors regarding the imaging, branding, and selling a city as a post-industrial city. Even the threat of terrorism is enough to dis-rupt any long-term revitalization projects anchored to the Olympics if that threat appears impending enough. Terrorist attacks—either potential or actual—will affect how a city is perceived in the eyes of highly valued tourists. As a result, the already-existing economic anxieties regarding how the city is represented—generated by post-industrialism—lends the threat of terrorism additional weight as a justification for the implementation of bigger and more technological security and surveillance systems needed to guard the Games. This is not to say that terrorism alone is not enough to justify greater security measures but terrorism becomes a focal point for officials and planners already concerned with urban representation. That they then deal strongly and unambiguously with the threat of terrorism through bigger and more sophisticated security and surveillance networks not only addresses terrorism but also offers a technological solution to the problem of maintaining favourable representations of the city.

Two sociological concerns arise from the implementation of mega-security systems, the first being how these systems actually work in practice. I've emphasized the importance of urban image and this preoccupation with image can affect the way these spaces are policed and secured by those charged with doing so to produce what Huey, Ericson, and Haggerty (2005) refer to as **image-oriented policing**. Image-oriented policing is a public–private partnership form of policing that is primarily about the maintenance of images through the selective policing of minor significations of disorder in order to create spaces conducive for consumption. Image-oriented policing rests on a valid assumption that if people are to be comfortable they must not only actually be safe from being shot or mugged, but they also must feel safe. For example, in their fieldwork, Huey et al. show how the private security guards that police a shopping district in downtown Vancouver focus on removing relatively harmless panhandlers and homeless people so that their presence does not deter tourists from visiting the area. Image-oriented policing, then, is not so much concerned with due process or justice. It is concerned with appearances. Huey et al. critique image-oriented policing for being concerned only with surface appearances rather than the deeper structural conditions that manifest as visible inequality.

Returning to mega-events and urban representation, the concern with mega-security is that it is not only terrorism that can disrupt the image of the city. Smaller, everyday, mundane activities common to cities everywhere, such as homeless people, panhandlers, and crowds of revelers—a whole range of potential significations of disorder—fall within the mega-security 'net', just as terrorism does. This is not to suggest that special-ops forces are dispatched for every homeless person sighted during the Olympics. Rather, image maintenance can be as much about policing the big disruptions as it can be the small disruptions, and insofar as image-oriented policing carries with it the potential for reinforcing already-existing stratifications through its inherent selectivity, then building bigger and more penetrating security systems must also carry with it the same potentials but on a much vaster scale. From a sociological standpoint, then, there is a danger of entrenching and furthering social stratifications with the implementation of mega-security networks due to the dangers that are associated with image-oriented policing.

The second sociological issue arises when mega-security systems brought in under the pretext of guarding a limited-duration event become long-term features of the host city. The basic elements of mega-event security—such as CCTV cameras, new public–private policing partnerships, Business Improvement Districts, or new information databases and sharing practices—can, like other infrastructural improvements, outlast the Games themselves to become solutions in search of a problem. That is, security technologies have a way of being redirected and justified for use in other contexts once their original justifications have faded away. For example, the C4I system put in place by SAIC in Athens is to be maintained and operated by SAIC for a period of up to four years after the Games, meaning that until 2008 the system will be operated by SAIC under the auspices of Greece and Athens. After 2008 there appears to be three potential courses of action: the contract to SAIC will be extended, the C4I system will be dismantled, or full control of the system will revert to Greece and the city of Athens. Given that part of SAIC's contract is to provide training for local operators, it appears that the system will probably not be dismantled but instead will be maintained indefinitely. This is not to suggest that the system will be operated with the same level of vigilance as during the Games or that the surveillance blimp from the Games will be continually hovering over Athens. Certainly, the system will be relaxed. Moreover, continuity of the system will undoubtedly have some beneficial outcomes in some respects, such as increased coordination between fire, police, and ambulance services. However, insofar as security and surveillance systems have the potential to create and entrench social stratifications in the urban landscape, a point well established by many authors (Mitchell, 2003; Gibson, 2004), the maintenance of the C4I system well into the future means that this divisive potential is also maintained.

Conclusion

Hosting the Olympics is not inherently negative. The problem, however, arises when the mix of post-industrial urbanism and terrorism produces conditions to justify the implementation of bigger and better security networks that are as much about urban representation as they are about terrorism. Although the expansion of state surveillance has traditionally been restrained by human rights and privacy appeals, mega-security networks compromise these arguments in two ways. First, the extraordinary conditions of mega-events such as the Olympics justify temporarily ratcheting forward the degree of surveillance penetration, marking the furthest advance of 'surveillance creep'. As I've argued, it may be difficult to roll back this creep given the governmental and corporate interests in maintaining such systems. Second, and of particular relevance to Canada, the public–private partnerships that are increasingly struck to police the Olympics and other mega-events mean that the traditional opposition between state and civil society is circumvented by quasi-governmental, quasi-private actors that engage in the duties of the public police. This throws into uncertainty the protections of liberalism (such as the right to privacy) when it is unclear just who is doing the policing and what their interests are. This is particularly true in Canada where the relationship of the private security agencies and officers with the protections offered by the Charter of Rights and Freedoms is ambiguous at best (Rigakos and Greener, 2000; Hutchinson and O'Connor, 2005). Given these concerns, and given that Vancouver will host the 2010 Winter Olympics, it is important that the long-term consequences of establishing mega-security networks under the extraordinary conditions of mega-events be kept in mind lest mega-security efforts become experimental models for ordinary urban security in the future.

References

Bell, D. 1976. *The Coming of Post-Industrial Society: A Venture in Social Forecasting*. New York: Basic Books.

Brenner, N. 2004. *New State Spaces: Urban Governance and the Rescaling of Statehood*. Oxford: Oxford University Press.

Castells, M. 2000. *The Rise of the Network Society*, 2nd ed. Oxford: Blackwell.

CNNTraveller. n.d. 'Old Flame, New Fame', *CNNTraveller*. Available at http://www.cnntraveller.com/2006/jan_feb/turin/ (accessed 2 March 2006).

Degen, M. 2004. 'Barcelona's Games: The Olympics, Urban Design, and Global Tourism', in *Tourism Mobilities: Places to Stay, Place to Play*, pp. 131–42, M. Sheller and J. Urry, eds. London: Routledge.

Fox Gotham, K. 2002. 'Marketing Mardi Gras: Commodification, Spectacle and the Political Economy of Tourism in New Orleans', *Urban Studies* 39, 10: 1735–56.

———. 2005. 'Theorizing Urban Spectacles: Festivals, Tourism and the Transformation of Urban Space', *City* 9, 2: 224–46.

Gibson, T. 2004. *Securing the Spectacular City: The Politics of Revitalization and Homelessness in Downtown Seattle*. Lanham, MD: Lexington Books.

Gold, J., and M. Gold. 2005. *Cities of Culture: Staging International Festivals and the Urban Agenda, 1851–2000*. Aldershot: Ashgate.

Hannigan, J. 1998. *Fantasy City: Pleasure and Profit in the Postmodern Metropolis*. New York: Routledge.

Harvey, D. 1989a. *The Condition of Postmodernity*. Oxford: Blackwell.

———. 1989b. 'From Managerialism to Entrepreneuralism: The Transformation of Urban Governance in Late Capitalism', *Geografiska Annaler* 71, 1: 3–17.

Hiller, H. 2000. 'Toward an Urban Sociology of Mega-Events', *Research in Urban Sociology* 5: 181–205.

Huey, L., R. Ericson, and K. Haggerty. 2005. 'Policing Fantasy City', in *Re-Imagining Policing in Canada*, pp. 140–208, D. Cooley, ed. Toronto: University of Toronto Press.

Hutchinson, S., and D. O'Connor. 2005. 'Policing *The New Commons*: Corporate Security Governance on a Mass Private Property in Canada', *Policing and Society* 15, 2: 125–44.

Knight, W. 2004. 'Colossal Surveillance Network Shields the Olympics', *New Scientist*. Available at http://www.newscientist.com/news/news.jsp?id=ns99996279 (accessed 1 November 2004).

Lash, S., and J. Urry. 1987. *The End of Organized Capitalism*. Madison, WI: University of Wisconsin Press.

———. 1994. *Economies of Signs and Space*. Thousand Oaks, CA: Sage Publications.

Lenskyj, H. 2002. *The Best Olympics Ever? Social Impacts of Sydney 2000*. Albany: SUNY Press.

Mitchell, D. 2003. *The Right to the City*. New York: Guildford Press.

Rigakos, G., and D. Greener. 2000. 'Bubbles of Governance: Private Policing and the Law in Canada', *Canadian Review of Law and Society* 15, 1: 145–85.

SAIC. n.d. 'A Gold-Medal Achievement: SAIC and the 2004 Summer Olympic Games in Athens', *Science Application International Corporation*. Available at http://www.saic.com/cover-archive/natsec/olympics. html (accessed 9 December 2004).

Sassen, S. 2001. *The Global City: New York, London, Tokyo.* Princeton: Princeton University Press.

Van den Berg, L., P.M.J. Pol, W. Van Winden, and P. Woets. 2005. *European Cities in the Knowledge Economy.* Aldershot: Ashgate.

Van Kempen, R., M. Vermeulen, and A. Baan, eds. 2005. *Urban Issues and Urban Policies in the New EU Countries.* Aldershot: Ashgate.

Questions for Critical Thought

RESISTANCE TO EDUCATION: SELF CONTROL AND RESISTANCE TO SCHOOL

1. Whether by the means of skipping class, talking back to our teachers, or falling asleep in class, we have all, at one time or another, resisted school and learning. What forces do you believe compelled you to act in these ways?
2. In what respects do parents' occupations serve as useful information? What can we or can't we deduce from occupation?
3. Why did the author think it was important to focus on Aboriginals?
4. According to Gottfredson and Hirschi (1990: 89), criminal acts provide immediate, easy, or simple gratification; are exciting, risky, and thrilling; require little skill or planning; result in pain and discomfort for the victim; and provide few or meagre long-term benefits. Account for this using the following theories of deviance: strain theory, cultural theory, and control theory.
5. Some students display low scholastic aspiration and high truancy, quite unlike the behaviour of students in other groups. Why do you think this is?

GENDER, CRIME, AND COMMUNITY: AN ANALYSIS OF YOUTH CRIME IN CANADA

1. What does it mean to say that a community is 'socially disorganized'? Why is crime more likely to occur in disorganized communities?
2. How are community social networks, social cohesion, and informal social control related to teenage delinquency?
3. Would social disorganization theory favour efforts to fight crime by 'getting tough' and locking more youth offenders up in prison? Why or why not?
4. In your viewpoint, why are young males (compared to young females) more likely to engage in behaviours considered delinquent?
5. The cost of crime prevention in Canada is a major part of government budgets. Debate whether crime prevention strategies should increase the number of police officers in the community or increase funding for community programs to bring neighbours together.

KEEPING AN EYE ON CRIME CONTROL CULTURE: THE RISE OF OPEN-STREET CLOSED-CIRCUIT TELEVISION SURVEILLANCE IN CANADA

1. How does open-street camera surveillance differ from other types of camera surveillance?
2. What is problematic about Orwell's and Giddens's characterizations of surveillance?
3. How does the Panopticon assure the functioning of power?
4. What is the relationship between intensified surveillance and media communication?

5. What are some strategies for resisting intensified surveillance in societies where surveillance is not simply generated by state agencies?

MEGA-SECURITY: CONCEPTS AND CONTEXT FOR OLYMPIC-SIZED SECURITY NETWORKS

1. A central argument in this chapter is that we are living in post-industrial times. Do you consider this argument to be valid in the Canadian context? Why or why not? What regions or economic sectors, if any, could be considered post-industrial?
2. Discuss the central links between urban policy, urban representation, and security provision. How do major events such as the Olympics intensify these links? What are the implications for social equality?
3. As described by Huey et al. (2005), image-oriented policing is policing that is concerned more with surface appearances and minor infractions than traditional policing concerns such as justice and due process. Why should this change worry sociologists and criminologists?
4. Think of the city you live in and its attempts to portray a certain image. Why is it important that the city have this image? Who is the imagined audience for such an image? Who are these images intended to attract?
5. Vancouver will host the Olympic Games in 2010. How might the Games benefit the city? What aspects of hosting the Games can we criticize?

Part V

Families

amily life has undergone major transitions in the past century. Given the multiplicity of current models, sociologists and others continue to debate exactly what a family is meant to be. Some base their definitions on sentiments and identities. Others base their definitions on family activities—for example, on shared earnings and the domestic division of labour. Still others define them by co-residence, parenthood, or emotional bonds. In the midst of all this confusion, the meanings of family and marriage continue to change.

Traditions of marriage and family change in response to changes in economy and cultural expectations; for example, the processes of entering marriage in many societies have changed with the spread of Western ideas. In Part 5, Nancy S. Netting explores current views and practices of the arranged-marriage tradition in India, where educated young adults try to negotiate between the expectations of parents and tradition with their own needs for intimacy and compatibility. While they consider personal input important, they also believe that choosing a partner should not be based on selfish individual decisions. Thus, the traditional arranged-marriage model has effectively developed into qualitatively different processes of family-directed engagement.

With easier transnational migration, preserving relationships with family and friends in both countries has been important among first generation migrants. However, transnational ties are also important to the experiences of their children. Kara Somerville's essay explores how second-generation South Indian migrants to Canada begin lasting transnational ties with family and friends in parental homelands through two important life cycle events: marriage and the birth of a child.

While many look within their culture and community to find suitable partners, Randal F. Schnoor and Morton Weinfeld's study shows that most gay Jewish Canadian men find partners outside their ethnic community. This is despite the fact that most respondents express the wish for a culturally compatible Jewish partner. Schnoor and Weinfeld attribute this high exogamy rate to 'identity ambivalence' in Jewish gays who find it difficult to reunite Jewish and gay wishes with little support from their Jewish community.

A community's economic well-being is associated with its children's health and academic attainment. Patrizia Albanese's pilot study into Quebec's childcare program assesses its impact on the children, domestic relations, and the community. Under this system, mothers are able to continue their employment, allowing improvements in both family finances and domestic relations.

While employment for women—especially, mothers of young children—is valuable, Canadian women also face difficulties. A dual-shift exists for women with paid work; they keep most of the responsibility for unpaid work done in the home, such as childcare, cooking, and cleaning. A. Bruce Arai's essay explores the way women respond to dual-shifts by turning to self-employment, and it examines the relationship between self-employment and child rearing in these families.

While Canadian families have changed greatly from the traditional breadwinner–caregiver model, there are still inequalities in the distribution of housework and caregiving between partners in a two-worker household. Roderic Beaujot's essay explains that the inequalities in paid work between genders are connected to inequalities in unpaid work. There are several models of the family's distribution of paid and unpaid work, yet important policies are still based on the breadwinner model. Beaujot suggests that policies that will discourage dependency of one partner, and dissociate gender and caregiving, can help promote equality both in the home and in the workplace.

Thus, even though there have been changes that promote equality and choice in marriage and family, there are still barriers in social policies and lack of support for non-traditional models. The chapters in Part V explore the evolution of the family's relationship with community, work, and equality.

CHAPTER 19

Love- and Arranged-Marriage in India Today: Negotiating Adulthood

Nancy S. Netting

Until the present time, Indian society has maintained the tradition of arranged marriages (Dion and Dion, 1993; Derné, 1995), even among highly educated professional youth who are fluent in English, adept at electronic communication, and very familiar with global youth culture. Since this group is clearly exposed to conflicting values, their continued adherence to Indian marriage customs becomes problematic. This research asks what is happening to the arranged-marriage tradition in the current environment of rapid economic change.

This paper examines two opposing hypotheses offered by sociological theory. **Modernization theory** predicts the collapse of the arranged marriage system and its replacement with Western-style individual choice; ideologies of individualism and romantic love are intricately imbedded in the global market system (Inkeles and Smith, 1974; Illouz, 1997; Nolan and Lenski, 1999). **Neo-traditionalism** predicts that Indian youth will instead see individualism as destructive of Indian family and religion, and thus strengthen their support of customs like arranged marriage. Commentators on contemporary Indian society provide various examples of such reaction (Derné, 1995; John and Nair, 1998, Kishwar, 1999; Harriss-White, 2001). This study also addresses a gap identified by Patricia Uberoi, who wrote, 'our sociological reflection on family and kinship . . . is [missing] the qualitative dimension of love, sex, marriage, and family life . . . the [whole] emotional tenor of [Indian] family relations' (Uberoi, 1993: 36).

This research is based on intensive **open-ended interviews** with 30 never-married upper-middle class educated youth in their twenties from Vadodara (formerly known as Baroda), a prosperous city in the west Indian state of Gujarat. The sample consisted of 15 men and 15 women, chosen via the snowball procedure. They ranged from 22 to 29 years old; most had professional BA or MA degrees. Twenty-five were Hindu, two were Christian, and one each came from the Jain, Muslim, and Sikh faiths. Questions covered parental marriage; respondents' romantic history; attitudes on mate-selection and desirable qualities; and opinions about premarital sexual experiences, **dowry**, horoscopes, woman's employment and residence after marriage, number of desired children, and individualism. The results showed that arranged marriages, as they exist in today's India, are a product of ongoing evolution. It is still socially expected that marriages will be arranged, but the process has changed considerably over the past generation.

Arrangements have evolved into a system of introductions, in which parents first pre-approve potential partners, then formally introduce the young people. Parental criteria are based on education, income (especially of the man), religion, **caste**, and reputation of the other family. Youth can veto someone at the start, or, if they think a match is possible, can hold several subsequent private sessions. When such meetings—more like interviews than dates—have continued for about six weeks, they are expected to announce their engagement. During the engagement period, the couple is allowed to go out together frequently but is expected to refrain from sexual activity. While there is more free choice at every stage than in the past, parents still expect to initiate the process and reserve the right to terminate any relationship of which they disapprove. There also exists in Indian cities a competing 'underground' system of romantic relationships, in which young people meet at college or work and sometimes develop serious feelings for each other. Two-thirds, or 20, of the respondents had been involved in at least one romantic relationship which they judged important. Over half (13/23) of these self-chosen couples were not traditionally acceptable in Indian culture: ten because the partners came from different castes, and another three because their partners were from different religions. If parents disapproved, the usual reason was incompatibility of the partner's family. The second most frequent cause was that the boy was too young and without a stable job.

Most (16/26) of the relationships had broken by the time of the interview, 13 for reasons internal to the couple. Three had been forced apart by disapproving parents, while another three were struggling with parental objections and admitted they were likely to separate. In this sample, no respondents believed they would marry if their parents continued to disapprove.

Most respondents (16) preferred a love-match, provided they could eventually get parental approval, but only nine expected one. Although a self-chosen marriage provided more equality and intimacy, they recognized that a parental introduction guaranteed similarity of backgrounds and ongoing parental support, while still offering them a degree of choice.

In many ways, the predictions of modernization theorists have been realized. Parents still play a decisive role in most marriages, but they put more emphasis on achieved characteristics such as education and occupation, rather than on ascribed ones. Arranged marriage has evolved to allow more input from youth, and there also exists a parallel system of dating that is growing in prevalence. To a lesser extent, neo-traditionalism is present as well; horoscopes, premarital virginity, and the requirement of parental support remain important.

Mainly the interviews showed young people living within the intersections of the familial and the individualistic systems, and at times attempting to create and navigate structures that are qualitatively different from any pre-existing model. One such innovation is the self-arranged marriage, in which a young person accepts the rules and values of an arrangement, but manages to control the procedure. More common is the 'love-cum-arranged' scenario, widely considered the best possibility. This includes the emotional high of falling in love, continues into an extended period of getting to know each other, and concludes with the winning of parental support. Whether either of these combinations, or some other possibility, will emerge as a stable norm, or whether they simply represent intermediate points on the way to Westernization, is, as yet, impossible to predict.

It is also apparent from the respondents' replies that decisions about marriage do not occur in isolation; they are made in the context of changes in the pace and pattern of growing up. Long years of education have brought India's middle-class youth more physical independence, modern skills, and intellectual sophistication than earlier generations ever experienced. Their desire for a greater share in the marriage decision is part of a growing demand for more equality in general. Young women want the rights to continue their careers, to have a small number of children, and to maintain responsibility for their own parents after marriage. Men want more freedom of sexual expression for themselves and their partners, not only before but also during marriage. Youth of both sexes insist they will use their new-found voices not as selfish individualists, but as responsible members of a family unit. They will listen to their parents, but they also want their parents to listen to them. In short, they want to be treated as full adults. If youth of both sexes, and eventually women of all ages, gain this equality, then Indian families will be qualitatively different from their predecessors.

In their responses, love emerged not only as romantic passion, but also as the quiet trust that grows slowly between classmates or during a family-directed engagement. An ongoing theme was the need to prevent emotion from carrying the self into unknown, dangerous territory. Instead the emphasis fell on mutual understanding and respect. Respondents spoke of their hopes to create an intimate space where emotion, sexuality, ideas, and needs, could be safely expressed. Such a conjugal relationship is problematic in India because it was not a major goal of the **patrilocal multigenerational** family (Singh and Uberoi, 1994). Today, however, both men and women want a partner who is caring, understanding, honest, and respectful. Compatibility of backgrounds, interests, values, and education were valued because they made intimacy possible.

The prevailing tone expressed by Indian youth approaching marriage is not one of defiance or rebellion, but of conscious attention to their own needs and empathy for those of their parents. They do not want to abandon a cherished home, but to renovate it to accommodate modern requirements. Freer communication between generations, based on respect and trust, as well as assured space for intimacy between marriage partners, are key goals to be achieved. As this study demonstrates, Indian youth of today are embarking on this great task of cultural reconstruction with confidence and courage.

References

Derné, S. 1995. *Culture in Action: Family Life, Emotion, and Male Dominance in Banaras*, India. Albany, NY: SUNY Press.

Dion, K.K., and K.L. Dion. 1993. 'Individualistic and Collectivistic Perspective on Gender and the Cultural Context of Love and Intimacy', *Journal of Social Issues* 49, 3: 53–69.

Harriss-White, B. 2001. 'Gender-cleansing: The Paradox of Development and Deteriorating Female Life Chances in Tamil Nadu', in *Signposts: Gender Issues in Post-independence India*, pp. 125–54, R.S. Rajan, ed. New Brunswick, NJ; London: Rutgers University Press.

Illouz, E. 1997. *Consuming the Romantic Utopia: Love and the Cultural Contradictions of Capitalism*. Berkeley, CA: University of California Press.

Inkeles, A., and D.H. Smith 1974. *Becoming Modern: Individual Change in Six Developing Countries*. Cambridge, MA: Harvard University Press.

John, M.E., and J. Nair. 1998. *A Question of Silence? The Sexual Economies of Modern India*. London and New York: Zed.

Kishwar, M. 1999. *Off the Beaten Track: Rethinking Gender Justice for Indian Women*. Delhi: Oxford University Press.

Nolan, P., and G. Lenski. 1999. *Human Societies: An Introduction to Macrosociology*, 8th ed. New York: McGraw-Hill.

Singh, A.T., and P. Uberoi. 1994. 'Learning to "Adjust": Conjugal Relations in Indian Popular Fiction', *Indian Journal of Gender Studies* 1, 1: 93–120.

CHAPTER 20

Life Cycle Events and the Creation of Transnational Ties among Second Generation South Indians

Kara Somerville

Relationships with family and friends, in the home and in host societies, provide important resources for migrant families. Research has recorded the importance of **transnational ties** among first-generation migrants, but much less is known about the experiences of their children. Transnationalism refers to the social relationships that are forged across national borders. This paper provides some clues as to how the new **second-generation migrants** are living their lives in ways that traverse borders. This study finds evidence of enduring ties between second-generation migrants and their parents' homelands, developed primarily through two important life-cycle events: marriage and the birth of a child. Both the frequency and intensity of cross-border relationships increase during these events, cementing **transnational identities**. Further, transnational ties are initiated and sustained among second generation migrants.

Sample

This paper is based on a larger study of 53 first- and second-generation immigrants from South India who are currently living in Toronto. Findings for this paper are based on in-depth interviews with a sub-sample of 18 second-generation migrants from Karnataka, India. Karnataka was selected for two main reasons. First, Karnataka has a stronger religious homogeneity—86 per cent Hindu—compared to other Indian states. Peggy Levitt (2004) has pointed out how religion exercises significant influence over the ways in which migrants are incorporated into host societies and stay attached to their homelands. The predominance of the Hindu religion in Karnataka makes religious variability less of an issue despite the small-scale sample. Second,

Karnataka is a source country for highly educated, economic class immigrants. Much existing transnational research is on refugees, whose reasons for maintaining ties to their homeland are arguably different.

Findings

Researchers debate whether transnationalism persists among the second generation. Some argue that the children of immigrants are not involved in transnational communities, or that their involvement is small (Portes 2001; Kasinitz, et al. 2002; Rumbaut, 2002); others argue that transnational communities are maintained among the second generation (Levitt 2002; Portes 2001). This study argues that not only are transnational ties maintained, they are also initiated by the children of migrants. In other words, second-generation youth generate and engage in cross-border ties, and they do so at very specific times in their lives.

Transnational engagement varies over the life cycle (Levitt 2002; Smith 2002; Levitt and Glick Schiller 2003); at certain times migrants are more or less inclined to have a physical or symbolic connection to their homeland. Researchers have begun to identify how unexpected opportunities, political upheavals, and elections—events that change throughout a person's life—can influence the likelihood that someone would engage in transnational practices. This is important research and it indicates how certain political and social events can trigger or suspend transnational ties. Less is known, however, about how the family as a social institution, shapes the life course trajectory of transnational ties among migrants and their children.

Second-generation Indo-Canadians have times in their life cycle when their transnational ties are symbolically heightened and physically accelerated. This study has identified two key life course events that prompt transnationalism: wedding plans and marriages and the birth of children. For second generation migrants from Karnataka, elections, political turmoil, or new business relationships are not the life course events that trigger transnationalism.

MARRIAGE

Family in both Canada and India play a central role in the marital preferences of the second generation. Immigrant youth seek approval from family members living in both countries to help them find a prospective mate and to plan an authentically Indian ceremony. Marriages serve as events that create a new social network of people located in India as the rituals of finding a partner, planning the ceremony, and shopping for wedding attire—create a set of relationships that involve frequent interaction with India. These relations are generated and maintained by the second-generation members themselves, and are not strictly mediated by the migrant generation.

Children of migrants often initiate new contact with family residing in India during the period of time in which they are arranging their marriage. They phone India more frequently to discuss their wedding plans, they travel to India to meet potential partners, they begin learning how to cook Indian dishes, they learn or re-learn Indian customs for the purposes of an authentic ceremony, and they more generally broaden their social network of people to include those who are physically located in India. Once created, these cross-border ties endure.

Too much research dealing with Indian marriages focuses on the traditional arranged marriage versus the Western love marriage. The assumption hidden within this dichotomy of arranged-versus love-marriages is the notion that arranged marriages are exclusively linked to India and love marriages are confined to Western countries.

Revisions to this approach explore the ways the second-generation migrants are negotiating arranged marriages in Western countries. What both the traditional conceptualization and its revised alternative fail to explore are the ways that marriages, in general, are being conducted between nation-states. Second-generation migrants are trying to sort through their own desires and contextualize them in relation to family and friends in both Canada and India. Marriages, therefore, act as a catalyst for cross-border relationships. Furthermore, once these ties are initiated, they remain significant. This desire of the second generation to draw on their 'Indianness' to define themselves, their marriage preferences, and their future married lives, help explain why weddings are a life course event that cultivate transnational ties among the children of migrants.

THE BIRTH OF CHILD

The second life course event that triggers transnationalism is the birth of a child. One possible reason why the birth of children is an important trigger is because the second-generation feel that their child(ren) will benefit from the reconnection with India and family in India. It is a way to expand the social network of their child without sacrificing the associations they have built in Canada. By raising their children within a social context that includes people in both their parents' countries of origin and settlement, the second-generation hopes to instill 'Indianness' into their children. Second-generation migrants discuss the importance of taking the best from both cultures and societies, which transnational ties allow them to do. They do not, however, want to adopt the old, traditional Indian culture, but would rather incorporate the contemporary Indian culture into their Canadian lives.

Therefore, the culture that they want to pass on to their children is different than what their own parents remember. Making sure the most 'current' Indian culture is passed on requires constant contact with people in India. Frequent visits to India; phone calls to relatives; and email correspondences with people in India for the purposes of informal conversations, recipe requests and constant updates, are necessary means for the second-generation members to recreate ties to a country from which their third-generation children would be otherwise disconnected. These daily, informal cross-border practices allow them, as parents, to demonstrate a connection to contemporary India. In order to communicate effectively during these transnational transactions, the second generation also has to maintain or relearn ethnic languages and etiquette. In this way, the desire to create transnational ties for their third-generation children prompts the second generation to become transnational.

Conclusion

Cross-border ties between India and Canada are initiated by the second-generation society members during very specific times in their lives—marriage rituals and the birth of children—which lead to an increase in cross-border practices and transnational identities. The symbolic and physical connection to family in both India and Canada is crucial to understanding the experiences of second-generation migrants in Canada. Understanding how these connections are influenced by important life course events that take place within the family provides a glimpse into the ways the second generation is using, and initiating, the **transnational social field**. These ties are not fleeting, and do not end when the event itself ends; they are sustained after the individual has passed through that particular life-cycle stage. Life-cycle events act as catalysts for enduring transnationalism, and not merely as periods of temporary transnational engagement. The recognition that the children of migrants maintain strong, enduring ties to their country of origin, even as they are incorporated into the country of settlement, indicates the need to continue exploring questions related to long-term migrant incorporation.

References

Kasinitz, P., M. Waters, J. Mollenkopf, and M. Anil. 2002. 'Transnationalism and the Children of Immigrants in Contemporary New York', in *The Changing Face of Home: The Transnational Lives of the Second Generation*, pp. 96–122, P. Levitt and M. Waters, eds. New York: Russell Sage Foundation.

Levitt, P. 2002. 'The Ties That Change: Relations to the Ancestral Home over the Life Cycle', in *The Changing Face of Home: The Transnational Lives of the Second Generation*, pp. 123–44, P. Levitt and M. Waters, eds. New York: Russell Sage Foundation.

———. 2004. 'Redefining the Boundaries of Belonging: The Institutional Character of Transnational Religious Life', *Sociology of Religion* 65, 1 (Spring 2004): pp. 1–18.

Levitt, P., and N. Glick Schiller. 2003. 'Transnational Perspectives on Migration: Conceptualizing Simultaneity', *Working Paper #03-09j, The Center for Migration and Development Working Paper Series*. Princeton: Princeton University.

Portes, A. 2001. 'Introduction: The Debates and Significance of Immigrant Transnationalism', *Global Networks* 1, 3: 181–93.

Rumbaut, R.G. 2002. 'Severed or Sustained Attachments? Language, Identity, and Imagined Communities in the Post-Immigrant Generation', in *The Changing Face of Home: The Transnational Lives of the Second Generation*, pp. 43–95, P. Levitt and M. Waters, eds. New York: Russell Sage Foundation.

Smith, R.C. 2002. 'Life Course, Generation, and Social Location as Factors Shaping Second-Generation Transnational Life', in *The Changing Face of Home: The Transnational Lives of the Second Generation*, pp. 145–67, P. Levitt and M. Waters, eds. New York: Russell Sage Foundation.

CHAPTER 21

Balancing Ethnicity and Sexuality: Gay Jewish Men Seek the Same

Randal F. Schnoor and Morton Weinfeld

While documentation and discussion of **out-marriage** rates among heterosexual Jews is widespread, very little such analysis exists for inter-group partnering patterns of gay Jews. Using both quantitative and qualitative data, this study addresses this void. 2001 Canada Census data reveal that Canadian gay and lesbian Jews are 'out-marrying' at a rate of approximately 89 per cent. This can be compared to an out-marriage rate of approximately 30 per cent for Canadian heterosexual Jews. A qualitative sociological study on gay Jewish men both corroborates the Census finding that gay Jews 'out-marry' at a very high rate and offers a rich and nuanced account of the forces that lie beneath this statistic. We found that the majority of the gay Jewish men interviewed expressed a desire for a Jewish partner, but only a very small proportion of these men actually had Jewish partners. Several reasons are cited to explain this discrepancy. Findings about gay Jews are compared to both heterosexual Jews and to other minority gay men.

This study examines the partnering practices among a small sample of gay Jewish males, a double minority. The specific topic of concern is the extent to which these partnerships involve Jews or non-Jews and the factors associated with these exogamous and endogamous relationships. Questions of Jewish identity will be explored as these relate to the partnership decisions of gay Jews. Comparisons will be made with both heterosexual Jews as well as gay individuals of other ethno-religious minorities.

Out-Marriage in the Jewish Community

While the issue of the extent to which gay Jewish men form inter-group partnerships has never been systematically examined, much attention has been devoted to the question of out-marriage rates among Jewish heterosexuals. The 2000–1 National Jewish Population Survey in the United States reported that, from the period between 1996 and 2001, approximately 47 per cent of American Jews were married to non-Jews (National Jewish Population Survey, 2003). Recent figures for Canada tell us that in the mid-1990s Canadian Jews were out-marrying at a rate of approximately 30 per cent (Weinfeld, 2001).

Inter-group Partnerships Among Minority Gay Men and Lesbians

In the social scientific literature that deals with the gay experience, little discussion presently exists on the subject of the ethno-religious composition of gay partnerships. Bell and Weinberg (1978: 85) reported that the majority of their gay black sample claimed that most of their romantic partners had been white. Two decades later, Peplau et al. (1997) found that 'committed interracial relationships occur at a higher rate among African-American lesbians and gay men than among black heterosexuals' (21). Greene (1995) reported that lesbians of colour have a greater tendency to partner with women who are not members of their ethno-religious group than do white lesbians.

Same-Sex Common-Law Relationships

The 2001 Canadian Census provided data, for the first time, on Canadians who report to be in common-law same-sex relationships. From this we can learn the rate at which Canadian Jews involved in common-law same-sex relationships partner with non-Jews. The Census found that 590 out of 660 gay and lesbian Jews did not partner with a fellow Jew. This corresponds to an 'out-marriage' rate of 89 per cent (Statistics Canada, 2004). This can be compared to the rate at which Canadian heterosexual Jews out-marry, reported above to be approximately 30 per cent.

Methodology

The qualitative component of this study encompasses in-depth interviews with thirty gay Jewish men in Toronto. Gay Jewish respondents were distributed evenly by age and religious background. These data both corroborate the Census finding that gay Jews 'out-marry' at a very high rate and offer a rich account of the factors influencing this statistic.

Findings

DESIRE FOR JEWISH PARTNER

Two-thirds of the respondents reported that if they were to be involved in a long-term relationship, they would prefer their partner to be Jewish. The most common reasons offered by respondents for their desire for Jewish partners had to do with issues of cultural affinity. There is no reason to believe that these factors are any different than the factors considered important by heterosexual Jews.

INTER-GROUP REALITIES

While we have evidence suggesting that gay Jews have a relatively strong desire to partner with other Jews, the realities of the situation do not reflect this desire. Of the ten respondents in the sample that had partners, eight of them had non-Jewish partners. While one must be cautious to generalize based on a small *non-probability sample*, this finding—combined with supporting interview data—provides some corroboration for the high rate of 'out-marriage' among gay Jews indicated by Census data. This phenomenon is, of course, consistent with the findings noted above, that minority gay men and lesbians tend to partner with those outside their cultural group more so than do heterosexual minority individuals.

ANALYSIS OF INTER-GROUP PARTNERING PRACTICES

The remainder of this work explores this question of why gay Jewish men demonstrate a strong inter-group partnering tendency. Analysis of the data identified five possible reasons for this phenomenon.

Small number of openly gay Jews

The obvious factor seems to be the sheer lack of eligible gay Jewish men. Simply stated, gay men are already restricted to a small part of the male population. To then desire a Jewish partner limits one's choices quite a bit more. As several respondents reported, gay Jews suffer from being a 'minority within a minority'. Finding a Jewish partner can be especially difficult if one lives away from the major urban centres, where most Jews reside (Dworkin, 1997).

Non-acceptance by the Jewish community

While small numbers may seem like the obvious reason, the data reveal that lack of acceptance by Jewish families and the larger Jewish community of their gay members can have a very strong effect on whether gay Jewish men seek out other Jews. Negative experiences in the Jewish community simply make it easier for gay Jews to seek partners elsewhere.

Lack of gay Jewish infrastructure

Another reason why gay Jewish men who wish to find Jewish partners are not successful in doing so is the lack of a gay Jewish organizational infrastructure in Toronto to facilitate social interaction between gay Jews. As opposed to the high priority put on the Jewish community to develop and fund dating services and matchmaking services for heterosexual Jews, no community-endorsed service exists for matching gay Jews. One can reasonably speculate that this is directly related to the community's non-acceptance of homosexuality and gay partnerships. This phenomenon is not unique to the Jewish community. Peplau et al. (1997) and Greene and Boyd-Franklin (1996) report the same situation in black communities, as does Chan (1989) for Asian communities.

Internalized distaste or discomfort with Jewishness

Gay Jews have double the reason to feel ambivalent about or devalue their own Jewish identities. Firstly, as any Jew, they may feel some discomfort due to a perceived Christian-normative climate in general society. Secondly, they can feel ambivalent as Jews because of a perceived lack of acceptance of their homosexuality from within their own Jewish community. Following from this, we observed some resentment towards Judaism or a devaluing of one's Jewish identity on the part of some respondents. Sometimes this resentment manifests itself as a strong subconscious distaste or discomfort for things Jewish, such as Jewish partners.

Internalized homophobia

When a gay individual is living in a community that does not support homosexuality, this person may start to internalize these negative messages and develop shame and guilt about his or her homosexuality. One respondent reported that he developed guilt because he believed that by being gay he was shirking his responsibility to fulfill the requirement within the Jewish community to procreate to ensure Jewish continuity. Interestingly, this attitude had a strong bearing on his choice of partner. He would not date a fellow Jew because he felt this would 'contaminate' another Jew and thus

cause further damage to the possibility of Jewish continuity.

Conclusion

This study has attempted to make a contribution to the under studied topic of the ethno-religious composition of minority gay male relationships. It illustrates that while the majority of gay Jewish men may desire a Jewish partner, there are a number of reasons why these partnerships are not actually occurring.

The study pieces together different aspects of the gay Jewish experience and illustrates the links to the larger phenomenon of inter-group partnering practices. Besides the more obvious factors at work, such as small numbers of gay Jews, the study uncovers more subtle underlying dynamics that are at play. The theme of non-acceptance of homosexuality by the Jewish community sometimes creates a situation where gay Jews are turned away from Judaism and Jewish life and find it more comforting to seek a partner outside of this oppressing milieu. The fact that the Jewish community chooses not to develop a social infrastructure to allow its gay members to meet one another, accentuates the situation. The study suggests that a perceived Christian-normativity in Canadian society combined with a perceived rejection of gay identity in the Jewish community can bring about internalized oppression on the part of gay Jews. Expressions of internalized distaste or discomfort with Jewishness or internalized homophobia can contribute to inter-group partnering.

Overall, the study provides an example of the way that some gay Jews suffer from what could be termed 'identity ambivalence'. The ambivalence is caused by conflicting or competing desires: on the one hand they want Jewish partners for cultural reasons, but on the other hand there are forces at work that do not allow this to happen. Respondents often experience a clash between their Jewish and gay desires and are forced to struggle to find ways to negotiate this difficult divide. These circumstances make it difficult for gay Jews to develop personally meaningful Jewish identities that successfully integrate their gayness. Further research is recommended to explore the strategies gay Jews use to negotiate these conflict-

ing commitments. Additional research on partnering in other gay and lesbian minority groups can explore the extent to which comparable identity ambivalence might exist.

References

Bell, A.P., and M.S. Weinberg. 1978. *Homosexualities: A Study of Diversity among Men and Women*. New York: Simon and Schuster.

Chan, C. 1989. 'Issues of Identity Development among Asian American Lesbians and Gay Men', *Journal of Counselling and Development* 68: 16–20.

Dworkin, S.H. 1997. 'Female, Lesbian and Jewish: Complex and Invisible', in *Ethnic and Cultural Diversity Among Lesbians and Gay Men*, pp. 63–87, B. Greene, ed. London: Sage Publications.

Greene, B. 1995. 'Lesbian Couples', in *Dyke Life: From Growing Up to Growing Old—A Celebration of Lesbian Experience*, pp. 97–106, K. Jay, ed. New York: Basic Books.

Greene, B., and N. Boyd-Franklin. 1996. 'African-American Lesbians: Issues in Couples Therapy', in *Lesbians and Gays in Couples and Families: A Handbook for Therapists*, pp. 251–71, J. Laird and R.J. Green, eds. San Francisco: Jossey-Bass Publishers.

Peplau, A., S.D. Cochran, and V.M. Mays. 1997. 'A National Survey of the Intimate Relationships of African-American Lesbians and Gay Men: A Look at Commitment, Satisfaction, Sexual Behavior and HIV Disease', in *Ethnic and Cultural Diversity among Lesbians and Gay Men*, pp. 11–38, Beverley Greene, ed. London: Sage.

Statistics Canada. 2004. 'All Persons by Selected Religion and Ethnic Origins, Showing Ethnic Origins and Religions of Same Sex Common Law Partners—for Canada and Selected Census Metropolitan Geography'. Table No. E741tbB.

'The National Jewish Population Survey 2000–1: Strength, Challenge and Diversity in the American Jewish Population', *A United Jewish Communities Report* in Cooperation with The Mandell L. Berman Institute–North American Jewish Data Bank.

Weinfeld, M. 2001. *Like Everyone Else . . . But Different: The Paradoxical Success of Canadian Jews*. Toronto: McClelland and Stewart Ltd.

CHAPTER 22

Earning and Caring

Roderic Beaujot

Defining Families

Families are people who mange, together, the central life-maintaining activities of earning a living and caring for each other. Families that do not succeed to earn a living and care for each other are, at the very least, under significant stress. Thus,

in the General Social Survey on families, we should probably pay less attention to the 'frequency of visits and telephone contact', and pay more attention to the financial transfers and the caring activities within and across households. We should also pay less attention to the specific nature of relationships or forms of families, and more attention to the earning and caring links across individuals who form families.

GENDER AND EDUCATION

In 1960 only a quarter of post-secondary students were women, now that number has risen to 56 per cent. At the undergraduate level, there are two areas where women remain in the minority: in engineering and applied sciences the progress is slow such that only 21 per cent of degrees were granted to women in 1995, and in mathematics/physical sciences proportions seem stalled at some 30 per cent women since 1980.

Without considering all the reasons for this change or lack of change, part of the explanation may relate to the extent to which various professions have become family friendly. When there are few women in a field, as in engineering or physical sciences, there may be less pressure to adopt family friendly provisions. Thus a circularity may exist wherein certain professions are slow at adopting family friendly orientations because the workers are mostly men, which in turn discourages women from entering the field.

GENDER AND WORK

The labour force participation patterns of women and men have become more similar, but there remain differences in levels and intensity (Beaujot, 2000: 144), and although the earnings ratios are on a converging path, the differences remain large.

There is both continuity and change, depending on the indicator to which one pays attention. In 1976, women comprised only 40 per cent of managers and professionals (white collar workers), compared to over half in 1996 (Beaujot, 2000: 147). On the other hand, while women are 45 per cent of the labour force, they comprise only 12 per cent of 'power jobs' (corporate officer positions in Canada's 560 largest corporations) and only 3.4 per cent of the 'clout positions' such as executive vice-presidents and chief executive officers (Church, 2000).

Earnings ratios are less pronounced at younger ages. At ages 25–34, the 1998 hourly earnings ratio of women was 92 per cent of that of men if they were single, and 96 per cent if they were unionized workers (Galarneau and Earl, 1999: 26). While marital status and parental status have come to play lesser roles, they continue to operate in opposite directions in the lives of men and women. For women, being married and having children reduces their labour force participation, but for men the same conditions—being married and having children—increases the labour force participation. Consequently, the smallest sex differences are for persons who are single without children and the largest differences are for the married with children (Beaujot, 1995).

Among couples with children under 16 years of age, there were dual-earners in 36 per cent of cases in 1961 compared to 62 per cent in 1997 (Marshall, 1998: 10). There are also more cases of wives earning more than their husbands (Crompton and Geran, 1995). However, in the combined average incomes of husbands and wives, wives contributed 16.2 per cent in 1970 and 30.5 per cent in 1990 (Rashid, 1994: 9). Even when wives worked full-year full-time, their average income only comprised 40 per cent of average family income.

Equal opportunity in education has largely arrived, and it has also advanced in terms of work, but this is complicated by family questions. It is by looking at paid and unpaid work together that we can get a better sense of the situation.

GENDER AND EVERYDAY LIFE

We have much poorer statistics on unpaid work than on education and paid work, making it more difficult to measure change. We now have three national-level time-use surveys, for 1986, 1992, and 1998. These are based on time-use diaries where respondents are asked to indicate their activity over a specific 24-hour day.

Time use in *paid work* includes driving to and from work, and it also includes time spent in education. *Unpaid work* is all other work, including housework, child care, and even volunteer work, performed as a main activity at given times of the day. These two together can be called *total productive time*. In contrast, the other two categories are down time: *personal care* along with *leisure and free time*.

All three surveys show an important result: for the total population aged 15 and over, the average productive time of men and women is very similar. The asymmetry is in terms of the division of this time into the paid and unpaid components. Nonetheless, there has been some convergence.

Marital status and the presence of children influence the total time in productive activities and the distribution into paid and unpaid components. At ages 25–44 in 1998, the greatest gender symmetry can be observed for those who are unmarried (neither married nor cohabiting) with no children. Compared to the category of unmarried without children, married without children increases the total productive time for both men and women, but it also brings more asymmetry, with the increase being in the category of paid work for men and unpaid work for women. Children further increase the total productive time for both sexes, but this increase is all in the unpaid work category, and especially for women.

It is noteworthy that, except for lone parents, the average time in total productive activity is very similar between men and women within these categories of marital and parental status for the population aged 25–44. Nonetheless, both marriage and children, but especially children, bring change in the direction of greater complementary or specialization.

The stalled revolution?

At stake are questions of both **dependency** and gender display (Brines, 1994). Durkheim (1960 [1893]) had elevated dependency to a universal principle, suggesting that without a division of labour, marriages would be transient. Nonetheless, there are powerful economic and cultural forces pushing in the opposite direction, especially women's labour market opportunities, and the cultural interest in greater equality by gender. Thus, in his article on 'The Future of Fatherhood', Coltrane (1995) observes various pressures for change, including economic ones with more time

in paid work by wives and greater commitment to women as full-time providers, and cultural questions like new ideals of sharing, less rigid gender attitudes, and men taking pride in their ability to do domestic work and being involved fathers. Other life course changes are pushing in the same direction, with more sharing associated with cohabitation, remarriage, and later births, where women are in a better position to negotiate the division of costs.

Family models in paid and unpaid work

The study of family models has paid much attention to the transition from a breadwinner model to dual-earner families. Thus it is important to analyze the extent of accommodation between families and the world of work.

Sullivan (2000) observes that concepts such as double burden, second shift, or stalled revolution have contributed to the understanding of the division of domestic work and related issues of power, but these ideas correspond to a 'no change' model that tends to ignore the potential for and possibilities of change. On the basis of American data from 1965 and 1998, Sayer (2002) finds that the relation between time-use and gender has changed since the 1960s. Men have increased their time in core non-market tasks (cooking, cleaning, and daily child care), marriage increases housework for both women and men, and both married mothers and married fathers of young children are putting in a second shift of work. She concludes that non-market work may be shifting from representing gender subordination to representing family caring.

In the **traditional or complementary roles** model, one person does more paid work and the other more unpaid work. This is the dominant category, amounting to 54 per cent of couples in 1998, with 10 per cent of cases showing the man doing more unpaid work and the woman doing more paid work. In the **double burden**, a given person does the same amount (or even more) paid work, and more unpaid work. This is the second largest category, corresponding to 33 per cent of the sample, with 30 per cent of the cases showing the man having the double burden. We can classify persons in a **collaborative** or more egalitarian model where both do the same amount of unpaid work. This model represents 13 per cent in 1998, including 5.7 per cent where they do the same amount of both paid and unpaid work. The comparisons between 1992 and 1998 show only slight change, but this tends to be in the direction of somewhat greater symmetry with only a slight reduction in complementary roles and a greater proportion of men among persons with a double burden. Further analysis suggests that the egalitarian model is most common at younger ages, when both are employed full-time, and for couples with children (Beaujot and Liu, 2001).

Policy Thoughts

Policy probably needs to work at three fronts. It is important to seek to achieve more individual self-sufficiency. It is also important to have families that look after individuals, and it is important to have a social safety net. As in any difficult policy area, there are contradictions. In particular, encouraging families to look after individuals can undermine the self-sufficiency of the person who takes the largest responsibility for this care.

The complexity of policy derives in part because various family models co-exist. Clearly, there needs to be support for those who have lived their lives under the assumptions of the breadwinner or neo-traditional patterns. At the same time, the de-gendering of caring activities is important to achieving equality of opportunity. Another problem is that many policies are based on a family wage model, which promotes dependency of one spouse on the other rather than self-sufficiency.

It is hard to put policy ideas into a few words. Clearly, family policy needs to relate both to families and to the labour market. My main point is that there is need for more discussion of provisions that would further modernize the family in the direction of co-providing and co-parenting. Might we look forward to a world where earning is as important as caring, and where men and women let each other into both spheres? Just as policy has promoted the de-gendering of earning, might the de-gendering of caring be promoted through a public education system that starts at a younger age, along with the better sharing of leaves and part-time work associated with children?

References

Beaujot, R. 1995. 'Family Patterns at Mid-life (Marriage, Parenting and Working)', in *Family Over the Life Course*, R. Beaujot, E.M. Gee, F. Rajulton, and Z. Ravanera, eds. Catalogue 91-543. Ottawa: Statistics Canada.

————. 2000. *Earning and Caring in Canadian Families*. Peterborough: Broadview Press.

Beaujot, R., and J. Liu. 2001. 'Models of Earning and Caring: Evidence from Canadian Time-Use Data'. Paper presented at the meetings of the International Union for the Scientific Study of Population, Salvador, Brazil, August 2001.

Church, E. 2000. 'Women Hold just 12% of Power Jobs, Survey Finds', *Globe and Mail* 9 February 2000: A1, A9.

Coltrane, S. 1995. 'The Future of Fatherhood', in *Fatherhood*, William Marsiglio, ed. Thousand Oaks, CA: Sage.

Crompton, S., and L. Geran. 1995. 'Women as Main Breadwinners', *Perspectives on Labour and Income* 7, 4: 26–9.

Galarneau, D., and L. Earl. 1999. 'Women's Earnings/Men's Earnings', *Perspectives on Labour and Income* 11, 4: 20–6.

Marshall, K. 1998. 'Stay-at-home Dads', *Perspectives on Labour and Income* 10, 1: 9–15.

Sayer, L. 2002. 'Nonmarket Time and Iinequality: Trends and Gender Differences in Men's and Women's Housework, Child-care and Shopping'. Paper presented at the meetings of the Population Association of America, Atlanta, May 2002.

Sullivan, O. 2000. 'The Division of Domestic Labour: Twenty Years of Change?', *Sociology* 34, 3: 437–56.

CHAPTER 23

Assessing Quebec's $7/day Childcare: Some Preliminary Findings

Patrizia Albanese

Introduction

Economically 'healthy' neighbourhoods result in healthier populations (Robert, 1999; Ross, Tremblay, and Graham, 2004; Hou and Myles, 2005), children's academic success (Garner and Raudenbush, 1991; Rosenbaum, Reynolds and Deluca, 2002) and children's better overall development and well-being (see Haveman and Wolfe, 1995). Higher family incomes are also associated with children's higher cognitive test scores and better child outcomes (Smith, Brooks-Gunn, Klebanov, and Lee, 2000; Carlson and Corcoran, 2001; Yeung, Linver, and Brooks-Gunn, 2002; Mistry, Biessanz, Taylor, Burchinal, and Cox, 2004). My project sought to assess whether Quebec's $7/day childcare program has helped to create 'healthier' neighbourhoods. Below is a summary of my preliminary research findings.

Project Overview

The overall goal of this **pilot study** was to assess the impact of $5/day ($7) childcare at the community and inter-personal levels using a series of **qualitative interviews** with mothers and childcare providers living in a community located on the Quebec–Ontario border. The study was conducted in a community made up of two adjoining towns. The larger of the two conjoined communities (472.85 km^2), a canton, had 2,007 inhabitants in 2001 (Statistics Canada, 2004), and the smaller of the two (3.19 km^2), a village, had a population of 1,661 inhabitants (Statistics Canada, 2004a). The communities are predominantly francophone, and are located on the Ottawa River—an ideal location for the logging industry (part of the

primary sector of our economy). They were prosperous logging towns until recently. Many of the town's men still work in the economically hard-hit (soft-wood) lumber industry, in one of the remaining paper and lumber mills in the region. Many women work in traditional **service sector** jobs, including retail sales, food services, health, beauty/ hair dressing and childcare, others commute to jobs in Ottawa/Hull/Gatineau, about an hour and a half away (Statistics Canada, 2004; Statistics Canada 2004a).

Interviews and printed (background) **questionnaires** were available in English or French depending on the language preference of respondents. A **non-probability sample** (a snowball sample) was collected. I began by interviewing mothers of children currently in $7/day childcare and asked them for names of others—either mothers or childcare providers. I interviewed 16 mothers and 17 childcare providers. As a result of snowball sampling, the research findings are not **generalizable** to the community at large. However, they still provided valuable information. My goal was to assess the economic and social impact of $7/day childcare on children, families, and their community.

Preliminary Findings

The two conjoined towns had a total of 12 childcare centres in operation in the summer of 2004 while I interviewed there—11 were home childcare centres (5 in the smaller town and 6 in the larger) and one was a large, newly built centre ('childcare centre facility'). The home and larger centres are regulated by one of two regional agencies that are in place to enforce government regulations; license new facilities; perform regular spot checks of the existing centres; provide information, training, and support to paid caregivers; and respond to parental concerns.

The home and larger centres were required to remain open for 10 consecutive hours. Women working at the centres provided basic childcare, as well as all planning of activities and menus, cooking, cleaning, shopping, laundry, book keeping, providing regular updates to parents, etc. All this was done for an average province-wide salary comparable to that of a parking lot attendant ($20,667 in 1998; Tougas, 2002).

SELECTING A CENTRE

I asked mothers how they selected their childcare providers and if they had a preference for home care or for a larger facility. Being a small town, many mothers told me that they selected their childcare provider based on information they had about the individual caregiver. This was especially true of home care. Often, the centre's hours of operation was the main determining factor for selecting one centre over another. That is, while all centres had to stay open for 10 hours, individual centre operators could choose when to open and close (example 7am–5pm or 6:30am–4:30pm, etc.).

Most mothers had clear preferences for either home care or larger centre care. Those who preferred home care argued that it was most like a real family setting and less like an institution or school ('there was plenty of time for that,' some argued). A few new mothers in the study explained that they felt that their home childcare provider was like a second mother to their children, and even a second mother to themselves, as some provided advice and support on neo-natal care, child development, toilet training, etc. Those who preferred and selected the larger childcare centre liked the 'school-like' routine and setting of the centre, and felt that it was better at preparing children for elementary school schedules. These mothers also liked that each child was grouped with other children of the same age group and developmental level.

MOTHERS' VIEWS ON THEIR CHILD'S DEVELOPMENT

Regardless of whether the child was in home care or at the larger centre, all mothers believed that $7/day childcare was not only a necessity—for them to be able to work or study—but beneficial to their children as well. All mothers recognized that their children were acquiring skills that they could not acquire with a baby sitter or grandparent/relative who provided care. By far, social skills (interacting and sharing with other children) were the most often mentioned and valued skills that mothers believed that their child(ren) developed. One mother of two explained that in $7/day childcare, her youngest child learned to play co-operatively and share with other children, while her older child, who needed childcare before this program was introduced and who was cared for by his grandmother is, to this day, less co-operative.

DOMESTIC RELATIONS

Some mothers also explained that, to a certain extent, this program has improved domestic relations because they are experiencing less financial stress, and therefore less conflict at home. Two mothers explained that they were frustrated when they were home and not working for pay. They believed that their husbands appreciated them more when they were contributing to household income. Mothers were not only able to seek or return to paid work (improving household income), but they could justify and 'afford' working part-time, or taking minimum wage jobs. Two mothers mentioned that it gave the couple more time to talk and more to talk about—one mother mentioned that it gave her and her partner more time to 'be a couple again'. One mentioned that her and her partner were able to build a new home in the town without childcare being a major financial consideration.

THE COMMUNITY

Five mothers mentioned that this program kept them in Quebec, or mentioned that while one or both partners worked in Ontario, they could not afford to live there due to the high cost of childcare. Most mothers mentioned that this program has created jobs for the town and made it possible for people—especially women—to find paid work. Overall, the towns benefited by retaining employed young couples. Local businesses benefited from female labour and the circulation of local dollars.

CHILDREN, FAMILIES, AND THEIR COMMUNITY

One mother concluded her interview by saying that her child is learning a lot, but most of all, he sees his mom and dad work. It was clear from this study that $7/day childcare made exposure to 'educationally stimulating experiences and materi-

als' (Mistry, Biesanz, Taylor, Burchinal, and Cox, 2004: 742) possible for a larger number of families. I found that the program had an overall positive effect: as children benefited from childcare, so did their mothers. Some found it easier to return to work, and some found employment in the childcare industry. With mothers' employment came improvements in household finances and domestic relations (to a certain extent) and this resulted in more disposable income. More children experienced a community where 'mama and papa' have paid work. Quebec's $7/day childcare program has not, and will not, solve all of this community's problems, but it allowed residents to tackle some of them.

References

Carlson, M., and M. Corcoran. 2001. 'Family Structure and Children's Behavioral and Cognitive Outcomes', *Journal of Marriage & the Family* 63, 3: 779–92.

Garner, C.L., and S. Raudenbush. 1991. 'Neighbourhood Effects on Educational Attainment: A Multilevel Analysis', *Sociology of Education* 64: 251–62.

Government of Quebec. 2003. 'Development and Funding Scenarios to Ensure the Permanence, Accessibility and Quality of Childcare Services: Consultations 2003'. Québec: Ministère de L'Emploi, de a Solidarité Sociale et de al Famille.

Haveman, R., and B. Wolfe. 1995. 'The Determinants of Children's Attainments: A Review of Methods and Findings', *Journal of Economic Literature* 33: 1829–78.

Hou, F., and J. Myles. 2005. 'Neighbourhood Inequality, Neighbourhood Affluence and Population Health', *Social Science & Medicine* 60, 7: 1557–69.

Mistry, R., J. Biesanz, L. Taylor, M. Burchinal, and M. Cox. 2004. 'Family Income and Its Relation to Preschool Children's Adjustment for Families in the NICHD Study of Early Child Care', *Developmental Psychology* 40, 5: 727–45.

Robert, S. 1999. 'Socioeconomic Position and Health: The Independent Contribution of Community Context', *Annual Review of Sociology* 25: 489–516.

Rosenbaum, J.E., L. Reynolds, and S. Deluca. 2002. 'How Do Places Matter? The Geography of Opportunity, Self-efficacy and a Look Inside the Black Box of Residential Mobility', *Housing Studies* 17, 1: 71–82.

Ross, N.A., S. Tremblay, and K. Graham. 2004. 'Neighbourhood Influences on Health in Montreal, Canada', *Social Science & Medicine* 59, 7: 1485–94.

Smith, J., J. Brooks-Gunn, P. Klebanov, and K. Lee. 2000. 'Welfare and Work: Complementary Strategies for Low-Income Women', *Journal of Marriage & the Family* 62, 3: 808–21.

Statistics Canada. 2004. 2001 *Community Profile—M.P.* Available at http://www12.statcan.ca/english/profil101/Detials/details1.cfm.

———. 2004a. 2001 *Community Profile—F.C.* Available at http://www12.statcan.ca/english/profil101/Detials/details1.cfm.

Tougas, J. 2002. 'Reforming Quebec's Early Childhood Care and Education: The First Five Years', Occasional Paper 17, Childcare Resource and Research Unit. Toronto: Centre for Urban and Community Studies.

Yeung, W.J., M.R. Linver, and J. Brooks-Gunn. 2002. 'How Money Matters for Young Children's Development: Parental Investment and Family Processes', *Child Development* 73, 6: 1861–79.

CHAPTER 24

Self-Employment as a Response to the Double Day for Women and Men in Canada

A. Bruce Arai

There is wide agreement that women still retain responsibility for much of the work that is done in the home (Kalleberg and Rosenfeld, 1992; Blain, 1993). Balancing the demands of this '**double day**' (Luxton, 1980: 179) or '**second shift**' (Hochschild, 1989: 3) is not always easy for women. Ginn and Sandall (1997) speculate on some of the reasons that meshing home and work demands may be even more problematic now than in the past.

Ginn and Sandall further claim that the conflicting demands of work and home lead to greater stress levels for both men and women, and when women are faced with a conflict between rigid demands in the home and rigid demands at work, they are under more pressure than men to find a way to accommodate those demands. Some of the ways in which women in their sample responded to these pressures were to move into part-time work, or into lower-level positions.

DEALING WITH STRESS

While these findings are instructive, there are other issues that must be considered when we move from documenting stress levels to ways in which women attempt to diffuse this stress. First, when faced with competing demands from home and work, women may use many techniques to introduce some flexibility into the demands from one or both sides. A second issue concerns the composition of the second shift. That is, household tasks are not completely interchangeable, and transferring some of these tasks to others can be difficult. The inflexibility of domestic demands may also depend on the age and number of children in the home.

Crompton and Harris (1998) have further argued that some occupations allow women to

plan their careers around family aspirations while others do not. They show that in professional occupations such as medicine, women can '**satisfice**' or reach some level of accomplishment in both their domestic and work spheres. By satisficing, women attain a level of satisfaction in their home and work lives, but also realize that to do so they must sacrifice some initial goals or hopes in each sphere.

The reason that occupation is important, Crompton and Harris contend, is that certain occupations are structured such that pre-planning of families and careers is possible.

While their argument is interesting, there is another way to explain Crompton and Harris's difference between professional and managerial women. The differences they find could also be due to the distinction between employment and **self-employment**. Although self-employment does not usually involve a long training period, the portability of skills, flexibility of hours, and ability to choose one's work could produce the satisficing pattern found among Crompton and Harris's doctors.

The Self-employment Option

So part-time employment, moving into lower-level positions and choosing family-friendly occupations may not be the only work-based responses of Canadian women to balancing employment and family. It may also be the case that women turn to self-employment in these situations. In an analysis of earlier American data, Carr (1996) found that women, but not men, did turn to self-employment in these situations (see also Jurik, 1998). There are

Table 24.1 Main Reason for Choosing Self-Employment, Women and Men

Reason	Women	Men
Make more money	7.8	9.3
Enjoy independence	29.0	46.0
Flexible schedule	9.6	4.2
Work from home	15.5	2.1
Family business	21.1	21.5
Other	16.4	17.0

Source: Survey of Work Arrangements, 1995.

at least three reasons why the odds that a woman will become self-employed should increase when faced with inflexible schedules.

First, one of the primary reasons that many entrepreneurs (both male and female) give when asked why they are self-employed is the flexibility that this form of work offers (Bechhofer and Elliott, 1978; Nisbet, 1997). Second, as job-related networks deteriorate, women often replace them with other networks, usually based around family and community contacts (Munch et al., 1997). These networks may lead to increased chances of self-employment. Finally, self-employment for women is more of an option now than in the past.

However, there are also good reasons for believing that women will not turn to self-employment as a way of balancing home and work responsibilities. First, the supposed flexibility of being an independent business operator who can set one's own hours and conditions of work may be largely illusory. Second, the appeal of decent earnings in self-employment is also problematic, especially in relation to the flexibility of running a business. Given what is known about the general characteristics of the self-employed population, it is not clear whether women turn to it to balance work and family.

The major question to be addressed in this paper then is whether Canadian women with children turn to self-employment as a way of easing the demands of the double day. Four specific hypotheses will be tested:

1. Women with children have greater odds of being self-employed than women without children.
2. The more children a woman has, the greater her odds of being self-employed.
3. Women with young children have greater odds of self-employment than women with older children.
4. Having children will increase the odds of self-employment for women more than for men.

Each of these hypotheses investigates a different dimension of the potential flexibility of self-employment for women, and in all cases the hypotheses apply only to people who are employed.

Data and Methods

Studies of the self-employed sector are notorious for being fraught with definitional concerns, and the potential inadequacy of a single concept to cover the extreme diversity involved in working for oneself (Steinmetz and Wright, 1989; Linder, 1992; Arai, 1995; Giles and Preston, 1996).

Data for this paper come from Statistics Canada's 1995 Survey of Work Arrangements (SWA). The SWA data are not ideal for investigating the hypotheses above.

Logistic regression models were estimated for women and men separately. The final sample, after excluding those people who were unemployed or not in the labour force, and those with missing data (118 women, 157 men) comprised 11,828 women and 13,766 men.

Conclusion

The significant and positive effect of the number of children on the odds of self-employment for women supported hypotheses 1 and 2. That is, having children increased a woman's odds of being self-employed, and the more children a woman had, the greater were her odds of self-employment.

Hypothesis 3 however, did not receive unqualified support. While women with very young children had higher odds of self-employment than women without children, women with preschoolers had the same odds of self-employment as women without kids. Women with school age kids again had greater odds of self-employment than women without children. Having preschoolers suppressed the positive effect of having very young children when children of both ages were present in the home, but it did not eliminate the increase in the odds when both preschoolers and school-age children were present. It was suggested that this situation is not well explained by existing theory, and an alternative argument about the duration and frequency of long-term work interruptions was proposed.

Finally, hypothesis 4 was also supported by the data. It is clear that women turn to self-employment as a way to manage the double day much more so than men.

In general, the results presented in this paper confirm previous findings on the ways in which men and women balance home and work responsibilities, as well as adding a new dimension to these debates. There are four main points that deserve consideration.

First, one of the clearest messages to emerge is that it is women, and not men, who make adjustments in their work situation when the demands of home and work are in conflict. The relatively inflexible demands of having children, especially very young children, increases a woman's odds of self-employment versus women without children, but having children, of any age, has no effect on men's odds of self-employment. The results show that in addition to some of the other ways in which women adjust to the demands of the double day (Kalleberg and Rosenfeld, 1992; Ginn and Sandall, 1997), they also turn to self-employment to alleviate these pressures, at least in Canada, and in the US (Carr, 1996).

Second, Crompton and Harris point out that women in certain occupations are able to 'satisfice' by achieving an acceptable level of performance in both the home and work. The same may be true of self-employment because it likely gives women all of the 'planning' benefits that Crompton and Harris found for doctors.

Third, Ginn and Sandall point out that women often end up taking lesser jobs when they are forced to make adjustments to balance home and work. If self-employment offers women the ability to satisfice between home and work, then it may be a preferable option to taking on lesser jobs. A woman's odds of self-employment increase if she works part-time, but part-time self-employment may be a more desirable form of work than part-time salaried or waged employment.

Finally, the results reveal that the relationship between childrens' ages and the odds of a woman being self-employed is not straightforward. Ginn and Sandall (1997) and Carr (1996) suggest that the presence of younger children should elevate stress levels and demands because young children require more sustained attention than older children. However, the results show that among younger children, this positive effect is only present for children under two, but not for three- to five-year-olds. In addition, older children increase a woman's odds of self-employment, which is not consistent with the ideas of Ginn and Sandall (1997) and Carr (1996).

Women turning to self-employment as a way to balance the pressures of the double day may be a peculiarly North American phenomenon, albeit with variations between Canada and the US.

References

Arai, A.B. 1995. Self-employment and the Nature of the Canadian Economy. PhD Dissertation. University of British Columbia.

Bechhofer, F., and B. Elliott. 1978. 'The Voice of Small Business and the Politics of Survival', *Sociological Review* 26, 1: 57–88.

Blain, J. 1993. ' "I can't come in today, the baby has chicken pox!" Gender and Class Processes in How Parents in the Labour Force Deal with the Problem of Sick Children', *Canadian Journal of Sociology* 18, 4: 405–30.

Carr, D. 1996. 'Two Paths to Self-employment? Women's and Men's Self-employment in the United States, 1980', *Work and Occupations* 23, 1: 26–53.

Crompton, R., and F. Harris. 1998. 'Gender Relations and Employment: The Impact of Occupation', *Work, Employment and Society* 12, 2: 297–316.

Giles, W., and V. Preston. 1996. 'The Domestication of Women's Work: A Comparison of Chinese and Portuguese Immigrant Women Homeworkers', *Studies in Political Economy* 51: 147–82.

Ginn, J., and J. Sandall. 1997. 'Balancing Home and Employment', *Work, Employment and Society* 11, 3: 414–34.

Hochschild, A., with A. Machung. 1989. *The Second Shift: Working Parents and the Revolution at Home*. New York: Viking.

Jurik, N.C. 1998. 'Getting Away and Getting By: The Experiences of Self-employed Homeworkers', *Work and Occupations* 25, 1: 7–35.

Kalleberg, A.L., and R.A. Rosenfeld. 1992. 'Work in the Family and in the Labour Market: A Cross-national, Reciprocal Analysis', *Journal of Marriage and the Family* 52 (May): 331–46.

Linder, M. 1992. *Farewell to the Self-Employed: Deconstructing a Socioeconomic and Legal Solipsism*. New York: Greenwood.

Luxton, M. 1980. *More than a Labour of Love*. Toronto: Women's Press.

Munch, A., M.J. McPherson, and L. Smith-Lovin. 1997. 'Gender, Children and Social Contact: The Effects of Childrearing for Men and Women', *American Sociological Review* 62, 4: 509–20.

Nisbet, P. 1997. 'Dualism, Flexibility and Self-employment in the UK Construction Industry', *Work, Employment and Society* 11, 3: 459–80.

Steinmetz, G., and E.O. Wright. 1989. 'The Fall and Rise of the Petty Bourgeoisie: Changing Patterns of Self-employment in the Postwar United States', *American Journal of Sociology* 94, 5: 973–1018.

Questions for Critical Thought

Love- and Arranged-Marriage in India Today: Negotiating Adulthood

1. How do you think the results of this study addressed the gap identified by Patricia Uberoi?

2. How does each theory—modernization and neo-traditionalism—describe the current practices? What are the limits in their individual descriptions? Which of the two theories do you think is more relevant to the current model of arranged marriage?

3. How do the educated Indian youths' ideas of love and marriage compare to Western notions? What do you think Indian youths' without exposure to global youth culture think about love and marriage?

4. What are the pros and cons of either a love- or arranged-marriage in Indian society? In Western society?

5. What are two innovations to arranged-marriage? In what ways do the innovations reflect the traditional arranged-marriage? The love-marriage?

LIFE CYCLE EVENTS AND THE CREATION OF TRANSNATIONAL TIES AMONG SECOND GENERATION SOUTH INDIANS

1. Why do second-generation South Indians sustain connections with people in their parents' homeland—instead of connecting to their own parents—as a means to 'revive' their traditional cultural identity?
2. Some researchers argue that second generation migrants are not transnational, while others argue that they are important transnational actors. Explain how this debate can be explained through a consideration of life-cycle stages.
3. Which two life course events activate the transnational social field and lead the second generation to have increased ties with their parents' country of birth? Explain why these particular events are important.
4. How are transnational family relationships maintained by the second generation?
5. Discuss how the transnational literature presented in this chapter 'fits' in relation to other immigration theories.

BALANCING ETHNICITY AND SEXUALITY: GAY JEWISH MEN SEEK THE SAME

1. This chapter examines the intersection of two types of individual identities—ethnicity and sexuality—and demonstrates that some people struggle to find a satisfactory balance between these identities. What are some other examples of identity intersections that individuals attempt to negotiate?
2. Why do you think ethnic minority groups (such as Jews) place importance on marrying someone from the same minority group? Is this a reasonable position in a multicultural society like Canada?
3. How important is it for you to marry someone of the same ethnic or religious group? Why do you feel that way?
4. In the decade of the 2000s there has been considerable debate in Canada on the question of same-sex marriage. Do you think Canada's traditional definition of marriage—the marriage of a man to a woman—should be enlarged to include the marriage of a gay male couple or lesbian couple? Justify your opinion.
5. The article suggests that community leaders of Canadian ethnic minority groups, such as Jews, blacks, and Asians do not actively support gay partnerships within their own communities. Why do you think this is the case? Is this a reasonable position?

DEFINING FAMILIES

1. How are gender and education related in discouraging women from certain professions?
2. Describe the effect on paid and unpaid work hours for women when children are in the family. Describe the effect for men.
3. What are some cultural barriers to men taking pride in domestic work and care-giving? What are some common justifications for this?
4. Are there societal backlashes to fathers taking time off work for the home and children? Are there societal backlashes for the home and children to mothers *not* taking time off work or using other means of childcare?
5. Discuss some policies that promote the de-gendering of earning and caring. What are the ways in which they are effective?

ASSESSING QUEBEC'S $7/DAY CHILDCARE: SOME PRELIMINARY FINDINGS

1. Do you think daycare helps or harms children? Why do you think this? What evidence can you use to support your argument?
2. If you were to do a follow-up study, what kind of study would you do? What kinds of questions might you ask? Of whom?
3. Do you agree or disagree with the idea that 'all other provinces should follow Quebec's lead and provide $7/day childcare to all parents regardless of economic need, employment status, etc.'? Why or why not?
4. 'People on social assistance should not have access to $7/day childcare. Spots should be reserved for working parents only.' Do you agree or disagree? What argument would you use to support your view?
5. Why do you think childcare workers earn incomes comparable to parking lot attendants? What do you think is a fair salary for childcare workers? Why?

SELF-EMPLOYMENT AS A RESPONSE TO THE DOUBLE DAY FOR WOMEN AND MEN IN CANADA

1. What are some ways women try to balance pressures from home with those from work? What do men do?
2. What are the effects of this balancing act on children in the home? How are the effects significant to a woman's or a man's current career and future prospects? Does it affect men as much?
3. What are the pros and cons of self-employment for women with children? In your opinion, is a change to self-employment generally a good idea for women with children?
4. What are some 'family friendly' workplace policies? Why do you think that few employees actually take advantage of them if many companies use them?
5. Describe the relationship between the age of children and the rate of self-employment for women. What explains the difference between the US and Canada in this respect?

Part VI

Education

Sociologists study education because it plays a vital role in socializing individuals, transmitting social values, and providing young people with the skills they need to function economically. The social importance of education is obvious in the sheer amount of time students spend in the classroom throughout their lives, and the social significance of material students are taught. Education has the power to influence the economic development of a society and the disparity of resources in the population. Education also gives people the skills to question the organization of society, and we see this questioning in the following chapters.

Sociologists use different approaches to ask questions about the social role of education, using different analytical lenses. Structural functionalists, for example, analyze the roles of the education system for society as a whole and the relationship between education and other parts of society. A founder of sociology, Émile Durkheim, saw education as a means to pass on society's norms and values, and in this way, to preserve social cohesion. Durkheim believed that society can survive only if there exists among its members a sufficient degree of homogeneity; education perpetuates and reinforces this homogeneity. Conflict theorists, on the other hand, view education as a social (also economic and political) resource to which groups have differential access. Therefore, they explore how some people benefit from having a privileged access to education, and how other groups fail to benefit. Symbolic interactionists show how students perform differently in school given their daily experiences interacting with others. They also explore factors like the time students spend outside school earning money to pay their tuition fees, and the role of family influence on a student's performance in education.

Sociologists use various sociological approaches in the following discussions to understand the present-day social role of education. In his chapter, Robert Prus looks at the different viewpoints that students assume during the learning process, and explores how an ideal educational experience can only come about through congruent student–teacher roles. Rebecca Raby analyzes how a school board's code of conduct shapes the idea of citizenship and contributes to creating an uncritical and passive student population. In their contribution, Marilee Reimer and Adele Mueller explore how 'first in the family' women are disadvantaged during the transition from university to careers because they lack the necessary skills that students from higher income families have, such as organizational literacy. In her chapter, Janice Aurini examines the legitimacy of the rapidly growing private schooling business. And in the final chapter in the section, Arnaud Sales, Réjean Drolet, and Isabelle Bonneau explore how the modern student is markedly changed from previous decades because of the average increase in students' ages.

Like other conflict theorists, Reimer, Mueller, and Raby all note inequalities and disadvantages within the education system, and explain how both intentional and unintentional aspects of education disproportionately affect the opportunities given to individuals. For his part, Prus stresses the importance of a symbolic interactionist assessment of the education system. He looks at the role of daily interaction in the education system and its effect on the individual. As we have said, the study of the education system is crucial because of its fundamental role in society—regardless of the sociological approach we take. In fact, all of the sociological approaches interact with one another to provide a richer sociological perspective on the education system.

CHAPTER 25

Activities and Interdependencies in the Educational Process: An Interactionist Approach to Student Ventures in Learning

Robert Prus

Assuming a **symbolic interactionist** approach, this paper outlines an **ethnographic approach** to studying the ways that 'people engage roles as students'. In contrast to most research on education that focuses on outcomes of instructional programs and the factors presumed to account for those outcomes, the emphasis is on the ways that people 'experience and accomplish the activities, interchanges and relationships' that are so integral to the educational process. Likewise, rather than deny or disregard the complexity of the learning process as this occurs within the context of the human group, this paper focuses on learning (and education) *as an enacted, adjustive social process* that is more or less continuously 'in the making'. In developing this statement, I rely on Chicago-style symbolic interactionism (see Mead, 1934; Blumer, 1969; Prus, 1997) wherein the emphasis is on (a) approaching human group life as a linguistically-informed realm of activity, (b) examining human group life in sustained ethnographic terms, and developing sets of process-related concepts (i.e., **generic social processes**) that not only (c) address the full range of human association but that also (d) explore an extended transsituational relevance.

Concentrating on 'what is', rather than 'what should be', the present statement encourages a more thorough, detailed, coherent approach to the study of learning. Likewise, while attending to the ways that people make sense of the situations in which they find themselves as these unfold, the focus is on examining the ways that people develop their activities in process terms.

Although virtually all of the topics considered here will be familiar to readers as long-term participants in student and/or instructional roles, it is essential to provide a more systematic and coherent means of approaching the fuller range of activities that constitute the student role as well as a mechanism for explicitly, directly, and centrally focusing research and analysis on activities.

Ironically, while it is only as people engage in activity that the student role assumes its primary essence, those studying education have given only marginal attention to the processes by which people (students and instructors) actually accomplish their activities. Thus, this statement represents an attempt to 'reclaim authenticity', to focus on the things that people actually do (and do not do) as students. Still, because student activities are at least partially, if not more centrally, contingent on the emphases and practices of their teachers, it is necessary to give consideration to the things that instructors do.

Acknowledging Instruction and the Quest for Mutuality

First, irrespective of the potentially differing objectives, concerns, and emphases of program directors and front-line instructors that one might encounter in more complex organizational environments, there is the matter of setting the parameters of instruction to be applied in the settings at hand. Typically, this involves such things as determining who will be taught (and by whom); deciding on the objectives, contents, and emphases of instruction; considering the methods of instruction; finding settings or forums for instruction; attending to the materials and technologies to be implemented; setting standards or levels of expectation for students; judging competence or assessing student performance; dealing with student weaknesses and failures; and certifying student performance.

Whereas researchers and analysts who focus on the outcomes of educational programs (as in completion rates, grades, student satisfaction) frequently emphasize instructor backgrounds and presentational styles, a more consequential feature of the instructional role from the viewpoint of those involved in teaching is apt to revolve around the matter of dealing with students.

Thus, beyond any concerns with their own preparations and presentations, virtually all instructors face the tasks of accessing and accommodating particular people as students, defining and adjusting the particular subject matters for instruction relative to those with whom they work, pursuing quality, maintaining instructional focus, and dealing with an assortment of student associates. As well, instructors commonly encounter a variety of individual and collective instances of disruption, resistance, and associated obstacles. Further, because of the outsiders (e.g., administrators, parents, politicians) who may make demands on their time, efforts, and priorities, individual instructors often face the task of achieving desired levels of autonomy in pursuing instances of instructional endeavour.

Still, to be effective in their roles as instructors (and communicators), a great many of the activities performed by teachers require that instructors 'take the role' (Mead, 1934) or adopt the standpoint of their students. To teach, therefore, requires that one think and act toward the instructional process 'as a student'.

Relatedly, in assuming the teaching role in more direct and central terms, instructors are faced with the need to consider the ways that students might comprehend and engage the subject matter at hand and make adjustments to offset counterproductive tendencies on the part of those they instruct. Instructors need not be particularly effective in meeting these objectives, but their earlier involvements in student roles normally provide instructors with more viable sets of student perspectives than 'the sets of instructor perspectives' with which their students typically work.

However, if instruction is to be effective, students also must take the role of the teacher. In more comprehensive terms, this means being attentive to concerns that they, 'as students', not only learn things but also do so in more competent manners. In actual practice, though, this often seems implicit and even when students adopt standpoints of these sorts they may find that these are difficult to sustain, particularly if their fellow students do not share these emphases.

Thus, while the educational process is contingent on people achieving a unity of the student-instructor roles, it is necessary to be mindful that the unity is problematic and can only be achieved through enterprise of a mutually focused, coordinated sort. Because instructor–pupil roles assume both an interactional interdependence and a content-based mutuality of focus, instructional unity depends on the willingness and abilities of both parties to enter into and sustain the many points of contact that constitute the educational venture.

Focusing on Student Activities

Recognizing that learning is a social process, we now consider the ways that people engage the educational process as students; how people enter into, make sense of, and otherwise implement roles as students.

When one approaches the student role mindful of people's activities therein, the following processes assume particular prominence: entering into the student role, attending to instruction, learning things, being assessed, sustaining efforts, attending to one's peers, encountering difficulties, experiencing failure and termination, and pursuing subsequent studies. To more effectively understand student roles, it will be necessary to examine ethnographically each of these realms of activity, to take each of these broader activities apart piece by piece and to consider instances of each in comparative analysis.

Thus, whereas these activities may be used as departure points for ethnographic inquiry, they also represent focal points for synthesizing (accumulating, comparing, assessing, qualifying, and extending) concepts that address people's participation in student roles.

When one envisions learning as activity, it also becomes apparent that attempts to reduce learning to psychological or other individual qualities are most inadequate for comprehending people's roles as students. Thus, although learning often assumes solitary dimensions (as in reading to oneself, studying for tests, interpreting assignments, and experiencing frustration in instances of learning), none of these activities could be meaningfully engaged, or would have any relevance, apart from people's associations with the other.

Although it is not possible to provide a more detailed research agenda that addresses these processes in the immediate statement (readers are referred to the full conference paper), the task is to examine all the things that people do in each of the preceding areas of student activity while not only sustaining an emphasis on 'what is' rather than 'what should be', but also attending to the developmental flow of the instances in which people do things, maintaining a concentrated focus on the ways that the participants make sense of, give meanings to, and adjust to the situations at hand, and developing research and analysis in ways that have a more generic, more enduring relevance. By pursuing these emphases, researchers not only would be better able to examine student activities in more authentic terms, but could also develop more precise, refined comparisons and conceptual understandings of the activities that constitute the student role.

Conclusion

In contrast to those who emphasize the outcomes of particular educational programs and seek out sociological and/or psychological factors as mechanisms for explaining differentials in program outcomes, the interactionist perspective adopted herein approaches education as a multiplistic, collectively engaged, and developmentally achieved process.

By examining education within the more generic conceptual frame of symbolic interaction, rather than envisioning education as an exclusive realm of endeavour itself, researchers and analysts are able to access and build on a literature that deals with parallel processes in a broad array of contexts. As well, by locating specific studies on student activities in this conceptual and methodological tradition, these scholars also can more directly contribute to the broader understanding of human knowing and acting.

References

Blumer, H. 1969. *Symbolic Interaction*. Englewood Cliffs, NJ: Prentice-Hall.

Mead, G.H. 1934. *Mind, Self and Society*, C.W. Morris, ed. Chicago: University of Chicago Press.

Prus, R. 1997. *Subcultural Mosaics and Intersubjective Realities: An Ethnographic Research Agenda for Pragmatizing the Social Sciences*. Albany, NY: SUNY Press.

CHAPTER 26

Polite, Well-dressed, and On Time: Secondary School Conduct Codes and the Production of Docile Citizens

Rebecca Raby

This paper examines *Ontario's Safe Schools Act* (2000), and the codes of conduct of school boards and high schools in the Niagara and Toronto regions. I investigate how these codes are organized, justified, and presented to students and, in the process, what kind of students (and adolescents) are assumed and created, particularly in terms of citizens and future workers. Codes of conduct are sites of knowledge production, fashioning middle-class, normative, gendered citizens, and marginalizing those who do not easily conform. These codes also suggest a government of young people through their capacity to act and consequent self-regulation, alongside more 'top-down' techniques.

High school codes of conduct, outlining expectations for how students should behave, may seem both necessary and benign. This article examines such codes (including dress codes) more critically, through a discursive analysis of Ontario's Safe Schools Act, Toronto and Niagara school board policies, and individual rules from secondary schools in Toronto and Niagara. I examine these rules with a focus on rights, responsibilities, and self-government. Age, class, race, sexuality, and gender relations are also produced within these specific deployments (and exclusions). I argue that dress and discipline codes are sites of knowledge production and attempts to secure internalized discipline.

Dress, Discipline, and Citizenship

A small number of researchers have studied general (non-uniform) dress and discipline codes similar to those I examine here. Yet a tension between inculcation into neo-liberal self-governance and concomitant shaping and **punishment** of teenagers

is evident in the dress and discipline codes that are enforced in **educational** facilities. Governance does not replace sovereign, top-down and disciplinary power, but rather these forms of power work in combination (Hannah-Moffat, 2000). Within various institutions, including schools, young people's selves are constituted through techniques that foster self-governance. However, schools also punish, through more sovereign and disciplinary means, those who fail to self-govern, dividing the 'good' citizens from the 'bad' (Hannah-Moffat, 2000: 528). The self-governing subject is again complicated when addressing adolescence, a time of life discursively framed as irrational, becoming, and in need of discipline (Lesko, 1996). The presentation of rules blends assumptions of autonomous and rational self-regulation with those of the developing, un-self-regulated teenager. Schools' rules, therefore, are particularly interesting sites for examining how sovereignty, discipline, and governance intertwine.

Making Citizens

In their overt linkage of rights and responsibilities, school rules are examples of attempts at neo-liberal governance 'in which the active citizen is required to self-regulate and self-manage as a "responsible citizen"' (Kemshall, 2002: 43). This citizenship is about governmentality, with young people's agency harnessed to a narrow, individualized, and obedient self-discipline through a discourse of responsibility. This citizenship reflects 'prudentialism', in which the individual 'becomes responsible and accountable for the proper management of her own risk or potential risk' in the interest of 'a responsible, self-sufficient future'

(Hannah-Moffat, 2000: 522). When people take responsibility for their own actions the state can govern at a distance, ideally well beyond a young person's time at school. Codes of conduct thus blend assumptions of an autonomous, self-regulating adolescent who must be responsible in the present with the guidance of an un-self-regulated teenager into becoming a self-regulating adult, legitimizing, and reproducing conflicting assumptions about adolescents.

One other consequence of such self-regulation is that the person (Other) who does not adequately respond to neo-liberal techniques is blamed and subjected to mechanisms of control and repression. This Other is managed through school rules, with those who fail to self-regulate experiencing the more sovereign power of the school, such as suspension, expulsion, or other consequences outlined in the schools' conduct codes and the province's zero tolerance policy. Later, I examine ways in which more 'petty' rules, including dress codes, can succeed in creating such Others.

Making Workers

Not only do these codes fashion a certain kind of citizen, but also a certain kind of worker. The link between schools and the creation of workers is prominent and blunt in many codes. First, student conduct is routinely linked to eventual employment especially through emphasis on punctuality (in almost all schools) and, occasionally, supported through overt gestures to the workplace: 'Punctuality is a good habit, which will be expected of you, both in your personal relationships and on the job' (Avenue Secondary, Niagara Region).

Secondly, a number of schools—particularly business and technical institutes in Toronto— frame the school as a place of business, usually as an explanation for dress codes and sometimes with reference to preparing students for the workplace. As stated by Chelsea secondary (Niagara Region), '[w]e expect students to dress in a socially acceptable manner similar to that of the world of work.'

Third, particularly in Niagara schools, the links between school and preparation for work are secured through what the school is defined against, specifically the street: 'Dress should be appropriate to an academic setting, [creating a] separation between street and school . . .' (Fleet Secondary and This Town Secondary, Niagara Region).

Through these rules we see a (not so) hidden curriculum in which students are groomed to be certain kinds of workers (and citizens): punctual, restrained in dress, and obedient. Rather than shaping young people for self-employment, focus on dress (especially uniforms) suggests links to the service industry or white-collar work, supported by the fact that this emphasis is quite evident in the business and technical schools.

Restraint and Docility

The production of a docile citizenry is further evident through emphasis on restraint, which will be examined here through the middle-class morality of dress codes, emphasis on asexual space, and repeated references to respect. Moral regulation can be seen as an instance of governmentality. A. Hunt defines moral regulation as 'practices whereby some social agents problematise some aspect of the conduct, values or culture of others on moral grounds and seek to impose regulation upon them' (1999: ix). Processes of moral regulation construct us as subjects who internalize forms of conduct, drawing us into practices of normalization. We see this here in relation to middle-class standards, and exhortations to self-govern as a marker of maturity. Such normalization processes invariably also create an 'outsider'—those who do not succeed in (or comply with) such practices.

Some dress codes are attentive to regulatory detail, significantly guiding a normative presentation of the body:

Halter-tops, tube tops, tank tops, one shoulder tops . . . muscle shirts, see-through or mesh tops (unless underneath a shirt) aren't to be worn. Blouses, shirts or tops that reveal bare backs, midriffs, undergarments, or that have spaghetti straps or revealing necklines are not to be worn in Trent's classes, hallways, class activities, or on field trips (Trent Secondary, Niagara Region).

Yet such rules are at least clear, in contrast to vague rules couched in middle-class language that can leave some students uncertain of expectations and provide teaching authorities with significant discretion.

Students should be clean and neatly dressed in a manner which maintains the good moral tone of the school (General Brock Secondary, Niagara Region).

. . . good common sense, good taste, decency and socially acceptable attire (Quarry View Secondary, Niagara Region).

In these latter examples, one must ask whose standards of 'good taste', 'common sense' or 'socially acceptable' apply. Taste is not neutral, but reflects a habitus linked to class (Bourdieu, 1984). The language of 'good taste' is slippery and flexible in its application. It also presumes a previous, shared knowledge of what it means.

Several other concerns are raised in reaction to these criteria. First, sexual expression, particularly female sexual expression, is presented as incompatible with self-respect. By linking displays of sexuality to a lack of self-respect, the marginalization and problematization of female sexuality is reinforced. The links between dress codes and gender are clear, even if rarely spelled out directly (students must avoid showing too much cleavage, for example). Significant popular commentary on the need for dress codes indicates concern with girls' skimpy clothing (McGovern, 1998; Page, 2002). Columnist Shelley Page (2002) argues that parents and school officials are anxious about young people's dress because they are uncomfortable with girls' sexuality, even if, for the girls themselves, their clothes are more about fashion than sex.

Conclusion

The citizenship being created through school dress and discipline codes in the Niagara and Toronto regions is premised on predefined responsibilities overtly linked to passive rights. The attempt is for students to internalize such responsibilities through self-respect, self-regulation, and self-discipline, as well as obedience to **authority**. These rules include regulation of dress, space and time, emphasize the productivity of work, and link responsibility to respect for nation and property. I have argued that a docile, productive citizenry is thus envisioned, with those Others who fail to self-govern (or to display prescribed self-respect) disciplined through more sovereign applications of tools such as the zero tolerance policy. Such a shaping of the lives of adolescents is justified on the grounds that they are in the process of becoming citizens and therefore need the guidance of rules. Yet there is little in these rules to suggest an active citizenship based on involvement in decision-making, challenge to the status quo or authority, independent thought, equality, or genuine democracy.

School rules are not only about constructing citizens, but also adolescence: teenagers are presented as becoming employees or citizens, at-risk from other students or from outsiders and as a social problem to the community and to each other. These representations complicate the role of school rules: is punishment about grooming for the future, safety, or controlling behaviour in the present? Further, school dress and discipline codes involve rules that are directly applied to young people, often covering activities not considered infractions for adults. Such rules participate in creating a delinquent 'other' based on age, particularly in the case of dress or actions acceptable among adults, such as 'horseplay', throwing snowballs, or displays of affection. What does it mean to young people when such petty rules are presented alongside much more serious ones, such as those addressing violence? And, more broadly, how are such rules applied in schools, and experienced, embraced, or resisted by young people? This analysis is only the first step in a wider project investigating how rules are deployed within the school setting and how students perceive, experience, conform to, and potentially resist these rules.

References

Bourdieu, P. 1984. *Distinction: A Social Critique of the Judgement of Taste*. Richard Nice, trans. Cambridge, MA: Harvard University Press.

Hannah-Moffat, K. 2000. 'Prisons that Empower: Neo-liberal Governance in Canadian Women's Prisons', *British Journal of Criminology* 40, 3: 510–31.

Hunt, A. 1999. *Governing Morals: A Social History of Moral Regulation*. Cambridge, UK: Cambridge University Press.

Kemshall, H. 2002. 'Effective Practice in Probation: An Example of "Advanced Liberal" Responsibilization?', *The Howard Journal* 41, 1: 41–58.

Lesko, N. 1996. 'Denaturalizing Adolescence: The Politics of Contemporary Representations', *Youth and Society* 28, 2: 139–61.

McGovern, C. 1998. 'Busting Out All Over: Teachers Struggle with Girls' Halter Tops and Hot and Bothered Boys', *British Columbia Report* 9, 50: 46.

Ontario Government. 2001. *Ontario Schools Code of Conduct*. Toronto: Queen's Park.

Page, S. 2002. 'School Dress Controversy Reflects the Fears of Adults', *Northern Daily News*, 26 April: 7.

CHAPTER 27

Crafting Legitimation Projects: An Institutional Analysis of Private Education Businesses

Janice Aurini

Introduction

Institutional analyses of education systems typically examine how schools conform to their environment (isomorphism), often privileging external legitimacy over internal efficiency or goals. Accordingly, education systems develop along standard lines of acceptable 'school-like' forms that include adopting concepts such as 'teachers' and 'students' and broad social goals such as 'equity' and 'inclusiveness'. Schools also 'loosely couple' their formal structure with outcomes by avoiding performance indicators such as standardized tests. These strategies permit schools to integrate multiple and conflicting goals and ward off inspection that may expose inefficiencies and inconsistencies (Meyer and Rowan, 1978).

When these insights were first developed in the 1970s, public schools dominated the educational landscape, and alternatives consisted of a peppering of elite and religious private schools and tutoring and test-prep businesses. Today, parents can now select from a growing array of education options such as charter schools, niche curricula private schools, learning centers and home schooling (Stevens, 2001; Aurini, 2004; Davies and Quirke, 2005). The expansion of these alternatives is complimented by the mounting strength of choice and 'pro-market' movements that champion the benefits of markets in encouraging innovation, variety and higher standards (Chubb and Moe, 1990). **Institutional theory** (IT) would predict that these forms would aspire to adopt as many legitimated elements as possible into their institutional structure to boost their legitimacy and survival chances. This necessity would be amplified in countries with strong public school systems such as Canada, where private enterprises must compete for enrolments.

Despite these predictions, private education alternatives routinely shed some of the most sacred elements of traditional schooling such as libraries, credentialed staff, mandated curriculum, and social programs. Privates are also free to adopt policies that may limit the range of students who are eligible to enroll, and remove students and policies that compromise their organizational goals. Despite this 'deviance', these forms are flourishing and enjoying increased legitimacy. In recent surveys, 46 per cent of Canadian parents said they would prefer to send their child to a private school if they could afford it while 66 per cent of Ontarians agreed with the statement, 'private school students receive a much better education than public school students' (Angus Reid, 2000; Davies, 2004).

If these forms deviate from traditional schooling templates, how do private education alternatives garner legitimacy? This paper examines this process as a 'legitimation project'—the on-going process of interpreting, incorporating, and influencing environmentally defined elements into an organization's institutional structure. Legitimation projects engage three under-analyzed processes central to IT: myth-making, 'coupling', and the logic of confidence (Meyer and Rowan, 1977; 1978).

This paper also examines two forms of private education that have enjoyed unprecedented popularity and growth in recent years: private tutoring businesses and learning centre franchises. Recent data shows that 24 per cent of Ontario parents have hired tutors in the past three years (Livingstone, Hart, and Davie, 2003), and 50 per cent of parents would hire a tutor if they had the resources (Davies, 2004). Since the 1970s, tutoring businesses have grown between 200–500 per cent in three major Canadian cities, and by over 90 per cent in Ontario between 1996 and 2004, an increase to 483 (from 250) locations (Aurini and Davies, 2004). Such recent growth makes them an ideal test case to examine a legitimation project from the 'ground up' and operationalize concepts that have often been cited as ambiguous and 'taken-for-granted' (see Perrow, 1985; Hirsch, 1997).

I draw on 40 interviews and site visits with tutoring business and franchise owners in Toronto and 5 interviews with representatives from private education and franchise associations. I also draw on the observations made during one year of participant observation in which I tutored for a major learning centre franchise that I will refer to as the 'Ontario Learning Centre'.

Crafting Legitimation Projects

The chart below summarizes the argument.

MYTH-MAKING

IT posits that in modern societies many policies, programs, and organizational forms behave as

	Public Education	Private Education
Myth-making	Adopt standard templates Social betterment	Strategic and selective adoption
Loose Coupling	Avoid performance indicators Symbolic coupling through adoption of standard templates	Avoid performance indictors Symbolic coupling through personal service
Logic-of-Confidence	Adherence to standard templates Teacher professionalism	Education consumerism

'institutional myths' that are adopted 'ceremoniously' regardless of their need or effect on organizational activities. Myths identify prescriptions to a particular end, and their adoption is argued to establish an organization as 'appropriate' and 'rational' (Meyer and Rowan, 1977).

Public schools incorporate widely held myths that include credentialed teachers, age-defined grades, and courses such as math and science (Meyer and Rowan, 1978). More recently, Ontario public schools have introduced standardized curriculum and tests and a parenting council in accordance to broader trends that frame the necessity for public sectors to demonstrate competency to their constituents (see Chubb and Moe, 1990; see Stein, 2001). These initiatives have been advanced as instruments to measure the ability of schools in delivering outcomes that are consistent with their institutionalized myths (e.g. learning). These myths have been adopted regardless of whether they effectively measure learning outcomes or improve the quality of education.

Conversely, the private education industry in Ontario is not required to hire certified staff, nor conform to government imposed curriculum guidelines. Among the interviewees, only eight of the owners were certified teachers, while the remaining hailed from areas such as psychology, business, and physics. Moreover, franchisers consider teachers undesirable franchise owners, citing them as lacking the 'ambition' and 'entrepreneurial spirit' necessary to run a profitable business. Of the six franchise brands examined, only two favoured tutors with teaching certification, since the highly standardized nature of franchise services leaves little discretion to the individual tutor. While smaller independent businesses tend to follow the school curriculum, learning centres also typically develop their own curriculums and fail to follow schools' instruction and exam timetable. These strategies permit these businesses to standardize their product across schooling districts and hire 'cheaper' labour.

LOOSE COUPLING

Myth-making gives rise to technical and coordination challenges for organizations because myths present themselves from different parts of the environment and may contradict one another or be ineffective. For instance, schools' 'inclusion' goals conflict with tracking systems and grading schemes which systematically differentiates students. To resolve inconsistencies, schools 'loosely couple' by building gaps between activities (e.g. curriculum) and outcomes (e.g. standardized tests) and by adopting vague and expansive goals that are difficult to measure such as 'citizenship' and 'socialization' (Weick, 1976; Meyer and Rowan, 1978).

Many learning centres create rituals that are supposed to serve as evidence of their programs' effectiveness. At the Ontario Learning Centre, students 'reflect' during the last five minutes of every tutoring session by taking turns relaying what they have accomplished during the session (e.g. 'I worked on book "X"') and how it will help them in school (e.g. 'It will help me sound out words and I'll do better on my spelling tests'). This ritual serves as an accountability function by seemingly coupling the institutionalized program with an 'outcome'. Once this ritual is performed, students are equipped with two or three phrases to tell their parents about what they learned in that session and how it will help them in school because '. . . the worst thing that can happen is that the kid comes out of the tutoring session and when asked by mom or dad "What did you work on tonight honey?", and they get an "I dunno, nothing much". After a parent has spent $300–400 [per month], they don't want to hear that" (fieldnotes, 2001). Thus, like public schools, environmental pressures to couple activities with outcomes encourage largely symbolic responses.

LOGIC-OF-CONFIDENCE

According to IT, myth-making and loose coupling permit stakeholders to believe that the organization is operating in good faith—referred to as the logic-of-confidence. This 'trust' permits organizations to ward off inspection and stabilize in form and practice (Haveman, 2000). In public schools the logic-of-confidence traditionally rests on the adherence to common templates of 'how' schooling should be done and teacher-professionalism (Meyer and Rowan, 1978).

In part, education consumerism has been facilitated by the emerging culture of intensive parenting and educational customization. These new childrearing ideologies stress the necessity for parents to attend to their children's intellectual development and unique personalities, and provide highly customized schooling (Zelizer, 1985; Wrigley, 1989; Stevens, 2001; Lareau, 2003). As one franchiser explained, parents are cognizant of their educational 'needs' and 'shop around' as they would for any other product or service (Interview: 14), and seek education that matches their value systems (see Brown, 1990).

Learning centres respond to this new consumer environment by offering a wide range of programs and services and small student–teacher ratios. These businesses espouse broad mission statements and market their services as highly customized. Common themes include: 'Developing your child's gifts and talents' (Academy for Mathematics and Science, 2004); 'personalized programme(s) to meet his or her individualized needs' (Sylvan, 2004); and programs that foster creativity, confidence, and self-esteem (Oxford Learning Centre, 2004).

The smaller student–teacher arrangement also permits more one-on-one attention that is not possible in the public school system. As one entrepreneur who developed his tutoring franchise into a private school explained, parents today 'micromanage their children', and 'when they come to a school they expect their kid to be micro-managed as well' (Interview: 10). Thus, rather than measured effectiveness, private educators garner high degrees of confidence by advancing their products as customized and responsive to the needs of each 'unique' child.

Conclusion

This analysis highlights how IT must be more cognizant of the variations within sectors such as education. These variations provide organizations with alterative sources of legitimacy and hence, 'appropriate' legitimation projects. Myth-making, coupling, and the logic-of-confidence are not static givens, but rather are in a constant flux, and can be highly sensitive to their position in the institutional environment.

References

Academy for Mathematics and Science. 2004 'FastTrackKids International'. Available at http://www.acadfor.com/index.htm (accessed 14 January 2004).

Angus Reid. 2000. 'A Failing Grade for Ontario's Public School System'. Available at http://www.angusreid.com/search/pdf/media/mr000303%5f1.pdf (accessed 20 January 2003).

Aurini, J. 2004. 'Educational Entrepreneurialism in the Private Tutoring Industry: Balancing Profitability with the Humanistic Face of Schooling', *Canadian Review of Sociology and Anthropology* 41, 4: 475–91.

Brown, P. 1990. 'The Third Wave: Education and the Ideology of Parentocracy', *British Journal of Sociology of Education* 11, 1: 65–81.

Chubb, J., and T. Moe. 1990. 'Politics, Markets and American Schools', *American Political Science Review* 84: 549–67.

Davies, S. 2004. 'School Choice by Default: Understanding the Demand for Private Tutoring in Canada', *American Journal of Education* 110, 3: 233–55.

Davies, S., and L. Quirke. 2005. 'Providing for the Priceless Student: Ideologies of Choice in an Emerging Private School Market', *American Journal of Education* 111, 4: 523–47.

Fuller, B. 2000. *Inside Charter Schools: The Paradox of Radical Decentralization.* Cambridge, MA: Harvard University Press.

Haveman, H.A. 2000. 'The Future of Organizational Sociology: Forging Ties among Paradigms', *Contemporary Sociology* 29, 3: 476–86.

Hirsch, P.M. 1997. 'Sociology Without Social Structure: Neoinstitutional Theory Meets Brave New World', *American Journal of Sociology* 102, 6: 1702–23.

Lareau, A. 2003. *Unequal Childhoods: Class, Race and Families*. Los Angeles: University of California Press.

Livingstone, D.W., D. Hart, and L.E. Davie. 2003. *Public Attitudes Towards Education in Ontario 2002: The 14th OISE/UT Survey*. Toronto: Orbit.

Meyer, J., and B. Rowan. 1977. 'Institutionalized Organizations: Formal Structure as Myth and Ceremony', *American Journal of Sociology* 83: 340–63.

———. 1978. 'The Structure of Educational Organizations in Environments and Organizations', in *Environments and Organizations*, pp. 78–109, Marshall W. Meyer and Associates, eds. San Francisco, CA: Jossey Bass.

Oxford Learning Centre. 2004. 'Improved Grades, Improved Confidence'. Available at http://www.oxford.ca (accessed 14 January 2004).

Perrow, C. 1985. 'Review Essay: Overboard with Myth and Symbols', *American Journal of Sociology* 91, 1: 151–5.

Stein, J.G. 2001. *The Cult of Efficiency*. Toronto: Anansi Press Limited.

Stevens, M. 2001. *Kingdom of Children. Culture and Controversy in the Homeschooling Movement*. New Jersey: Princeton University Press.

Sylvan Learning Centers. 2004. 'Senior Math'. Available at http://www.educate.ca (accessed 14 January 2004).

Weick, K.E. 1976. 'Education Organizations as Loosely Coupled Systems', *Administrative Science Quarterly* 21: 1–19.

CHAPTER 28

University Restructuring and the Female Liberal Arts Undergraduate Student: Does She Get 'Value for the Money' at Corporate U?

Marilee Reimer and Adele Mueller

This paper is a preliminary report on a research project on the university-to-career transition for an important group of 'non-traditional' students: young women who are the first in their families to go to university. In Atlantic Canada, where economic restructuring has eliminated many traditional 'working class' jobs and where universities compete for the limited 18–19-year-old pool, the draw of university reaches into new populations. For young women in rural areas coming from families with no higher education experience, university offers a door into the wider world of careers about which they know little. At the same time, restructuring is creating a polarization between well-funded research universities and primarily teaching universities and faculties. That the latter are particularly popular with first-in-their-family women students means that they are encountering universities with less funding for the very services they need to develop their university experience to facilitate the transition to careers. In this research we are concerned with how it actually works that many students in this group reach the landmark of graduation with no plans and few prospects for careers. We also want to understand what makes it possible for other students to build career planning into their university experiences.

The University to Career Transition

Much of the considerable body of literature on the university-to-career transition builds in a **human capital** approach that links well with the individualized, free choice model of rational decision-making that characterizes policy discussions. Individuals are seen as possessing equal awareness and abilities to assess the full range of opportunities. Sociological research using large databases, on the other hand, is able to discern socially structured pathways such as class, gender, race, and geographic location that shape young people's transition experiences. The first approach emphasizes agency, the second structure. Recent work has sought to link agency and structure to gain a deeper understanding of the university and transition experiences of specific groups of 'non-traditional students'.

The method of **Institutional Ethnography** (Smith 1999) is used to investigate how what the women say and do in their everyday lives and experiences is shaped and organized for them in their encounters with the range of institutional supports in building their university experience. We want to see how they talk about the local, everyday actualities of moving through university experience, thus breaking out of the 'rational decision making model' and the socially structured pathways to see how it actually works when some make a clear transition to career and others don't. In this phase of our research, which this paper presents, we have conducted 17 in-depth interviews and numerous follow up discussions with undergraduate and graduate students at three New Brunswick universities and interviews with professionals in student services at two of the schools.

We are beginning to see that the organization— a wide range of institutional supports—is not neutral and generalized: it embodies the social inequalities pervasive in society. Students coming from families with a high level of organizational literacy (Darville, 1995) have an awareness of the connectedness of university experience to career development. Organizational literacy 'in, for example, job applications, legal documents, and union contracts, is concerned with effecting organizational process . . . with the ways that experience is managed, ordered, regulated and controlled' (Darville, 1995: 254). Such students are in a better position to tap the institutional supports for careers throughout the university experience.

Students who are first-in-the-family attendees, on the other hand, are less familiar with how to operate in an organizational context that requires a grasp of how careers are organized in a textual medium. The following two narrative summaries display how university does not provide the essential supports for these students.

First, let's consider 'Joanne's' university experience, that is, the experience of a student whose parents attended university. The organizational structure that accomplishes the link between higher education and specific careers is no mystery to Joanne. It is constantly present in her family; her mother is a teacher and her father, who also went to university, works in IT at the Local University. Moreover, her transition skills have been honed over a lifetime of family coaching on the purpose of education. Joanne' graduated from high school in the academic stream as an 'A' student and was accepted to the university of her choice, where her father works. Her family continued to provide numerous material supports while she attended university: room and board, tuition, career advice, etc. She was an English major, but when she found the marking practices in that department to be 'brutal' and was unable to get the good grades she would need to qualify for post-graduate studies, she transferred to History. But she didn't just randomly select History one day. She first met with the department chair for academic counselling. In other words, she searched for a major where she would do well and get the good grades to facilitate further studies toward a teaching career. Every summer she found employment working with children and gaining the teaching experience that would contribute to her résumé. She researched teacher training programs early, and to further enhance her chances of getting into that program, she identified an exchange program that allowed her to spend her fourth year at the university that provided that particular course. In the end, Joanne was one of the few young women accepted right out of her BA into that Bachelor of Education program. She exemplifies how students who are prepared to benefit from the process of undergraduate studies are able to apply it to a future career.

In contrast, 'Heather' had a lack of career planning skills. Heather is one of the first-in-the-family students for whom the career process remains largely invisible; the university has not been able to make this a topic that students can see they have to address. Heather's manner of looking for career information does not put her in touch with either institutional supports or student services. Her two visits to a student advisor, for example, were to address basic survival issues on the way to graduation—how to register late and whether she met the requirements for graduation.

As for many young people in rural areas, where the range of jobs is limited, one of Heather's early career plans was to join the military or the RCMP. Indeed, she took the first test but failed and 'just never bothered to go back and do it again'. Still, the idea of law enforcement as a career remained with her throughout her first three years of university. It played a part in where she went to university, in the selection of her major and minor, and in how she thinks about a future career as a crime scene investigator.

Once at university, she had limited encounters with institutional supports. For instance, she never went to see the faculty advisor. Her isolation was a particular problem during her third year when she nearly missed registration; she learned it was underway from another student. During this time, she worked four days a week while carrying a full course load. From the beginning of her university experience, she was highly dependent upon word-of-mouth communication from other students and people in her community who went to Big City University.

Conclusion

We can see a clear difference between students who understand what a BA is and how it is organized in relation to a career process and those who do not. For many first-in-the-family students in New Brunswick, the university-to-career transition remains invisible. When administrators speak in parent information sessions or when student advisors talk about the Bachelor of Arts as a universal degree that will prepare students for a list of jobs, these students still remain outside the organizational procedures that accomplish the translation of degree to job. Omitted is the context, for example, of the New Brunswick labour market, where a limited range of professional and entry-level managerial careers are represented and there are few such jobs available.

Universities are not set up to meet the specific needs of many small town, rural women from working class backgrounds. These young people have few organizational literacy skills that would allow them to manoeuvre through the university-to-career transition. If first-in-the-family women students had greater access to the transitional process, it would be possible for them to situate themselves differently in the early stages of the university experience. Our research suggests that it would be beneficial if an emphasis on the transitional experience began early—at the very least during student orientation—and was continued throughout the first year and beyond.

References

Darville, R. 1995. 'Literacy, Experience, Power', in *Knowledge, Experience, and Ruling Relations: Studies in the Social Organization of Knowledge*, M. Campbell and A. Manicom, eds. Toronto: University of Toronto Press.

Smith, D.E. 1999. *Writing the Social: Critique, Theory and Investigations*. Toronto: University of Toronto Press.

CHAPTER 29

Academic Paths, Aging, and the Living Conditions of Students in the Late Twentieth Century

Arnaud Sales, Réjean Drolet, and Isabelle Bonneau

Student life is profoundly marked by the diversity of individual trajectories, which are in stark contrast with the linear path traditionally taken by students. The impact on the age of the student population is significant: indeed, student life can no longer be qualified as strictly for the young. Between the ages of 20 and 30 years, different imperatives come into play in terms of living conditions and lifestyle. These imperatives are not always compatible with the conditions of classic student life. This study of the academic paths and the financial situation of Quebec university students shows how the disconnection between student condition and youth occurs and how this disconnection impacts the differentiation of student's living conditions and modes of financing university studies.

In the collective imagination, the student condition is traditionally associated with youthfulness. In Canada, and more specifically in Quebec, the way university studies are carried out and the timing of studies as adopted by many individuals within the framework of the institutional rules and practices of the universities have progressively resulted in a relative disconnection from the traditional student condition/youth link. The student population is getting older. In fact, an increase in the proportion of students over 25 years of age has been observed with regard to full-time students: in Canada, the proportion of students aged 18–21 years dropped between 1980 and 1993 from 54.57 per cent to 47.91 per cent, and to as low as 38.4 per cent in our Quebec student sample. On the other hand, the numbers in all age groups 22 years and over have increased, and the 25-years-and-over group now represents 25 per cent of the student

population in Canada and 31 per cent in Quebec. In this chapter, we will show how the disconnection between student condition and youth comes about by examining the individual micro-actions which determine academic paths and how this disconnection impacts the differentiation of students' living conditions, in particular from the perspective of modes of financing for university studies.

The Extension of Youth and the Jumbling of the Stages of Life

The redistribution of age classes within the student population can be interpreted, first of all, from the perspective developed by Cavalli and Galland (1993) with regard to the extension of youth. Under a 'translational logic', this phenomenon pushes forward the 'thresholds of entry into adult life' to a more advanced age (Galland, 1996: 41). Two of the four main movements at the source of the extension of youth theory certainly play a role in the aging of the student population: (1) prolongation of studies which, in principle, postpones the age of entry into the job market; and (2) a more difficult insertion into the job market for young people, due to the impact of unemployment and the casualization of labour.

With regard to (1), it is obvious that the considerable development of graduate programs at the master's and doctoral levels implies admitting older students than in the undergraduate programs. Indeed, the number of students at the master's level increased by a factor of 1.6, and at the doctoral level by 2.25, between 1980 and 1993. What are the consequences of this on the age of the student population? The extension of youth

Table 29.1 Average and Median Age by Level of Study and Student Status, Quebec, Autumn 1994

| Study Level | Full-time | | | Part-time | | | Total | | |
	Age Mean	Age Median	N	Age Mean	Age Median	N	Age Mean	Age Median	N
Undergraduate	23.1	22.0	1,499	30.4	27.0	297	24.3	22.0	1,795
Master's	28.5	26.0	283	36.9	36.0	167	31.6	29.0	450
Doctoral	32.5	31.0	128	42.7	44.0	12	33.3	32.0	140
Total	24.5	22.0	1,910	33.0	31.0	476	26.2	23.0	2,385

hypothesis and its translational logic correlate to imply linearity and continuity of academic paths. We must therefore define the requirements of a model linear trajectory, examine how individual academic paths are adjusted in relation to this model, calculate the proportion of students following or not following this model, and draw conclusions as to the consequences of the types of paths chosen on the age of the student population. However, the extension of youth hypothesis cannot, a priori, account for the fact that the average age of full-time students is 23.1 years in undergraduate programs, 28.5 years in master's programs, and 32.5 years in doctoral programs (see Table 29.1). If the prolongation of studies was the only factor involved, the radical changes in living conditions would not be observed because the effects of age would be limited.

With regard to (2), it should be noted that students differ in several ways from other young people who do not go on to university studies. While it is more difficult today than at the beginning of the 1980s, the professional insertion of university graduates in full-time or permanent jobs is much easier than for other young people (Sales, 1998, 2001; Audet, 1995). The extension of youth hypothesis with its translational logic correlate regarding the thresholds of entry into adult life seems, a priori, to apply only partially to students. What might be a more productive hypothesis is the idea of desynchronization and complexification in the ordering and arrangements of these thresholds so that their structural organization is modified under

the effect of individual behaviors and institutions (Galland, 1996: 41). The traditional model of entry into adult life, characterized by the relative synchronization of living with one's parents and studying, then living as a couple and working, has given way to more varied and often more complex paths, especially for students. From this, the aging of the student population could be considered not solely as a result of the extension of youth, but much more as a result of the 'jumbling of the stages of life' (Attias-Donfut, 1996: 16)—the mechanisms of which need to be understood.

Academic Paths and the Aging of the Student Population

To first understand the disconnection between student condition and youth, we examined academic paths and their effect on the age of the student population, based on the aggregate of individual micro-actions which are embedded in the personal logics of their lives and supported by aptitudes, motivations, orientations, and living conditions linked or not linked to family or professional contexts. These micro-actions cannot, however, be disassociated from the institutional context in which they are carried out, especially university regulations, nor from, it is also probable, the models of behaviour adopted by the student milieu within a specific institution. Indeed, universities differ with regard to the linearity of the academic paths of their students (see Sales, Drolet, and Simard, 1997).

Academic Paths of Students in Undergraduate Programs

In order to understand how approaches to studies impact the academic paths and the age of students, we defined the requirements of a model linear path, the most direct path that a student can follow from his or her initial registration in CEGEP to the completion of university studies. We then compared the paths of full-time students holding a general DEC to this model, taking into consideration each of the requirements. From the outset, we note that three quarters of the students in their third year respected the normal rhythm of studies for the bachelor's program in which they were registered. However, when the requirements inherent to a linear academic path were integrated into the analysis, we noted that this proportion decreased. Respecting the prescribed rhythm of studies for a bachelor's program, without any prior interruption, except for summer sessions (first requirement) only holds for 68.9 per cent of third-year students. This is due to the fact that even if a student respects the prescribed time limit for completing the current program, it does not mean that he or she never interrupted his or her university studies. For example, a student could have done a certificate program, then worked for a year before registering in the current program. If we consider students who have never changed programs (second requirement), the proportion decreases to 62.5 per cent. When the two requirements (1 and 2) are taken into consideration together, the proportion decreases very slightly from 62.5 per cent to 62 per cent. This minimal shift simply indicates that almost all the students who changed programs also interrupted their studies at least once. The accumulation of these short breaks and delays as of their initial registration at university means that about 40 per cent of students in their third year of a bachelor's program did not respect the three conditions of a linear academic path, that is, completing the program within the prescribed time limit, without a program change, and without an interruption of studies.

Conclusion

In this article we have underscored the fact that university studies are no longer the privilege of youth and in fact, students 20-years-old and younger are a minority when the student population is looked at in its entirety. The continuation of university studies at the graduate levels, which fits into the extension of youth general phenomenon, is not enough to explain the trend of an aging student population today, which stems more from a jumbling of the stages of life by the desynchronization of the thresholds of entry into adulthood. We therefore sought to understand this aging of the student population by analyzing the academic paths adopted by a sampling of students on the basis of micro-decisions such as the choice of student status, the extension of the duration of studies by assuming a lighter course load, reorientation into another discipline, interruption of studies, especially between levels, and of course, adults returning to the classroom. This has resulted in very diversified academic paths breaking with the traditional linear and uniform progression of studies previously practiced. For several reasons, the most important being economic (the desire to obtain a job, financial problems, and so on), a considerable portion of students attends university according to their own temporality. This has a major impact on the average age of the student population, so much so that the student condition can no longer be defined as being strictly an experience of youth.

References

Attias-Donfut, C. 1996. 'Jeunesse et Conjugaison des Temps', *Sociologie et Sociétés* XXVIII, 1: 13–22.

Audet, M. 1995. *Qu'advient-il des Diplômés des Universités? La Promotion de 1992, 19 Secteurs, 128 Disciplines.* Quebec: Les Publications du Québec.

Cavalli, A., and O. Galland, eds. 1993. *L'allongement de la jeunesse.* Arles: Actes Sud.

Galland, O. 1996. 'L'entrée dans la Vie Adulte en France. Bilan et Perspectives *Sociologiques', Sociologie et Sociétés* XXVIII, 1: 37–46.

Sales, A. 1998. 'The New Challenges of the Employment Markets of Knowledge Workers', Paper presented at the 10th International Conference of Socio-Economics, Research Network on Knowledge, Economy and Society of The Society for the Advancement of Socio-Economics. Vienna, Austria, July. Published in 2001 in Spanish under the title 'Desafíos del mercado de empleo para los trabajadores del conocimiento', in *Universidad, Sector Productivo y Sustentabilidad*, Miguel Ángel Briceño Gil, ed. Caracas: Universidad Central de Venezuela Press.

Sales, A., R. Drolet, and G. Simard. 1997. 'La Différenciation de la Population Universitaire au Québec'. Report submitted to the Ministère de l'Éducation du Québec. Montreal.

Wu, Z. 1999. 'Premarital Cohabitation and the Timing of First Marriage', *Canadian Review of Sociology and Anthropology* 36, 1: 109–27.

Questions for Critical Thought

ACTIVITIES AND INTERDEPENDENCIES IN THE EDUCATIONAL PROCESS: AN INTERACTIONIST APPROACH TO STUDENT VENTURES IN LEARNING

1. What views might students assume in the learning process? How do these differing perspectives relate to people's abilities to comprehend, learn, remember, retain, or otherwise use the matters learned in class?

2. How important is background preparation (stocks of knowledge, fluency with concepts, familiarity with procedures) for specific courses? What does this suggest about students who are passed to the next grade without a sufficient base at earlier levels?

3. In what ways might students intentionally and unintentionally disrupt the learning process for others and/or themselves? What things might make it more unlikely that people will develop a more sustained interest in learning?

4. How do students tell if they are doing a good job or making progress in learning class-related materials? Of what value is learning that does not show up on grades on people's tests and assignments or report cards?

5. Is there a more general 'character of learning' that some students develop more than others? If so, how might students pursuing learning acquire characters of these sorts?

POLITE, WELL-DRESSED, AND ON TIME: SECONDARY SCHOOL CONDUCT CODES AND THE PRODUCTION OF DOCILE CITIZENS

1. In what ways do the Toronto and Niagara school boards' codes of conduct influence the idea of citizenship, the level of restraint and docility amongst students, and a student's preparedness for future careers?

2. Sociologist Robert Merton described manifest and latent functions in society. (A manifest function is a function that is obvious, for example, the military defends the nation. A latent function is a function that is unrecognized or unintended, for example; the military creates new jobs in certain industries.) Describe the manifest and latent functions of the Toronto and Niagara school boards Code of Conduct.

3. How might someone's past experience, ethnicity, or socio-economic status serve as a disadvantage in school as a result of the code of conduct?
4. How does a vague dress code affect the ways women perceive themselves?
5. What amendments would you make to the school boards' code of conduct so that students have an optimal learning and socialization experience?

CRAFTING LEGITIMATION PROJECTS: AN INSTITUTIONAL ANALYSIS OF PRIVATE EDUCATION BUSINESSES

1. How do schools resolve the contradictions in their myth-making?
2. How do private education businesses craft their legitimation projects to resonate with wider understandings of social reality?
3. How do myth-making, coupling, and the logic-of-confidence influence legitimation projects?
4. Does the private status of tutoring businesses entail potentially different legitimation projects than traditional (public) schooling structures?
5. If private education businesses fail to adhere to education standards, how do they garner public confidence?

UNIVERSITY RESTRUCTURING AND THE FEMALE LIBERAL ARTS UNDERGRADUATE STUDENT: DOES SHE GET 'VALUE FOR THE MONEY' AT CORPORATE U?

1. What are the main challenges for first-in-the-family women during the transition from university to careers?
2. How does a person's organizational literacy demonstrate that educational institutions are not neutral and generalized? What does a person's organizational literacy indicate about social equality?
3. What type of socially structured pathways shape young people's university-to-career transition? Why are these socially structured pathways so significant?
4. The narratives of Joanne and Heather demonstrate a disparity between class and advantage-level that is the product of socialization in the home environment, among other factors. What additional challenges can you think of that Heather might face in the university-to-career transition?
5. Suggest ways that learning institutions can help first-in-the-family women acquire greater capacity to handle the university to career transition.

ACADEMIC PATHS, AGING, AND THE LIVING CONDITIONS OF STUDENTS IN THE LATE TWENTIETH CENTURY

1. What two examples of youth theory play a role in the aging of the student population?
2. What shortcomings are there with the extension of youth hypothesis? What alternative model does the author suggest using to understand the increasing age of university students?
3. In addition to observing the micro-actions of individuals, why is it also important to observe the institutional role of universities as it relates to the increasing age of the student population?
4. What relationship exists between strict academic paths and the amount of student compliance?
5. How might other social trends change as a result of an increasingly older student population?

Part VII

Work

Most people have to work to gain the necessities of life. The four general economic sectors of employment are primary and resource, manufacturing, service, and social reproduction. As dramatic changes in the state of these sectors have occurred throughout Canadian history, sociology's understanding of both work and the workplace has continued to evolve.

For most, work life, like family life, is a social context where macrosociological processes meet microsociological experiences. We all know something about work, whether from first-hand experience or the accounts others provide us. Working together in large numbers, we create goods and services, earn a wage for ourselves, and produce a profit for the company. The daily work routine is so common that people who break the pattern seem abnormal. No wonder so many unemployed and retired people feel like outsiders to the 'real' business of society.

It is at work that we experience control or freedom from control, social integration or isolation. We form unions or associations to look after our interests; in this way we develop a sense of ourselves as workers, managers, or employers. In the end, our job identity is a key part of our social selves. Evident in the essays in this section, research on the sociology of work is increasingly concerned with new occupations and the relationship between work and 'new technology'.

For example, Margrit Eichler and Ann Matthews criticize the neglect with which sociological dialogue on work has treated unpaid work. They then explore the distinction some people make between unpaid work and what they consider 'real work', and the effect this distinction has on social policy. For her part, Alexandra Marin documents the processes of social capital transfers of job availability information. Her study finds the flow of information from network information-holders to be structured by both their knowledge and motivations.

With the arrival of computer-mediated communication, sociologists have studied how this new technology affects workplace relations. Anabel Quan-Haase addresses the impact of computer-mediated communication on work interactions, communities, and trust in organizations.

Antonie Scholtz and David W. Livingstone, for their part, re-examine the knowledge-based economy advocates' claims that knowledge leads to greater employee decision-making power in the workplace, and that there is a shortage of skilled workers. They find that existing power dynamics in the workplace are still similar to those in the past.

These studies all show there has been much change in the definitions and dynamics of work. However, the studies also note how much remains the same, and how working life affects employees and social policy in general.

CHAPTER 30

What is Work? Looking at All Work through the Lens of Unpaid Housework

Margrit Eichler and Ann Matthews

Introduction

Without any doubt, work is one of the most important topics in sociology. But what is work? Various sociological dictionaries define work in a manner that includes paid work as well as unpaid housework, only to proceed to immediately exclude the latter from consideration (Nolan, 1993; Marshall, 1998; Johnson, 2000). Reskin (2000), for instance, suggests:

> Although the term 'work' generally is used to denote the exertion of effort toward some end, economically it refers to activities oriented toward producing goods and services for one's own use or for pay. The conception of work as a means of generating income underlies most sociological scholarship on work and most of the available statistics. Unpaid productive work, including that done in the home (indeed, homemaking is the largest occupation in the United States) and volunteer work, tends to be invisible. This article focuses primarily on paid work (3261).

The sociology of work, likewise, focuses on paid work. Unpaid housework and care work, though not entirely ignored, are circumscribed in a particular way. Discussion focuses on the movement of women into paid work and the effect this has on home life (Abbot, 1993; MacBride-King and Paris, 1993; Neuman, 1995; Valente, 1995; Auster, 1996). Thus, unpaid housework is formally acknowledged as work but, in fact, not considered relevant in the discussion of work—a neglect with a long history (Eichler, 1978).

Housework has been explored as a specific type of work (Lopata, 1971; Oakley, 1974, 1990; Eichler, Guppy, and Siltanen, 1977; Luxton, 1980, 1997; Hochschild, 1989; DeVault, 1991; Shelton and John, 1996). The majority of sociological studies use a list of concrete and specific housekeeping tasks that focus on such things as preparing meals, cleaning, going shopping, etc. Childcare may or may not be included in these lists. (It is for this reason that we talk consistently about housework and care work together.) The lists typically do not include the cognitive and planning work and the time management that lie behind these concrete and very mundane tasks (Hessing, 1994). **Feminist scholars** have argued for decades that unpaid housework and care work is real work by pointing out parallels between paid work and unpaid work. In this paper, we do the opposite: starting with unpaid housework and care work, we explore what makes some activities work and others not for our respondents.

The Study

The project on Unpaid Housework and Lifelong Learning is part of a large-scale study on Work and Lifelong Learning (WALL). A description of the complete project can be found on WALL's website at http://wall.oise.utoronto.ca/. The unpaid housework study consists of four phases. At the time of writing this paper, we have completed the data collection for phases 1 and 2. The first phase involved sending **questionnaires** to members of various women's groups, asking about the nature of their unpaid housework and community work and the learning attached to it. The second phase involved 11 **focus groups** that followed up on some of the findings of the questionnaires. In this paper, we draw primarily on the focus groups.

We posed eight questions in the focus groups. We asked participants to list some of the unpaid housework and care work they normally did, and received. As expected, the tasks listed were similar to those identified in the literature. We then asked: 'Did you do any of the following tasks: provide emotional support; organize, plan, manage or arrange matters; deal with crises; maintain contact with family members or friends; take care of yourself; resolve conflicts?' Without exception, people in each of the groups would agree that this was what they did. One participant exclaimed spontaneously 'This is my life!' while the others in the group nodded and agreed verbally. We discussed in some detail the ways in which people engaged with these tasks, and then discussed whether or not this constituted work and why or why not.

Definitions of Work

There were five distinct conceptions of work that emerged from the 11 groups. These are not mutually exclusive definitions. Instead, they represent conceptions of work that draw the boundaries differently in each case, including and excluding different sets of activities and utilizing different rationales:

a) the conventional definition (activities that are paid are work);

b) the extended conventional definition (activities are work if they either could be paid or are directly related to paid work, even though unpaid);

c) the goal achievement definition (purposeful activities that are oriented towards achieving some goal without being enjoyable at the moment);

d) the social coercion definition (activities that are unpleasant, would not be done by choice, but must be done); and

e) the energy expenditure definition (any activity that requires energy and effort is work).

The energy definition jives with that given in various social science dictionaries and encyclopedias (Nolan, 1993; Marshall, 1998; Reskin, 2000). The difference, of course, is that they then proceed to ignore the unpaid dimension of it, while in the focus groups the whole discussion centered on this type of work.

WHAT IS NOT WORK?

What is perceived as not-work is clearly contingent on one's definition of work. If the definition of work is that it is paid or that it supports paid work, then activities that are not paid and do not support paid work are not work (the conventional and expanded conventional definitions). If activities are defined as work if they are directed towards achieving a specific goal, then those activities which are engaged in because of immediate gratification, where the activity itself is the goal, are not work (the goal-achievement definition). If work is defined as undesired activities that are engaged in because of some external or internal constraint, those activities that are freely chosen are defined as not-work (the social coercion definition). And finally, if work is defined as energy expenditure, then those activities that regenerate our energies are defined as not-work (the energy expenditure definition).

While respondents varied in their conceptions of what constituted work, two criteria were accepted by most of them: First, for whom the work was performed. Though not consistent among all respondents, a dividing line was drawn between self-care and care for others. Secondly, it became abundantly clear in the focus groups that it is not the activity per se that determines whether an activity is perceived as work or not, but the conditions under which it is performed. Whatever the definition of work employed, the vast majority of participants did regard unpaid housework and care work as work and not as non-work or leisure.

Consequences of the Definitions of Work

Definitions are not right or wrong—they are useful or useless. The definitions generated by the focus groups open up new questions and new perspectives on old questions about work. When the sociology of work considers only one slice of the total work performed and unpaid housework is ignored, we cannot adequately assess the effect of various policies. For instance, the Canadian health system is currently being squeezed in terms of money and available staff, with the effect that patients are discharged to their homes much earlier than used to be the case. This results in a steep increase in the intensity of the unpaid care work performed by family and friends. A decrease in paid work leads to a direct increase in unpaid work. This should be factored into policy decisions. Similarly, we found in our questionnaires that mothers of young children engaged in an astonishing amount of so-called voluntary labour on behalf of their children's schools.

Conclusion

The energy expenditure definition is put forward by the sociology of work but promptly forgotten in any discussions. Yet, this definition was important to our focus group participants. What would happen if we were to take it seriously? If we define work as energy expenditure towards a particular goal, the line between paid and unpaid work would not disappear, but would lose a fair amount of its significance. We would routinely look at all work performed by people, rather than just one segment, and consider all work of equal relevance for understanding how societies work. Energy expenditure raises the question of energy regeneration. Energy may be expended—and re-generated—through either paid and/or unpaid work or neither, depending on the nature of the work and the circumstances under which it is performed. Furthermore, energy depletion and regeneration would suggest that we should look at the sustainability of our work environments (paid and unpaid). We could also take into account the variable amounts of energy that are available to specific groups of people. People with disabilities, for instance, have long argued that we may have to re-define what counts as full-time work for particular subgroups. Such an approach would also let us integrate an equity concern. It takes energy to deflect discrimination on the basis of race, age, sex, disability, etc. Taking the energy expenditure definition of work seriously would encourage us to ask some interesting, important, and innovative new questions.

References

Abbot, A. 1993. 'The Sociology of Work and Occupations', *Annual Review of Sociology* 19: 187–209.

Auster, C.J. 1996. *The Sociology of Work: Concepts and Cases*. Thousand Oaks, CA: Pine Forge Press.

DeVault, M.L. 1991. *Feeding the Family: The Social Organization of Caring as Gendered Work*. Chicago: University of Chicago Press.

Eichler, M. 1978. 'Women's Unpaid Labour', *Atlantis* 3, 2: 52–62.

Eichler, M., N. Guppy, N., and J. Siltanen. 1977. 'The Prestige of the Occupation Housewife', in *The Working Sexes*, pp. 151–75, P. Marchak, ed. Vancouver: UBC Institute for Industrial Relations.

Hessing, M. 1994. 'More than Clockwork: Women's Time Management in their Combined Workloads', *Sociological Perspectives* 37, 4: 631–3.

Hochschild, A. 1989. *The Second Shift: Working Parents and the Revolution at Home*. New York: Viking.

Johnson, A.G. 2000. *The Blackwell Dictionary of Sociology: A User's Guide to Sociological Language*, 2nd ed. Oxford, UK: Blackwell Publishers.

Lopata, H.Z. 1971. *Occupation: Housewife*. Oxford: Oxford University Press.

Luxton, M. 1997. 'The UN, Women, and Household Labour: Measuring and Valuing Unpaid Work', *Women's Studies International Forum* 20, 3: 431–9.

———. 1980. *More than a Labour of Love: Three Generations of Women's Work in the Home*. Toronto: Women's Press.

MacBride-King, J., and H. Paris. 1993. 'Balancing Work and Family Responsibilities', in *Work in Canada: Readings in the Sociology of Work and Industry*, pp. 53–9, G.S. Lowe and H.J. Krahn, eds. Scarborough, ON: Nelson Canada.

Marshall, G. 1998. 'Work', in *Oxford Dictionary of Sociology*, New ed., pp. 706, G. Marshall, ed. Oxford: Oxford University Press.

Neuman, E. 1995. 'Stay-at-home Mothers Benefit Families', in *Work: Opposing Viewpoints*, pp. 278–85, D. Bender and B. Leone, eds. San Diego, CA: Greenhaven Press.

Nolan, P. 1993. 'Work', in *The Blackwell Dictionary of Twentieth-century Social Thought*, pp. 715–17, W. Outhwaite and T. Bottomore, eds. Oxford: Blackwell Publishers.

Oakley, A. 1974. *The Sociology of Housework*. New York: Pantheon Books.

———. 1990. 'What is a Housewife', in *British Feminist Thought*, pp. 134–50, T. Lovell, ed. Oxford: Basic Blackwell.

Reskin, B.F. 2000. 'Work and Occupations', in *Encyclopedia of Sociology*, 2nd ed., pp. 3261–9, E.F. Borgatta and R.J.V. Montgomery, eds. New York: Macmillan Reference USA.

Shelton, B.A., and D. John. 1996. 'The Division of Household Labor', *Annual Review of Sociology* 22: 299–322.

Valente, J. 1995. 'Working Mothers Benefit Families', in *Work: Opposing Viewpoints*, pp. 278–85, D. Bender and B. Leone, eds. San Diego, CA: Greenhaven Press.

CHAPTER 31

How Job Information Enters and Flows through Social Networks: The Role of Labour Market Characteristics and Tie Strength

Alexandra Marin

Theories of **social capital** contend that individuals and groups benefit from social networks that allow access to resources that others control. My research examines the processes involved in such transfers of resources, stressing the agency of the parties involved. My premise is that three nested sets of resources constitute social capital: the 'latent resources' controlled by a person's contacts, the 'available resources' to which contacts permit access, and the 'accessed resources' actually activated via contacts. Existing social capital research focuses on the existence and consequences of each kind of social capital and neglects the processes through which social capital is created and transformed from latent resources into available and accessed resources.

I examine these neglected processes empirically in the substantive setting of job searches, focusing on informational resources. I conducted interviews with both information holders and job seekers in the market for entry-level white collar work in Toronto. The portion of my research discussed here is based on data from in-depth interviews with 37 insurance agents employed in a Toronto call centre. Interviews focus on these respondents as information holders who sometimes know of job openings and who might sometimes share this information with job seekers. I examine how they learn about job openings, how they determine who might be interested in those openings, and how they decide whether or not to share information about openings. In the interest of brevity, I omit here the supporting quotes from interviews that are included in the full version of this paper.

Getting In-the-Know

I asked each respondent to list job openings that they had known of in the past year and to explain how they had learned of each. All respondents had known of job openings in the past year, and particularly of openings in the insurance company that employed them or the bank that was its parent company. Information holders learn of job openings through three primary methods. First, they encounter them in the course of their own job searches, which most respondents conduct, though some more actively than others. Second, some learn of openings because they actively solicit job information on behalf of their job-hunting network members. Finally, almost all occasionally learn of openings by some method of passive reception—noticing a sign or advertisement, receiving an unsolicited email, or hearing an opening mentioned in conversation.

Passive reception of job information is common among these information holders. Most commonly they receive information through emails from their own human resources department or from lunchroom gossip about openings for similar jobs at competing insurance companies or banks. These jobs are similar to the positions the information holders currently occupy.

While many information holders also passively learn of other kinds of jobs, my interviews suggest that these openings are not often noted and are effectively forgotten immediately after they are encountered. Respondents remember jobs when they are interested in the jobs for themselves or when they can mentally link the job to a network member. To the extent that information holders do not retain information about some jobs, this information is not at risk of being available or accessed by their network members, and therefore does not constitute a latent resource. Therefore, the existence of latent information in the network

depends on information holders who are not only exposed to information but who retain it.

Getting the Word Out

While information holders have not often been studied directly, research that has considered their motivation has focused on their pre-screening behaviour, testing the hypothesis that information-holders pre-screen potential applicants and withhold information from those who they believe will perform poorly and damage the referer's reputation. While respondents did allude to concerns about their reputation when providing referrals, this is not the primary factor they take into account. Further, respondents are more likely to say that they would refer someone because they believe the person would not damage their reputation than to report declining to refer someone who they believe would do damage.

A more salient factor when determining whether or not to refer someone is information holders' reluctance to share job information that network members might not want. Information holders are reluctant to provide information about jobs unless they believe that the person would be interested in that particular job. They fear appearing intrusive if they suggest a career area not already being actively considered, or being insulting if they suggest a lower-status job than the job-seeker had in mind. As a result information holders report, even when they believe one of their network members may be suitable for a job, that they would not mention the job unless the person asked for information or had specialized training or clear interest in the particular kind of job.

Labour Market Characteristics and the Role of Tie Strength

I have argued that information holders are more likely to retain information about job openings when they are interested in pursuing the jobs or when they know someone who they can mentally tie to the opening. I have also argued that information holders are reluctant to pass information to network members who they do not know to be interested in similar jobs. The key variable that affects information flow in both cases is the information holders' understanding of their network members' information needs. The likelihood that information holders have this understanding depends on the strength of their tie to job-seekers and the kind of labour markets in which job seekers sought employment.

In **open labour markets** credentials and job requirements are loosely linked and jobs are open to people with assorted qualifications. Because there is no obvious required credential, there are no obviously ideal candidates. As a result network members are not likely to come immediately to mind when information holders learn of these jobs, and information about these jobs is consequently less likely to be retained. Furthermore, because the people who are qualified for these jobs are also qualified for a variety of other jobs, information holders are not able to accurately evaluate whether or not a particular person would be interested in a particular job. Information holders are less likely to share information under these circumstances because they cannot be sure the information will be welcome.

However, both of these obstacles to information-flow in open labour markets are partially removed when information holders deal with their strong ties. Information holders are more willing to risk providing unsolicited career advice to strong ties because closer relationships allow them to take some liberties. Also, information holders have greater knowledge of their strong ties' career intentions and therefore less cause to worry that they will inadvertently provide unwelcome information. This greater knowledge also makes it more likely that information holders will link information that they encounter to these network members and therefore retain the information.

In **closed labour markets** credentials and job requirements are more tightly linked. Jobs require specialized credentials or training and job-seekers have qualifications that are useful to them in a nar-

row field of jobs. In these markets, information holders with even superficial knowledge of the job and the applicant can more easily evaluate the fit between them. Job requirements are more obvious and network members with those requirements are more likely to be linked to job information, increasing the likelihood that this information will be retained. In addition, information holders are more willing to share information because they can be more certain that the information will be appropriate and therefore welcome or at least inoffensive.

Searching in closed labour markets advantages weak ties, but it does not disadvantage strong ties who are still the most likely to be informed of jobs for which they are suitable. However, because the pool of qualified applicants for these jobs is more restricted, information holders are more likely to find a qualified network member among their more diverse weak ties than among a smaller group of strong ties. This is especially the case when information holders know of jobs related to their own work where the network members most likely to be qualified are work-related ties with whom they may not be close.

Conclusion

I find that the flow of information from these information holders is structured and that this structure is shaped by information holders knowledge and motivations. Their understanding of their network members' needs influences the information they retain and can subsequently disseminate. Their reluctance to risk awkwardness by providing inappropriate information results in different kinds of job information flowing towards different segments of their networks. This is one of the first studies of social capital to directly study the network members who provide resources in addition to the network members who benefit from them (see also Flap and Boxman, 2001). The findings suggest that this approach will be fruitful in gaining a more detailed and empirically-informed understanding of how resources flow through social networks.

References

Flap, H., and E. Boxman. 2001. 'Getting Started: The Influence of Social Capital on the Start of the Occupational Career', in *Social Capital: Theory and Research*, N. Lin, K. Cook, and R.S. Burt, eds. New York: Aldine de Gruyter.

Lin, N. 2001. *Social Capital: A Theory of Social Structure and Action*. Cambridge: Cambridge University Press.

Lin, N., J.C. Vaughn, and W.M. Ensel. 1981. 'Social Resources and Occupational Status Attainment', *Social Forces* 59, 4: 1163–81.

CHAPTER 32

The Use of Communication Media: A Case Study of a High-Tech Organization

Anabel Quan-Haase

Working in an Internet Era Organization

Computer-mediated communication, for example, e-mail and instant messaging, has become an essential element of many organizations. The Internet and internal Intranets have the ability to link everyone in an organization, from managers to professionals to line workers (Sproull and Kiesler, 1991). This type of communication media provides speed, flexibility, and connectivity. But, how do workers use computer-mediated communication? What media are used to communicate with workers within a group? And, are different media used to communicate with workers outside the organization? For what purposes are computer-mediated communication used? How does computer-mediated communication change the nature of relations that link workers? Or, are relations between workers unchanged?

There is little evidence in the literature demonstrating how computer-mediated communication is used in work settings and how it affects work relations. In order to address this gap, a case study of media use in a medium-sized high-tech firm was conducted to learn more about how computer-mediated communication affects interactions, community, and trust in organizations. A high-tech firm of knowledge workers was analyzed because its technologically savvy employees routinely use computer-mediated communication. The firm shall be referred to as Knowledge Media Enterprises (KME), a pseudonym.

Studying Employees' Uses of the Internet

To learn more about the use of computer-mediated communication at KME and how its use affects work relations and organizational structure, we used three forms of data collection: surveys, interviews, and observations. A total of 27 departmental employees, 11 from software development and 16 from client services, took part. Participants had worked for KME an average of 28 months (range: 5–48 months). The participants' education level and positions at KME varied. This allowed us to obtain a broad **sample** within the organization. The survey gathered information regarding communication with individuals located in three settings: those within the group, those located in the wider organization, and those outside the organization. Participants were asked to report how frequently they used three types of communication media: face-to-face or telephone, e-mail, and instant messaging. Five survey participants from each department (10 in total) were interviewed, with each interview lasting approximately 45 minutes. Everyday work practices were observed in order to learn how participants managed and used computer-mediated communication, and to learn how computer-mediated communication fit into their work relationships. Observations started at 9:00 AM and concluded when the employee left the office (approximately 4:30 PM). The observations allowed for face-to-face, telephone, e-mail, and instant messaging interactions to be analyzed.

Working in a Hyperconnected Environment

We found that KME is a hyperconnected organization (Castells, 1996). **Hyperconnectivity** can be described as the availability of people for communication anywhere, anytime. Adding computer-mediated communication to face-to-face and telephone contact has resulted in workers always being available for communication. Employees can easily send an e-mail or instant message to any other member of the organization, regardless of status or role. This hyperconnectivity means new forms of collaboration or teamwork are possible.

Although a large proportion of communication is with colleagues elsewhere in KME, most communication continues to be within the work group (see Figure 32.1). Even in this high-tech organization, where employees have diverse computer-mediated communication tools available to them for **boundary-spanning communication**, they continue to exchange information primarily with other group members. This suggests communication with other colleagues in the organization has not replaced group-based communication.

Most communication in KME is done via computer-mediated communication, even if fellow workers are sitting across the hall. The high use of

computer-mediated communication within the work group is surprising given theoretical arguments maintaining that computer-mediated communication primarily supports global, boundary spanning exchanges of information while face-to-face and the telephone support local, group-based exchanges. Why would workers talk to each other via e-mail or instant messaging if they are sitting next to one another when they could just get up and walk over to their colleague's desk? We found three main reasons. First, over time, computer-mediated communication has become the expected way of communication. The implicit norms of the organization dictate that computer-mediated communication is the easiest and most appropriate way of getting in touch with others. People feel more comfortable talking to each other over e-mail and instant messaging. Second, computer-mediated communication does not interfere with others' work because they can respond to the email or instant message when it is convenient for them. Thus, it is a much more flexible form of communication. Third, e-mail and instant messaging require less time investment and effort. It takes less time to send an e-mail than it does to walk over to a colleague's desk. Often colleagues are unavailable or in a meeting and time would be wasted trying to locate them.

WHAT MEDIA ARE USED MOST OFTEN?

Figure 32.1 shows how often workers at KME use different media (Quan-Haase and Wellman, 2004). The graph shows that computer-mediated communication accounts for a large proportion of all communication within the group, elsewhere in the organization, and outside of the organization. In particular, employees use instant messaging to communicate with co-workers in the same group and elsewhere in the organization. KME's culture and fast-paced environment emphasizes using instant messaging. It takes priority over e-mail, face-to-face conversation, and the telephone. This is not only a matter of individual discretion, but also an important organizational norm. Employees rely on instant messaging because of its speed and

Figure 32.1 Communication by Media and Distance

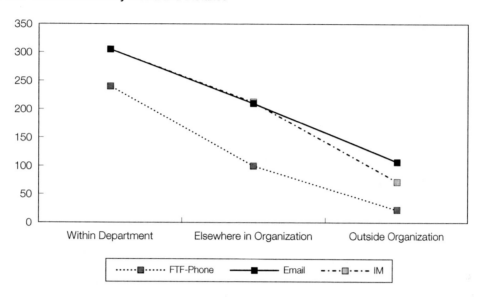

its real-time (nearly **synchronous communication**) nature. We observed that people would often prioritize instant messages. For example, during an interview, one of the employees said she needed to interrupt the conversation in order to read an instant message. She said it was something urgent and it would only take her a minute to respond. In this case, instant messaging clearly took priority over the face-to-face conversation in which she was engaged.

Communication outside the organization occurs more frequently via e-mail (103 days per year) than by face-to-face and the telephone (21 days per year). Similarly, instant messaging (72 days per year) is used more frequently than face-to-face and the telephone for communicating outside the organization. The difference between computer-mediated communication and traditional means of communication for outside communication are large: e-mail is used 4.9 times more frequently than face-to-face and the telephone, and instant messaging is used 3.4 times more frequently than face-to-face and the telephone. This is consistent with the notion that electronic networks support boundary-spanning communications at KME with customers,

partners, and users who are distributed globally. As expected, face-to-face is used less for communication outside the organization.

WHAT MEDIA ARE USED FOR WHAT PURPOSES?

KME people communicate a great deal for informing, coordinating, and collaborating. Employees use computer-mediated communication regularly as a convenient means of collaborative communication, creating a dense virtual network of exchange. Yet computer-mediated communication does not function as an independent communication system at KME. Computer-mediated communication, face-to-face contact, and the telephone serve different communication purposes and hence are not in competition with one another. For example, e-mail is used to send more detailed messages and to provide explanations. E-mails can be stored on the hard drive and thus be kept for future reference. By contrast, instant messaging is used for short communications. It serves at least 4 purposes: (1) for finding out if someone is available for communication via the telephone or to arrange to meet at a nearby coffee shop for a break or go out for lunch; (2) to get in touch with someone and see how they are doing and how their work is progressing; (3) for social purposes, for example exchanging jokes, gossip, and greetings; and (4) to send information about an e-mail that was sent earlier. Face-to-face and the telephone are used for dealing with complex problems that require extensive discussion. Employees often use the telephone or walk to their colleagues' desks to ask questions. They see such encounters as good occasions to chat and connect on a more personal level. Although there are no formal rules at KME for which media to use for communication, employees have tacitly adopted conventions about which media to use for what purposes.

Conclusion

Although computer-mediated communication provides new and alternative ways for communication that facilitates easy and effective bridging of group and organizational boundaries, most communication takes place within the work group, rather than with others in or outside the organization (Monge and Contractor, 2003). Despite the need for boundary-spanning communication and the technological ease for doing it with computer-mediated communication, the work group is still the most important source for information at KME. It is where employees find community, build friendships, and get work done. That boundary-spanning interactions did not occur at the expense of local interaction suggests groups are not a relic of the past, but constitute the central focus of communication. This suggests that boundaries of distance and group continue to constrain communication. We found that e-mail and instant messaging support communication at all distances; it is used more frequently than face-to-face and the telephone for communicating within the group, elsewhere in the organization, and outside the organization (Wellman, 2002). At KME, hyperconnectivity affords more active use of networked relationships within and between workgroups. Media are used for different purposes and thus do not compete with each other. E-mail is used for longer messages, while instant messaging is used for short exchanges.

References

Castells, M. 1996. *The Rise of the Network Society*. Cambridge, MA: Blackwell Publishers.

Monge, P.R., and N.S. Contractor. 2003. *Theories of Communication Networks*. Oxford: Oxford University Press.

Quan-Haase, A., and B. Wellman. 2004. 'Networks of Distance and Media: A Case Study of a High-tech Firm', *Analyse und Kritik* 28: 241–57.

Sproull, L.S., and S.B. Kiesler. 1991. *Connections: New Ways of Working in the Networked Organization*. Cambridge, MA: MIT Press.

Wellman, B. 2002. 'Designing the Internet for a Networked Society', *Communications of the ACM* 45, 5: 91–6.

CHAPTER 33

'Knowledge Workers' and the 'New Economy': A Critical Assessment

David W. Livingstone and Antonie Scholtz

Advocates of an emerging knowledge-based economy (KBE) claim the link between knowledge and power is growing stronger. Many employees, especially the professionals who make up a rising class of '**knowledge workers**', are alleged to be gaining unprecedented powers in the workplace. Skeptics dismiss these claims as wishful thinking in hierarchically organized **capitalist mode of production** economies. Using data from a recent national survey of learning and work, we find that current patterns of discretionary power in the labour process remain very similar to those characterizing prior periods of industrial capitalism. In contrast to KBE concerns about skill and training deficits, much greater numbers of workers, including professional employees, appear to have more job-related skill and knowledge than significant opportunities to apply them in current paid workplaces.

Head from Hand

All humans possess some capacity for logical thinking, decision-making, and abstract conceptualization (Gramsci, 1971). Within industrial capitalism, however, conception and planning have been separated from execution through the detailed division of labour. By 'scientifically' identifying and embedding workers' knowledge in the design of work and/or in machines, early industrial capitalists were able to reduce the skill necessary to perform tasks while increasing productivity (Braverman, 1974; Sohn-Rethel, 1978). However, owners have increasingly required skilled managers and professionals to run their growing organizations, and to develop and sell products (see Beniger, 1986; Schement and Curtis, 1995; Cortada, 1998).

An occupational hierarchy structured around ownership and, secondly, around a complex delegation of decisions-making power emerged. We distinguish eight major class groupings: *corporate executives, small employers, the self-employed, managers, supervisors, professional employees, service workers,* and *industrial workers* (see Livingstone and Mangan, 1996). The first three groups have historically enjoyed the most decision-making power and opportunity to use their own and others' technical skill, while industrial and service workers have been largely dispossessed of discretionary control in both respects. Managers, professionals, and supervisors have been delegated more decision-making power to carry out management's objectives, yet remain vulnerable (e.g., downsizing, outsourcing).

A New Socio-Economic Epoch?

Over the last half-century, workplaces have transformed in the face of globalizing competition and the generalization of information technology (OECD, 1996). For those proclaiming a KBE, these changes signify deep, systemic change. The social relations of production—the structure of authority—and the technical relations of production—the complexity of tasks—under industrial capitalism are being transcended. Knowledge is now the 'intangible' key to profit, productivity, and power, no longer capital or the physical means of production. The necessity of problem-solving and creative activity by highly educated 'knowledge workers' is argued to demand constant learning and greater discretionary power in order to add value to new products or services (Drucker, 1993; Cortada, 1998; Klein, 1998). Increasingly these discretionary benefits are being attributed to all workers via flattened management structures and employee-involvement initiatives (OECD, 1999; Black and Lynch, 2003). The only barrier to the spread of knowledge-based work practices, we are told, is lack of education and skills among the general workforce (Stewart, 1997; Neef, 1999).

More critical theorists argue the organizing principles of industrial capitalism remain intact. We may be witnessing a relatively rapid period of technical change but this is simply a progression within a capitalist system that has always depended upon innovation for competitive advantage (Schement and Curtis, 1995). The introduction of software into the manufacturing process in the 1960s enabled greater automation via flexible manufacturing systems and manufacturers quickly found their ability to increase profit via lowered direct labour costs gone. Since then, corporate owners/executives have experienced a more intense need to gain competitive advantage through increased productivity in their administrative offices, service departments, and product development divisions (Morris-Suzuki, 1984; Kenney, 1997) as the production process itself has become more global or transnationalized (Robinson, 2004).

Déjà Vu

Ensuring the creative process of innovation proceeds efficiently in a profit-making direction is not an easy task. An increasingly dominant response has been **knowledge management**, where 'backroom software' (Baldoz, Koeber, and Kraft, 2001) serves to centralize decision-making by capturing and harnessing the knowledge of workers, including professionals and managers. One theorist suggests to 'support the monitoring, valuation, and reporting of intellectual capital, management ultimately will need systems and processes that support knowledge accounting with a rigor comparable to our traditional systems for managing hard assets' (Klein, 1998: 6). This rhetoric surrounding knowledge management is eerily reminiscent of the 'knowledge capturing' and micro-planning of

scientific management a century earlier (see Chumer, Hull, and Prichard, 2000). We might well begin to describe it as 'scientific knowledge management'. More educated knowledge workers may be required to exercise more technical skill, but management may be using information technology to track activity and dictate a quite limited number of choices (Aneesh, 2001; Colley, Hodkinson, and Malcom, 2003; Huws, 2003). In spite of many arguments and pro and con anecdotes, empirical research on discretionary intellectual activity of knowledge workers and others in current paid workplaces remains under-researched.

Researching Knowledge Work

One approach has studied those occupations involved in the production and dissemination of knowledge (Machlup, 1962; Porat, 1977). A second, increasingly dominant approach has defined knowledge workers according to the education and skill they bring to their jobs. Canadian studies have been among the most extensive to date. These suggest that routine data processing has become the dominant occupation and that 'professional' occupations, while growing relatively quickly, still make up a very small portion of the labour force (Lavoie and Roy, 1998; Baldwin and Beckstead, 2003). The evidence suggests the occupational structure in advanced capitalist countries is not changing nearly as fast or to the extent that many KBE theories claim. Neither approach, however, tells us much about changing opportunities for discretionary activity or new divisions of labour.

Towards an Activity-Based Measure of Knowledge Work.

To estimate whether an increase of discretionary, non-routinized work has occurred, we must examine knowledge in action. Some management theorists (Carlsen, Klev, and von Krogh, 2004) argue that knowledge cannot be understood as an object or possession, instead we must study it as activity. Collins (1998) suggests we study the 'working

Table 33.1 Class Position by Decision-making Power, Employed Labour Force, Canada, 2004

	None (%)	Advice (%)	Make Decisions (%)
Small employers	6	7	87
Self-employed	27	10	63
Managers	23	24	53
Supervisors	40	25	36
Professional employees	51	24	26
Service workers	68	16	16
Industrial workers	74	11	15
TOTAL	43	18	39

Source: WALL National Survey of Learning and Work, 2004 (N = 5,344). (http://www.wallnetwork.ca). Note: Row percentages may not equal 100 due to rounding.

knowledge' possessed by all employees instead of rehabilitating ambiguous, confusing, and elitist conceptions of knowledge workers.

Our own empirical study uses data from the 2004 WALL Learning and Work Survey (N = 9,063 adult Canadians). We have examined several items that estimate respondents' discretionary control and opportunity to perform complex technical tasks. Here we only have space to present findings on employees' opportunities to make policy decisions regarding human resources, budgets, and the products or services their organization offers.

As Table 33.1 indicates, the power relations of the traditional class hierarchy are largely intact in the employed Canadian labour force. Ownership of property remains a dominant structuring force, with most industrial and service workers having little opportunity for decision-making input and most owners indicating full control. The professional and managerial employees who are typically the focus of knowledge worker discussions still tend to have very limited decision-making power. Just half of managers indicate any direct involvement in significant organizational decisions, while about 20 percent indicate no participation in decision-making. Among professional employees, over half report no involvement whatsoever in organizational decision-making, a quarter may play an advisory role and only a quarter are directly involved in organizational decisions. The vast

majority of both service workers and industrial workers, by their own accounts, remain fully excluded from organizationally meaningful decision-making.

Even among the highly skilled, possession of technical skills is no guarantee that one has opportunities to use them. According to WALL respondents' own assessments, around 40 per cent of Canadian jobs now require a post-secondary level for adequate performance. However, well over 50 per cent of the employed labour force has obtained this level of formal education. While there are always some job mismatches, there is a very substantial and growing proportion of employees whose skills are underemployed in Canada, as in other advanced industrial societies (see Livingstone, 2004). The proportion of under-qualified is substantially less than the underemployed and is declining. Advocates of KBE posit exactly the converse condition. More specifically, service and industrial workers, whose jobs have the lowest performance requirements, have among the highest rates of underemployment. There is little support in such evidence for the general skill deficit often assumed by KBE promoters.

The evidence so far suggests that the irony of current visions of the knowledge-based economy is how much knowledge is going to waste. Globalization and information technology have undeniably impacted the paid workplace. Yet many more workers appear to have kept ahead of knowledge demands than have fallen behind. Those who may have fallen behind are often making extensive formal and informal learning efforts to compensate (see Livingstone, 2002). This demand for more equitable advanced education must be honoured in a democratic society. This national survey suggests that, aside from endemic shortage in skilled trades, lack of technical skills is not a fundamental problem. The actual problem appears to be the real lack of a knowledge-based economy in which those who have skills could apply them and more effectively use this knowledge to contribute to decision-making in their workplaces.

References

Aneesh, A. 2001. 'Skill Saturation: Rationalization and Post-industrial Work', *Theory and Society* 30: 363–96.

Baldoz, R., C. Koeber, and P. Kraft. 2001. 'Making Sense of Work in the Twenty-first Century', in *The Critical Study of Work: Labor, Technology, and Global Production*, pp. 3–17, R. Baldoz, C. Koeber, and P. Kraft, eds. Philadelphia: Temple University Press.

Baldwin, J.R., and D. Beckstead. 2003. *Knowledge Workers in Canada's Economy, 1971–2001*. Ottawa: Statistics Canada.

Beniger, J.R. 1986. *The Control Revolution: Technological and Economic Origins of the Information Society*. Cambridge, MA: Harvard University Press.

Black, S.E., and L.M. Lynch. 2003. 'The New Economy and the Organization of Work', in *New Economy Handbook*, pp. 545–63, D.C. Jones, ed. San Diego, CA: Academic Press.

Braverman, H. 1974. *Labor and Monopoly Capital: The Degradation of Work in the Twentieth Century*. New York: Monthly Review Press.

Carlsen, A., R. Klev, and G. von Krogh. 2004. 'Living Knowledge: Foundations and Frameworks', in *Living Knowledge: The Dynamics of Professional Service Work*, pp. 1–19, A. Carlsen, R. Klev, and G. von Krogh, eds. New York: Palgrave Macmillan.

Chumer, M., R. Hull, and C. Prichard. 2000. 'Introduction: Situating Discussions about "Knowledge"', in *Managing Knowledge: Critical Investigations of Work and Learning*, pp. xv–xxx, C. Prichard, R. Hull, M. Chumer, and H. Willmott, eds. New York: St Martin's Press, Inc.'

Colley, H., P. Hodkinson, P., and J. Malcom. 2003. *Informality and Formality in Learning: A Report for the Learning and Skills Research Centre*. London, England: Learning and Skills Research Centre.

Collins, D. 1998. 'Knowledge Work or Working Knowledge? Ambiguity and Confusion in the Analysis of the "Knowledge Age"', *Journal of Systemic Knowledge Management* (March): 10–22.

Cortada, J.W. 1998. 'Introducing the Knowledge Worker', in *Rise of the Knowledge Worker*, pp. xii–xix, J.W. Cortada, ed. Boston: Butterworth-Heinemann.

Drucker, P.F. 1993. *Post-capitalist Society*. New York: HarperCollins.

Gramsci, A. 1971. 'The Intellectuals', in *Selections from the Prison Notebooks*, pp. 3–23, Q. Hoare and G.N. Smith, eds and trans. New York: International Publishers.

Huws, U. 2003. *The Making of a Cybertariat: Virtual Work in a Real World*. New York: Monthly Review Press.

Kenney, M. 1997. 'Value Creation in the Late Twentieth Century: The Rise of the Knowledge Worker', in *Cutting Edge: Technology, Information Capitalism and Social Revolution*, pp. 87–102, J. Davis, T.A. Hirschl, and M. Stack, eds. New York: Verso.

Klein, D.A. 1998. 'The Strategic Management of Intellectual Capital: An Introduction', in *The Strategic Management of Intellectual Capital*, pp. 1–7, D.A. Klein, ed. Boston: Butterworth-Heinemann.

Lavoie, M., and R. Roy. 1998. *Employment in the Knowledge-based Economy: A Growth Accounting Exercise for Canada*, Catalogue no. R-98-8E. Ottawa: Human Resources Development Canada.

Livingstone, D.W. 2002. *Working and Learning in the Information Age: A Profile of Canadians* (No. W/16). Toronto: Canadian Policy Research Network.

———. 2004. *The Education–Jobs Gap: Underemployment or Economic Democracy*, 2nd ed. Aurora, ON: Garamond Press.

Livingstone, D. W., and J.M. Mangan. 1996. 'Men's Employment Classes and Class Consciousness: An Empirical Comparison of Marxist and Weberian Class Distinctions', in *Recast Dreams: Class and Gender Consciousness in Steeltown*, D.W. Livingstone and J.M. Mangan, eds. Toronto: Garamond Press.

Machlup, F. 1962. *The Production and Distribution of Knowledge in the United States*. Princeton, NJ: Princeton University Press.

Morris-Suzuki, T. 1984. 'Robots and Capitalism', *New Left Review* 147: 109–21.

Neef, D. 1999. *A Little Knowledge is a Dangerous Thing: Understanding Our Global Knowledge Economy*. Boston, MA: Butterworth-Heinemann.

OECD. 1996. *The Knowledge-based Economy*. Paris: Organisation for Economic Co-operation and Development.

———. 1999. *OECD Employment Outlook 1999: Giving Youth a Better Start*. Paris: Organisation for Economic Co-operation and Development.

Porat, M.U. 1977. *The Information Economy: Definition and Measurement*. Washington, DC: US Department of Commerce.

Robinson, W.I. 2004. *A Theory of Global Capitalism*. Baltimore: Johns Hopkins Press.

Schement, J.R., and T. Curtis. 1995. *The New Industrial Society*. New Brunswick, NJ: Transaction Publishers.

Sohn-Rethel, A. 1978. *Intellectual and Manual Labour: A Critique of Epistemology*, M. Sohn-Rethel, trans. New York: The MacMillan Press Ltd.

Stewart, T.A. 1997. *Intellectual Capital: The New Wealth of Organizations*. Toronto: Doubleday/Currency.

Questions for Critical Thought

WHAT IS WORK? LOOKING AT ALL WORK THROUGH THE LENS OF UNPAID HOUSEWORK

1. What are some parallels between paid work and unpaid work?
2. List and describe the five definitions of work that the focus groups provided. How does each affect the conception of what not-work is?
3. What are the two criteria of work that all respondents accepted?
4. How is the sociological definition of work relevant to policy? Give some examples.
5. What are some benefits of using the energy expenditure model of work? Can you think of any counter-arguments?

HOW JOB INFORMATION ENTERS AND FLOWS THROUGH SOCIAL NETWORKS: THE ROLE OF LABOUR MARKET CHARACTERISTICS AND TIE STRENGTH

1. List and describe the three resources that constitute social capital. Give an example of each.
2. Why might job information remain latent?
3. How might people differ in their sensitivity to being perceived as intrusive when passing on job related information?
4. Thinking of jobs that you might seek when you graduate, will these be open labour market jobs or closed labour market jobs? What strategy might you adopt in seeking information from your friends or family members?
5. What might these findings suggest about how social capital operates with regard to resources other than job information?

THE USE OF COMMUNICATION MEDIA: A CASE STUDY OF A HIGH-TECH ORGANIZATION

1. Discuss advantages and disadvantages of relying on computer-mediated communication for local communication and distant communication.
2. To what extent does computer-mediated communication increase worker productivity?
3. To prevent employees from using instant messaging for personal use, should employers be allowed to regulate their employees' conversations? In what ways?
4. What are the pros and cons of working in a hyperconnected organization?

5. Why does instant messaging take priority over email? Why does instant messaging take priority over face-to-face conversations?

'Knowledge Workers' and the 'New Economy': A Critical Assessment

1. Make a list of the practical and theoretical knowledge possessed and used by both a skilled machinist and an engineer working in an auto factory. Discuss who likely has the most control over their work, who makes the most money, and who has higher occupational status. How might the social and technical relations of production within capitalism explain issues of control, financial reward, and status?

2. Consider your current job or a job you have had in the past. Were you able to apply your knowledge? Why or why not? How might the organization you work(ed) for make better use of your practical and theoretical knowledge?

3. Computers and other information communication technologies are changing the way we work and the way businesses and governments operate. Think of a likely occupation you will have in the future: how has technology improved and degraded that job? What changes might technology create in the future?

4. How can you explain the existence of growing numbers of underemployed people in an economy increasingly based on workers' knowledge?

5. What sort of reforms might increase workers' opportunities to use their knowledge and skill in contemporary paid workplaces?

Part VIII

Aging

The average age of Canadians increases each decade. Because of increased longevity and smaller family sizes, the proportion of seniors in Canada is rapidly increasing, yet many Canadians openly practise ageism—direct or indirect discrimination against people based on their age. This includes denying qualified and willing candidates employment because of stereotypical attitudes toward older or younger people—indeed, toward any person who appears to violate the age norms and expectations that are common in our society.

Aging is not merely a biological phenomenon—it also involves the psychological and social processes that affect people as they age. Aging affects, and is in turn affected by, interactions between individuals and their family, friends, communities, and the whole of society. As with other topics, there are various sociological approaches to understanding aging. Functionalists sometimes contend the devaluation of people as they age is harmful to society because older individuals have a wealth of knowledge and experience they can pass on. Conflict theorists view aging as problematic because the power and influence necessary to effect change decreases as people age. Symbolic interactionists focus on how an individual's roles change because of and in response to aging. Applying feminist theory to the analysis of ageism can provide insight into the social forces that affect older women and their experiences in a gendered world.

For many obvious reasons, sociologists are paying increased attention to the social process of aging and to related issues such as retirement and the older individual's sense of identity. Since a large portion of the senior population is composed of older immigrants, there has also been interest in how these older citizens experience aging in a foreign society.

Better health has resulted in fewer activity-limited years in old age for many seniors. In Part 8, David MacGregor and Thomas R. Klassen explore the effects of compulsory retirement, the policy most English-Canadian universities have followed up to now. They contend that forcibly retiring scholars at an arbitrary age of 65 years is discrimination based on age—or ageism—and results in Canadian universities losing productive members that have much to contribute to academia.

The devaluation of older individuals not only has an effect on their employment status, but also on their sense of self and identity when such ideas are internalized.

Laura Hurd Clarke explores the relationship between an older woman's sense of self and her body. While worsening of health and functionality frustrate, societal ideas of beauty as youth and stereotypes of older women also contribute to the divorce between the inner self and the aging body. As her sample group was mostly socially homogeneous, Clarke suggests further research on aging women of other backgrounds and circumstances.

There has been little research on seniors in subcultures, though these make up a large part of the senior population. Neena L. Chappell looks at the experience of older Chinese Canadians in comparison to other Canadians. The essay dispels common false assumptions about subcultural difference in the use of health care services, examines indicators of quality of life for Chinese immigrants, and looks at the changing structure of traditional kin-related caregiving.

In this section, the different sociological approaches are usefully combined to study aging. For example, Clarke uses a combination of symbolic interactionism and feminist theory to examine the construction of meaning and identity about the body within a gendered and ageist social world. Her interviews with elderly women show that socially constructed meanings that refer to women, aging and older women's bodies add to the tensions and conflicts between the self and the body as well as felt age and appearance in later life. In taking a more traditional functionalist approach, Chapell points to the endurance, resourcefulness and adaptability of Chinese immigrant families within the structural constraints that they face.

CHAPTER 34

The Great Purge: Forced Retirement and the 'Succession Question' in Canadian Sociology

David MacGregor and Thomas R. Klassen

In 1990 the **Supreme Court of Canada** ruled that mandatory retirement policies do not offend against the **Canadian Charter of Rights and Freedoms**, which expressly forbids discrimination on the basis of age. One of the plaintiffs was Professor Bernard Blishen from York University. With his close friend and colleague, John Porter, Blishen was a key builder of the discipline of sociology. Among his many achievements, he was Research Director of the Hall Commission that in 1964 created the national medicare program. None of this seemed to matter in Canada's highest court (*McKinney v. University of Guelph*).

Blishen's fate will likely be shared by thousands of scholars in Canadian universities who pioneered their fields in the 1960s and 1970s. However, forced exit encounters hardly any opposition from social scientists and specifically from sociologists. This article traces the overall dimensions of **ageism** in Canadian universities with special emphasis on sociology—a discipline justly proud of its advocacy of social justice. In a coda to this paper, we suggest factors that may avert a human rights disaster in Canadian universities.

Age Purge

The Association of Universities and Colleges of Canada estimates that some 12,000 professors will reach retirement age by 2011 (2002). Excluding the University of Toronto, which abolished forced exit in 2005, 400–500 Ontario professors annually will reach 65 in the next half-decade. At the University of British Columbia alone some 425 faculty will mark their 65th birthday by 2011 (Spencer, 2001; Senate Ad Hoc Committee, 2002).

About 22 per cent of female faculty and 37 per cent of male faculty will celebrate their 65th birthday by 2011. Women faculty will make up over a quarter (26 per cent) of those experiencing forced exit between 2006 and 2011. Because women often begin university teaching later in life, mandatory retirement likely comes when their pension accumulations are low; moreover, they 'are forced to retire at what could be the peak of their careers' (Sussman and Yssaad, 2002: 16). Based on United States retirement patterns, Spencer estimates that in Ontario alone 1,100 professors would continue to work in the absence of mandatory retirement between 2005 and 2011 (Spencer, 2001).

Forced retirement will have a devastating effect on sociology. Over 40 per cent of Canadian sociologists (about 330) will reach retirement age in this time period. One third of those facing forced retirement will be women (about 110). After hard struggles, these women scholars created a feminist standpoint within sociology, transformed the discipline, and will be asked to leave.

The age purge that current legislation, administration, and faculty association policies make possible ensures that professors age 65 and older never reach sufficient numbers to effect a radical change in how elders are viewed, treated, and studied in academia. Women's participation in higher education needs to reach a critical mass 'in the fundamental pillars of academic appointment—research, teaching and service' before awareness and self-awareness of gender issues in academe is possible (Donaldson and Emes, 2000). The same is true of age issues—unexamined stereotypes of older people may be common in ivory towers since older people are shut out.

'The Succession Question'

In *Society/Societe*, the official newsletter of the Canadian Sociology and Anthropology Association, Bruce Curtis and Lorna Weir opened a debate about 'the **succession question** in Canadian sociology' (2002: 3). They pointed to 'a wholesale transfer of authority and leadership' as the cohort hired in the 1960s and 1970s withdraws and a new generation takes the wheel (2002: 3).

Oddly, Curtis and Weir never mention forced retirement. Their view is identical to the **managerial perspective** of the Association of Universities and Colleges of Canada (AUCC), which celebrates 'revitalizing the universities through faculty renewal' (Elliott, 2000). Hidebound older sociologists, write Curtis and Weir, compare badly with the 'energy' and 'inventiveness' of new faculty. Observing that the stratification of university positions 'is largely mapped on the generational divide', Curtis and Weir lament the 'gross indignity' suffered by deserving job candidates rejected by 'selection committees whose members are less qualified than they are' (Curtis and Weir, 2002: 7, 8).

They marvel at the 'radical chic' of sociology from the 1960s to the 1980s when it was ' "sexy"; oppositional; boundary-pushing'. What happened? The discipline has grown old and decrepit, apparently, and thirsts for fresh blood. Some departments have already 'managed generational renewal by hiring entrants with diverse and novel interests, committed to a collegial and re-energized sociology' (Curtis and Weir, 2002: 12).

United States Comparisons

Partly in response to Curtis and Weir, Neil McLaughlin compared university systems in the United States and Canada. Structural factors make the Canadian academic scene 'flat', while the American system encourages elite achievement. As a result, Canadian sociology's scholarly integrity and innovation may be more easily compromised. As in Canada, American sociology may have low prestige compared to other disciplines, but a sociologist from Harvard is still a Harvard professor (McLaughlin, 2005: 13). Without elite institutions, Canadian sociology lacks that kind of clout.

McLaughlin missed a key difference—one that is shaking up the Canadian post-secondary system from British Columbia to Ontario and the Atlantic provinces. For American universities, the compulsory retirement age rose from 65 to 70 in 1986, and disappeared altogether in 1993. The American system allows unhindered intercourse between academic generations. At age 65 an American professor might be contemplating career moves and new vistas of research; in Canada—instead of being offered 'a performance incentive of further employment opportunities' (Senate Ad Hoc Committee, 2002: 6)—the professor is shown the door, and (if lucky) condemned to part-time teaching and a shared office.

In American universities, older professors attract and supervise top graduate students. Many institutions rely on established faculty with more time for students than younger faculty who must concentrate on research and publications. There is concern that senior scholars will not stay long enough to avert a near-future shortage of qualified faculty replacements. While Curtis and Weir (and the AUCC) doubt the quality of older scholars, research in the United States indicates that senior professors are 'highly productive, hard-working', and deeply committed to their institutions (O'Brien, 2004). A Canadian Federation for the Humanities and Social Sciences report—'The Academy as Community'—finds an urgent need for mentoring new scholars by experienced professors, but never mentions that, unlike in the United States, mandatory retirement policies will decimate senior professors in the Canadian academic 'community' (Bailey, et al., 2004).

Canadian universities are finding it difficult to recruit anyone from the United States much older than 50 while American institutions are attracting middle-aged scholars. A 62 year-old Nobel Prize winner vaulted to the United States from the University of British Columbia when he discovered he would be forcibly retired at age 65. One of the leading thinkers on political thought abandoned Canada for the University of Texas 'because he wanted to work beyond 65 . . . Others have left Ontario universities for campuses in Quebec' (Armstrong and Sax, 2004). The University of Toronto decision in the spring of 2005 to eliminate mandatory retirement reflected its inability to draw high profile scholars with a retirement regime that differed from other Anglo-Saxon nations.

Conclusions

Several forces have brought the debate about mandatory retirement to the forefront at the beginning of the twenty-first century, including the aging baby boom generation and a greater awareness of human rights. Sociologists have, for the most part, been silent in this debate that includes ageist preconceptions of older workers, both in academia and outside it. As a recent federal report suggests, 'stereotypical views may often lead to discriminatory practices that negatively affect older workers in terms of hiring, promotions, job security, access to training and other benefits, and remuneration' (Fourzly and Gervais, 2004). Sociology must go beyond managerial perspectives and offer a progressive model confronting the age purge and reintegrating older faculty into the discipline, and more generally other workers who wish to work past an arbitrary retirement age.

Sociologists can rebuke the mythology that resistance to mandatory retirement involves only a few privileged (male) professors brazenly hanging onto high salaries and comfortable jobs. Prominent mandatory retirement legal cases have involved bus drivers, hospitality workers, firefighters, sanitation engineers, and police officers (MacGregor, 2005). The majority of older workers 'would prefer to leave the labour force under terms and conditions of their own choosing rather than being forced to leave' (Schellenberg and Silver, 2004). As with the age purge in the discipline of sociology, women workers are often hurt the most by forced exit.

Sociologists can also undertake research on how ageist attitudes and stereotypes of older workers have come to arise and been taken for granted by many, including Supreme Court justices, university administrators, and some social scientists. Lastly, sociologists can ensure that the debate over mandatory retirement is clear: removing forced retirement to allow those who wish to work longer is not to suggest that they must work longer. As the recent University of Toronto agreement illustrates, eliminating arbitrary retirement at age 65 can go hand-in-hand with providing all faculty (and more generally, all workers) with greater flexibility as to when to retire.

Governments, such as Ontario and New Brunswick, may soon legislate against mandatory retirement. Alberta, Ontario, and British Columbia are pumping up investment in higher education. Even to restore the student/teacher ratios of the early 1990s, universities would have to hire an additional 10,000 to 20,000 faculty, perhaps more. This could mean doubling the whole system within five or six years. Without adequate numbers of new PhD graduates to fill the demand, universities (following Toronto's lead) may turn to their older faculty and abandon forced exit policies. This would not only prevent a human rights disaster, it would allow more orderly turnover, with professors leaving gradually rather than all at once at age 65— partially obviating the dysfunctional boom and bust hiring patterns of the 1960s to the 1990s.

References

Armstrong, J., and D. Sax. 2004. 'Age Rule Costs UBC a Laureate', *Globe and Mail*, 30 October.

Association of Universities and Colleges of Canada (AUCC). 2002. *Trends in Higher Education*.

Bailey, A., et al. 2004. 'The Academy as Community: A Manual of Best Practices for Meeting the Needs of New Scholars', Canadian Federation for the Humanities and Social Sciences, Fall.

Curtis, B., and L. Weir. 2002. 'The Succession Question in English Canadian Sociology', *Society/Societé* 26 (October): 3–12.

Donaldson, E.L., and C. Emes. 2000. 'The Challenge for Women Academics: Reaching a Critical Mass in Research, Teaching, and Service', *The Canadian Journal of Higher Education* 30, 3: 33–56.

Elliott, L. 2000. 'Revitalizing Universities Through Faculty Renewal', *Research File*, Association of Universities and Colleges of Canada 4, 1 (March).

Fourzly, M., and M. Gervais. 2004. *Collective Agreements and Older Workers in Canada*, Labour Program at Human Resources Development Canada. Available at http://www.hrsdc.gc.ca/asp/gateway.asp?hr=/en/lp/spila/wlb/caowc/10chapter_5.shtml&hs=lxn (accessed 24 May 2005).

MacGregor, D. 2005. 'The Ass and the Grasshopper: Universities and Mandatory Retirement', in *Time's Up: Mandatory Retirement in Canada*, C.T. Gillin, D. MacGregor, and T. Klassen, eds. Toronto: Lorimer.

McKinney v. University of Guelph, [1990] 3 S.C.R. 229. (Supreme Court of Canada).

McLaughlin, N. 2005. 'Canada's Impossible Science: Historical and Institutional Origins of the Coming Crisis in Anglo-Canadian Sociology', *Canadian Journal of Sociology* 30, 1.

O'Brien, R.D. 2004. 'Older Faculty Stay On at Harvard', *Harvard Crimson*, 12 February.

Schellenberg, G., and C. Silver. 2004. 'You Can't Always Get What You Want: Retirement Preferences and Experiences', *Canadian Social Trends* 75 (Winter), Catalogue No. 11-008.

Senate Ad Hoc Committee on the Academic Implications of Mandatory Retirement at Age 65. 2002. University of British Columbia, 3 May.

Spencer, B.G. 2001. 'Student Enrolment and Faculty Recruitment in Ontario: the Double Cohort, the Baby Boom Echo, and the Aging of University Faculty', *Ontario Confederation of University Faculty Associations*, October.

Sussman, D., and L. Yssaad. 2002. 'The Rising Profile of Women Academics', *Perspectives* 6, 2 (February). Catalogue no. 75-001-XIE.

CHAPTER 35

Older Women's Bodies and the Self: The Construction of Identity in Later Life

Laura Hurd Clarke

The conflictual relationships that adolescent and middle-aged women have with their bodies have been widely discussed in the literature (Myers and Biocca, 1992; Bordo, 1993; Abell and Richards, 1996; Hesse-Biber, 1996; Brumberg, 1997; Morgan, 1998). Whereas declines in health and functional abilities are normative in later life (Novak, 1997), today's cultural standard of physical attractiveness is that of a youthful, toned, thin, and healthy body (Bordo, 1993; Brown and Jasper, 1993). Moreover, there is a 'double standard' of aging (de Beauvoir, 1972; Sontag, 1972) whereby

physical signs of advanced age are more harshly judged in women than in men. Despite the fact that attention to appearance and the pursuit of physical attractiveness are key aspects of the feminine **gender role** and **identity** (Rodin, Silberstein, and Striegel-Moore, 1984; Franzoi, 1995), older women's feelings about and experiences in their bodies have been largely unexplored.

To date there has been little attention paid to the interrelationships between the body and identity in later life or the influence of the changing, lived body on an older adult's sense of **self**. Questions remain as to how an older woman's changing physical appearance and functional abilities shape and constrain her construction of identity. This paper draws on the concepts of age identity, the body as mask (Featherstone and Hepworth, 1991) and felt identity (Goffman, 1963) versus chronological age to address the following research questions: (1) How do women perceive their changing appearances and what impact do these perceptions have on their sense of identity?, and (2) What is the nature of the relationship between an older woman's sense of self and her body? The relationship between the body and identity is discussed in terms of **Cartesian mind/body dualism**, the women's perception of having 'inside' selves that are separate from their bodies and the experience of the body as a prison of the self.

Theoretical Framework

Predominantly informed by symbolic interactionism, this study integrates the latter with **feminist** theory and an analysis of systemic ageism such that it focuses on the construction of meaning and identity (Berger and Luckmann, 1967; Blumer, 1969) in relation to the body within a gendered and ageist social world (Stewart, 1994; Ginn and Arber, 1995). Symbolic interactionism is particularly adept at elucidating the social construction of reality and identity (Ryff, 1986; Denzin, 1992; Charmaz, 1994). However, symbolic interactionism has been criticized for failing to account for social structure and power (Meltzer, Petras, and Reynolds, 1975; Coser, 1976; Stryker, 1981; Denzin, 1992). Indeed, symbolic interactionism has tended to pay insufficient attention to sexism and ageism. In contrast, feminist theory and analyses of ageism provide important insights into the social structural forces that impinge upon older women (Ginn and Arber, 1995; McMullin, 1995; Garner, 1999). Jagga and Rothenber (1993) argue that feminist theory is a useful 'lens' through which to focus social theory on the gendered nature of the social world. Nevertheless, feminist theory has tended, until recently, to ignore the experiences of older women (McMullin, 1995; Reinharz, 1997) and discussions of ageism have tended to ignore the unique issues facing older women (McMullin, 1995). Because of the respective strengths and weaknesses of symbolic interactionism, feminist theory and analyses of ageism, I argue that taken together they are a powerful means of making sense of older women's lives.

Data

Striving to share in their 'definition of the situation' (Thomas, 1972: 331) and to focus on the lived realities of 'the everyday world' (Smith, 1987: 88), I conducted 96 hours of semi-structured interviews with 22 women aged 61 to 92. Given the importance of appearance to women's sense of self as well as existing time constraints, the study focused on older women. I interviewed each of the women for three to six hours across two or three sessions. With the consent of each participant, all of the interviews were tape-recorded and transcribed verbatim. The use of multiple interviews fostered the validation of data by allowing for the clarification of emergent themes, meanings, and inconsistencies raised in previous interviews.

Discussion

The majority of the women in my study argue that there is a disparity between their bodies and their sense of identity. The women tend to distinguish between an 'inside' self and an 'outside' self. The 'inside' self is reminiscent of Kaufman's (1986) **'ageless self'**, Strauss's (1959) **'essential self'** and de Beauvoir's (1972) distinction between 'the Other . . . who is old' and the 'private, inward experience' (284). The 'outside' self is described as a mask or physical container of the 'inside' self, which is hidden, if not trapped, within the aging body and is similar to Featherstone and Hepworth's (1991) **'mask of aging'**.

The women account for the tension between the body and the self, or the 'inside' and 'outside' selves, in five different ways. To begin with, the youthful older adults contend that they feel like teenagers on the inside despite declining levels of health and functional abilities and the changes that have occurred in their appearances. Thus, the relationship between the body and identity is articulated in terms of a discrepancy between chronological age and felt age. The emphasis on being youthful on the inside despite one's chronological age highlights the strength of the devaluation of later life. The women differentiate themselves from the appearances, chronological ages, and functional abilities of their bodies. In this way, the women distance themselves from the stereotypes concerning older adults as well as the physical realities of growing older.

The masked older adults suggest that what they look like on the outside belies their true identities within. The idea that the body masks an individual's felt or 'true' identity is similar to Gubrium's (1986) research on individuals suffering from Alzheimer's disease and senile dementia. Gubrium suggests that Alzheimer's disease has been socially constructed such that the disease is distinguished from the person, or 'victim', that is hidden within the diseased and failing body. Conceiving of Alzheimer's disease as 'an enemy' (99) that is to be fought against and resisted by all those concerned, Gubrium (1986) contends that the body and the self are separate from each other such that the former masks, traps and betrays the latter. Unlike Strauss's (1959) concept of the mask with which individuals voluntarily hide their 'real' selves by concealing, suppressing or manipulating their 'identifying signs of status' (Glaser and Strauss, 1967: 83), Gubrium (1986) suggests that individuals with Alzheimer's disease are forcibly masked. Both Strauss (1959) and Gubrium (1986) argue that beneath the masks, whether they be socially constructed and presented or forcibly assigned through physical aging, is a true self, distinct from what others perceive in the behaviour and body of the individual. Similarly, the women in my study assert that aging involves an inevitable, undesirable, and uncontrollable status passage (Glaser and Strauss, 1971) in which the true self becomes less

visible in the aged shell of the body and the masks of their bodies become more impenetrable over the life course.

The entrapped older adults express the sense that their bodies have become prisons that constrain the ability of their youthful selves from participating in activities they once engaged in freely and easily. In contrast to ongoing health problems, many of the women refer to those periods of time when they have influenza and other common viruses as moments in their lives when they feel old. Illness renders chronological age more salient than felt age, albeit temporarily. Cremin (1992) reports that the older adults in her study indicate that they feel old in 'specific and transient' (1305) situations such as unsettling, embarrassing, or conflictual situations or in specific interactions or difficulties that arise due to the loss of independence which results from memory loss, declining functional mobility, and acute health problems. Declining health and functional abilities make the body more visible and palpable to the individual and underscore the 'relatedness of self and world, mind and body, inside and outside' (Williams and Bendelow, 1998: 160).

In contrast, some elderly people—call them 'the fighters'—struggle against the implications of having to appear young in order to avoid patronizing, if not discriminatory, behaviour in our youth-oriented society. Similar to the masked older adults, one of the youthful older adults yearns for the recognition of her true inner self by members of younger generations. She struggles with the standards of attractiveness that she has internalized. While she continues to mask her chronological age with make-up, hair dye, and youthful attire, she also expresses the wish that she did not feel that she had to do so in order to remain visible and socially valued.

Finally, the 'realists' argue that who they are on the inside is congruent with their chronological ages on the outside. Notably few in number, the two women who exemplify this category are pragmatic about the physical realities of aging. The women stress the importance of being aware of one's age so as not to feel inadequate or frustrated with declining physical abilities. The women also acknowledge that they do, at times, experience a disparity between their sense of identity and their bodies. While the women concede that it is difficult to achieve and maintain, realism is perceived as the desired approach to body-self dichotomy.

The five ways of expressing the tension between the body and the self are not mutually exclusive and share a number of elements in common. The youthful older adults, the masked older adults, the entrapped older adults, and the fighters all tend to express frustration and pain over the limiting nature of the body. The body as camouflage serves to conceal the self and to enable younger generations to see the women as 'old ladies', and thereby as devalued and frequently invisible. Reflected images confront the women with the physical changes that accompany aging and challenge their imagined, youthful internal images of themselves. The reflected image generates angst, bewilderment, and even despair and has the power to contradict an older woman's sense of self, if not social worth, in relation to her changing body. Similarly, the body as prison restrains and betrays the youthful and vibrant inner self. Unlike individuals with advanced Alzheimer's disease or senile dementia, the women are acutely aware of their changing realities and I would suggest that the awareness of the prison that the body constitutes for some older women makes the distress experienced by them more acute. One might speculate that the women might progress through the body-self typology

from fighters and masked older adults to entrapped older adults as their bodies increasingly constrain their behaviour and their energy becomes more focused on basic activities of daily living.

At the same time, the women argue that the 'inside' self, as the source and interpreter of meaning of lived reality, is what is most important. Perhaps the valuing of the self over the body is a means of negotiating the loss of physical attractiveness and functional abilities that occurs in later life. Indeed, the women describe having re-evaluated their priorities such that individuality and personality come to be esteemed over the fleeting beauty and energy of youth. The prioritization of the self over the body may also be the outcome of socialization in which the Cartesian perspective predominates and the women have been taught to value character over appearance.

Conclusion

In conclusion, this paper has addressed a gap in the body-image literature that has tended to ignore the experiences and perspectives of older women. The paper situates the complexities and contradictions in the construction of a sense of self within the broader social context that devalues age, women and frailty. The application of symbolic interactionism through a feminist lens illuminates the ways in which socially constructed meanings pertaining to women, aging and older women's bodies augment the tensions and conflicts between the self and the body, as well as felt age and appearance in later life.

References

Abell, S.C., and M.H. Richards. 1996. 'The Relationship between Body Shape Satisfaction and Self-esteem: An Investigation of Gender and Class Differences', *Journal of Youth and Adolescence* 25, 5: 691–703.

Berger, P.L., and T. Luckmann. 1967. *The Social Construction of Reality: A Treatise in the Sociology of Knowledge*. Garden City, NY: Doubleday and Company.

Blumer, H. 1969. *Symbolic Interactionism: Perspective and Method*. Englewood Cliffs, NJ: Prentice-Hall.

Bordo, S. 1993. *Unbearable Weight: Feminism, Western Culture and the Body*. Los Angeles, CA: University of California Press.

Brown, C., and K. Jasper. 1993. 'Introduction: Why Weight? Why Women? Why Now?', in *Consuming Passions: Feminist Approaches to Weight Preoccupation and Eating Disorders*, pp. 16–35, C. Brown and K. Jasper, eds. Toronto: Second Story.

Brumberg, J.J. 1997. *The Body Project: An Intimate History of American Girls*. New York: Random House.

Charmaz, K. 1994. 'Discoveries of Self in Illness', in *Doing Everyday Life: Ethnography as Human Lived Experience*, pp. 226–42, M.L. Dietz, R. Prus, and W. Shaffir, eds. Mississauga, ON: Copp Clark Longman.

Coser, L.A. 1976. 'Sociological Theory from the Chicago Dominance to 1965', *Annual Review of Sociology*: 145–60.

Cremin, M. 1992. 'Feeling Old versus Being Old: Views of Troubled Aging', *Social Science and Medicine* 34, 34: 1305–15.

de Beauvoir, S. 1972. *Old Age*, P. O'Brian, trans. London: Cox and Wyman.

Denzin, N.K. 1992. *Symbolic Interactionism and Cultural Studies: The Politics of Interpretation*. Cambridge, MA: Blackwell.

Featherstone, M., and M. Hepworth. 1991. 'The Mask of Ageing and the Postmodern Life Course', in *The Body: Social Process and Cultural Theory*, pp. 371–89, M. Featherstone, M. Hepworth, and B.S. Turner, eds. Newbury Park, CA: Sage.

Franzoi, S.L. 1995. 'The Body-as-object versus the Body-as-process: Gender Differences and Gender Considerations', *Sex Roles* 33, 5/6: 417–37.

Garner, J.D. 1999. 'Feminism and Feminist Gerontology', in *Fundamentals of Feminist Gerontology*, pp. 3–12, J.D. Garner, ed. New York: Haworth.

Ginn, J., and S. Arbor. 1995. '"Only connect": Gender Relations and Ageing', in *Connecting Gender and Ageing: A Sociological Approach*, pp. 1–14, S. Arber and J. Ginn, eds. Philadelphia: Open University Press.

Glaser, B.G., and A.L. Strauss. 1967. *The Discovery of Grounded Theory*. Chicago: Aldine.

———. 1971. *Status Passage*. New York: Aldine Atherton.

Goffman, E. 1963. *Stigma: Notes on the Management of Spoiled Identity*. Englewood Cliffs, NJ: Prentice-Hall.

Gubrium, J.F. 1986. *Oldtimers and Alzheimer's: The Descriptive Organization of Senility*. Greenwich, CN: JAI Press.

Hesse-Biber, S. 1996. *Am I Thin Enough Yet? The Cult of Thinness and the Commercialization of Identity*. New York: Oxford University Press.

Jagger, A.M., and P.S. Rothenberg. 1993. 'Introduction', in Feminist Frameworks: *Alternative Theoretical Accounts of the Relations between Women and Men*, 3rd ed. New York: McGraw Hill Humanities.

Kaufman, S.R. 1986. *The Ageless Self Sources of Meaning in Late Life*. Madison: University of Wisconsin Press.

McMullin, J. 1995. 'Theorizing Age and Gender Relations', in *Connecting Gender and Ageing: A Sociological Approach*, pp. 30–41, S. Arber and J. Ginn, eds. Philadelphia: Open University Press.

Meltzer, B.N., J.W. Petras, and L.T. Reynolds. 1975. *Symbolic Interactionism: Genesis, Varieties and Criticism*. Boston: Routledge and Kegan Paul.

Morgan, K.P. 1998. 'Women and the Knife: Cosmetic Surgery and the Colonization of Women's Bodies', in *The Politics of Women's Bodies: Sexuality, Appearance and Behavior*, pp. 147–66, R. Weitz, ed. New York: Oxford University Press.

Myers, Jr., P.N., and F.A. Biocca. 1992. 'The Elastic Body Image: The Effect of Television Advertising and Programming on Body Image Distortions in Young Women', *Journal of Communications* 42, 3: 108–33.

Novak, M. 1997. *Aging and Society: A Canadian Perspective*. Toronto: ITP Nelson.

Pearsall, M., ed. 1997. *The Other within Us: Feminist Explorations of Women and Aging*. Boulder, CO: Westview.

Reinharz, S. 1997. 'Friends or Foes: Gerontological and Feminist Theory', in *The Other within Us: Feminist Explorations of Women and Aging*, pp. 73–94, M. Pearsall, ed. Boulder, CO: Westview.

Rodin, J., L. Silberstein, and R. Striegel-Moore. 1984. 'Women and Weight: A Normative Discontent', *Nebraska Symposium on Motivation* 32: 267–307.

Ryff, C.D. 1986. 'The Subjective Construction of Self and Society: An Agenda for Life-span Research', in Later Life: *The Social Psychology of Aging*, pp. 33–74, V. Marshall, ed. Beverly Hills, CA: Sage.

Smith, D.E. 1987. *The Everyday World as Problematic: A Feminist Sociology*. Boston: Northeastern University Press.

Sontag, S. 1972. 'The Double Standard of Aging', *Saturday Review of the Society* 1, 1: 29–38.

Stewart, A.J. 1994. 'Toward a Feminist Strategy for Studying Women's Lives', in *Women Creating Lives: Identities, Resilience, and Resistance*, pp. 11–35, C.E. Franz and A.J. Stewart, eds. San Francisco, CA: Westview.

Strauss, A.L. 1959. *Mirrors and Masks: The Search for Identity*. Glencoe, IL: The Free Press.

Stryker, S. 1981. 'Symbolic Interactionism: Themes and Variations', in *Social Psychology: Sociological Perspective*, pp. 3–29, M. Rosenberg and R.H. Turner, eds. New York: Basic Books.

Thomas, W.I. 1972. 'The Definition of the Situation', in *Symbolic Interaction: A Reader in Social Psychology*, pp. 331–6, J.G. Mania and B.N. Meltzer, eds. Boston: Allyn and Bacon.

Williams, S.J., and G. Bendelow. 1998. *The Lived Body: Sociological Themes, Embodied Issues*. New York: Routledge.

CHAPTER 36

Aging among Chinese Canadian Immigrants— Reflections

Neena L. Chappell

A Bit of History, Chinese Seniors in Canada

Chinese immigration to British Columbia began in 1858, 9 years prior to Canadian confederation; nevertheless, 63 per cent of current Chinese immigrants arrived after 1970; and fully 73 per cent were born outside of Canada (Li, 1998). That is, Chinese Canadians, and Chinese Canadian seniors in particular, are likely to be immigrants who relocated here from another country. Immigration is believed to be especially important for Chinese seniors because of their unique history in Canada. Mainly men were initially recruited to assist in building the national railway; upon its completion in 1885 the federal government began passing Anti-Chinese legislation including a head tax and lack of entitlement to vote, though they nevertheless remained eligible for conscription, and culminating in the 1923 Chinese Immigration Act prohibiting the Chinese to enter the country. The period 1923–47 of Chinese exclusion consisted primarily of married-bachelors living alone in Canada, inhibiting the growth of a second generation born in Canada. This Act was repealed 24 years later and the discriminatory laws and abuse of civil rights were slowly rescinded. By the late 1950s most were removed from provincial and federal books. In 1967, revisions to immigration

regulations made it virtually impossible to discriminate on the basis of country of origin or racial background. Further changes in the late 1970s and early 1980s saw immigrants enter both as refugees and as businesspersons with substantial investment capital.

Importantly, the **institutional racism**—discrimination that is state-sanctioned—against the Chinese was more extreme than against any other ethnic group in Canada's history (Li, 1998). It included a legally sanctioned withdrawal of citizenship rights, exclusion from immigration, and restrictions on occupational competition. This applied equally to Chinese who were Canadian by birth or naturalization (Li, 1998).

Selective Substantive Research

Research consistently shows that current Chinese Canadian seniors reflect their immigration history: most (71.3 per cent) immigrated due to family reunion; most (78.3 per cent) speak Cantonese at home; and only a quarter (23.1 per cent) understand English well. Despite this language barrier, examination of health service use by Chinese Canadian seniors in British Columbia shows that, with similar health as other seniors, they utilize western health services to the same extent as other

Canadian seniors. The vast majority sees a physician, under half use medical support services, and around 15 per cent use home care services (Chappell and Lai, 1998). This contradicts the prevalent belief that sub-cultural groups under-use our western health care services. It might be noted that recent research by Chen and Kazanjian (2005) reports preliminary results that Chinese immigrants use less health care with regard to mental health problems.

Chinese Canadian seniors have a strong preference for western treatment over traditional Chinese medicine and for western trained doctors over Chinese practitioners, but they prefer to use western practitioners who have Chinese-speaking staff. Furthermore, the predictors of utilization are similar to those reported throughout the western world; need or ill health is the strongest predictor of physician services and need together with enabling and predisposing factors predict use of medical support services and home care services. Neither age at immigration nor period of immigration is related to use of services, suggesting an assimilation interpretation is not warranted. The tendency of researchers to continue embracing a belief in the under-use of services by subcultural groups warrants an examination of researchers' own assumptions.

Half of Chinese Canadian seniors also engage in traditional Chinese care for both minor and major illnesses, predicted by their religious beliefs and their preference for traditional Chinese medicine. **Socioeconomic status** (SES) is unrelated to the use of either western or traditional services. This finding, though, should be treated with caution given that the sample consists largely of relatively poor seniors (79.7 per cent reported income of less than $1,000/month).

In terms of quality of life, when compared with Chinese elderly living in selected locales in China (Souzhou, Hong Kong, and Shanghai), Canadian Chinese seniors experience greater quality of life as measured by subjective well being but lower than that reported for Canadian seniors generally. However, the predictors of quality of life, and the factors that help create that quality, are similar—health, social support, and economic circumstances (Chappell and Lai, 2000).

For those living in Canada, how does involvement in traditional Chinese culture, given their relative inability to speak English and the relative value placed on elders historically in Chinese culture, affect their quality of life? Research (Chappell, 2005) demonstrates that, in addition to the standard predictors of health and SES, involvement in the culture, such as participation in celebrations and social functions, frequenting Chinese senior centres, and other similar activities, but not adherence to beliefs—especially **ethnocentric beliefs**—is important overall and for specific domains such as social relationships, community participation, attitude towards life, and spirituality (but not family relationships). Homeland visits, immigration for family reunion, and ancestor worship are differentially related depending on the domain examined. Interestingly, year of immigration and period of immigration are unrelated to quality of life in Canada.

Chinese culture is perhaps nowhere epitomized more than in terms of *xiao*—filial piety— a Confucian concept encompassing a broad range of beliefs and behaviours including children's respect, obedience, loyalty, material provision, and physical care to parents within a traditional patriarchal system whereby sons are valued over daughters. While the practice of filial piety is changing within China, for the Chinese diaspora exposure to different forms of thinking and behaviour are inevitable. Chen (1997) characterizes the diasporic Chinese in North America as living in an environment of democracy, capitalism, and individualism on the one hand together with anti-Chinese prejudice and discrimination on the other, resulting in a hybridizing of Chinese and Western cultures.

Unlike most Canadian seniors, most Chinese Canadian seniors do not live with only their spouse and very few live alone; most live either with their children or with both children and a spouse. Similar to the west, daughters and spouses are involved in assistance with **basic and instrumental activities of daily living** (ADL and IADL) and perceptions of support and their involvement increases as more assistance is provided while that from sons decreases. The participation of daughter-in-laws tends to be lower than that of sons or daughters, a clear departure from traditional norms (this shift is also documented within China). However, sons are more involved than we typically find among North American families; they are slightly more likely to be providing assistance with ADL/IADL than is true of daughters or spouses. The traditional Chinese son/daughter-in-law caring unit is most likely to be evident in terms of support with IADL but not in terms of support with ADL (typically much heavier care) or emotional support. If the parent lives alone, sons are much more likely to provide support. Spouses predominate in the provision of emotional support (similar to the west but a departure from traditional Chinese culture).

The future of aging among Chinese Canadians promises to be profoundly different from that experienced today. The reason lies in the distinct types of immigration taking place in the latter part of the twentieth century. Recent Chinese immigrants are better educated, wealthier, and come with their families to a country that accords them the same rights as others. Independent living requires economic sufficiency and is at least aided by knowledge of the host language, two characteristics that the current cohort of diasporic Chinese seniors lack but future cohorts will possess. Indeed, aging among Chinese Canadians who immigrated during and after the late 1970s is likely to be more similar to that of other Canadians.

What does this research tell us? It reveals the endurance, resourcefulness, and adaptability of families within the structural constraints they face. Despite experiencing a history of extreme institutional racism, Chinese Canadian families, drawing on traditional culture plus their new host society culture, create strategies for coping that reflect a new reality from a blending of two different cultures, both of which embrace the informalization and gendering of the responsibilities of caregiving within the private rather than the public domain.

A METHODOLOGICAL NOTE

Conducting research with subcultural groups when one is not a native member of the group (and in this instance cannot speak the language) is challenging. It necessitates collaboration with those who know the language and the culture intimately. At least in Chinese culture, official interpreters do not necessarily provide the meanings as expressed by in-group members. Furthermore, western devised measures cannot be simply applied within the subcultural context. Especially in Mainland China, the willy-nilly use of western measures is cause for grave concern and requires a questioning of some of the research. Data must be interpreted with a knowledge of the culture; one example, empirical studies of assistance (caregiving) with ADL and IADL among Chinese seniors both in China and overseas consistently report extremely high disability. This though seems to reflect high levels of support but not of disability as children and others show traditional respect by assisting seniors, irrespective of their capability. Great pains to train interviewers to record levels of ability/disability distinct from levels of actual assistance have thus far been to no avail.

References

Chappell, N.L. 2005. 'Perceived Change in Quality of Life among Chinese Canadian Seniors: The Role of Involvement in Chinese Culture', *Journal of Happiness Studies* Forthcoming.

Chappell, N.L., and D. Lai. 1998. 'Health Care Service use among Chinese Seniors in British Columbia, Canada', *Journal of Cross-Cultural Studies* 13: 21–37.

Chappell, N.L., and K. Kusch. (Under review.) 'Gendered Caregiving to Chinese Canadian Elderly'.

Chappell, N.L., D. Lai, G. Lin, I. Chi, and S. Gui. 2000. 'International Differences in Life Satisfaction among Urban-living Elders: Chinese and Canadian Comparisons', *Hallym International Journal of Aging* 2, 2: 105–18.

Chen, A.W., and A. Kazanjian. 2005. 'Rate of Mental Health Service Utilization by Chinese immigrants in British Columbia', *Canadian Journal of Public Health* 96, 1: 49–51.

Chen, S. 1997. 'Being Chinese, Becoming Chinese-American: The Transformation of Chinese Identity in the United States, 1910–1928'. PhD Dissertation. Salt Lake City: University of Utah.

Li, P. 1998. *Chinese in Canada*, 2nd ed. Don Mills, ON: Oxford University Press.

Questions for Critical Thought

The Great Purge: Forced Retirement and the 'Succession Question' in Canadian Sociology

1. Would you rather hire someone age 25 or someone age 60 for a job? Why? Should people employed in physically demanding roles, such as firefighters, retire at a predetermined age? What about an even earlier age than 65?
2. After being interviewed for a job that you really want, you are told that you are 'too young'. How do you feel? What, if anything, would you do in this situation?
3. When you see an elderly person driving a car, what thoughts go through your mind? Why might you have those thoughts, and not others?
4. At what age would you like to retire? What does this reveal about your conception of your post-graduation full-time permanent employment?
5. Ontario will ban mandatory retirement, effective 12 December 2006. Do you think this is the beginning of a renewed movement to eliminate forced retirement across Canada and the rest of the world?

Older Women's Bodies and the Self: The Construction of Identity in Later Life

1. What are five ways the interviewed women account for the tension between the body and the self? What are the limitations of each in adequately dealing with the changing circumstances of ageing women?
2. What is 'Cartesian duality', and how is it evident in the women's reactions to aging?
3. What are some of the ways in which Western society devalues age, women, and frailty? Based on those interviewed, how well has this devaluation been internalized by women?
4. Have there been changes in how the media portray older women? Has there been an increase or decrease of older women in significant movie roles?
5. Would there be differences in how women relate body to self-identity if the interviewed women were from another culture? Why?

Aging among Chinese Canadian Immigrants—Reflections

1. Discuss the distinctiveness of older Chinese adults as a cultural group in Canada today.
2. What are some possible reasons many people, including researchers, think Chinese Canadian seniors do not use our western health care system.
3. Discuss the factors that potentially impact the quality of life of Canadian Chinese seniors.
4. What are some of the cultural differences evident between care provided by children of seniors among Chinese and other Canadian groups? How would you explain the differences?
5. How and why do we expect aging to be a different experience in the future for Chinese Canadian seniors?

Part IX

Health

Evidence-based practice is currently the central paradigm influencing health care decisions and actions. It is premised on the belief that the use of scientific evidence ultimately leads to better health outcomes. Subjective knowledge possessed by individuals, therefore, is treated as irrational or irrelevant. Scientific knowledge, however, is applied in various ways to meet specific interests. This raises the question as to whose interest is served by the application of scientific knowledge in the form of medical expertise in contemporary society.

The authors in Part IX provide a sociological rationale into scientific knowledge application in diverse areas within the health care industry—sexual pharmacology, preventive medicine, chronic pain treatment, complementary and alternative medicine, and medicalization of disability.

Medical experts apply scientific knowledge for various reasons. To Barbara L. Marshall, medical experts use scientific knowledge to advance their scientific and commercial interests rather than patients' well being. In her paper, she sees the re-fashioning of sexual dysfunctions to age-related organic diseases as a professional strategy to create an endless chain of possibilities for medical intervention that potentially places individuals at risk.

Kimberley-Anne Ford adds to the discussion by indicating that government agencies also apply scientific knowledge or expertise to gain power and govern themselves accordingly. In using the prevention of malaria by Canadian travellers as a case study, Ford shows how power operates through application of scientific knowledge by travel medicine providers. The paper, however, highlights the critical role of subjective knowledge in the governance of health.

Like Marshall, David Lewis, Kevin Brazil, and Paul Krueger believe that medical experts apply scientific knowledge to advance their scientific interest, and to justify their actions, even if their actions are incorrect. Using the 'money matters' thesis as benchmark, they argue that money does not matter in predicting outcome of chronic pain treatment. This finding lessens the suspicion surrounding pain as 'subjective', 'unreal', and 'money driven' when treatment for chronic pain fails or when medical experts fail to diagnose pain objectively.

Sandy Welsh, Heather Boon, Merrijoy Kelner, and Beverley Wellman also discuss a possible fit of complementary and alternative medicine into the mainstream health care system. They identify inter-professional battles between conventional medicine and complementary and alternative medicine as one of the main barriers of complementary medicine's entrance into the mainstream of medicine. This is not astounding because medical experts are more than likely to reject any complementary and alternative medicine as non-scientific and subjective in order to maintain their dominance in the health care jurisdiction.

Governments also hide behind scientific knowledge to justify their decisions and actions. Tanya Titchkovsky makes this point in her study of disability and 'people-first language'. She shows how disability is organized as a medicalized and individual matter and, as such, takes shape as an abnormal limitation and lack of function that some four million Canadians 'just happen to have'. This notion of disability removes the possibility of understanding disability as a social, and thereby complex, political phenomenon requiring an action, rather than 'people-first language'.

In general, the following essays argue that the interests of various groups and stakeholders influence how scientific knowledge, in the form of medical expertise, is applied in various contexts.

CHAPTER 37

An Epidemic in Search of a Disease: The Construction of Sexual Dysfunction as a Social Problem

Barbara L. Marshall

Introduction

This paper explores the phenomenon of 'epidemic-making' in relation to the growth of sexual pharmacology and the related manner in which sexual bodies are constructed and regulated. I argue that a convergence of scientific and commercial interests has liberally deployed **epidemic** rhetoric, expanded horizons of 'risk', and newly responsibilized individuals and health care practitioners to increase surveillance and intervention.

Widely circulated are figures that suggest an 'epidemic' of **sexual dysfunction**, with almost half of women and more than a third of men reported to be afflicted. Yet epidemics imply contagion. While 'miasma' theories were largely superceded by infectious disease theories as epidemiology developed (Terris, 2001), 'miasmas' of various sorts have resurfaced as a range of ills, which straddle the medical and the social (e.g., teen pregnancy, obesity, alcoholism, depression, social phobia) are enfolded into the rhetoric of epidemics. I argue that the interface between academic researchers, pharmaceutical industries, and health promotion discourses has contributed to a miasma for the development of sexual dysfunction. In disorders like female sexual dysfunction, 'distress' is a diagnostic criterion, so *creating* distress is essential to the creation of treatable disorders and their growth into epidemic conditions. As Linda Singer has argued, 'An epidemic emerges as a product of a socially authoritative discourse in light of which bodies will be mobilized, resources will be dispensed, and tactics of surveillance and regulation will appear to be justified' (Singer, 1993: 117).

Sexual Dysfunction as a Social Problem

Clinical research articles, popular science and health reporting, and the myriad of reports from pharmaceutical research firms widely reiterate the 'epidemic' rates of sexual dysfunction. The source of the epidemiological statistics can generally be traced back to two studies. The Massachusetts Male Aging Study established the widely cited rates of erectile dysfunction in men and also established that erectile function was age-related, with older men reporting much higher rates of erectile dysfunction than younger men. What never seems to get reported in the ubiquitous citations to this study is that 'despite the marked declines in actual events and behavior and in subjective aspects of sexuality, men in their sixties reported levels of satisfaction with their sex lives and partners at about the same level as younger men in their forties' (McKinlay and Feldman, 1994: 272).

Even more widely cited is the National Health and Social Life Survey (Laumann, Paik, et al. 1999) which gave us the figures of 31 per cent of men and 43 per cent of women suffering from sexual dysfunction. However, discrete sorts of problems (desire, arousal, orgasm, pain) are collapsed into homogenous categories of male and female 'sexual dysfunction'. Also, there is no indication (because these data were not collected) of whether or not problems experienced were a source of distress to those surveyed. The creation of 'distress' from these data has been the task of careful public relations.

This is not to suggest that people do not have sexual difficulties that cause them concern. My interest here is in the *ontology* of these disorders and related questions: What is their nature? Who has the authority of defining them and treating them? How has deploying the rhetoric of epidemics acted so as to mobilize resources and increase surveillance?

Some analyses of the social construction of disease have argued that the proliferation of disease categories has resulted in shrinkage of what might be considered 'normal'. However, Stephen Katz and I have argued that the very binary of normal/abnormal appears to be giving way to a different binary—that of functional/dysfunctional (Katz and Marshall, 2004). The shift from normality to functionality opens new spaces for the politics of disease construction and for the deployment of the rhetoric of epidemics to flourish as an increasing array of behaviours or physical states deemed to be dysfunctional can be enfolded into the logic of epidemic-construction. 'Functionality' does not require any correlate of normality. Sexual function, in fact, is defined largely in the absence of any normative data, and much of the research has proceeded on the basis of redefining what might be statistically normal as dysfunctional. Sexual function is a cultural ideal. One of the demands of successful biosocial citizenry is an acceptance and literate understanding of functional states as naturally adaptable. Individuals must be aware of how highly undesirable and prevalent a condition is, and how susceptible they are to it. As Andrew Webster notes, these new discourses of health and illness have created the 'worried well' as a significant market.

The construction of the 'active patient' with sexual dysfunction occurs against an expanded horizon of risk, a revision of the concept of '**sexual health**', and increasing responsibilization of both the individual and the health professional to undertake surveillance. The construction of sexual dysfunctions as organic, rather than psychogenic disorders, linked them with other bodily disorders that act as 'risk factors' (e.g., diabetes, prostate cancer, and obesity). However, 'age'—as the most apparent risk factor—embraces everyone. The spectre of sexual dysfunction has also been taken up by various health promotion discourses in terms of various lifestyle factors that may increase risk. These include both official campaigns, as in the case of Health Canada's anti-smoking campaign ('Tobacco use can make you impotent'), and unofficial ones, as in People for the Ethical Treatment of Animals' promotion of vegetarianism ('Eating meat can cause impotence'). Furthermore, the concept of sexual health itself has expanded from a concern with reproduction and absence of sexually transmitted diseases to focus on a concern with sexual function.

The discursive construction of problems or complaints into 'diseases', or what we might conceptualize here as the 'contagion' of the diseases, rests on a particular configuration of biomedical capital, academic researchers, and a burgeoning science and health reporting industry. The clinical and market success of Viagra® is significant in contributing to the rapid expansion of institutional and discursive spaces for the construction of sexual disorders and the legitimacy of talking about and treating them within a medical idiom.

Individuals are responsibilized for their own preventative and rehabilitative care, and they must become skilled at self-assessing their sexual functionality aided by the resources of medical informatics, marketing and health promotion literature, and their myriad of self-tests and questionnaires. While many of these were developed as aids in clinical diagnosis, they now circulate widely, often in abbreviated form, in promotional and health education materials.

Pfizer's 'three steps to better erections' plan illustrates well the construction of the 'active patient' in this respect:

1. Rate your sexual health (in this case, by filling out a short form of the International Index of Erectile Function),
2. Talk to your doctor, and
3. Ask about pharmaceutical treatments.

Physicians too, are encouraged to be proactive in eliciting information about sexual function as 'part of the routine medical history' (Lightner, 2002), and to use questionnaires to identify symptom complexes—either physician administered or left in the waiting room.

Pharmaceutical companies have invested heavily in the development of diagnostic instruments, and they are central to the construction of dysfunctions. From this perspective, worries about the potentially distorting role of industry funded research should extend to their active role in creating diagnostic tools and promoting patient identity formation around disorders long before the clinical testing—or even development—of any treatment.

Conclusion

The rhetoric of an 'epidemic' of sexual dysfunction has been deployed to create a miasma of contagion against the backdrop of an expanded horizon of risk. This has shifted meanings of the very concept of 'sexual health', and an increasing responsibilization of both individuals and health professionals to engage in preventative and rehabilitative protocols. The convergence of scientific and commercial interests in the re-fashioning of sexual dysfunctions as age-related organic diseases consigns us to always think of bodies as unfinished, puts all men and all women potentially at risk, and provides for an endless chain of possibilities for intervention.

References

Katz, S., and B.L. Marshall. 2004. 'Is the functional "normal"? Aging, Sexuality and the Biomarking of Successful Living', *History of the Human Sciences* 17: 53–75.

Laumann, E.O., A. Paik, and R.C. Rosen. 1999. 'Sexual Dysfunction in the United States: Prevalence and Predictors', *Journal of the American Medical Association* 281: 537–44.

Lightner, D. 2002. 'Female Sexual Dysfunction: A Concise Review for Clinicians', *Mayo Clinic Proceedings* 77: 698–702.

McKinlay, J.B., and H.A. Feldman. 1994. 'Age-related Variation in Sexual Activity and Interest in Normal Men: Results from the Massachusetts Male Aging Study', in *Sexuality Across the Life Course*, pp. 261–85, A.S. Rossi, ed. Chicago: University of Chicago Press.

Pfizer Inc. n.d. 'Three Steps to Better Erections'. Available at http://www.viagra.com/steps/index.asp (accessed 25 April 2005).

Singer, L. 1993. *Erotic Welfare: Sexual Theory and Politics in the Age of Epidemic*. London: Routledge.

Terris, M. 2001. 'The Changing Relationships of Epidemiology and Society', *Journal of Public Health Policy* 22: 441–63.

CHAPTER 38

Citizenship and Health: The Governance of 'Imported Malaria' and the Safety of Anti-Malarial Drugs

Kimberly-Anne Ford

Introduction

Using the prevention of **malaria** by Canadian travellers as a case study, this paper shows how power operates through agents of governance—in this case travel medicine providers—who encourage 'free' citizens to act in accordance with dominant public health campaigns. The paper underscores the dichotomous role of subjective knowledge in the **governance of health**—to be at once 'officially' dismissed, while simultaneously feeding into **health discourse** and performing a critical function in the creation of healthy democracies.

The Case Study

Western countries are increasingly concerned with growing rates of 'imported malaria', a term used to designate cases of malaria that are 'brought back home' from malaria-endemic parts of the world, by travellers (Rowlands, 2001; Health Canada, 2002). An increase in chloroquine-resistant malaria has led Health Canada to endorse the use of the anti-malarial drug mefloquine (sold in Canada under the brand name Lariam™) by people travelling to most malaria-endemic regions of the world (Health Canada, 1995, 2000). Mefloquine is highly effective, but it is also known to cause potentially serious neuropsychiatric side effects in some users (Canadian Pharmacists' Association [CPA], 2002). The rates and severity of mefloquine side effects reported by manufacturers have been called into question in numerous investigative journalism reports that suggest that the drug may be more dangerous than admitted by Health Canada (e.g. CTV, 1997; Gartner, 2002). Travellers are increasingly outspoken about the

pros and cons of mefloquine, most often describing negative side effects in their 'weblogs'. However, Health Canada continues to make sweeping statements in support of its use, claiming, for example: 'Myth: Most people who take mefloquine have serious side effects. Fact: For travellers to high-risk areas, the risk of acquiring malaria and dying is significantly greater than the risk of experiencing a serious side effect from mefloquine' (Health Canada, 2002). Consequently, travel medicine providers (hereafter TMPs) in Canada continue to prescribe it. In fact, a large majority (22/26) of the TMP survey respondents identified mefloquine as the most commonly prescribed anti-malarial drug in Canada.

Data reviewed for the case study is drawn from two primary qualitative sources. A detailed questionnaire consisting of 35 open- and closed-ended questions was mailed to 142 TMPs across Canada. Semi-structured telephone and face-to-face interviews with eight malaria 'experts'—health care providers, individual travellers, members of parliament, and members of advocacy groups—were also conducted. In addition, 284 pages of weblog text were downloaded from the Internet and saved into Word files, and approximately 1,200 pages of government documents pertaining to mefloquine were obtained through Access to Information Act requests.

The Notion of 'Governmentality' and the Governance of Malaria

Michel Foucault (1980, 1991) as well as scholars such as Mitchell Dean (1994), Colin Gordon (1991), and Nicholas Rose (1993, 1994) have argued that power is not antithetical to freedom, but that it indeed depends upon the freedom of citizens to govern themselves along the lines established in 'discourses of power'. Rose (1993), therefore, argues that we should not understand our freedom as illusory. Instead, we should be aware that freedom is crafted by the tension between liberty and governance. In order for the citizens of advanced democracies to be disease-free, individual liberty is impinged upon by health discourse, norms, and regulations. Citizens then come to internalize these norms and regulations and to incorporate them into their usual healthy behaviours and routines. However, in healthy democracies, citizen criticism feeds back into the process of governance, norms, regulations, and discourses are thereby transformed.

In order to excavate the ways in which this construction of 'free citizens' comes about in the arena of malaria prevention campaigns, it is necessary to examine the 'assemblages'—the medico-administrative apparatuses for regulating social space, the 'strategies' by which medical knowledge becomes actualized in public health campaigns, and the deployment of agents of governance that create public health campaigns and ensure their actualization (Rose, 1994).

A network of institutional and individual agents of public health, including Health Canada, international health agencies (WHO, CDC and others), North American military organizations, medical doctors and nurses, pharmaceutical corporations, TMPs, and individual travellers themselves are all enmeshed in the governance of malaria among Canadian travellers. These agents are, to varying degrees, responsible for approving, authorizing, testing, using, and/or endorsing the various anti-malarial drugs that are prescribed.

Health Canada's Population and Public Health Branch draws upon research and data from the Centre for Disease Control (CDC), the Canadian Institutes for Health Research, the World Health Organisation (WHO), pharmaceutical corporations and regional health institutes in order to devise malaria prevention campaigns. TMPs affirm that it is access to the most up-to-date informa-

tion that allows them to claim expertise in the area of malaria prevention, and that this information is provided through the aforementioned sources and the US-manufactured software program Travax™.

In order for public health campaigns to develop, individual travellers must also share their subjective experience with the medical establishment and health institutes. This subjective knowledge is then transformed into statistics on disease prevalence and drug side effects, and is coded and recorded. This 'clinical knowledge' upholds or transforms health discourse (Foucault, 1973).

Present-day guidelines from Health Canada identify mefloquine as the 'first line of defence' drug for Canadian travellers who are heading to regions of the world with chloroquine-resistant strains of malaria. All of the TMPs who responded to the survey acknowledge the importance of their clients' direct experience with anti-malarial drugs, or travel to a malarial country. For example, TMPs recognized that travellers having experienced a side effect directly affects their choice of a new prophylactic; one TMP refers to the old adage: 'once bitten twice shy' (Survey respondent #83). However, intuition, 'interactive knowledge' (i.e., knowledge that is gained by sharing a life world with others [Park, 1993]), and common sense are all disavowed by TMPs.

Discussion

To borrow from Beck (1992), TMPs act in accordance with, and want to uphold, the dichotomous view that 'science "determines risk" and the population "perceives risk"' (57). This division between experts and non-experts, in Beck's view, shapes an image of the public as ignorant, but well intentioned. It encourages the belief that 'protests, fears, criticism or resistance in the public sphere are *pure problems of information*. If the public knew what the technical people know, they would be at ease—otherwise they are just hopelessly irrational' (58). Although TMPs affirm that information about malaria and the various ways to prevent it is available, they see their patients as misinformed or ignorant.

The science of risk, which encompasses public health, is inherently political. This is particularly clear in the case of mefloquine and malaria prevention. To make their recommendations, Canadian TMPs rely on Travax™ software, which uses data supplied by the US government through the CDC. United Press International has noted that the US government has a lot at stake in avowing the safety of mefloquine (Benjamin and Olmsted, 2003).

Compounding this problem, it has been suggested that Canadian institutions do not welcome dialogue with the public, and lack transparency, in particular with respect to drug regulation (Lexchin and Mintzes, 2004). This poses a problem, since citizens have the important potential role of ensuring the accountability of public health agencies. Some regulators, however, do not always acknowledge the role of the public with respect to their accountability. One Health Canada advisor stated the following:

> Health Canada wants to increase transparency and to involve the public, but the public's role cannot always be high. . .The experts are more competent than we (the public). To place trust in the population would be an error (interview respondent #5.2, male, Health Canada advisor).

TMPs survey respondents do acknowledge that the individual has control over his or her own body and thus is free to choose which anti-malarial drug to use. However, they do not concede that citizens can have any role in the broader realm of public health, and they dismiss the knowledge possessed by individual travellers as being mythical or non-factual. Without a doubt certain modes of knowledge (intuitive and subjective) are necessarily outwardly marginalized and discredited in order to encourage compliance with mainstream public health campaigns. However, it is important to note that these subjugated knowledges are not excluded from the governing process; rather they

are fundamental to the development of knowledge and discourse (Foucault, 1980). This knowledge is thus enmeshed in the re-creation of discourses of power and may lead public health institutes to re-evaluate their strategies.

Slowly but surely, this is taking place in North America. Public pressure has led to a number of Food and Drug Administration (FDA) warnings about mefloquine and there have been a number of changes in the product insert, including information about the potential risk of suicidal ideation. Moreover, the FDA has recently allowed the Glaxo-Welcome pharmaceutical corporation to market the drug Malarone® as the 'safer anti-malarial drug' in the US, and to state that it has a better safety profile than mefloquine (GlaxoSmithKline, 2002). In Canada, one public health official noted:

> Health Canada will post new guidelines for Canadian travellers for the prevention of malaria on their website. These new guidelines will have myths about malaria and also more complete information about the three 'first line drugs'— mefloquine, malarone and doxycycline. These three drugs are all between 90 and 95 % effective (interview respondent #3.1, female, medical doctor).

Conclusion

Although it is outwardly dismissed by TMPs as irrational and counterfactual, citizen concern over the safety of mefloquine is actually contributing to a shift in Canadian malaria prevention strategies. This is taking place with respect to other pharmaceutical drugs and health issues as well (for example, see CBC, 2004).

Non-expert knowledge, then, is publicly disparaged. Perhaps this is a key part of the strategy to make people listen to the 'experts' and govern themselves accordingly. Meanwhile, power 'recuperates' non-expert subjugated knowledge, recoding and reinterpreting it, and finally giving it a stamp of approval, before enfolding it into the strategies and mechanisms of governance.

References

Beck, U. 1992. *Risk Society: Towards a New Modernity*. London: Sage.

Benjamin, M., and D. Olmsted. 2003. 'Navy Cover-up Alleged on Side Effects', *UPI Online*. Available at http://www.upi.com/view.cfm?StoryID=20030907-042825-2777r (accessed 16 March 2006).

Canadian Pharmacists' Association (CPA). 2002. *Compendium of Pharmaceuticals and Specialities—The Canadian Drug Reference for Health Professionals*. Ottawa, Canada: CPA.

CBC. 2004. 'Pushing for Change', *CBC Disclosure*. Available at http://www.cbc.ca/disclosure/archives/040217_adr/change.html (accessed 16 March 2006).

CTV. 1997. 'Mefloquine Nightmare', *W5*. Ottawa. 14 October 1997.

Dean, M. 1994. *Critical and Effective Histories: Foucault's Methods as Historical Sociology*. London: Routledge.

Foucault, M. 1973. *The Birth of a Clinic: An Archaeology of Medical Perception*, A. Sheridan, trans. New York: Pantheon Books.

———. 1980. *Power/Knowledge: Selected Interviews and Other Writings 1972—1977*, C. Gordon, ed. New York: Pantheon Books.

———. 1991. 'Governmentality', in *The Foucault Effect: Studies in Governmentality*, pp. 87–112, C. Gordon, P. Miller, and G. Mitchell, eds. London: Harvester Weatsheaf.

Gartner, H. 2002. *Fifth Estate: The Nightmare Drug*. Ottawa. 16 October 2002.

GlaxoSmithKline. 2002. 'FDA approves new safety data for Malarone™'. Available at http://www.gsk.com/press_archive/press_08232002.htm (accessed 1 December 2005).

Gordon, C. 1991. 'Governmental Rationality: An Introduction', in *The Foucault Effect: Studies in Governmentality*. London: Harvester Wheatsheaf.

Health Canada. 1995. *Canadian Recommendations for the Prevention and Treatment of Malaria Among International Travellers 1995* [Original online source is no longer available] (accessed 3 March 2002).

———. 2000. *Canadian Recommendations for the treatment and Prevention of Malaria*. Available at http://www.phac-aspc.gc.ca/publicat/ccdr -rmtc/00vol26/26s2/ (accessed 4 October 2003).

———. 2002. *Misconceptions about Malaria and Mefloquine*. Available at http://www.phac-aspc.gc.ca/publicat/ccdr-rmtc/00vol26/26s2/26s2n_e.html (accessed 1 December 2002).

Lexchin, J., and B. Mintzes. 2004. 'Transparency in Drug Regulation: Mirage or Oasis?', *Canadian Medical Association Journal* 171, 11: 1503.

Park, P. 1993. 'What is Participatory Research? A Theoretical and Methodological Perspective', in *Voices of Change: Participatory Research in the United States and Canada*, pp. 1–201, P. Park, ed. Westport, CT: Bergin and Garvey.

Rose, N. 1993. 'Government, Authority and Expertise in Advanced Liberalism', *Economy and Society* 22, 3: 283–99.

———. 1994. 'Medicine History and the Present', in *Reassessing Foucault: Power Medicine and the Body*, pp. 48–72, C. Jones and R. Porter, eds. London: Sage.

Rowlands, B. 2001. 'A Better Pill for Preventing Malaria', *The Daily Telegraph*, 27 April 2001: 20.

CHAPTER 39

The Impact of Financial Compensation on Treatment Outcomes for Chronic Pain: A Test of the 'Money Matters' Thesis

David Lewis, Kevin Brazil, and Paul Krueger

Introduction

Several interventions are available for pain management. To get them, a simple declaration that one is in pain is usually sufficient. If a health care professional observes signs of a tumour, fracture, fever, or heart attack, he or she can imagine that pain accompanies those signs and respond. By contrast, chronic pain is problematic. Claims of chronic pain are not always accepted; if they are, then treatments can impair normal functioning. Surgery, for example, can increase disability, while medications can lead to altered cognition, addiction, or compromised liver and kidney function (Fries, 1983; Williams, 1988; Jayson, 1992).

If the pain can be shown to be disabling, support for persons with chronic pain often extends beyond treatment to income support. For payers, there is a financial incentive to remove the client from compensation if possible. However, treatment is often ineffective in the sense that it does not lead to reported pain relief in chronic cases. Even if treatment relieves pain, side effects can impair functioning.

The payers' interest corresponds with the deviance control elements of the 'sick role' (Parsons, 1981). While sufferers are rewarded by being excused from usual roles (such as employee, mother, and the like) they must sincerely co-operate in efforts to make them well again.

Health care in Canada is currently dominated by an 'evidence-based' approach. With its language of scientific precision, impartiality, and objectivity, it remains a persuasive discourse. However, the approach confronts a problem in that pain can only be measured 'objectively', by self-report. Resuming one's activities of daily living, on the other hand, is observable by others.

Thus, the goal of treatment in an evidence-based approach is to restore function as indicated by resumption of roles, because that is an 'objective' **outcome** of treatment; treatment fails if the release from role obligations is permanent. This dovetails neatly with the funders' need to remove clients from financial support.

Reactivation strategies are one form of therapy for chronic pain. They are aimed at helping individuals live with their pain by increasing activity and exercise, while minimizing side effects by weaning them from medication. They may be employed for 'recalcitrant' chronic pain, where other treatments have failed. Miller (1961) used the term 'accident neurosis' to refer to people whose reported back pain seems disproportionate to observable evidence of spinal damage. Finding that those seeking compensation had significantly greater pain, disability, psychological disturbance, and lost work time than those who were not, Miller (1961) suggested that the process of compensation-seeking might exacerbate symptoms.

Since then, there has been ongoing interest in examining the extent to which financial compensation was associated with prolongation of claimed disabling pain. There are over 1,180 articles on malingering in the clinical literature; Rohling, Binder, and Langhinrichsen-Rohling (1995) called it 'money matters' (see also Harris, 2005).

Because of the suspicion that reported chronic pain could be 'deliberate malingering associated with the prospects of compensation' (Jayson,

1992), litigation, pre-treatment compensation, and changes in compensation brought about by treatment have entered the pantheon of outcome measures for chronic pain assessment and outcomes research (Williams, 1988). Other outcome measures involve role functioning, and, of course, pain.

Using an axiomatic theory testing approach, we set out to test the 'money matters' thesis that better treatment outcomes for chronic pain would occur in the absence of litigation or other financial compensation (such as disability insurance, workers' compensation, and the like).

Methods

This was a prospective quasi-experimental non-equivalent group design (Cook and Campbell, 1979). The site was a multi-disciplinary reactivation pain management program located in southern Ontario, and the data collection took place between June 1997 and July 1999. Those in litigation, receiving financial support as a result of their pain occurrence, or otherwise were in one group; those not receiving such support were in another.

MEASUREMENT

The Functional Activities Confidence Scale (FACS) and the Resumption of Activities of Daily Living Scale (RADL) (Williams and Myers, 1998) are condition-specific measures. The Zung Depression Index (Zung, 1974) was applied because clinicians believed that depression often accompanies chronic pain. The Short-Form 36 item questionnaire (SF-36) (Ware, 1996) is a generic indicator of health status. It divides into 8 'domain' scales: Physical Functioning, Role Physical, Role Emotional, Pain, General Health, Vitality, Mental Health, and Social Functioning. In addition, there are two 'summary' scales: the Physical Component Scale and the Mental Component Scale. With all of these scales except the Zung, a higher score is better. All these tests were administered at enrolment and de-enrolment by clinical staff, who also collected consents, socio-demographics and clinical

histories. The outcomes were the health status indicators—FACS, RADL, Zung, and SF-36 calculated as change scores. They were analyzed using student's t-test with Bonferonni correction, repeated-measures ANOVA, and logistic regression. In each case, they were compared by group (no compensation versus compensation).

Results

A total of 90 consecutive clients enrolled in the treatment program between July 1997 and June 1999 were included in this study. Mean time in program was 76 days (95 per cent, C.I. 42–109). As many as 76 (88 per cent) completed the program; there were no significant differences between completers and dropouts.

Clients' ages ranged from 26 to 63 years of age; 38 per cent were men; and 29 per cent did not complete high school, while 27 per cent had completed college or university. Twenty-two per cent had been white-collar workers. Less than 7 per cent were in full-time employment and another 12 per cent were on restricted duties. A little over half were receiving some **financial compensation** for their disability; of these, about 34 per cent were in ongoing litigation. On average, they had been off work for 3.9 months (range 0–13 months).

Ninety-five per cent experienced pain in their back or neck and 86 per cent had tried some form of therapy before enrolment; 59 per cent found that at least one of these therapies helped. Even so, 79 per cent used medication for pain several times a week or more. There were no differences between compensation and no compensation groups on any of these traits, except that there were more men in the compensation group.

Bivariate (t-test) analyses showed that most changes in outcomes measured were in the desired direction, but small: only the SF-36 domain 'physical functioning' and the summary 'physical components scale' changed significantly (p < .05). Only 3 clients from each of the groups had resumed at least some paid employment by program end;

similarly, 3 clients from the no compensation group and 7 from the compensation group had reduced their frequency of medication use.

Variables for compensation and litigation yielded no significant difference. There were no significant effects by gender on any outcome. As would be expected, age and education co-varied with general health, and job class with RADL score. Almost all of the ratios of the study's variables approach unity, except for gender. The study further showed no significant change in medication use or in numbers working at paid employment.

Conclusion

By clinical definition, pain is 'that experience we associate with actual or potential tissue damage' (cited in Merskey and Bogduk, 1994). There are those, admittedly, who report pain 'in the absence of tissue damage or any likely pathophysiological cause [and] there is usually no way to distinguish their experience from that due to tissue damage if we take the subjective report' (Merskey and Bogduk, 1994; see also Haugli and Steen, 2001). Such reports are usually due, not to failures in clinicians' detection or inadequacies in treatment, but to 'psychological reasons' (Merskey and Bogduk, 1994) such as factitious disorder, which is deliberate simulation of illness (Merck Medicus Online, 2005).

When a motive can be attributed, then what clinicians believe to be falsely reported pain is not factitious disorder but malingering. Thus, Parsons' sick role becomes psychiatry's 'illness affirming behaviour' (Eisendrath, 1995, 2002) or 'secondary gains of illness' (Gatchel, 2005), or 'malingering'.

However, this study indicates that money does not matter in predicting outcome; financial compensation was an unimportant variable in this study. It showed no significant associations with any other. Our results are limited by time and place, but they do constitute a challenge to the axiom that financial support limits outcomes in **chronic pain treatment**.

The measured changes in all domains were small, so the actual intervention may be seen as unsuccessful by some standards. Indeed, there is no 'evidence-based' support for a physiotherapeutic approach to pain management (Koes, Bouter, et al., 1991). Even so, no pain management program can fail, because of the ideology surrounding pain as 'subjective': if the client reports improvement in pain, it is because of treatment. If, on the other hand, there is no reported improvement, then the pain is not 'real': the client is attempting to gain attention or money.

References

Cook, T.D., and D.T. Campbell. 1979. *Quasi-Experimentation: Design and Analysis Issues for Field Settings*. Boston: Houghton-Mifflin.

Eisendrath, S.J. 1995. 'Psychiatric Aspects of Chronic Pain', *Neurology* 45, 12 (Suppl 9): S26–34.

Eisendrath, S.J., and D.E. McNiel. 2002. 'Factitious disorders in civil litigation: Twenty Cases Illustrating the Spectrum of Abnormal Illness-affirming Behaviour', *Journal of the American Academy of Psychiatry and the Law* 30, 3: 391–9.

Fries, J.F. 1983. 'The Assessment of Disability: From First to Future Principles', *British Journal of Rheumatology* 22 (suppl): 48–58.

Gatchel, Robert J. 2005. 'The Step-Care Framework of Pain Treatment', in *Clinical Essentials of Pain Management*, pp. 111–39, R.J. Gatchel, ed. Washington: American Psychological Association.

Harris, I., J. Mulford, M. Solomon, J.M. van Gelder, and J. Young. 2005. 'Association Between Compensation Status and Outcome After Surgery: A Meta-analysis', *JAMA* 293: 1644–52.

Haugli, L., E. Steen, E. Laerum, R. Nygard, and A. Finset. 2001. 'Learning to Have Less Pain—Is It Possible? A One-year Follow-up Study of the Effects of a Personal Construct Group Learning Programme on Patients with Chronic Musculoskeletal Pain', *Patient Education and Counselling* 45, 2: 111–8.

Jayson, M.I. 1992. 'Trauma, Back Pain, Malingering, and Compensation', *British Medical Journal* 305, 6844: 7–8.

Koes, B.W., L.M. Bouter, H. Beckerman, G.J.M.G van der Hiejden, and P.G. Knipschild. 1991. 'Physiotherapy Exercises and Back Pain: A Blinded Review', *British Medical Journal* 302: 1572–6.

Merck Medicus Online. 2005. Available at http://www.merckmedicus.com/pp/us/hcp/thcp_dorlands_content.jsp (accessed 28 February 2005).

Merskey, H., and N. Bogduk, eds. 1994. *Classification of Chronic Pain*, 2nd ed. Seattle: IASP Press.

Miller, H.G. 1961. 'Accident Neurosis', *British Medical Journal* 1: 992–8.

Parsons, T. 1981. 'Definitions of Health and Illness in Light of American Values and Societal Structure', in *Concepts of Health and Disease*, pp. 70, A.L. Caplan, H.T. Engelhardt, and J.J. McCartney, eds. Reading, MA: Addison-Wesley.

Rohling, M.L, L.M. Binder, and J. Langhinrichsen-Rohling. 1995. 'Money Matters: A Meta-analytic Review of the Association between Financial Compensation and the Experience and Treatment of Chronic Pain', *Health Psychology* 14, 6: 537–47.

Ware, J.E., Jr. 1993. SF-36 *Health Survey Manual and Interpretation Guide*. Boston: The Health Institute, New England Medical Centre.

Williams, R.C. 1989. 'Toward a Set of Reliable and Valid Measures for Chronic Pain Assessment and Outcome Research', *Pain* 35, 3: 239–51.

Zung, W.W. 1974. 'The Measurement of Affects: Depression and Anxiety', *Modern Problems of Pharmacopsychiatry* 7: 170–88.

CHAPTER 40

Where Will the Jurisdiction Fall? The Possible Regulation of Traditional Chinese Medicine/ Acupuncturists in Ontario

Sandy Welsh, Heather Boon, Merrijoy Kelner, and Beverley Wellman

Introduction

As the use of **complementary and alternative medicine** (CAM) by members of the public, and the number of CAM practitioners, both continue to increase across North America (Gilmour, Kelner, and Wellman, 2002) and Europe, how CAM fits (or does not fit) into existing **health care systems** is becoming a more important topic of discussion both practically and theoretically. Practically, patients are already using CAM combined with conventional (usually Western) medical products and therapies together in their efforts to treat and prevent illness, as well as to maintain and enhance their health (Tataryn and Verhoef, 2001). Our paper attempts to deal with two distinct, yet related, issues concerning one CAM group, Traditional Chinese Medicine/Acupuncturists (TCM/As), and their role in the health care system. First, we use the work of Abbott to help us address how room may be created for TCM/As in the Ontario health care system. Because this is a process that has not finished, our analysis is speculative. Second, we examine how internal and external jurisdictional battles as well as the **professionalization process** of TCM/As are playing out to affect which TCM/A groups will be in a position to move into any potential vacancy in the health care system. This also allows us to move beyond social closure perspectives and to assess the usefulness of Adams' (2004) approach for studying CAM.

Methods

Data for this paper were derived from five sources: personal interviews with CAM practitioner group leaders, conventional health care practitioner group leaders, government representatives, a focus group with TCM/A practitioners, and archival material. Detailed description of the methods used to collect these data is available elsewhere (Kelner, et al., 2002; Boon, et al., 2004; Kelner, et al., 2004a; Kelner, et al., 2004b; Welsh, et al., 2004). The final source of data was the Health Professions Regulatory Advisory Council report on TCM/A (HPRAC, 2001) published in 2001.

The Case of Acupuncture: A Profession or a Treatment Modality?

One of the key issues for the regulation of acupuncture in Ontario is the question of whether acupuncture is a profession or a treatment modality. If acupuncture was determined to be a profession, this would imply full jurisdictional rights. But if acupuncture is a treatment modality, it sets the stage for others also to claim acupuncture as part of their jurisdiction. In its April 2001 report, HPRAC concluded 'that for the purposes of regulation, acupuncture is best viewed as a treatment modality rather than a profession' (HPRAC, 2001a). HPRAC suggested that acupuncture should be part of the existing controlled act of 'performing a procedure on tissue below the dermis'. This sets up TCM/As to share jurisdiction over this controlled act with a variety of health care professions, including medical doctors, nurses, and massage therapists.

Although shared tenancy is less than desirable for many TCM/As, this may be the only way for these groups to enter the system of professions in Ontario. Most government officials interviewed recognized the competing jurisdictional interests within the various health care practitices and the difficulty that new CAM professions may have in finding a place within the system: 'It is harder for them to squeeze in because it is musical chairs and 99 per cent of the chairs are taken.'

Despite acknowledging the public support for the regulation of some CAM groups, government officials seemed aware of the impending difficulties of implementing regulation of TCM/As should that decision be made: 'A problem is the controversy within the groups themselves. They are not the easiest groups to deal with and that in itself is a challenge. They are not willing to work together and they argue and don't present their issues clearly.'

The discussion above highlights the need for the CAM practitioner groups to find a way to 'fit' into the existing system of professions and the role the provincial government may play in that. There are no obvious vacancies in the current health care system in Ontario. However, the decision to regulate these TCM/As is ultimately a political one—the state has the power to create space in the system.

Jurisdictional Battles and Professionalization Process

While the government contemplates establishing jurisdictions for TCM/As, the TCM/As are also involved in pitched battles for shaping this jurisdiction. The debate over whether acupuncture is a modality or profession in its own right is far from over. With TCM/As, we see issues of inter-professional and intra-professional conflict over jurisdiction that is mixed in with the TCM/A groups' professionalization process (e.g., Adams 2004).

In terms of inter-professional conflict, TCM/As were aware that they were trying to carve out 'turf' in a health care system already overflowing with professions. 'Other professions are trying to squeeze acupuncture and other parts of TCM into their scope of practice. You see that happening with physiotherapy, chiropractors and massage therapists' (TCM/A leader). At the same time, intra-professional conflict also hindered TCM/As ability to gain jurisdictional control.

I see lots of conflicts in the group: one is standards: we don't want those who don't know acupuncture to practice acupuncture; we don't want those who don't know traditional Chinese Medicine to practice it (Acupuncture Focus Group).

The professionalization process also was viewed as impinging on the scope of the practice, or jurisdiction, of certain practitioners (e.g. Adams, 2004). Some practitioners feared a loss of freedom to practice if their practitioner group was regulated. Other practitioners, those that viewed their standards were the 'highest', believed there needed to be constraints on the jurisdictional claims of some TCM/As. Overall, TCM/A practitioners felt that regulation would solve all their problems by bringing increased legitimacy to their practice: 'We want the profession to be recognized and standardized and put in legal status. . . .We need the medical doctors to recognize us' (Acupuncture Leader).

Conclusion

Our findings suggest that the state may be favourable toward the regulation of TCM/A practice, primarily because of increasing public pressure. The Ontario context for CAM professions, for that matter, demonstrates both the usefulness and limits of the social closure perspective. Some degree of social closure will occur when the goal of statutory self-regulation is achieved, but it will not create a monopoly for many of the acts claimed by the CAM groups, acupuncture in particular. Due to the way regulation is structured in Ontario, other medical professions will still have the right to include some types of CAM work in their practices. This is where an analysis that includes the complex system of professions is needed—in particular where more attention to the work of Andrew Abbott may shed light on the continuing jurisdictional battles between CAM groups themselves and between CAM and conventional medicine

Adams's (2004) work encourages scholars to link professionalization projects with inter-professional conflicts. Our study supports taking the study of CAM occupations in that direction. Similar to the dentists and dental hygienists in Adams's study, we find that the jurisdictional battles between TCM/A groups and others in the medical profession are shaping what the jurisdictions will look like. In Ontario, this will probably result in a form of shared tenancy, where TCM/A groups and other medical professionals share control over acupuncture. At the same time, the professionalization process of TCM/A is also pushing the issue onto the agenda of the state. Where our study differs from Adams's dental hygienists is in the role of internal jurisdictional battles. TCM/A practitioners are far from being a cohesive group able to present a united front to the state and to other medical professions (Welsh et al., 2004). This lack of cohesion is also not likely to end anytime soon, and may be a unique characteristic of many CAM occupations. Future studies of CAM should continue to build on the work of Adams (2004) as well as incorporate internal jurisdictional battles where warranted.

References

Adams, T. 2004. 'Inter-professional Conflict and Professionalization: Dentistry and Dental Hygiene in Ontario', *Social Science and Medicine* 58: 2243–52.

Boon, H., S. Welsh, M.J. Kelner, and B. Wellman. 2004. 'Complementary/alternative Practitioners and the Professionalization Process: A Canadian Comparative Case Study', in *The Mainstreaming of Complementary and Alternative Medicine in Social Context: An International Perspective*, P. Tovey, G. Easthope, and J. Adams, eds. London: Routledge.

Gilmour, J., M.J. Kelner, and B. Wellman. 2002. 'Opening the Door to Complementary and Alternative Medicine: Self-regulation in Ontario', *Law and Policy* 24, 2: 150–74.

Health Professions Regulatory Advisory Council (HPRAC). 2001. 'Traditional Chinese Medicine and Acupuncture. Advice to the Minister of Health and Long Term Care'. Available at http://www.hprac.org/english/reports.asp.

Kelner, M., H. Boon, B. Wellman, and S. Welsh. 2002. 'Complementary and Alternative Groups Contemplate the Need for Effectiveness, Safety and Cost-effectiveness', *Complementary Therapies in Medicine* 10: 235–9.

——. 2004a. 'The Role of the State in the Social Inclusion of Complementary and Alternative Medical Occupations', *Complementary Therapies in Medicine* 12: 79–89.

——. 2004b. 'Stakeholders' Responses to the Professionalization of Complementary and Alternative Medicine', *Social Science and Medicine* 59: 915–30.

Tataryn, D., and M.J. Verhoef. 2001. 'Combining Conventional, Complementary and Alternative Health Care: A Vision of Integration', in *Perspectives on Complementary and Alternative Health Care*, pp. VII.87–109. Ottawa: Health Canada.

Welsh, S., M. Kelner, H. Boon, B. Wellman. 2004. 'Moving Forward? Complementary and Alternative Practitioners Seeking Self-regulation', *Sociology of Health & Illness* 26, 2: 216–41.

CHAPTER 40

Disability: A Rose By Any Other Name? 'People-first' Language in Canadian Society

Tanya Titchkosky

> How we are seen determines in part how we are treated, how we treat others is based on how we see them; such seeing comes from representation.
>
> —Dyer, 1993: 1

Introduction

There is pervasive representation of **disability** found in organizationally produced pamphlets and guidelines regarding how to 'name' disability in Canada. There is currently an unified attempt—coming from seemingly everywhere—to make sure that anyone who has anything authoritative to say about disabled people publicly does so in the language of 'people with a disability', or people-**first language**. 'People with disabilities' is the dominant linguistic formulation of disability in Canada, and deserves sociological consideration.

The phrase 'people with disabilities' has been in circulation since at least the 1970s, but until the 1990s such phraseology was one of a number of ways to make reference to disabled people (see Canada, 1981). Since sometime after the 1983

International Year of the Disabled, these various expressions of disability have been supplanted almost entirely by 'people-first' phraseology (see Canada, 1996; 1998; Human Resources Development Canada, 1995). This is a representation of disability approaching hegemonic proportions, and there are sometimes formal sanctions—and many informal ones—for not using it.

My work here, however, flows from the assumption that all speech gives rise to and reflects a particular re-presentation of the meaning of people. This assumption grounds the need to analyze the consequences of the current linguistic formulation of disability. The two fundamental questions of this paper are what representation of disability undergirds the people-first language and what representation of disability does this language game (re)insert into the world?

Touched by the Other

A current Canadian government document, (Canada, 1998) claims to represent the status and desires of disabled people in Canada and does so through a typical and exemplary use of people-first language. The introductory line of *In Unison* (1998) proclaims, 'Disability touches everyone' (11). Yet some Canadians—according to the government, over four million—have been touched with more force than others and have 'reported some level of disability'. Reporting on a level of disability is presented by *In Unison* as quite distinct from being touched by disability. 'People with disabilities' are, first and foremost, reportable: people who can be counted by measuring and surveying levels of impairment. Such counting requires that disability be conceptualized as a measurable condition—as possessing a level. One key way this measurement was accomplished by the Canadian government was through the Health and Activity Limitations Survey (HALS), which aimed at ascertaining individuals' functionality.

Again, despite the fact that *In Unison* begins by reminding readers of everyone's connection to disability, and even informs readers that 'Most individuals experience some form of functional incapacity or limitation as a normal part of aging,' the report does make clear, through its constant use of 'they', that it is written by, and directed at, non-disabled people. In this enterprise of othering, people-first language ensures that some clear and certain image of bodily limitation or sensorial lack is re-inscribed only on 'them'. In other words, the mythical dichotomy, if not the chasm, between the pathological and the normal is reinforced (Goffman, 1963; Foucault, 1970; Canguilhem, 1991 [1966]; Davis, 1995; Thomson, 1997).

Of course, there is nothing new about non-disabled people speaking about the nature of the hardship that disabled people face. Moreover, it is not typical that an authoritative voice is a disabled one, except perhaps when one speaks of 'personal' stories of 'suffering' a disability. Habit and power relations are certainly at play. Nonetheless, the question remains: If disability touches everyone, how, in particular, does disability touch non-disabled people through people-first language?

The Social Significance of 'People with . . .'

As a way to draw out the social organization accomplished through people first language and to address the various questions I have raised, I will more explicitly address the representation of disability found in *In Unison*. Here is the introductory paragraph of *In Unison* in its entirety:

> Disability touches everyone. In 1991, 4.2 million (16%) Canadians reported some level of disability. Aboriginal Canadians are particularly affected with over 30% of Aboriginal persons reporting a disability-almost double the national average. All Canadians have some experience with disability through their own experience, contact with relatives, colleagues or friends. Most individuals experience some form of functional incapacity or limitation as a normal part of aging (11).

How ever disability touches the non-disabled reader, the very fact that it does touch is certainly taken for granted. Non-disabled people are positioned as those who need to be reminded that they do now and will in the future be in contact with 'people with disabilities'. Statistically speaking, the probability of spending at least part of one's life as a disabled person is close to 100 per cent (Zola, 1982). This probability is closer to a certainty if one is Aboriginal. Despite the statistical normalcy of living in and beside disability, *In Unison* believes that all Canadians need to be reminded that 'they do indeed have some experience with disability'.

In Unison implies that touched as people are by disability, non-disabled Canadians rarely see a disabled person, since disabled people rarely participate in the institutions of society, especially in employment. They face personal, social, and economic disadvantages and barriers that prevent access to the same opportunities as other

Canadians. Women and Aboriginal persons with disabilities, in particular, experience greater disadvantages, reporting higher incidences of unemployment and poverty (11).

Despite *In Unison*'s hint that the difference disability makes might best be located in disabled peoples' common fate as an isolated and excluded minority group, this is not the way that the report represents the issue of diversity with respect to disability. *In Unison* represents the diversity of 'Canadian citizens with disabilities' strictly in terms of the variation of and in conditions of individuals with physical, sensory, and mental disabilities. The version of diversity that disability is said to represent is thus uniform in character. Difference is located only in conditions of bodily or sensorial impairments. The only diversity that this group conceived of as 'people with disabilities' represents is a decontextualized, depoliticized, and ironically, depersonalized one.

Normalcy and Personhood

What is reflected in organizations such as WHO and the Canadian government in their conceptions of disability is a medicalized version of impairment. According to this medical logic, what is most important and most deserving of emphasis is a shared unified stance in 'personhood'. James Overboe (1999) criticizes this view:

> I believe that the term 'person with a disability' demonstrates and is underscored by a 'normative' resemblance that we can attain if we achieve the status of being deemed 'people first' (with the term's emphasis on independence and extreme liberal individualism) in the eyes of an ableist-centered society (24).

People-first language makes the claim that a resemblance of normalcy can be attained if all people and institutions emphasize, over and over again, that disabled people are indeed 'people'. What people-first language aims to bring non-disabled people 'in touch with' are representations

of normalcy as closely as is possible. While 'disability touches everyone,' and while 'most people experience some form' of disability, readers of *In Unison* are still positioned as those who stand in need of convincing that when the touch or experience of disability comes around, they should only focus on an extreme liberal and abstractly independent form of personhood.

Disability is not being noticed, characterized, defined, measured, or responded to by anyone outside of the people who embodied it. For example, there is no hint that disability is best conceptualized as a relation between people and the environment (Gadacz, 1994), or that environments are disabling (Oliver, 1990, 1996), or that disability is a policy matter beset by conflicting models of how difference and inequality ought to be addressed (Bickenbach, 1993). Further, there is no hint that disability is constituted from taken-for-granted notions of normalcy (Davis, 1997; Thomson, 1997; Linton, 1998), or that disability always appears through narrative in social life and should be examined as such (Zola, 1982; Mitchell and Snyder, 1997; Michalko, 1998, 1999; Titchkosky, 1998, 2000, 2001; Corker and French, 1999; Michalko and Titchkosky, 2001). All of these alternative ways of locating the social significance of disability share a bracketing of the taken-for-granted good of medical versions of disability, and an insistence that how disability is interpreted and represented is of primary concern.

The consequence is that disability is conceived and programmatically treated as an individual trouble and not a public issue. 'People with disabilities' language makes two central interpretive moves: first, it separates the individual from disability and, second, it circumscribes disability as some-thing (bad) that is only understood in relation to its attachment to individuals. While ironic, this is also political and, while political, its politics are hidden.

Conclusion

It is undoubtedly true that people-first language originated in the desire to resist disability as a master-status, and thus to reject images of people completely mastered by disability defined as a set of embodied limitations. Note, however, that through people-first language the concept of disability has remained the same-only a little distance has been enforced between it and its possessor.

However, an analysis of disability discourse can help disabled people and non-disabled people 'get in touch with' the manner and form of constituting the meaning of people. Still, whatever else disability has to offer to collective understandings of the human condition, it is 'high time' (almost 20 years after the International Year of the Disabled) to understand people-first language as one of the dominant ways to maintain clear, certain and manageable boundaries around bodies, minds and senses while denying disability any positive actuality.

References

Bickenbach, J. 1993. *Physical Disability and Social Policy*. Toronto: University of Toronto Press.

Canada. 1996. *Equal Citizenship for Canadians with Disabilities: The Will to Act. Federal Task Force on Disability Issue*. Ottawa: Minister of Public Works and Government Services Canada.

Canada. 1998. *In Unison: A Canadian Approach to Disability Issues. A Visionary Paper of Federal/Provincial/Territorial Ministers Responsible for Social Services*. Hull, QC: Human Resources Development Canada.

Canguilhem, G. 1991 [1966]. *The Normal and The Pathological*, C. Fawcett and R. Cohen, trans. New York: Zone Books.

Corker, M., and S. French, eds. 1999. *Disability Discourse*. Buckingham: Open University Press.

Davis, L., ed. 1995. *Enforcing Normalcy: Disability, Deafness and the Body*. London: Verso.

———. 1997. *The Disability Studies Reader*. New York: Routledge

Foucault, M. 1970. *The Order of Things: An Archaeology of the Human Sciences*, A.S. London, trans. London: Tavistock Publications.

Gadacz, R. 1994. *Re-Thinking Dis-Ability: New Structures, New Relationships*. Edmonton: University of Alberta Press.

Goffman, E. 1963. Stigma: *Notes on the Management of Spoiled Identity*. Englewood Cliffs, NJ: Prentice-Hall.

Human Resources Development Canada (HRDC). 1995. *Vocational Rehabilitation and Disabled Persons Act: Annual Report 1994–95*. Ottawa: Human Resources Development Canada.

Linton, S. 1998. *Claiming Disability: Knowledge and Identity*. New York: New York University Press.

Michalko, R. 1998. *The Mystery of the Eye and the Shadow of Blindness*. Toronto: University of Toronto Press.

———. 1999. *The Two-In-One: Walking with Smokie, Walking with Blindness*. Philadelphia: Temple University Press.

Mitchell, D., and S. Snyder, eds. 1997. 'Disability Studies and the Double Bind of Representation', in *The Body and Physical Difference: Discourses of Disability*, pp. 1–31. Ann Arbor, MI: University of Michigan Press.

Michalko, R., and T. Titchkosky. 2001. 'Putting Disability in Its Place: It's Not a Joking Matter', in *Embodied Rhetorics: Disability in Language and Culture*, pp. 200–28, J. Wilson and C. Lewiecki-Wilson, eds. Carbondale, IL: University of Southern Illinois Press.

Oliver, M. 1990. *The Politics of Disablement: A Sociological Approach*. Hampshire and London: Macmillan.

———. 1996. *Understanding Disability: From Theory to Practice*. New York: St Martin's Press.

Thomson, R.G. 1997. *Extraordinary Bodies: Figuring Physical Disability in American Culture and Literature*. New York: Columbia University Press.

Titchkosky, T. 1998. 'Women, Anorexia and Change', *Dharma* 23, 4: 479–500.

———. 2000. 'Disability Studies: Old or New', *Canadian Journal of Sociology and Anthropology* 25, 5: 197–224.

———. 2001. 'Cultural Maps: Which Way to Disability?', in *Disability/Postmodernity: Embodying Disability Theory*, pp. 145–60, M. Corker and T. Shakespeare, eds. London: Continuum.

Zola, I.K. 1982. *Missing Pieces: A Chronicle of Living with a Disability*. Philadelphia: Temple University Press.

Questions for Critical Thought

An Epidemic in Search of a Disease: The Construction of Sexual Dysfunction as a Social Problem

1. Sexual dysfunction is a socially-constructed problem. Discuss.
2. Most diseases in contemporary society are socially constructed to serve primarily the interest of those constructing these diseases. How far do you agree with this statement?
3. How has the rhetoric of an epidemic of sexual dysfunction been deployed to affect the actions of both individuals and health professionals?
4. How does the interface between academic researchers, pharmaceutical industries, and health promotion discourses contribute to the miasma for the development of sexual dysfunction?
5. Critically evaluate the two sources of epidemiological statistics used in defining the epidemic rate of sexual dysfunction.

Citizenship and Health: The Governance of 'Imported Malaria' and the Safety of Anti-Malarial Drugs

1. Why would agents of governance want to uphold the dichotomous belief that science determines risk and the public perceives risk?
2. How can Canadian citizens influence discourses of health?
3. Define the five types of knowledge mentioned in the text and discuss how they are related to one another.
4. Referring to the case study, discuss the dualistic idea of subjective knowledge in the governing process.
5. Discuss the relationship between power and freedom in contemporary forms of governance.

The Impact of Financial Compensation on Treatment Outcomes for Chronic Pain: A Test of the 'Money Matters' Thesis

1. How does the 'money matter' thesis affect pain management?
2. What is the role of subjective rationality in evidence-based pain management?
3. Pain assessment should only be made based on evidence-based physiotherapeutic approaches. How far do you agree with this statement?
4. How far do you agree with the assertion that better treatment outcomes for chronic pain are attainable in the absence of litigation or other financial compensation?
5. Explain the difference between clinical and social definitions of pain. What accounts for the difference in the definition of pain?

Where Will the Jurisdiction Fall? The Possible Regulation of Traditional Chinese Medicine/Acupuncturists in Ontario

1. Acupuncture is both a profession and a treatment modality. Discuss.
2. How does the professionalization process of TCM/As affect their potential entry into mainstream health care system?
3. Why and how should the practice of CAM be regulated?
4. What are the social and political barriers affecting the incorporation of TCM/As in the Ontario health care system?
5. How does the internal jurisdictional battles among TCM/As contribute to their exclusion from the health care system?

DISABILITY: A ROSE BY ANY OTHER NAME? 'PEOPLE-FIRST' LANGUAGE IN CANADIAN SOCIETY

1. How does disability touch non-disabled people through people-first language?
2. How do we address the personal and socio-economic barriers confronting people with disabilities?
3. Assess the efficacy of people-first language as a remedy for social and political barriers confronting people with disabilities?
4. What representation of disability does the people-first language seek to introduce into the world?
5. What are the alternative ways of understanding the social significance of disability in the Canadian society?

Part X **Inequality and Stratification**

Much of Canadian social policy has been directed at addressing problems associated with inequality and stratification across social groups. Despite this intervention, inequality and stratification with their attendant social cankers still endure. This calls for a sociological analysis into why the problems of inequality persist in spite of state intervention and the current dimensions of inequality. The following chapters deliberate pertinent problems associated with inequality that visit some social groups on a daily basis but are easily ignored by many in the society.

Krista Robson sets the ball rolling by using the Renee Heikamp ordeal as a case study in understanding the role of motherhood to explain her son Jordan's death as a consequence of his mother's action, as opposed to a consequence of an inadequate welfare system. Robson concludes that the labelling and criminalization of poor and marginalized mothers in Canadian society serves a political purpose by blaming these women, rather than the state, for their predicaments.

Solutions to problems of social exclusion do not rest only on the state, but also on the civil society. This calls for a multi-levelled approach in addressing the problems. Stephen W. Baron takes up the challenge by examining the unemployment experiences of homeless male street youth and how their labour market experiences and interpretations of unemployment are linked to criminal behaviour. Understanding social exclusion from the perspective of those excluded is critical in ultimately addressing the problems associated with it.

Grace-Edward Galabuzi explores how crime-labelled communities feature in the crusade against gun violence in Toronto. A Building Hope Coalition, formed in the Black community in Toronto to address gun violence, serves as the reference for Galabuzi's paper. J.L. Deveau takes the discussion of inequality from the communities to the workplace. He ponders on how workplace accommodation works to the disadvantage of people with disabilities. Deveau, therefore, contends that people with disabilities be involved in strategies geared towards making workplaces accommodating for all, irrespective of who you are as a person.

Workplace inequalities come in different forms. Amber Gazso offers a sociological interpretation of how gender as a social structure explains, and gets reconstructed, by news discourse on women's inequality in the workplace.

Aside from gender, income is one of the major arrangements that bring about inequality in society. Paul S. Maxim and his colleagues examine the income disparity within and between Aboriginal groups as well as the income disparity between the general Canadian population and the different Aboriginal groups. Even though income is mainly held as an economic variable, this study assesses income disparity among various social groups from a purely sociological standpoint.

The discussions presented in this Part investigate how victims of inequality are easily held responsible for their conditions, thus releasing the state from the responsibility of accounting for this phenomenon and its attendant social ramifications. This exploration is likely to trigger further debate on the role of the state and communities in dealing with inequalities in Canadian society.

CHAPTER 42

'Canada's Most Notorious Bad Mother': The Newspaper Coverage of the Jordan Heikamp Inquest

Krista Robson

Introduction

When reading the news coverage surrounding the inquest into the starvation death of an infant in a homeless women's shelter, it became clear that this case was a horrifying example of how the **discourse of motherhood** and the individualization of responsibility can work together to regulate the behaviour of mothers. The purpose of this paper is to ponder the role that the concepts of motherhood played in portraying this infant's death as a consequence of the actions of his '**bad mother**', as opposed to a consequence of an inadequate welfare system.

This paper will first outline the details surrounding this infant's death. Second, the discourse of mother blame and how it intersects with neoliberalism's individualization of responsibility will be summarized. Third, evidence will be presented of the cultural norms pertaining to mothers that dominated the media coverage of the Heikamp inquest. Finally, this individual case study will be situated within a broader discussion of how the 'bad mother' label is currently being used for political purposes not only by the public at large, but also by the state.

Jordan and Renee Heikamp

Renee was 19 years old when her infant son, Jordan, died of starvation in a women's shelter in downtown Toronto in 1997. Renee was homeless at the time and had been for about four years prior to becoming pregnant. Upon Jordan's birth, hospital staff called the Catholic Children's Aid Society (CAS) to intervene because of their concerns about Renee's ability to care for her son. Nine days after the birth, the CAS social worker assigned to the case, Angela Martin, arranged for Renee and Jordan to be discharged and moved into a women's shelter. Thirty-seven days later, Jordan was rushed to the hospital and pronounced dead on arrival. An autopsy revealed that Jordan died of chronic starvation. Renee had been breastfeeding Jordan, but her breast milk had dried up and the formula that she was feeding him was over diluted.

Both Renee and the social worker were charged with criminal negligence causing death. In 1998, after a 13-month preliminary hearing into the death, Madam Justice Mary Hogan of the Ontario Court of Justice ruled that the case would not proceed to trial because of a lack of evidence of 'wanton and reckless disregard' for the life of another person, the requisite element for criminal negligence causing death, on the part of either Renee or the social worker. The judge ruled that 'the death of baby Jordan was a terrible tragedy—one made even more so by the fact that it might have been prevented' (*R. v. Heikamp and Martin*, 1999). In April 2001, after a four-month investigation, a coroner's inquest ruled that the starvation death of Jordan was a homicide and made recommendations for changes to the child protection system to prevent similar deaths in the future.

Discourse of Motherhood

The contemporary discourse of motherhood rests on several core assumptions that constitute the belief system against which women's lives are judged. First, a considerable weight of responsibility is placed onto the mother for the healthy development of children. Second, mothering is considered to be socially very important work; consequently, the characteristics of motherhood are strongly associated with the idea of self-sacrifice (Barrett and McIntosh, 1982; Rich, 1986; Glenn, Chang, and Forcey, 1994; Ladd-Taylor and Umansky, 1998). Third, the characteristics of motherhood invoke the idea of maternal instinct (Rich, 1986; Glenn, Chang, and Forcey, 1994; Connolly, 2000a). A final core assumption is that the '**good mother**' can only exist in the two-parent heterosexual family form.

These ideas, which constitute the dominant discourse of motherhood, have shaped and limited the choices that women make about their lives (Rich, 1986; Glenn, Chang, and Forcey, 1994). Women who deviate from the ideals of motherhood are subject to social and legal regulation.

Individualization of Responsibility

Actual mothering, however, 'occurs in specific social contexts that vary in terms of material and cultural resources and constraints' (Glenn, Chang, and Forcey, 1994: 3). As a result, the dominant standards of the 'good mother' often become a 'source of injury for mothers whose finances, education, age, living conditions, marital status . . . render such standards impossible to achieve or counter-productive' (Connolly, 2000b: 263).

Reliance on the myths of 'good motherhood' encourages the denial of economic, political, and social barriers to good parenting. And these barriers have intensified throughout the past two decades. The pressures of economic recessions, the globalization of production, and growing government deficits have challenged the viability of the traditional welfare state in Canada (Cossman and Fudge, 2002). With federal and provincial governments reducing their role in the delivery of social services, a massive shift in form and governing practices has seen the emergence of a neo-liberal state (Brodie, 1995; Bakker, 1996). Two overarching government practices promoted by neo-liberalism are privatization and familialization.

Methodology

For this examination, articles from three Canadian newspapers (*Globe and Mail*, *National Post*, *Toronto Star*) that appeared during the final month of the coroner's inquest were reviewed. These three newspapers were chosen because they each had significant coverage of the inquest and, in particular, each had columnists who wrote extensively and regularly on the case during the inquest. The coroner's inquest sat for 64 days from January to April 2001, with the verdict and recommendations released on 13 April 2001. Any article that included a mention of the Heikamp inquest that appeared between 12 March and 30 April 2001 was selected for analysis. In total, there were 63 articles that appeared during this time period. Qualitative content analysis was used to understand how this sample of news items communicated various 'truths', about mothering. Each article was read with the purpose of identifying the presence of themes that would reflect the main conceptual ideas that constitute mothering discourse, and how the 'myths' of mothering were invoked and if (and how) these contributed to labelling Renee as a 'bad mother'.

'Canada's Most Notorious Bad Mother'

When women 'refuse to behave according to the 'rules' of good mothering' (Steedman, 1987: 84) and 'when this behaviour is reported, it is seen as *truly newsworthy*' (Steedman, 1987: 150, emphasis added). I would suggest that this is how Renee Heikamp became front-page news for four months in 2001. To make sense of this death, the press consistently relied upon the pervasive societal discourses of mother blame, intersected with the neo-liberal concept of responsibility. According to the media, Jordan's death was directly attributable to his starvation, for which his mother was to blame. Thus, Renee was represented as having killed her son through bad mothering and, in particular, through her negligence.

The 'bad mother' label operates to shift attention away from a specific act to the whole person (Ladd-Taylor and Umansky, 1998); as a result, every aspect of Renee's behaviour was up for scrutiny and all of her actions during Jordan's short life were identified, according to the press, as signs of her 'bad mothering'. For instance, Renee's incapacity to be a 'good mother' was apparently evident in the first few days of Jordan's life:

> During the last two weeks of Jordan's life, a time in which doctors testified his wasting would have become apparent, she was looking for apartments, asking to go to Blue Jays games, eating in restaurants, getting engaged, accompanying a male friend to the doctor for company, fighting with other shelter residents and, as a consequence, moving rooms, getting a sunburn (Coyle, 2001).

Being labelled a 'bad mother' meant that activities that seemingly fit the criteria of 'good mothering' become signs of deviant mothering. For instance, from the lists above, 'looking for an apartment' and 'getting engaged' would presumably be acceptable behaviour, since homelessness and single parenthood are certainly marks of deviant mothering. Yet Renee was unable to escape the label of 'bad mother' even when attempting to conform to the criteria of 'good mothering'.

Blaming Renee

Renee's status as a homeless woman led many to see her as 'ill-equipped for motherhood' (Philp, 2001). Homeless mothers cannot provide their children with adequate shelter and food. But it requires a leap to arrive at the assumption that they cannot deliver discipline, affection, or nurturance. A prevailing assumption within the discourse on mothering, however, is that all women should be able to provide a proper maternal environment, which is preferably represented by the traditional

nuclear family. This assumption is itself a contradiction that worked against Renee from the beginning.

However, Renee did admit that, as Jordan's mother, she took some responsibility, but she added that, 'I feel like I've been singled out quite a bit and I don't think it's appropriate at this time' (quoted in Huffman, 2001). She was not the only one, moreover, who was not willing to take all the blame in this case. The coroner's inquest was characterized as an exercise in 'buck passing' (Coyle, 2001; Wente, 2001) and 'finger pointing' (Philp, 2001), with no one person or agency assuming any responsibility, but instead all desperately trying to place blame on others.

The inquest's ruling disappointed those looking for the blame to land somewhere. Much like the preliminary judicial hearing in the case, however, the coroner's jury focused on a systems failure. For instance, the jury directed recommendations at child protection workers, every Children's Aid Society in Ontario, the Ministry of Community and Social Services, the Ministry of Health, the City of Toronto, staff at women's shelters, and hospitals/clinics.

In the media's reaction to this case, questions were not being asked in order to uncover and change the structural context in which this case arose. The question posed by the media— 'How could this happen?'—spoke more to a (over)reliance on the private organization of child care. Only three articles and one letter to the editor moved beyond blaming the mother and other individuals to look instead at systemic economic and societal barriers to good parenting.

Conclusion

Isolating the Heikamp case from the context in which it existed, and mounting a powerful moral campaign to blame the mother is more reassuring to the status quo because it does not implicate the systemic problems and disadvantages, or the 'network of circumstances' (Landsberg, 2001)—for instance, cuts to welfare, hospitals, legal aid, and agencies assisting the poor—that characterized this case. Yet even in the face of dwindling social support, when there is a perceived failure to care, the individuals and, especially, individual mothers who hold the burden of care, are blamed and the structural barriers and inequalities are ignored. Mother blaming in Renee's case, therefore, served a political purpose—attention was diverted away from the lack of resources for those women marginalized in our communities because of poverty and directed instead towards regulating and punishing this one woman.

References

Barrett, M., and M. McIntosh. 1982. *The Anti-Social Family*. London: Verso.

Connolly, D. 2000a. *Homeless Mothers: Face to Face with Women and Poverty*. Minneapolis: University of Minnesota Press.

———. 2000b. 'Mythical Mothers and Dichotomies of Good and Evil: Homeless Mothers in the United States', in *Ideologies and Technologies of Motherhood: Race, Class, Sexuality, Nationalism*, pp. 263–94, H. Ragone and F. Winddance Twine, eds. New York: Routledge.

Cossman, B., and J. Fudge. 2002. *Privatization, Law and the Challenge to Feminism*. Toronto: University of Toronto Press.

Coyle, J. 2001. 'Faint Gleams of Hope in a Day of Buck Passing', *Toronto Star*, 3 April: B1.

Glenn, E.N., G. Chang, and L.R. Forcey, eds. 1994. *Mothering: Ideology, Experience and Agency*. New York: Routledge.

Huffman, T. 2001. 'Heikamp Hurt by Request to Consider Homicide Verdict', *Toronto Star*, 5 April: B1.

Ladd-Taylor, M., and L. Umansky. 1998. *'Bad' Mothers: The Politics of Blame in Twentieth-Century America*. New York: New York University Press.

Landsberg, M. 2001. 'Save Some Wrath for Society that Failed Baby Jordan', *Toronto Star*, 21 April: L1.

Philp, M. 2001. 'Will There be More Baby Jordans?', *Globe and Mail*, 5 April: A13.

R. v. Heikamp and Martin. 1999. Ontario Court of Justice.

Rich. A. 1986. *Of Woman Born: Motherhood as Experience and Institution*. New York: W.W. Norton & Company.

Steedman, C.K. 1987. *Landscape for a Good Woman: A Story of Two Lives*. New Brunswick, NJ: Rutgers University Press.

Wente, M. 2001. 'Everyone is Nicely Off Hook in Death of Baby', *Globe and Mail*, 12 April: A1.

CHAPTER 43

Street Youth Labour Market Experiences and Crime

Stephen W. Baron

Introduction

Research indicates that advanced capitalist societies are experiencing a number of structural economic transformations leading to an increased non-standard employment and more poor-paying jobs (Tanner, 1996; Wilson, 1997; Hartnagel, 1998; Young, 1999). Simultaneously, there has been an increase in the importance of training and education required to obtain employment (Wilson, 1997). Evidently, these fundamental structural changes are creating a permanent group of under/unemployables locked out of the normal occupational structure of Canadian society (Box, 1987; Inciardi, Horowitz, and Pottieger, 1993; Wilson, 1997).

Young people have been hit disproportionately hard by economic restructuring (Wilson, 1997; Young, 1999). An extreme manifestation of this is the growing problem of 'street kids', youths under the age of 24 who have left school and 'hang out' on the street on a regular basis (Radford, King, and Warren, 1989; Smart et al., 1990; Hagan and McCarthy, 1997). The lack of access to meaningful employment in the regular economy leaves these marginal youths at risk for a number of social problems including street crime (Williams and Kornblum, 1985; Tanner, Krahn, and Hartnagel, 1995; Baron and Hartnagel, 1997, 1998; Wilson, 1997; Young, 1999).

Despite debates regarding the effects of these economic transitions on marginal youth, there has been limited research into how these youth react to **unemployment** and how this is linked to criminal activity (Craine, 1995). In this paper I examine the unemployment experiences of selected male **street youth** and explore how their labour market experiences and interpretations of unemployment are linked to criminal behaviour.

Research Evidence and Theory

Exploring the impact of economic restructuring on the lives of marginal youth, Anderson (1990), MacLeod (1987), Padilla (1992), Sullivan (1989), Williams (1989), and Wilson (1997) all outline the devastation resulting from economic change. In light of these findings, a number of researchers have called for greater attention to be paid to the variables linking unemployment and crime (Wright, 1981; Horowitz, 1984; Box and Hale, 1985; Box, 1987; Hartnagel, 1998;). For Box and others (see Wilson, 1997; Young, 1999), the apparent relationship between unemployment/ unemployability and crime is compounded by a subjective element. Box (1987; see also Box and Hale, 1985) further points out that people's

interpretations of their labour market situations plays a large role in shaping their responses to it.

Grounding this in a traditional criminological perspective, strain theorists stress material inequalities as the key to understanding crime (Cloward and Ohlin, 1960; Box, 1987). Strain theorists argue that the motivation to commit crime increases when legitimate opportunities to achieve culturally defined success goals, including material success, are restricted. Again, working from a control perspective, it can also be argued that unemployment reduces people's bonds to conventional societal institutions (Hirschi, 1969; Box, 1987; Hartnagel, 1998; Wilson, 1997). The unemployed have fewer stakes in conformity that might be jeopardized by criminal conduct.

Methods

Recognizing the heterogeneity of the street youth population, 200 male respondents were identified based on four sampling criteria: (1) participants must be male; (2) they must be aged 24 and under; (3) they must have left or finished school; and (4) they must spend at least three hours a day, three days a week 'hanging around' on the street or in a mall. The rationales for these criteria were: (1) to avoid the potential ethical and methodological problems of a male researcher inquiring about intimate lives of female respondents; (2) to cover the age range of those described as street youth (Caputo and Ryan, 1991); (3) to eliminate those not eligible for fulltime employment; and (4) to obtain a sample of 'serious', 'at-risk' youth and avoid the 'weekend warriors'.

The study's data were collected over a six-month period from January through June of 1993 in Edmonton, Alberta, a large Western Canadian city with a population of 800,000. The labour market at the time of data collection was extremely difficult for those less than 24 years of age, with their unemployment rate reaching 20.2 per cent in 1993. The snowball sampling technique was used to reach qualified respondents.

Background

The above procedures yielded a sample of 200 male street youths with an average age of almost 19 years (x = 18.86). The racial make-up of the sample was predominantly Caucasian (77 per cent), although almost a quarter (n = 46) were from other racial groups. Aboriginal youth made up the majority of these other respondents (n = 32). The average respondent had completed Grade 9. A full three-quarters of the sample had been with no fixed shelter during the previous year (n = 153). Respondents reported an average legal income of $335 a month in the previous year. Some of this was employment income and some was state support. At the time of the study, 59 respondents reported being on state support. Most respondents reported that state support was unsatisfactory and insufficient. A minority, however, indicated it was adequate enough to live on, and a positive alternative to hunger and homelessness.

The average respondent reported more than 1,600 offences in the prior twelve months—numbers comparable to the totals reported in other work using urban street youth (Inciardi, Horowitz, and Pottieger, 1993; Baron, 1995). The sale of illegal drugs made up the bulk of these offences (x = 1,200). Respondents also reported an average of 348 property offences and 48 robberies throughout the year. The former were primarily thefts from cars (57 per cent), shoplifting (including food), and break-and-enters. The primary motivation for these various offences was utilitarian: to gain money 'to live' and to purchase drugs and alcohol. Thus, we see evidence of an impoverished group supporting themselves through crime to compensate for their lack of legal resources.

Employment and Unemployment

Despite their meagre education, the respondents had extensive labour market experience, reporting an average of seven jobs in their lifetimes. While these jobs ranged in quality and status, most were concentrated in the lower end of the labour market. The majority of respondents provided economic reasons, including layoffs, temporary positions, and bankruptcies, for their previous employment ending. However, a number of respondents indicated that they had been dismissed from their jobs for tardiness, absenteeism, and serious personal differences with their managers. There were also others who indicated they left their jobs because they were unsatisfied with their wages and working conditions.

While these youths reported a great deal of previous employment, their current situations reflected some difficulties in obtaining work. The average youth in the study reported being out of work ten months out of the previous twelve. The average respondent indicated that he looked for work for three of those months, (x = 2.7 months), did not pursue work during six of those months (x = 5.5), and was unable to pursue employment because of incarceration the rest of the time (X = 1.75 months). Some respondents indicated they did not look for work during some of this time because they had become discouraged and given up their job search.

Lengthy unemployment appeared to destroy respondents' motivation. Many respondents blamed their periods of search inactivity on drug and/or alcohol abuse. A large number also implied that they did not search for employment because they did not require the 'meagre' financial rewards of a job. Some street youths also recognize the role that social and economic disadvantage plays in their unemployment. Furthermore, there was the impression from some of the youths that gaining employment had more to do with luck than anything else. This logic might have allowed the youths to downplay the role of some of the previously mentioned factors in their inability to secure employment.

Depression, Guilt, Emotional Indifference, and Unemployment

Another avenue researchers have been encouraged to explore surrounds people's emotional reactions to their unemployment (Box, 1987; Feather, 1990). It is suggested that being unemployed may have some effect on people's emotional states, which may in turn influence their behaviour. A few of the youths reported negative emotional reactions, including depression and/or guilt over their unemployment. For some, these emotions appeared to stem from the inability to fulfill societal expectations of work, self-sufficiency, and material success.

In spite of the negative emotional reactions expressed by some respondents, the majority of them expressed little affective response to their unemployment. They, however, were confident that they could get a job if they actually attempted to find one. There was also the impression that many of these jobs were to be found at the lower end of the labour market and, while easy to obtain, they were not the first choice for most of the respondents. A considerable number of the youths stressed the profitability of crime over legitimate work, thus making them successful entrepreneurs in an alternative economy.

Conclusion

The results of the choices made by street youths lead to some unintended consequences. First, some of the youths are incarcerated for their crimes. Thus their somewhat forced, somewhat chosen alternative economic routes eventually close off doors to legitimate employment, leaving them restricted to the criminal labour market. Second, while out of work they are not acquiring the education, job skills, and experience that might help them overcome some of the barriers in the tough labour market. In many ways, they have little chance of escaping the secondary labour market. The problem is that the choices they make leave them vulnerable to incarceration, which in turn creates more difficulty for their return to conventional society. In a sense, these youths are pushed to the margins of society and forced to live in extreme conditions, where they are then punished for trying to survive.

References

Anderson, E. 1990. *Streetwise: Race, Class and Change in an Urban Community*. Chicago: University of Chicago Press.

Baron, S.W. 1995. 'Serious Offenders', in *Canadian Delinquency*, J.H. Creechan and R.A. Silverman, eds. Scarborough: Prentice-Hall.

Baron, S.M., and T.Y. Hartnagel. 1997. 'Attributions, Affect and Crime: Street Youths' Reaction to Unemployment', *Criminology* 35: 409–34.

———. 1998. 'Street Youth and Criminal Violence', *Journal of Research in Crime and Delinquency* 35: 166–92.

Box, S. 1987. *Recession, Crime and Punishment*. Basingstoke: Macmillan.

Box, S., and C. Hale. 1985. 'Unemployment, Imprisonment and Prison Overcrowding', *Contemporary Crises* 9: 209–28.

Caputo, T., and C. Ryan. 1991. *The Police Response to Youth at Risk*. Ottawa: Solicitor General.

Cloward, R.A., and L.E. Ohlin. 1960. *Delinquency and Opportunity*. New York: Free Press of Glencoe.

Craine, S. 1997. '"The black magic roundabout": Cyclical Transitions, Social Exclusion and Alternative Careers', in *Youth, the 'Underclass' and Social Exclusion*, R. MacDonald, ed. London: Routledge.

Feather, N.T. 1990. *The Psychological Impact of Unemployment*. New York: Springer-Verlag.

Hagan, J., and B. McCarthy. 1997. *Mean Streets: Youth Crime and Homelessness*. Cambridge: Cambridge University Press.

Hartnagel, T.F. 1998. 'Labour Market Problems and Crime in the Ttransition from School to Work', *Canadian Review of Sociology and Anthropology* 35: 435–60.

Hirschi, T. 1969. *Causes of Delinquency*. Berkeley, CA: University of California Press.

Horowitz, A.N. 1984. 'The Economy and Social Pathology', *Annual Review of Sociology* 10: 95–119.

Inciardi, J.A., R. Horowitz, and A.E. Pottieger. 1993. *Street Kids, Street Drugs, Street Crime*. Belmont, CA: Wadsworth Publishing Company.

MacLeod, J. 1987. *Ain't No Makin It*. Boulder, CO: Westview Press.

Padilla, E.M. 1992. *The Gang as an American Enterprise*. New Brunswick, NJ: Rutgers.

Radford, J.L., A.A.C. King, and W.K. Warren. 1989. *Street Youth and AIDS*. Ottawa: Health and Welfare Canada.

Smart, R.G., E.M. Adlaf, K.M. Porterfield, and M.D. Canale. 1990. *Drugs, Youth and the Street*. Toronto: Addictions Research Foundation.

Sullivan, M.L. 1989. *Getting Paid*. Ithaca: Cornell University Press.

Tanner, J. 1996. *Teenage Troubles*. Toronto: Nelson.

Tanner, J., H. Krahn, and T.E. Hartnagel. 1995. *Fractured Transitions from School to Work: Revisiting the Dropout Problem*. Don Mills, ON: Oxford University Press.

Williams, T. 1989. *The Cocaine Kids*. New York: Addison-Wesley.

Williams, T., and W. Kornblum. 1985. *Growing Up Poor*. Lexington, MA: Lexington Books.

Wilson, W.J. 1997. *When Work Disappears*. New York: Knopf.

Wright, K.N. 1981. *Crime and Criminal Justice in a Declining Economy*. Cambridge, MA: Oelgeschlager, Gunn and Hain.

Young, J. 1999. *The Exclusive Society*. Thousand Oaks, CA: Sage.

CHAPTER 44

Building Hope: Confronting Social Exclusion and Violence in Toronto's Black Community, 2001

Grace-Edward Galabuzi

Introduction

The paper discusses the formation of the **Building Hope Coalition** in response to an upsurge in gun **violence** in the **Black community** in Toronto in the summer of 2001. It explores the Coalition's attempt to create a community anti-violence movement as a form of collective action response to the violence, which involved presenting an alternative ideological response through a restorative justice agenda, community autonomy, and a process of identity deconstruction and reconstruction as preconditions for movement mobilization. These efforts are complicated by opposition from within the Black community to the Coalition's community autonomy approach and charges that it was embracing 'collective responsibility' for the 'criminal acts of a few'. The efforts also confront a persistent anti-black discourse in the media, whose effect is to racialize crime and portray the Black community as a culturally deviant 'other',

prone to 'criminal behaviour'. The paper explores the concurrent processes of the racialization of crime and the racialization of poverty, and other social, ecological, and developmental factors in reproducing conditions that trigger the violence.

Gun Violence in Toronto's African Canadian Community

In the summer of 2001, Toronto's African Canadian community was engulfed in an undeclared crisis of internecine violence. About 16 Black youth lost their lives in gun violence over a period of four months. According to the Black Action Defense Committee, that loss of young life to violence simply added to one hundred such deaths in a 5-year period and 200 in the preceding ten years. While Canada's and Toronto's murder rates were stable for much of the 1990s, at about 2.5 per 100,000 for Canada and 2.4 per 100,000 for Toronto, the rates among Blacks in Toronto and particularly youths, have skyrocketed. According to Gartner and Thompson (2004), the rate for Blacks is four times that of the general population at 10.1 per 100,000. While the Black community represents just under 10 per cent of the city's population, it accounted for approximately 30 per cent of the murder victims annually between 1996 and 2004.

The upheaval set off alarms in the community and forced a renewed community focus on the condition of Black youth in the city. Their experience of marginalization, alienation, and social exclusion derives from a complex of social factors created by persistent high levels of poverty, youth unemployment, high school dropout rates, social service deficits, segregated neighbourhood selection leading to racialized low-income areas, and the experience of systemic racism that defined black youth interaction with mainstream institutions in the city. While the violence represented a crisis centred in low-income neigbourhoods, it was symptomatic of a persistent and pervasive condition of social exclusion that devalued Black life across the city, intensified periodically by institutional and media driven anti-black racist discourses.

Some members of the Black community, concerned that government authorities were ignoring the violence because of the marginal status of the Black community confronted officials from the city, province, and the federal governments to demand action. Acknowledging the limits of that strategy, others began to advocate an approach focusing on the mobilization of community resources for collective community action.

Building Hope Coalition

The emergence of the Building Hope Coalition represented the attempt to seek community-centred sustainable responses to the crisis. Initially, the coalition sought to organize a series of community meetings in the most affected low-income areas of the city and meetings with Black youth. The objective was to seek community specific alternatives to mainstream institutional responses

to the violence and mobilization of a community wide anti-violence campaign that would include forms of discourse intervention aimed at countering long standing characterizations of the Black community as crime 'prone'.

It advocated restorative justice measures to reconcile young perpetuators of violence to the community, by denouncing violent behaviour while holding them to community based social obligations. The Coalition also sought to develop a comprehensive community action plan to guide a broader and more systematic medium and long term response through partnership involving what it called the four levels of governance: federal, provincial, city, and Black community. It also focused on the need for strong community institutions to address the immediate well-being of families in grief (a mass memorial service was organized for the lost youth), offering counselling for the parents, relatives and friends dealing with the trauma of the loss of their loved ones to the fatal violence, as well as conflict resolution, anger management programs, and other supports for youth employment, recreation, and social services.

The paper considers the Coalition's social construction of the crisis as a Black community problem to which an Afro-centric solution needed to be articulated in the Garveyite tradition of self-reliance and community autonomy. It reviews the Coalition decision to take community action in response to state neglect and inaction and its objection to the relations of dependency with the dominant institutions which the Coalition claimed were responsible for maintaining and reproducing the subordinate position of the Black community in Canadian society.

It reviews the Coalition's process of social construction of a Black community on the basis of 'common experiences of a history of oppression' and 'self-definition', among an amalgam of various national and cultural groups and attempts to mobilize them for political action. Some in this community of communities consider the very concept of 'shared identity' lethal because in Canadian society generally, young black men, have been largely constructed as aggressive, violent and dangerous.

The Coalition approach met with criticism from within the community and beyond. Critics argued that the project represented a form of 'collective responsibility' for the actions of a few; an approach they claimed obviated their membership in the broader Toronto community and effectively ghettoized them. It played into the hands of the mainstream media, which had defined the shootings as an exclusively Black community concerns, and perpetuated a racist discourse of black criminality. Others resented the impact the stigma would have on their careers as the negative cross socio-class identity fused working class and low-income phenomenon into middle class Blacks' experiences. Others claimed it conflated a 'Jamaican' problem to all segments of the black community. Critics also identified media and government authorities' construction of the violence as un-Canadian—using characterization such as 'Black on Black' crime, or 'Black crime', which created a new category of **criminal activity** in which only Blacks were culpable.

For critics, the attention on the violence served to raise public anxiety about 'Black crime', at a time when it had been low because it was seen as intra-community violence. They argued that the mainstream media and civic leaders' applause of the Coalition 'Stop the Violence' campaign validated the position by the Toronto Police Force rank and file, that the Black community should 'take responsibility' for the criminal element in its midst. Critics argued that this was tantamount to imposing policing responsibilities on one of the most marginalized communities in the city. That it meant abandoning the community to deal with complex problems without the benefit of the resources and institutions established in society for this purpose, in essence the broader Toronto community excising the Black community from its civic body, as though it were a cancer.

The paper focuses on the tension in the community represented by these two positions, using the contending narratives to interrogate the media construction of the 'Black community' as monolithic, an aggressive and dangerous 'Other', and disproportionately prone to violent behaviour. It notes the vulnerabilities that arise out of generations of negative stereotypes in Toronto imposing a form of social deviance on the community. Coverage in major newspapers, referring to Blacks as culturally deficient, and sensationalizing criminal activities involving Black suspects, using repeated images to disproportionately portray and generalizing it as representative of the Black community's moral position provides a social cultural explanation for crime in Toronto in a period of moral panic, thereby racializing criminality and reinforcing the ideological position that 'racialized immigrant communities' exist outside the boundaries of normal Canadian behaviour. The effect of the racist anti-Black discourse intensified the alienation of the community youth, making nihilistic violence more likely.

Conclusion

From a social movement analysis standpoint, the paper explores the tension between structure and agency. How do socio-political structures and collective action interact in the push and pull struggles of subaltern movements? The contending positions in the Black community speak to the challenges of the identity formation process in movement building and the agency/structure debate manifests itself in the tension between autonomous action and the structural constraints of social exclusion. In that respect, a key question posed by the paper is: Are Black communities passive victims of their circumstances condemned to the vagaries of structural forces beyond their control or are they capable of an agency that could transform their reality?

References

Black Action Defense Committee. 2001. 'End The Shootings'. Toronto.

Gartner, R., and S. Thompson. 2004. 'Trends in Homicide in Toronto'. Paper presented at the U of T Centre of Criminology Research Colloquium on Community Safety: From Enforcement and Prevention to Civic Engagement, 25 June.

Garvey, A.J., ed. 1970. *Garvey and Garveyism*. New York: Collier-Macmillan.

Statistics Canada. 2001. 'Visible Minorities in Canada', *Canadian Centre for Justice Statistics Profile Series*. Ottawa: Ministry of Industry.

CHAPTER 45

Workplace Accommodation for the Disabled in the Federal Public Service: An Institutional Ethnography

J.L. Deveau

Introduction

Canadian workplaces have been designed for able-bodied persons. To work in these places, disabled Canadians need **workplace accommodation**. The Meiorin and Grismer Supreme Court of Canada rulings had a significant impact on accommodation for the disabled. Previous to these decisions, workplace accommodation was perceived as whatever concessions needed to be made to employees who, like me, had the misfortune of being disabled.

The Meiorin and Grismer rulings transformed accommodation into an inclusive process necessitating both systemic and individualized measures to enable the disabled to function in workplaces designed for persons who are able-bodied. Systemic measures include such things as wheelchair accessible washrooms in public places and the provision of alternatives to printed formats such as Braille, large print, audiocassette, and diskette. Individualized accommodations include such things as providing interpreters for deaf and hearing-impaired employees, adaptive technology, flexible work arrangements, and so on.

This article is based on the premise that 'texts' and the language they contain play an active role in the mediation of everyday government operations (Smith, 1990). Workplace accommodation is one such operation that is organized through text-based practices.

Theoretical/Methodological Framework

I used Institutional Ethnography (IE), a methodology advocated by Canadian sociologist Dorothy E. Smith (Smith, 1987, 1990). IE rejects the established scholarly way of validating knowledge by referring to ideas already established in the literature and relies on people's experience as a point of entry into sociological inquiry. This methodology investigates the connection among local settings of people's everyday life experiences, institutional processes, and 'ruling relations'—powerful outside forces that affect those experiences. Smith's concept of 'ruling' is derived from Marx. IE relies on a theorized way of exploring ruling practices—as people's social activities organized through texts, language and expertise.

In addition to using texts on workplace accommodation, I used my personal experience of what happened when I requested workplace accommodation as the basis for this investigation, combined with all documents kept on file by my workplace pertaining to this matter. The latter were obtained through Freedom of Information under Canada's Privacy Act.

During the first 10 years of my career, I had been able to work in an office that had an openable window that provided natural ventilation. Then, in 2001, I was relocated into an office that had no provisions for natural ventilation. The lack of natural ventilation caused me to experience a biomedical condition known as 'environmental sensitivity', a disability, which has been defined as:

> a chronic (i.e. continuing for more than three months) multi-system disorder, usually involving symptoms of the central nervous system and at least one other system. Affected persons are frequently intolerant to some foods and they react adversely to some chemicals and to environmental agents, singly or in combination, at levels generally tolerated by the majority. . .Improvement is associated with avoidance of suspected agents and symptoms recur with re-exposure.

This textually-mediated version of my condition brought me square against a line of fault between two opposing epistemologies: the heavily guarded ideological perception that the 'living flesh of disability' is an individualized problem (biomedical model of disability) against my embodied experience which viewed it as an interaction between my impairment and my physical environment (social model of disability).

Social Construction of Disability

Disability in everyday language is typically assigned to be a problem originating with the individual; it is something arising from bodily malfunc-

tion, an inability to do things in a way perceived to be 'normal', i.e., the biomedical model of disability (Linton, 1998; Titchkosky, 2003). Characterizing disability as 'inability' coincided with the ascendancy of bio-politics in the eighteenth century, when the body became identified as a social object to be managed in a manner that was consistent with its maximum functionality to the capitalist relations of production (Foucault, 1980).

This way of assigning meaning to the disabled achieved and preserved the state's power over the human body, which, from a structural functionalist perspective, has remained intact in today's society as 'an inevitable outcome of the evolution of contemporary society' (Barnes, 1996). Hence, the 'disability business' ensures that doctors, occupational therapists, physiotherapists, acupuncturists, and other professionals (ruling apparatus) maintain their status and positions in society. This functionalist account of the emergence of disability in society is an American perspective (Barnes, 1996); the British perspective draws on the materialist theories of Marx and Engels (1970) and suggests that disability is a function of industrial capitalism (Barnes, 1996; Oliver, 1996). Disabled people became severely disadvantaged because they were unable, rather than unwilling, to keep up with the dogma of capitalism: 'the speed of factory work, the enforced discipline, the time-keeping and production norms' (Oliver, 1996: 33).

The Work of Shielding the Institution from Inclusivity

It takes a lot of work to be disabled—people with disabilities are often not born that way (Titchkosky, 2003). It is a transformation process which involves continually invalidating one's self and validating the social and physical environments created for, and by, the able-bodied and normality itself. And since disability is perceived as being an individualized problem, we are expected to do this unpaid work in order to overcome that intrinsic flaw in our personhood—that 'thing' called disability.

After I discovered I could not function in my office at work, I spent a month 'working' to try and find an alternative office location. If people with disabilities are going to be able to receive the necessary accommodation, we—and not the institution—are the ones having to do the 'work' to try and get this accommodation. Our success is contingent upon our health capital. Given that the disabled are constantly involved in 'the work of being disabled' so that we are able to fit into a world designed for the able-bodied, this results in significant expenditures from our health capital. The amount of 'work' and resulting stress on persons with disabilities, who must fight for their workplace accommodation, often results in exacerbating the person's disability, overall health, and family life (Deveau, forthcoming). As a result, the disabled person may not be able to oppose the ruling apparatus. This in turn results in the person with disability not being able to obtain the necessary accommodation, having to possibly quit his/her job or goes on short- or long-term disability. Since disability is perceived as an individualized problem, the disabled person is then blamed for not having enough self-assertion required to overcome his/her impairment. The institution gets off the hook and continues to replicate itself in its image as if nothing ever happened.

Conclusion

The purpose of this investigation was to find out what happened when I requested workplace accommodation. Using institutional ethnography to conduct textual analyses of the forms, policies, standards, and texts used in my requests for workplace accommodation has enabled me to understand how the power of the biomedicalized model of disability, diffused in these texts, resulted in disavowing my lived experience of this phenomenon.

Since the hegemonic status of the biomedicalized model of disability is still too powerful, the Meiorin and Grismer Supreme Court of Canada decisions have had little effect on how workplace accommodation is administered in my workplace. Workplace accommodation is still considered to be a form of remedy for disabled employees who, like me, have the misfortune of having some sort of physical or mental limitation. Until such time as the disabled, not unlike the feminist movement of the 1970s and 1980s, are able to develop their own way of expressing what it means to be disabled and of how accommodation should be handled, the institution, as demonstrated in this institutional ethnography, will continue to utilize well-orchestrated manoeuvres to shield itself from inclusivity.

References

Barnes, C. 1996. 'Theories of Disability and the Origins of the Oppression of Disabled People in Western Society', in *Disability and Society: Emerging Issues and Insights*, pp. 43–61, L. Barton, ed. New York: Longman Publishing.

Campbell, M.L., and F. Gregor. 2002. *Mapping Social Relations: A Primer in Doing Institutional Ethnography*. Aurora: Garamond Press.

Deveau, J.L. Forthcoming. 'Duty to Accommodate Disabled Federal Public Service Employees'. Unpublished PhD dissertation, University of New Brunswick.

Foucault, M. 1980. *Power/Knowledge: Selected Interviews and Other Writings, 1972–1977*. New York: Pantheon Books.

Linton, S. 1998. *Claiming Disability: Knowledge and Disability*. New York: New York University Press.

Marx, K., and F. Engels. 1970. *The German Ideology: Students Edition*. London: Lawrence and Wishart.

Oliver, M. 1996. 'A Sociology of Disability or a Disablist Sociology?', in *Disability and Society: Emerging Issues and Insights*, pp. 18–42, L. Barton, ed. New York: Longman Publishing.

Smith, D.E. 1990. *The Conceptual Practices of Power: A Feminist Sociology of Knowledge*. Toronto: University of Toronto Press.

———. 1987. *The Everyday World as Problematic: A Feminist Sociology*. Toronto: University of Toronto Press.

Sine, D., L. Rotor, and E. Hare. 2003. 'Accommodating Employees with Environmental Sensitivities'.

Available at http://www.healthyindoors.com/english/resources/workplace1.pdf (accessed 11 November 2004).

Titchkosky, T. 2003. *Disability, Self, and Society*. Toronto: University of Toronto Press.

———. 2001. 'Disability-A Rose by Any Other Name? "People-First" Language in Canadian Society', *Canadian Review of Sociology and Anthropology* 38, 2: 125–40.

CHAPTER 46

Women's Inequality in the Workplace as Framed in News Discourse: Refracting from Gender Ideology

Amber Gazso

Introduction

Women's inequality in the workplace is a rich area of sociological discussion. Knowledge about this phenomenon is not merely limited to sociological discussion. Newspaper articles often delineate how women and men are faring in their workplaces, with a great deal of attention being placed on the issue of women's (predominantly white women's) inequality in professional positions.

This paper seeks to bridge these separate but not entirely disparate 'sociological' and 'news' discussions of women's inequality in the workplace. The following research questions guided the study: (1) How is news discourse on women's inequality in the workplace framed by **gender**, and (2) How does news discourse on women's inequality in the workplace further construct gender? I answered these questions by counterposing sociological interpretations of how gender as a social structure explains women's inequality in the workplace with what is present in the news discourse.

Contextualizing and Theorizing Women's Unequal Workplace Experiences

Post-1970, Canadian women have dramatically increased their labour market participation. In 1961,

labour force participation among women was below 30 per cent, compared to more than 75 per cent in 1996 (Fortin and Huberman, 2002). Heisz, Jackson, and Picot (2002) explain that, although wages do continue to remain lower for women, the gap between women's and men's wages is narrowing.

Despite these significant inroads made into the Canadian labour market, women continue to experience occupational segregation, income, and status inequality compared to men in their workplaces. The average income earned by women and men who worked full-time full-year in 2001 was $35,258 for women and $49,250 for men. Among all other earners (i.e., part-time, temporary, casual) the wage gap ($24,688 and $38,431, respectively) continues to exist for women and men (Statistics Canada, 2004). Of all adult workers earning less than $8 an hour in 2000, 69 per cent were women (Saunders, 2003).

Some theorists attribute women's unequal workplace experiences to the forces of globalization and economic restructuring that favour low-waged and unskilled workers (Armstrong, 1996; Moghadam, 1999; Anderson, 2000; Marshall, 2000). Other theorists postulate that women's primary responsibilities for family life create their unequal workplace experiences (Duffy, Mandell, and Pupo, 1989; Dunn, Almquist, and Chafetz, 1993). Still others maintain that workplace structures, for example, such promotional barriers as glass ceilings and 'mommy tracks' (Kanter, 1977; Cotter, Hermsen, Ovadia, and Vanneman, 2001) and gender cultures (Maddock and Parkin, 1994), reward and favour men over women.

Leibowitz (1997) acknowledges another dominant assumption that women and men experience unequal workplaces because their roles and capabilities are biologically determined. Again, the transfer of gendered expectations for and distinctions between women's and men's work through the processes of socialization (Connell, 1985; Nelson, 1994; Anderson, 2000) and the 'doing' of gender in everyday workplace activity (West and Zimmerman, 1987).

Methodology

This study examines the English-language newspaper articles on women's inequality in the workplace from two Canadian national newspapers, the *Globe and Mail* and the *National Post* from November 2000 to November 2002. Newspaper articles were collected from the Dow Jones Interactive database (which allows searches of several Canadian and US newspaper online archives via the Internet) by utilizing three broad 'search' terms—women and men and work; management and women; business and women. Articles retrieved using these search terms were deemed to be on 'women's inequality in the workplace' if they referred to employment status, gender norms and assumptions about behaviour in the workplace, and conflict between women and men in the workplace in their headlines. In total, 107 articles were collected. The analysis of these news articles was guided by the theoretical methods of Frame Analysis (Goffman, 1974; Pan and Kosicki, 1993) and Critical Discourse Analysis (CDA) (Fairclough, 1992; Teo, 2000).

Framing Women's Inequality in the Workplace

Gender frames and is further constructed in news discourse at individual, interactional, and institutional levels in three ways: 'Women Just Don't Fit In', 'Women's "Natural" Choice', and 'Women—Take Your Chances Juggling'.

WOMEN JUST DON'T FIT IN (IN A MAN'S WORLD)

News discourse that was situated in this frame suggested that workplace cultures uphold stereotypical assumptions that women are fundamentally different than men and so do not fit into a man's work world. Once these gender-stereotypical cultures are reflected in workplace structures, women get 'just so far and not further' (Lorber, 1994: 227) in their occupations, coming face-to-face with a 'glass ceiling'. In this frame, options for change are not directed at the structural level but rather at women's behaviour. News discourse suggests that women can possibly resist invisible barriers and, thus, experiences of not fitting in, if they act upon one option—they can crack the glass ceiling and advance up the corporate ladder through work performance that gets noticed. However, cracking the glass ceiling and keeping the doors open in gendered workplace cultures means not just functioning similar to men, it means acting like men.

Cracking the glass ceiling, however, does not guarantee that women will become more equal to men in their workplaces. Kanter (1977) explains that, even if women are in 'token' positions of power, several forces within organizations serve to maintain their inequality, such as increased visibility and the exaggeration of their differences. News discourse captures these forces and contains the implicit message that women may not necessarily want to or be capable of 'staying the course' in the fight to become equal or get ahead.

News discourse conveys a second optional response for women who don't fit in and dislike experiencing invisible barriers that impede their advancement—women can leave. This option surfaced in a news article on a study that revealed women's under-representation as partners in law firms.

> In November, Deloitte & Touche announced 30 new Canadian partners, including seven

women. . . . Such figures do not reflect the number of women who entered the professions 10 years ago. . . . Concerned about high attrition, it [Deloitte & Touche] set about understanding why women were leaving . . . many were departing because of unacceptable workplace culture. Women disliked the professional service firm culture because of its 'benevolent paternalism' and its not always subtle treatment of women as less than equal. They objected to receiving less desirable assignments or being denied valuable opportunities routinely available to men (Greenwood and Suddaby, 2001).

To summarize, the frame 'Women Just Don't Fit In' centres on the idea that workplaces themselves are gendered at the institutional level. It infers that these gendered workplaces are largely a result of women's and men's 'doing gender' (West and Zimmerman, 1987) in their micro-level interactions.

WOMEN'S 'NATURAL' CHOICE

Women's unequal workplace experiences are also framed as a result of their occupational choices. The idea that women choose occupations unequal to men's does at first appear to simply reflect women's individual agency. Upon more close inspection, these 'choices' are largely framed as a result of women's family responsibilities. News discourse does recognize, however, that women's differential occupational choices are informed by their anticipated responsibilities as mothers and caregivers for children and the elderly (Armstrong and Armstrong, 1993; Benoit, 2000; Luxton and Corman, 2001). However, these responsibilities are interpreted as choices. It is when women's caregiving responsibilities are acknowledged as affecting their choice of workplaces that news discourse implicitly suggests that women's choices and, thus, their inequality, are because they are essentially different than men.

In this frame, sexual dimorphism and essential differences between women and men are assumed to provide the bases from which women's and

men's differential social behaviour (Spanier, 1991) and experiences in workplaces originate. Gender is further shaped in this frame because it implicitly suggests that biological sex, as it informs individual agency, determines one's experiences in the work force.

WOMEN—TAKE YOUR CHANCES JUGGLING

Despite the influx of women into the labour market post-1970, women still spend far more time in domestic labour than men (Hochschild, 1989; Benoit, 2000; Gazso-Windle and McMullin, 2003). Not only do these women experience an unequal 'second shift' in their responsibility for family care giving (Hochschild, 1989), they also experience an unequal 'third shift', compared to men, that of juggling work–family conflict (Hochschild, 1997). As news discourse implicitly suggests, this juggling can actually ensure women's inequality in the workplace in that their actual or assumed family responsibilities can impede their advancement.

In summary, gender shapes this frame by suggesting that it is women's (not men's) juggling of paid work and family life that determines their inequality in the workplace. Since women's juggling appears to be a 'natural' choice, it should be of no surprise that there are not always provisions to manage this juggling, such as 'family-friendly' policies, in the decision-making cultures of workplaces. Gender is further shaped in this frame by the 'good'/'bad' dichotomization of the choices women have once their juggling creates experiences of inequality in their workplaces: (1) women can 'suck it up and deal'; and (2) women can leave. In acting upon either of these options, women invite others' definitions of them as 'good' mothers (those who leave to rear their children) or 'bad' mothers (those who juggle and 'deal') and further expose themselves to other inequalities.

Considering Gender Ideology

Despite women's increased labour force participation and men's child-rearing capabilities, women's mothering and caregiving in the domestic sphere and men's breadwinning in the public, paid work sphere are still upheld as gender appropriate behaviour (Hochschild, 1989). The tenacity of this male breadwinner/female caregiver ideology is demonstrated by the fact that there continues to be a gendered division of household and paid labour that is inherently linked to dominant assumptions about biologically determined femininity and masculinity (Gazso-Windle and McMullin, 2003).

Evident in the above analysis of the frame 'Women Just Don't Fit In', women who occupy upper-level positions in largely male-dominated workplaces are women who get noticed: by working long hours, 'shaking things up' with new and innovative ideas, and by displaying competitive personalities and level-headedness—qualities largely comparable to those stereotypical qualities that are assumed to lead to men's success.

This frame appears to suggest that notions about gender-appropriate behaviour are downplayed for these women in high-status positions because they act like men. The dominant ideological assumption that women are caregivers is also hidden, because news discourse shows that women are only successful 'ladder climbers' if they put off any plans to bear children and raise a family. Not surprisingly, however, problems abound when these high-power/high-status women choose to have families. It is here that the temporarily hidden male breadwinner/female caregiver ideology becomes fully visible for women who no longer act like men in a man's world.

Most assuredly, this gender ideology is interwoven with power. It is men who benefit from this ideological orientation to news discourse on women's inequality in the workplace, not women. The male breadwinner/female caregiver ideology that overshadows and/or underscores these frames, therefore, further shapes gender ideology, but in a largely regressive manner.

Conclusion

The news discourse analyzed in this study suggests that, overall, women's unequal workplace experiences result because women are crossing over clearly laid-out ideological boundaries of which sphere is appropriate for women and which sphere is appropriate for men. This study suggests that what may be underlying explanations of women's inequality in the workplace as a result of structural barriers, stereotypical assumptions, individual choice, and work/family conflict, are broader, power-implicated, ideological forces. Such forces are dependent upon the organization of practices according to assumed essential biological differences. I would add that it is how and why we value and assign legitimacy to these differences and uphold them as superior or inferior in ideology that remains at the crux of the problem of gender inequality in our workplaces, and in our society as a whole.

References

Anderson, M.L. 2000. *Thinking about Women: Sociological Perspectives on Sex and Gender*. Boston: Allyn and Bacon.

Armstrong, P. 1996. 'The Feminization of the Labour Force: Harmonizing Down in a Global Economy', in *Rethinking Restructuring: Gender and Change in Canada*, pp. 29–54, I.C. Bakker, ed. Toronto: University of Toronto Press.

Armstrong, P., and H. Armstrong. 1993. *The Double Ghetto: Canadian Women and Their Segregated Work*. Toronto: McClelland & Stewart.

Benoit, C.M. 2000. *Women, Work and Social Rights: Canada in Historical and Comparative Perspective*. Toronto: Harcourt Brace & Company, Canada.

Connell, R.W 1985. 'Theorizing Gender', *Sociology* 19, 2: 260–72.

Cotter, D.A., J.M. Hermsen, S. Ovadia, and R. Vanneman. 2001. 'The Glass Ceiling Effect', *Social Forces* 80, 2: 655–82.

Duffy, A., N. Mandell, and N. Pupo. 1989. *Few Choices: Women, Work and Family*. Toronto: Garamond Press.

Dunn, D., E.M. Almquist, and J.S. Chafetz. 1993. 'Macrostructural Perspectives on Gender Inequality', in *Theory on Gender/Feminism on Theory*, pp. 69–90, P. England, ed. New York: Aldine de Gruyter.

Fairclough, N. 1992. *Discourse and Social Change*. Cambridge: Polity Press.

Fortin, N.M., and M. Huberman. 2002. 'Occupational Gender Segregation and Women's Wages in Canada: An Historical Perspective', *Canadian Public Policy* 27, Supp.: S11–39.

Gazso-Windle, A., and J.A. McMullin. 2003. 'Doing Domestic Labour: Strategising in a Gendered Domain', *Canadian Journal of Sociology* 28, 3: 341–66.

Goffman, E. 1974. *Frame Analysis: An Essay on the Organization of Experience*. New York: Harper Colophon Books.

Greenwood, R., and R. Suddaby. 2001. 'Doors Still Shut to Female Partners', *Globe and Mail*, 29 January: M1.

Heisz, A., A. Jackson, and G. Picot. 2002. *Winners and Losers in the Labour Market of the 1990s*. Ottawa: Analytical Studies Branch, Statistics Canada.

Hochschild, A.R. 1989. *The Second Shift: Working Parents and the Revolution at Home*. New York: Viking.

———. 1997. *The Time Bind: When Work Becomes Home & Home Becomes Work*. New York: Metropolitan Books.

Kanter, R.M. 1977. *Men and Women of the Corporation*. New York: Basic Books.

Leibowitz, L. 1997. 'Perspectives on the Evolution of Sex Differences', in *Gender in Cross-Cultural Perspective*, pp. 6–14, C.B. Brettell and C.F. Sargent, eds. Upper Saddle River, NJ: Prentice Hall.

Lorber, J. 1994. *Paradoxes of Gender*. New Haven: Yale University Press.

Luxton, M., and J.S. Corman. 2001. *Getting By in Hard Times: Gendered Labour at Home and on the Job*. Toronto: University of Toronto Press.

Maddock, S., and D. Parkin. 1994. 'Gender Cultures: How They Affect Men and Women at Work', in *Women in Management*, pp. 29–40, R.J. Burke, ed. London: Paul Chapman Publishing Ltd.

Marshall, B.L. 2000. *Configuring Gender: Explorations in Theory and Politics*. Orchard Park, NY: Broadview Press.

Moghadam, V.M. 1999. 'Gender and the Global Economy', in *Revisioning Gender*, pp. 128–60, B.B. Hess, ed. Thousand Oaks, CA: Sage Publications.

Nelson, L. 1994. 'Interpreting Gender', *Signs* 20, 11: 79–105.

Pan, Z., and G.M. Kosicki. 1993. 'Framing Analysis: An Approach to News Discourse', *Political Communication* 10: 55–75.

Saunders, R. 2003. *Defining Vulnerability in the Labour Market*. Ottawa: Canadian Policy Research Network, Inc.

Spanier, B.B. 1991. '"Lessons" from "Nature": Gender Ideology and Sexual Ambiguity in Biology', in *Body Guards: The Cultural Politics of Gender Ambiguity*, pp. 329–50, J. Epstein and K. Straub, eds. New York: Routledge.

Statistics Canada. 2004. 'Average Earnings by Sex and Work Pattern'. Available at http://www.statcan.ca.myaccess.library.utoronto.ca/english/Pgdb/labor01a.htm.

Teo, P. 2000. 'Racism in the News: A Critical Discourse Analysis of News Reporting in Two Australian Newspapers', *Discourse & Society* 11, 1: 7–49.

West, C., and D.H. Zimmerman. 1987. 'Doing Gender', *Gender & Society* 1, 2: 125–51.

CHAPTER 47

Dispersion and Polarization of Income among Aboriginal and Non-Aboriginal Canadians

Paul S. Maxim, Jerry P. White, Paul C. Whitehead, and Dan Beavon

Introduction

It is well established that, as a group, Canadians of Aboriginal origin are economically disadvantaged (INAC, 1989; Jankowski and Moazzami, 1994; George, Kuhn, and Sweetman, 1996; Frideres, 1998). The income differential across the Aboriginal and non-Aboriginal divide has received some attention (Gardiner, 1994; George and Kuhn, 1994; Bernier, 1997; De Silva, 1999), but not the disparity within the Aboriginal community and between Aboriginal groups.

We address three questions: (1) Why study intra-Aboriginal inequality? (2) What is the gap in wages and income between the general Canadian population and the different Aboriginal peoples? and (3) How much inequality exists both within and among the Canadian non-Aboriginal population and the Aboriginal groups? We also look at whether transfer payments reduce inequality.

Aboriginal Canadians 1986–1996: A Review of Previous Studies of Income Inequality

Given the interest of governments and attempts to reduce inequality, we are interested in whether the gap with non-Aboriginal Canada has diminished and whether the dispersion and polarization in the wages of Aboriginal peoples has become less pronounced. This involved looking first at the previous studies.

Clatworthy et al. (1995) found the mean income for workers of Aboriginal origin to be $17,367, but they also found variation between the various Aboriginal groups. Non-status Indians had a mean income of $21,035; registered Indians, a mean of $15,791; Métis, a mean of $18,467; and Inuit, a mean income of $15,690. They conclude that while the income gap for those with full-time/full-year employment (forty plus weeks) is smaller than those with other employment statuses, the earnings of registered Indians and Inuit lagged other Aboriginals and were even further behind the Canadian labour force as a whole.

George, Kuhn, and Sweetman (1996) draw similar conclusions in their report to the Royal Commission on Aboriginal Peoples. They argue that, conditional on full-time/full-year work, earnings of Aboriginal persons are 10.4 per cent below those of the non-Aboriginal population. This represents a slight improvement over their findings from 1986, where the differential was 11 per cent (George and Kuhn, 1994).

Bernier (1997) reports that workers claiming Aboriginal origins earned $6,500 less than Canadians as a whole in 1990. For those who identified with a First Nation in the Aboriginal People's Survey, the earnings were lower by an additional $2,900. In addition, she finds that inequality and polarization for Aboriginal peoples actually increases when Employment Insurance benefits are added to wages. Greater polarization suggests that general government transfers are less effective in reducing inequality in Aboriginal communities than in the non-Aboriginal population. One might speculate that the transfers based on employment participation effect a smaller number of more affluent Aboriginals due to lower labour force participation rates. Regardless of the cause, this could have important policy implications.

Comparative Earnings and Wage Dispersion

To maintain continuity with previous research, we have identified four analytically distinct groups within the Census Aboriginal population: status Indians, non-status North American Indians, Métis, and Inuits. Previous studies have consistently assessed the Métis and non-status Indians as having less income disparity and less polarization than the status Indians who inhabit the First Nations communities. Some research has also assessed status Indian and Inuit populations as having the greatest inequities among all aboriginal groups (Clatworthy et al., 1995; Bernier, 1997). In terms of change, we had expected that, given the recent policy interest in First Nation communities and their relative deprivation, there would be the greatest change in this group.

Dividing the Aboriginal population into four constituent groups permits intra-Aboriginal comparisons and inter-group comparisons on four economic measures for all persons 18–64 years of age for 1995: (1) Positive reported wage and salary income for 1995; (2) Wage and salary income, including zero income; (3) Positive total income (i.e., income from all sources); and (4) Total income, including zero income.

Results

The results show that, overall, **Aboriginal Canadians** report earnings that are lower than the non-Aboriginal population. Status Indians earn $10,325 less than non-Aboriginals, and they have the lowest earnings of any of the Aboriginal sub-groups. Non-status Indians fared best with a deficit of $6,353, but all the groups show a much lower level of wage and salary income than **non-Aboriginal Canadians**.

All of the measures of inequality are consistent in direction and relative size when we look at only those with positive wage and salary income. Greater inequality of wage income exists within each subgroup of Aboriginal people than for non-

Aboriginal Canadians. The measures of inequality among the group's registered Indians, non-status Indians and Métis, however, are not significantly different from one another. The most inequitable distribution of wages is among the Inuit. This finding is consistent with previous studies. Bernier (1997) concludes that the Inuit work fewer hours for higher wages in the lower quintile of earners. She speculated this may relate to an emphasis on artisan endeavours. While this may account for part of the difference we would argue that it cannot account for the entire gap. A more important factor is related, but somewhat different: the geography of being Inuit, which we will discuss later.

Status Indians experience the next greatest inequality. First Nations' communities are made up almost exclusively of status Indians. The reserve is a key contributor to the kinds of inequities observed. The non-Aboriginal to Aboriginal comparisons show serious inequity concerning polarization toward the bottom of the range for Aboriginals. Similar results are seen when zero incomes are included. The results indicate the mean income decreases for each category although the size of the decrease varies. We might expect that, because status Indians report many more zero incomes than do non-Aboriginal Canadians, the decrease in mean wage and salary income would be greater for status Indians. This is not so. Only a much greater proportion of earners at the low end of the income distribution among status Indians than for non-Aboriginals could produce this result. Inequality rises dramatically for status Indians particularly when the measures used are sensitive to the top of the income distribution.

How do government transfers and other sources of income influence polarization, dispersion, and the wage gap? In order to answer this we used total income, which would include wage and salary income plus transfer payment income. The wage gap decreases only slightly when total income, including the zero categories, are considered. This is the case across all the Aboriginal sub-groups. This is because the percentage of zero incomes is relatively low due to the effect of transfer payments.

The indices of inequality show the same patterns here as in the other scenarios. What is unexpected is that analyzing total income appears to make the dispersion of income slightly greater. Ironically, the 'top up' which results in total income, consists primarily of government transfers. Other sources, such as investment income, comprise only a small proportion of the residual between total income and wage and salary income only. This does not mean that transfer income creates inequities, but it does seem to indicate that the structure of transfer income does not significantly adjust inequity as measured by dispersion and polarization. This may be the result of so many incomes being clustered at the lower tail of the distribution both before and after transfer income is considered. However, given that the prevailing wisdom is that transfer payments are significant in closing inequalities this is a counterintuitive result that deserves further examination.

Assessing the Patterns of Inequality: Aboriginal Groups Compared to Non-Aboriginals

All Aboriginal Canadians are disadvantaged when compared with the non-Aboriginal Canadian population. The amount of disadvantage, as measured by the characteristics of income we are examining, differs for the different categories of Aboriginal peoples. It also varies depending on the assumptions we used to calculate income, i.e., whether transfer payments are included and how we define the lower limit of income.

If we think of the score for the non-Aboriginal population as the base or 'norm', how do different Aboriginal groups vary from this basic pattern of inequality? We find that in all cases there is greater measurable inequality for all groups when we compare them with the non-Aboriginal population. This is the case regardless of the assumptions. There is, however, variation in the magnitude of the relative inequality. In all four scenarios, registered Indians and Inuit show the greatest differences; hence, are at the greatest

disadvantage. Changing assumptions also affects the levels of measurable inequality. The inclusion of those with zero incomes, when other sources of income are not considered, increases the levels of inequality, except in the case of the Inuit. This may indicate that there are relatively fewer Inuit reporting zero incomes than non-Inuit Northerners doing so. The effect of using total income is that overall levels of relative inequality decrease in all cases. Transfers and other income sources appear to have the greatest impact on registered (status) Indians with relative rates of measured inequality decreasing by approximately 50 per cent. The case of the Inuit remains enigmatic as the inequality actually increases with the introduction of earners of zero income even with the inclusion of transfer payments and other sources in the income calculations.

The results we found when including all income sources, including transfers and investment income, deserve further comment. We see that the general pattern shows an increase in measured disparity and polarization in income for all Aboriginal groups, but not the non-Aboriginal population. The reason for this is twofold. First, while some sources of income, such as government transfers, are designed to target low-income individuals many non-wage and salary sources are non-discriminatory. Thus, they serve to shift the mean income up slightly but do little to reduce the overall gap. Furthermore, sources of income outside government transfers (such as investment income) are more accessible to upper income earners. This serves to move the upper end of the distribution even higher, thus increasing income polarization. Therefore, the greater the basic dispersion of wage and salary income the more likely we are to find an increase in equality as we add the non-wage and salary income.

Second, by looking beyond wage and salary income, we are invariably increasing the size of the target population. Almost all of those people outside the labour market either have no income at all or acquire small amounts primarily through government transfers. Very few people have substantial sources of income outside traditional wage labour. The 'idle rich' are exceedingly rare in general and even more rare in the Aboriginal population.

Conclusion

Further research is necessary to identify and measure the main causes of intra-Aboriginal variations in income. It is, however, useful to consider the potential reasons for the differences. The data indicate that the Aboriginal groups rank from Inuit at the high end, through status Indians, to non-status Indians and, finally, to Métis having the lowest levels of inequality. We would hypothesize that the spatial isolation of the Inuit and relative socio-spatial isolation of status Indians in comparison to non-status Indians and Métis may provide a

powerful explanation for the differences in inequality. The Inuit are clearly the most separated Aboriginal subgroup. The reserve community system functions in a similar way to the isolation of the North, creating sociocultural distances and fractures in the market of opportunity. Other factors such as discrimination can, and do, amplify this separation from market opportunities (Pendakur and Pendakur, 1996). The Métis are, on the other hand, the least separate given they are the 'least visible', live in close proximity to non-Aboriginal populations (Maxim and White, 2000), and, as a minority, have the greatest levels of assimilation and market integration. This isolation and lack of integration could result in human capital differences, socio-economic differentiation, and a range of other contributors to inequality.

References

Bernier, R. 1997. 'The Dimensions of Wage Inequality among Aboriginal Peoples', in *Research Paper Series*, No. 109. Ottawa: Statistics Canada, Analytical Studies Branch.

Clatworthy, S., J. Hull, and N. Laughran. 1995. 'Patterns of Employment, Unemployment and Poverty. Four Directions Consulting', *Report to the Royal Commission on Aboriginal People (1996): People to People, Nation to Nation*. Ottawa: Minister of Supply and Services Canada.

De Silva, A. 1999. 'Wage Discrimination against Natives', *Canadian Public Policy* 25, 1: 65–85.

Frideres, J.M. 1998. *Aboriginal Peoples in Canada*. Scarborough: Prentice-Hall.

Gardiner, P. 1994. 'Aboriginal Community Incomes and Migration in the Northwest Territories: Policy Issues and Alternatives', *Canadian Public Policy* 20: 297–317.

George, P., and P. Kuhn. 1994. 'The Size and Structure of Native–white wage Differentials', *Canadian Journal of Economics* 27: 20–42.

George, P., P. Kuhn, and A. Sweetman. 1996. 'Patterns of Employment, Unemployment and Poverty: A Comparative Analysis of Several Aspects of the Employment Experience of Aboriginal and non-Aboriginal Canadians using 1991 PUME', *Royal Commission on Aboriginal People: People to People, Nation to Nation*. Ottawa: Minister of Supply and Services Canada.

Indian and Northern Affairs Canada (INAC). 1989. *Highlights on Aboriginal Conditions, 1981–2001, Part III, Economic Conditions*. Ottawa: Indian and Northern Affairs Canada.

Jankowski, W.B., and B. Moazzami. 1994. 'Size Distribution of Income and Income Inequality among the Native Population of Northwest Ontario', *Canadian Journal of Native Studies* 14: 47–60.

Maxim, P., and J. White. 2000. 'Patterns of Urban Residential Settlement among Canada's Aboriginal Peoples', *Population Studies Centre Discussion Papers Series 00-08*. London: University of Western Ontario, Population Studies Centre.

Pendakur K., and R. Pendakur. 1996. *The Colour of Money: Earnings Differentials among Ethnic Groups in Canada*. Ottawa: Department of Canadian Heritage, Strategic Research Analysis.

Questions for Critical Thought

'CANADA'S MOST NOTORIOUS BAD MOTHER': THE NEWSPAPER COVERAGE OF THE JORDAN HEIKAMP INQUEST

1. Who do you think is responsible for the death of Jordan Heikamp and why?
2. The welfare system in Canada has outlived its usefulness. Discuss.
3. How can poor mothers in Canadian society be made more functional in 'mothering' their children?
4. Propose a solution to the increasing poverty confronting some mothers in Canadian society.
5. What, in your opinion, is a good mother and what conditions enable a mother to attain good motherhood?

STREET YOUTH LABOUR MARKET EXPERIENCES AND CRIME

1. Homelessness and unemployment situations do not justify criminal behaviour. Discuss.
2. Using two sociological theories, discuss how unemployment accounts for criminal activities in Canadian society.
3. Criminal behaviour is either an innate or acquired trait, or both. Discuss.
4. The labour market experiences of street youth and the interpretations they assign to unemployment contribute significantly to crime behaviour. Discuss.
5. How has economic restructuring affected marginalized youth in the Canadian society?

BUILDING HOPE: CONFRONTING SOCIAL EXCLUSION AND VIOLENCE IN TORONTO'S BLACK COMMUNITY, 2001

1. Who should take the lead in confronting the canker of gun violence in Canada's most populated city? The government or local communities? Discuss.
2. Negative stereotyping of a group of people impacts negatively on their actions. Discuss the statement with palpable examples.
3. Using the structure/agency debate, explain how social exclusion and violence can be addressed in Canada.
4. Community participation is critical in addressing increasing violence in major Canadian cities. How true is this statement?
5. What were the objectives of the Building Hope Coalition? Discuss the criticisms raised against the movement?

WORKPLACE ACCOMMODATION FOR THE DISABLED IN THE FEDERAL PUBLIC SERVICE: AN INSTITUTIONAL ETHNOGRAPHY

1. Social exclusion confronting people with disability must be approached from a systemic perspective, rather than at the individual level. Discuss.
2. What is social exclusion? With reference to people with disability, how does social exclusion play out in Canadian society?
3. How is the social construction of disability affecting the welfare of people with disability in Canada?
4. Disability is socially constructed. Discuss.
5. Inputs from people with disability must be involved in all programs geared towards their well-being. How far do you subscribe to this view?

Women's Inequality in the Workplace as Framed in News Discourse: Refracting from Gender Ideology

1. How does gender frame news discourse on women's inequalities in the workplace?
2. How does news discourse on women's inequalities in the workplace reconstruct gender?
3. Identify and discuss the mechanism(s) by which women's inequalities in the workplace could be addressed.
4. Use any sociological theory to explain why women are treated differently from men in the workplace.
5. What forces account for women's unequal workplace experiences in Canada?

Dispersion and Polarization of Income among Aboriginal and Non-Aboriginal Canadians

1. How far do you agree with the statement that government transfer payments are insignificant in addressing income inequalities in Aboriginal communities?
2. Suggest ways of addressing income inequality among Aboriginal Canadians.
3. Who is to be blamed—the state or Aboriginal Canadians—for the poor income status of Aboriginal Canadians?
4. How do government transfers and other sources of income affect polarization and wage gaps?
5. What factors account for income disparities between Aboriginal Canadians and non-Aboriginal Canadians?

Part XI

Sexuality and Gender

S ex and gender issues are deemed sensitive and are approached differently by many people to reflect their biological and social orientations. Sociologists interest themselves with sex and gender issues primarily to seek explanations to thorny issues that many people shy away from or present it to suit their respective interests. The following essays deliberate sex and gender from educational, economic, and medical perspectives.

Libby Alexander's chapter ponders the school-based sexuality education as a form of official discourse of sexuality. Based on teenage students' evaluation of school-based sexuality education, Alexander argues that sexuality education be made more relevant by connecting with students' experiences of sexuality and how these experiences are shaped by the dynamics of social relations.

From purely economic perspective, Susan Vincent explores Tupperware's image of gendered domesticity. Tupperware's business style of contracting mainly women as dealers for their products without employing them full-time is brought to question. The issue of whether Tupperware is capitalizing on gendered roles of women in North American society to advance their capitalist interest is thoroughly debated.

Mary Patton takes the baton from Vincent by examining how the biomedical and pharmaceutical communities take advantage of their expertise to medicalize menopause to the disadvantage of women by marginalizing women's situated knowledge. Patton uses Lana and Rebecca's encounters with biomedical experts when they sought help for menopause problems to challenge established socio-cultural structures that legitimize, disseminate and sustain gender structured biomedical knowledge.

Ann Duffy, Nancy Mandell, and Sue Wilson discuss the economic rationalization and interpretation of the roles of women in the Canadian society. They qualitatively assess how midlife women balance caring commitment and paid employment. How midlife women strategize to accommodate their dual roles is also made explicit in the chapter.

Altogether, the chapters in this Part combine to challenge the status quo, or the 'powers that be', in shaping sexuality and gender roles in society.

CHAPTER 48

'They should make it more normal': Young People's Critical Standpoints and the Social Organization of Sexuality Education

Libby Alexander

'School is supposed to prepare you for life, sex is a big part of life.'

—Kyle, early 20s

Introduction

Sexuality education is part of 'bio-power' (Foucault, 1984): ruling forms of knowledge with the aim of promoting life by telling us the correct way of living it. 'Knowledge is power' when it gains the status of *truth*. But how and for whom is this knowledge produced? Who produces it?

What we know about 'sexuality' is filtered through the languages we have access to, what Foucault calls *discourses*. School-based sexuality education is a form of 'official discourse' of sexuality. Rather than emerging from **young peoples'** experiences, official knowledge emerges from institutional relations, such as public health, with the aim of regulating youth sexualities.

Method

I recruited participants by approaching two community youth groups in Northern Ontario. The interviews were semi-structured focus groups in which I asked participants to describe and evaluate their experiences of sex education. The participants ranged in age from mid-teens to early 20s and came from both the public and Catholic boards.

I also tie these experiences to the textual analysis of both the *Canadian Guidelines for Sexual Health Education* (1994) and the *Ontario Ministry of Training, Colleges and Universities Secondary School Curriculum for Health and Physical Education* (1999). Sex education is organized by health curricula. Smith

(1990) argues that texts get constructed as official knowledge obscuring the activity of the people that goes into producing them. Thus, the power relations inherent in texts are concealed. In examining these texts, I map out the textual mediation of sex education: how sexual knowledge in schools is socially organized. What discourses of sexuality are activated through the use of curriculum texts?

Overview of Findings

What do these interviews reveal about the social organization of knowledge? The participants' experiences paint a picture of 'the facts of life', not as 'natural' or 'objective' but as a struggle between official and subjugated youth knowledges. Talking about **sex** in health class tended to be limited to discussions of anatomy, reproduction, and prevention. Most participants argued that this exclusive focus failed to relate to their everyday lives. What they wanted to discuss were things such as emotions, pleasure, sexual identities, relationships, and varieties of sexual practices. Iris, a young woman in her mid-teens said:

> We learned about protection, we don't have discussions about sex and how we shouldn't be judging other people, they don't talk about that at all and I think that's wrong because we should learn about that. We should learn about actual living skills like how we shouldn't be judging people but we learn math instead.

This comment expresses frustration, echoed by many participants, at what gets counted as 'the basics' in school. Sexuality is not given the same degree of legitimacy as other subjects such as mathematics. They learn about *protection*, which gets severed from sex itself as well as social contexts such as 'judging people'.

Sexuality was often presented in narrow and mechanical ways. Classroom sex education constructs 'sex' as heterosexual, penile–vaginal intercourse with an emphasis on negative consequences such as disease or unwanted pregnancy. Some mentioned teachers who were limited on what they could talk about; others said their sex education was cut short due to the teacher's embarrassment. Many described scare tactics that were used to deter them from sexual behaviour, such as graphic videos depicting childbirth. As one participant put it, it was like 'the worst case scenario was going to be you'.

Many participants described environments full of anxiety and embarrassment that discouraged open discussion about sexuality. The duration of sex education was often brief, ranging from one-day sessions to two weeks at most. Participants said that this was not enough time to 'get used to' the content and some said that this was overwhelming.

In response to a question on what would make it less embarrassing to seek out knowledge about safe sex, Audrey a tenth grader argues:

> I think they should make it more normal . . . like on TV, sex is supposed to be bad but everyone does it so it's not a bad thing. I just think if it was more out there, more people would be like 'ok, this is normal' kind of thing and they wouldn't be afraid.

If something is *made to be normal*, she reasons, it might be less frightening and stigmatizing. She informed me of how she believed that many young people are afraid to go to places like the local health unit for information because they don't want to seem 'promiscuous', a morally loaded

term. Importantly, this shows how 'access' to knowledge about sexuality is not simply about providing information but is also tied to the wider discourses that make youth sexuality out to be problematic rather than acceptable.

At the same time however, the young people's experiences show how sex education does *normalize* a particular form of sexuality. The omission of various knowledges and experiences is an active process of limiting the wide range of pleasures, identities, and meanings to construct a narrow definition of 'normal' sexuality. What emerged from these interviews was a picture of sexuality education that reproduced heterosexuality as a natural way of being while silencing any other possibilities. The 'facts of life' are not natural but a continual site of struggle that people actually live. For example Wesley recalls:

> I knew I was gay for a while and something had kind of, I don't know, upset me and confused me—they're talking about guys and girls. Guys getting girls pregnant, the girls already have their big boobs and—they talked about arousal too. Guys, you're going to see a girl and you're going to get really hot for her. That wasn't happening for me and I knew that wasn't going to happen for me and I felt left out.

Arousal is being taught in a particular way, to be specifically directed towards the 'opposite' sex. This particular construction of 'the basics' comes at a cost to Wesley and the many gay, lesbian, bisexual, transgender, and questioning young people who are marginalized by this silencing which preserves the idea of a natural heterosexuality and fixed notions of gender and sex.

Textual Mediation of Sexuality Education

When examining curriculum guidelines such as the *Canadian Guidelines for Sexuality Education* and the Ontario secondary school health curricula, one can note the language of rational choice being imposed on sexuality. For example, specific expectations of the grade 10 'Healthy Growth and Sexuality' unit include explaining the effects (e.g. STDs, HIV/AIDS) of choices related to sexual intimacy (e.g. abstinence, birth control) and demonstrating understanding of how to use decision-making skills effectively to support choices related to responsible sexuality. The focus is on individual behaviour change through the acquisition of decision-making skills. Informing students of the negative consequences of sexual behaviour is expected to help them make 'healthy choices'. However these interviews reveal the complexity of sexuality that troubles the notion of rational choice. The following quote gives an example:

> I felt like the way sex is presented in sex ed class is that it sort of leaves it kind of mysterious and kind of appealing, so when you're younger like 14, 13 . . . everyone's like 'yeah I gotta lose my virginity'. It's like you know? That's the thing you have to do, it's like a rite of passage. The one thing I probably needed to hear in sex ed was 'just don't worry about it man'. Even though they do say that but they don't say it in a way that really speaks to you . . . and I went out and had sex without a condom my first time and it just scared me for like a month (Theo, early 20's).

The sex education experiences described in these interviews were mostly concerned with the last line of this quote: the moment of unprotected sex and how to prevent it. However, this 'private moment' is embedded in a social context, constructed as a 'rite of passage'. How does heterosexual intercourse get taken for granted as a marker of adulthood? How is the concept of virginity organized by gender? Official sex education does not ask these questions but rather isolates *protection* from the 'mysterious' and 'appealing' context of sex.

Conclusion

These interviews have illustrated young people's critical insights about sexuality, which challenge the particular constructions of what counts as 'the basics' in school. Official sex education is a type of 'banking education' that deposits information into students' minds, denying their own forms of expertise (Freire, 1970). It is anchored in the aims to regulate, rather than explore, sexuality. The participants' insights support the argument for transforming sexuality education into a critical pedagogy to investigate the connections between how we 'know' and experience sexuality and the wider social relations that shape these experiences.

References

Foucault, M. 1984. *The History of Sexuality, Vol. 1*. New York: Vintage Books.

Freire, P. 1970. *Pedagogy of the Oppressed*. New York: Continuum.

Health Canada. 1994. *Canadian Guidelines for Sexual Health Education*. Ottawa: Health Canada.

Ministry of Training, Colleges and Universities. 1999. Toronto: Ministry of Training, Colleges and Universities.

Smith, D. 1987. *The Everyday World as Problematic: A Feminist Sociology*. Toronto: University of Toronto Press.

———. 1990. *Texts, Facts and Femininity*. London, UK: Routledge.

CHAPTER 49

Preserving Domesticity: Reading Tupperware in Women's Changing Domestic, Social, and Economic Roles

Susan Vincent

Introduction

Tupperware has a way of bringing women together, but not always for the expected reason. When a friend invited me to her Tupperware party some years ago, I felt uncomfortable and decided to investigate the reasons for my distaste. I decided to explore Tupperware's image of **gendered domesticity**. I did not take into account Tupperware's powerful snowballing effect. As other women learned that I was thinking about Tupperware, they approached me and I became a willing listener of their vituperative comments. I had extensive discussions with five women, and obtained other information through discussions at presentations I gave. This alternative 'Tupperware party', or group of women allied in our discomfort, shared certain characteristics. We were university-educated, Euro-Canadian professionals, some in the academy, one outside. I noted that the most pointed criticisms of the company came from a couple of older women who had spent their early adult years as housewives, although they later joined the ranks of academe.

When I moved to another part of Canada and started talking about Tupperware to younger Euro-Canadian university women, their reactions were quite different. The younger women's conversation was markedly less negative and personal. The very different reactions of my two generations of friends stemmed, I suspected, from their experiences in entering the work force. The older women had been expected to be, and had in some cases been, housewives. By contrast, the younger women had expected and been expected to pursue careers. My conversations with all of these women, some dozen or more, raised more questions than they could possibly answer—about women's changing work and domestic roles, and about why Tupperware's image seemed so stubbornly static. In this paper, 'Tupperware' is defined as the complex of product, company, strategy, and image associated with the company.

Women Then and Now: Domestic, Economic, and Social Roles

There are significant bodies of research on the history of women's domestic work, waged work, and social roles in North America over the last century (e.g., Luxton, 1980; Cowan, 1983; Hartmann, 1987; Armstrong and Armstrong, 1994; Sangster, 1995; Strong-Boag, 1995). Despite a continued elision between women and the domestic sphere, the domestic, economic, and social roles of white North American women have changed significantly over the last century. I comment here on factors that specifically relate to Tupperware.

DOMESTIC WORK

What constitutes domestic work has changed over the last century. Just as the workplace was being deconstructed to improve productive efficiency, the same process was being applied to the home. In the 1920s the science of home economics was born (e.g., see Andrews, 1923), calling attention to various household tasks and trying to manage them in ways similar to how industry was managed—the 'Fordification' of domestic work (Bose, 1982: 229).

WAGED WORK

While capitalist products and calculations were slowly entering the domestic sphere, women were quickly entering the work force. In the post-Second World War era, very few Canadian women had waged jobs. Indeed, many women, especially from the middle class, felt pressured not to take jobs, but to stay home with their children (Sangster, 1995; Strong-Boag, 1995). In 1960, only 30 per cent of Canadian women were in the work force (Boulet and Lavallee, 1984).

Despite the difficulties in entering the job market, women's participation in the work force increased. In 2001, 56 per cent of Canadian women over the age of 15 had entered the work force, accounting for 46 per cent of the total labour force (Statistics Canada, 2002). While their numbers increased dramatically, women's occupations did not change very much.

SOCIAL RELATIONS

One of the widely acknowledged components of North American women's gender roles is sociability (Stack, 1974; di Leonardo, 1987). I will point to some possible changes derived from two Canadian case studies.

The first case study deals with women living in Ontario suburbs in the 1950s. Strong-Boag (1995) describes the close informal reciprocal relationships between women. While not all of the women she interviewed agreed, there is a strong sense of knowledge, services, and goods being shared through ongoing sociability among women similarly situated as mothers without paid work. There is evidence that this intimate reciprocity has changed over the intervening period. Side (1999) describes friendships among a sample of mostly white, middle-class Ontario women in the 1990s: the women interviewed value their friendships with other women for the companionship, the emotional support, and the conversation that was exchanged within these relationships. Formal obligation of support between friends was regarded as imposition that threatened the voluntariness of these relationships and, as such, rarely occurred.

The discussion presented above demonstrates that while women entered the work force in large numbers over the last fifty years, they did not leave their domestic roles behind. This resulted in a tremendous dual pressure on women who needed to earn money and keep the house clean. Tupperware suggests that it is the solution to this problem.

What Is Tupperware?

The plastic that was used in early Tupperware was invented in 1938 by Earl Tupper, but the product really only took off in the 1950s when the party sales format was adopted. There are three important features of the company: the product, the sales organization, and the party.

THE PRODUCT

In North America, Tupperware consists of two types of products: kitchenware and toys for children. The kitchenware usually serves to store food or to serve it and often does both. The toys comprise a much smaller range of goods. A glance at the catalogue indicates that there has been significant change in Tupperware's offerings since the 1950s to keep up with advances in kitchen technology, but that the scope of the product has remained dedicated to kitchen and children.

THE SALES ORGANIZATION

Most typically, Tupperware is sold directly to the consumer, rather than to stores that would then do the work of retailing. There are nested pyramids of dealers and distributors. The distributors are actually independent contractors who buy the product wholesale from the company and make a commission. They also earn a commission on the sales of dealers they recruit, providing an incentive to expand the sales force. The sellers buy their own demonstration kits. The hostesses provide the location of the party and further subsidize sales by providing food. The hostesses, of course, also provide the customers.

THE PARTY

While Tupperware is now available in stores, on the Internet, and by catalogue, the quintessential and most common way to buy Tupperware is to attend a party. The parties follow a standard format. The hostess invites friends, family, colleagues, and acquaintances to the party and usually provides the locale and refreshments. The dealer sets up samples and then leads 'ice-breaker' games. As the party moves on, the dealer demonstrates the product and suggests potential uses to entice people to buy.

The Gender of Tupperware

The description given above makes it clear that Tupperware is a quintessentially gendered product. The expectation is so entrenched in North American culture that Tupperware dealers will be women that it is news when they are men (e.g., Streisand, 1996; Brown, 1999). Not only is the archetypal person called to mind by a mention of Tupperware a woman, she is also white (Clarke, 1999) and working- or middle-class (Biggart, 1989).

This Tupperware image of a white, middle-class 'Everywoman' corresponds to specific domestic and family roles. In particular, it targets women as household managers. The company's goal is 'to create exceptionally designed, great-looking products that make everyday living easier' (Tupperware, 1999: 2). 'Making everyday living easier' involves managing a budget, planning and cooking nutritious and delicious meals, keeping the house in order, attending to the needs of her husband and children, and maintaining social networks. The 'great-looking products' allow her to do all of this as stylishly and efficiently as possible.

Tupperware offers help with the domestic budget by helping to keep food fresh so that less is wasted, and providing women with a flexible way of earning income as dealers for Tupperware (Rapping, 1980; Biggart, 1989; Bingham, 1975; Clarke, 1999). Tupperware also saves women's time by exposing them to recipes that can be easily prepared using Tupperware products.

Tupperware's middle zone between domesticity and the market was a strategic one at a time when women were moving into the work force. In the process of selling for Tupperware, the gender features discussed above of managerial, organizational, culinary, consumer savvy, maternal, sociable housewives come into play. However, dealers' 'success stories'—given in company material designed to attract women to a career in Tupperware—emphasize the lack of special skills needed. In the case of Tupperware, as with the feminized workplace, certain skills and behaviours are necessary and expected, but not recognized as learned and specific to any particular woman. This allows employers to take advantage of these 'natural' skills, without having to recompense them.

Conclusion

As long as women continue to be responsible for the domestic sphere at the same time that they need to engage in income earning, Tupperware's fusion of the two will have practical and ideological salience. While Clarke (1999) suggests that Tupperware has been used by women as a saviour, solving their economic problems while giving the domestic sphere value and respect, I consider it more of a reverse canary in the mine shaft, strengthening when women's dual work/home pressures become overwhelming. The organization and gender segregation of the workplace that does not allow workers to engage in fulfilling personal lives is a major factor here. Tupperware's continued dependence on a mixture of domesticity and commodity indicates that women—and men—have not yet achieved a dignified balance between their roles in life.

References

Andrews, B. 1923. *Economics of the Household: Its Administration and Finance*. New York: The Macmillan Company.

Armstrong, P., and H. Armstrong. 1994. *The Double Ghetto: Canadian Women and their Segregated Work*, 3rd ed. Toronto: McClelland and Stewart.

Biggart, N.W. 1989. *Charismatic Capitalism: Direct Selling Organizations in America*. Chicago: University of Chicago Press.

Bingham, E. 1975. 'Letter to the Editor', *Ms* 4, 6: 4.

Bose, C. 1982. 'Technology and Changes in the Division of Labour' in *The Changing Experience of Women*, pp. 226–38, E. Whitehead, et al., eds. Oxford: Basil Blackwell and The Open University.

Boulet, J., and L. Lavallee. 1984. *L'evolution de la Situation Economique des Femmes*. Ottawa: Supply and Services Canada.

Brown, C. 1999. 'Tupperware Story', CBC radio 4644, 13 April.

Clarke, A. 1999. *Tupperware: The Promise of Plastic in 1950s America*. Washington: Smithsonian Institution Press.

Cowan, R.S. 1983. *More Work for Mother: The Ironies of Household Technology from the Open Hearth to the Microwave*. New York: Basic Books.

di Leonardo, M. 1987. 'The Female World of Cards and Holidays: Women, Families and the Work of Kinship', *Signs* 12, 3: 440–53.

Hartmann, H. 1987. 'Changes in Women's Economic and Family Roles in Post-World War II United States', in *Women, Households and the Economy*, L. Beneria and C. Stimpson, eds. New Brunswick, NJ: Rutgers University Press.

Luxton, M. 1980. *More than a Labour of Love: Three Generations of Women's Work in the Home*. Toronto: Women's Press.

Rapping, E. 1980. 'Tupperware and Women', *Radical America* 6, 14: 39–49.

Sangster, J. 1995. 'Doing Two Jobs: The Wage-earning Mother, 1945–70', in *A Diversity of Women: Ontario, 1945–80*, pp. 98–134, J. Parr, ed. Toronto: University of Toronto Press.

Side, K. 1999. 'Government Restraint and Limits to Economic Reciprocity in Women's Friendships', *Atlantis* 23, 2: 5–13.

Stack, C. 1974. *All Our Kin: Strategies for Survival in a Black Community*. New York: Harper and Row.

Statistics Canada. 2002. *Women in Canada: Work Chapter Updates*. Ottawa: Minister of Industry. Available at http://www.statcan.ca/english/freepub/89F0133XIE/89F0133XIE01001.pdf (accessed 7 October 2002).

Streisand, B. 1996. 'Pam Teflon Bowls 'em over', *US News & World Report* 121, 1: 16.

Strong-Boag, V. 1995. ' "Their side of the story": Women's Voices from Ontario Suburbs', in *A Diversity of Women: Ontario, 1945–80*, pp. 46–74, J. Parr, ed. Toronto: University of Toronto Press.

Tupperware. 1999. *Tupperware Catalogue Winter/Spring*.

CHAPTER 50

Analyzing Women's Situated Knowledge for Menopause Construction

Mary Patton

Introduction

Of concern for my feminist research is how women understand menopause in a society in which the dominant view of **menopause** is one of deficiency (Coney, 1994). Women develop understandings of menopause from that which is known in their local settings. Smith (1987) and Haraway (2001) refer to this as **situated knowledge**. The biomedical and pharmaceutical communities present the medicalized view of menopause through the media and the health care system as the superior representation of menopause, making it readily available and marginalizing other ideas (knowledge) about menopause (Hubbard, 2001).

An analysis of women's accounts of menopause offers an opportunity to explore the organized power relations that create the conditions and situated knowledge for women's menopause experiences. Women's experience of menopause cannot be separated from the broader social, economic, and political world and the social relations that structure the conditions for their understandings of menopause. Here I use the narratives of Lana and Rebecca, two of the 20 middle-aged women I interviewed, to show how different women's socio-economic and cultural locations, embedded in the broader socio-political world, offer varying constraints and possibilities for developing situated menopause knowledge. I emphasize Lana and Rebecca's active engagement with ideas about menopause to demonstrate that they are not passive recipients of knowledge.

The Medicalization of Menopause

Lana, a hairdresser who described herself as a woman of West Indian descent, spoke about her menopausal experience, which began after she experienced menstrual difficulties and had a complete hysterectomy at age 40, approximately 20 years ago. A complete hysterectomy involves removal of the ovaries that are required for estrogen production; therefore, following surgery, Lana was placed on hormone replacement therapy (HRT) for surgically-induced menopause. She explained:

The lady doctor examined me and said I had an infected [uterine] fibroid and it was better for me to get it out as fast as I could. . . . The [gynecologist] explained that it was better for me to have a complete hysterectomy because it was safer, no chance of cancer developing. As I wasn't planning

on having more children, because I was past childbearing, I considered that and said okay. He said that it wasn't going to be any problem just that I wouldn't have this monthly thing anymore. I said that's fine because I didn't want to have [periods] anymore because they were for me such a problem. . . . He suggested that I take estrogen. The estrogen [I take] is the lowest dose that you can have and it is better for me to take something to control the hot and cold perspiration.

Lana relied on biomedical expertise and agreed to a complete hysterectomy. Relying on a physician was the accepted way to deal with menopause in the 1980s and estrogen [HRT] was the standard remedy for hot flashes (Walters, 1994). Lana spoke about not being prepared for menopause and being unaware of the side effects of HRT. Menopause was not a media topic in the 1980s (Seale, 2002). Lana accepted a life on HRT, medicalizing her menopause, without being exposed to the estrogen problematization now available. She did not recall the physicians presenting options to a complete hysterectomy. Fisher (1986) documents the lack of choice given to women, concluding that clients' decision-making is disadvantaged when physicians have the authority to control information through the ways in which they answer questions and present material (1986).

Fisher (1986) further points out that women are not in positions to demand choices when they are in pain and distress. Lana explained that she did not explore alternatives:

The doctor said it was best to take everything out. I didn't know it was possible to take part of it only. I wasn't given a choice. Maybe I would have said just take a part . . . but then you're frightened and you don't want [pain].

Lana now recognizes the vulnerability of her position when she sought biomedical help, including her unease, uncertainty, and her reluctance to ask questions. According to Freidson (1970), clients from a social-cultural group differing from that of an upper-middle class physician often conceal and restrain their concerns and anxieties by passivity and granting deference to the physician's knowledge. Roberts (1996) also found in her study that poor women of colour frequently reported experiencing prejudice when seeking health care. Lana, however, denied experiencing prejudice during her care. While it is important to consider that Lana's position as woman of colour may have contributed to the physicians' recommendations for her care, it is important not to make assumptions about the centrality of race for her experience.

Lana's experiences draw attention to the ways in which a biomedical paradigm narrows treatment to surgery and drugs. This is not unexpected as physicians are trained in the biomedical approach to health issues. Yet the recommendation of a complete hysterectomy by the physician as the 'normal' practice eliminated choice for Lana. In Dyer's words, 'the establishment of normalcy is . . . according to [the physician's] own world view. . . . In so far as they succeed, they establish their hegemony' of **biomedical knowledge** and practices (1977: 30). Lana did not discuss knowing that when a physician recommends treatment, he or she controls the information given. Since part of a physician's role is providing information, the activity appears natural or inevitable, but he or she may present a limited or biased view (Hall, 1997).

Rebecca's account offers insight into the constraints and opportunities in her setting for developing menopause knowledge. Rebecca is a married Caucasian woman in her mid-fifties whose career has been in broadcasting. About six years ago, she experienced uterine hemorrhaging and fibroids, for which her physician recommended a complete hysterectomy. Rebecca elaborated:

> I ended up being hospitalized briefly because my hemoglobin count went down very low. . . . At that point, the surgeon wanted to do a hysterectomy and I said I had read about [laser] endometrial ablation. The doctor hadn't mentioned it but, it was new at this point. . . . So, I had an endometrial ablation to take care of things. The next year

I had the same experience all over again [hemorrhaging]. The doctor said, 'You have had two episodes where your hemoglobin has dropped dangerously low and you are going to risk heart damage. . . . You need to think about the hysterectomy option'. . . . So, when I was 49 years old I had a hysterectomy. . . . And just like that with the surgery, [I was in menopause].

Rebecca spoke about using her journalist research skills to inform herself about menopause, HRT, alternative solutions to a hysterectomy, and the surgery itself. Haug and Lavin (1983) note that knowledge increases 'patient power' and can be extensive if people are well educated, have sought information, and had experience with a condition for some time (39), thus enhancing client–physician power relations. How ever one theorizes that the relation, the important point for my research purpose is that Rebecca was able to influence the health care she received and delay having a hysterectomy. This does not mean that Rebecca was beyond the influence of medical authority. The physician still has the ultimate power. As Hall clarifies, 'power not only constrains and prevents; it is also productive. It produces . . . new kinds of knowledge . . . new objects of knowledge . . . [and] shapes new practices' (1997: 260). For example, Rebecca had a complete hysterectomy rather than leaving the ovaries intact. Rebecca did not describe debating the options here, even though it is known that physicians frequently present arguments for surgery based on their biases and assumptions that manipulate women's decision-making processes (Fisher, 1986).

Conclusion

Rebecca and Lana reported keeping current about menopause today and being aware of the Women's Health Institute Study that links long-term estrogen use with increased breast cancer risk (Wathen et al., 2004). Both women are decreasing their HRT dosage and anticipating quitting. Lana stated that she is dissatisfied with her physician who says, 'It's okay to stay on [HRT] because even women 80 years old take this and they're fine.' She is seeking a new physician. When women have access to credible resources and the support to use it, they are better able to make decisions that serve their needs. Yet, even then, validated biomedical knowledge about menopausal women's bodies traditionally constructed by the ideas and assumptions of elite white men—biomedical scientists, physicians, and pharmaceutical researchers—continues to dominate through the media and the healthcare structures so that other views are marginalized (Hubbard, 2001). Rebecca's narrative showed that it is not enough for a woman to construct herself as having the skills and 'know how' for informing herself about menopause. She medicalized her menopause experiences through surgery and drugs, as did Lana. Butler (2003) argues that women strategize and make the best decisions they can within the constraints of power, knowledge, patriarchy, economics, and freedom in their locations (123). Hegemonic biomedical knowledge and lack of choice both position women as subjugated, which underscores how knowledge is situated not only through women's locations but also through the established socio-cultural structures that legitimize, disseminate, and uphold gender-, race-, and class-structured biomedical knowledge.

References

Butler, J. 2003. 'The Question of Social Transformation', in *Women and Social Transformation*, pp. 1–28, E. Beck Gernsheim, J. Butler, and L. Puigert, eds. New York: Peter Lang.

Coney, S. 1994. *The Menopause Industry*, rev. ed. Alameda, CA: Hunter House Inc.

Dyer, R., ed. 1977. *Gays and Film*. London: British Film Institute.

Fisher, S. 1986. *In the Patient's Best Interests: Women and the Politics of Medical Decisions*. New Brunswick, NJ: Rutgers University Press.

Freidson, E. 1970. *Professional Dominance: The Social Structure of Medical Care*. Chicago: Aldine Publishing Company.

Hall, S. 1997. *Representation: Cultural Representations and Signifying Practices*. Thousand Oaks, CA: Sage Publications.

Haraway, D. 2001. 'Situated Knowledges', in *The Gender and Science Reader*, pp. 169–88, M. Lederman and I. Bartsch, eds. London: Routledge.

Haug, M., and B.Lavin. 1983. *Consumerism in Medicine*. Beverly Hills, CA: Sage Publications.

Hubbard, R. 2001. 'Science, Facts, and Feminism', in *Women, Science, and Technology*, pp. 153–9, M. Wyer, M. Barbercheck, D.Giesman, H. Örun Öztürk, and M. Wayne, eds. New York: Routledge.

Roberts, D. 1996. 'Reconstructing the Patient: Starting with Women of Color', in *Feminism and Bioethics: Beyond Reproduction*, pp. 116–43, S. Wolf, ed. New York: Oxford University Press.

Seale, C. 2002. *Media and Health*. Thousand Oak, CA: Sage

Smith, D. 1987. *The Everyday World as Problematic. A Feminist Sociology*. Toronto: University of Toronto Press.

Walters, V. 1994. 'Women's Perceptions Regarding Health and Wellness', in Health, Illness, and *Health Care in Canada*, pp. 307–25, B. Bolaria and H. Dickinson, eds. Toronto: Harcourt Brace and Company, Canada.

Wathen, C., D. Feig, J. Feightner, B. Abramson, and A. Cheung. 2004. 'Hormone Replacement Therapy for the Primary Prevention of Chronic Diseases: Recommendation Statement from the Canadian Task Force on Preventive Health Care', *Canadian Medical Association Journal* 170, 10: 1535–7.

CHAPTER 51

Balancing Work and Caring: Midlife Women Assess their Accommodations

Ann Duffy, Nancy Mandell, and Sue Wilson

How do midlife women talk about their past and current attempts to balance caring commitments with paid employment? Using a diverse sample of 25 Ontario women between the ages of 50 and 60 years, we consider (1) the specific strategies employed to balance caring and paid work obligations; (2) the emotive language with which women frame their retrospective evaluation of these strategies—notably, regret, necessity, frustration, and anger; and (3) their current evaluation of their past balancing acts—notably, remorse, necessity, satisfaction (Mandell, Duffy, and Wilson, 2006).

Balancing Strategies

The large-scale movement of married women into the labour market in the 1960s pushed women to find ways to balance the competing demands of caring work with paid work. Individual solutions include staying at home with young children, working part-time, choosing jobs viewed as more compatible with child care, utilizing formal and informal child care arrangements, delaying childbearing, reducing fertility, and using labour-saving services (Duffy and Pupo, 1989; Luxton 1987; Luxton and Corman, 1997; Statistics Canada 2000; Vosko, 2000).

Balancing strategies reflect women's care giving responsibilities. Purchasing support, calling on extended family, and using local community resources depend on the extent and intensity of women's engagement. Frequently within families, care giving moves back and forth across generational lines in a way that involves complex intergenerational linkages among relations (McDaniel, 2002).

Expressing Profound Ambivalence

Despite their diversity, midlife women experience and express profound ambivalence about their lifetimes of juggling of caring and paid work. Meeting the care giving needs of family members means women constantly make personal, family, and work decisions that leave them feeling frustrated and constrained. A pattern of **structured ambivalence** characterizes their lives (Connidis and McMullin, 2002). In trying to negotiate intimate relationships in terms of their needs and desires, midlife women run up against the needs and demands inherent in the structuring of work and family life. Mothers, for example, often express guilt at their absence from their children's lives at the same time as they express frustration at their lack of advancement, security, and recognition in their paid employment. Conflict coexists with contentment as women struggle to resolve **structural contradictions**.

Midlife women frequently describe their compromises in managing the burdens of care giving. A fifty-five-year old casino worker, who emigrated to Canada when she was two years old, emphatically lists the compromises she has made in order to fulfill her family and employment obligations:

> Many times, many, many times [I made compromises]. With a working mother you are always the last person that you are going to think about. You have to put your children first, your husband, your job, your parents, if they need you. So, yes . . . there were many, many compromises, many.

Compromise makes her long for the era when mothers stayed home with the children, saying that she 'would much rather have been in the other generation where the mother stayed home with the children'. Ambivalence characterizes same-sex relationships as well. A highly educated professional woman with a stay-at-home partner describes herself as having the 'good end of the stick in our family'. As she states, her partner is the one who 'certainly has to make compromises because of my job and my not being around and available and stuff'.

Inevitability permeates the assessments of midlife women. Making sacrifices is accepted as an inexorable social fact. Yet, ironically, this fixed reality is conceptualized as freely chosen. A respondent who gave up employment until her three children were grown describes this decision as solely her own: 'Yes, I did [give up my job when my first child was born]. By choice. . .I think. I've done it and I was happy when I did it and it was time to just move on.'

However, she later qualifies her 'choice' by explaining that her husband, who earned more money than she did, preferred her to stay home: 'He made more money than I did so it was better off that he worked and I stayed home with the kids.'

Her ambivalence is embedded in her very construction of her decision—it is embraced as a choice, as a statement of her agency, and of her belief in the value of full-time mothering and partnering while acknowledging her decision as a rock-hard necessity.

Frustration, conflict, and some resentment characterize these descriptions. A 56-year-old respondent currently employed part-time as a deli worker speaks of the personal sacrifices she made in being a full-time mother:

> You don't have time for yourself. It was a compromise, I suppose. You got three children running around and you have to take care of them. And, the household and the meals, and the soccer practices and the hockey and all that stuff. It was good, but at the same time you did give certain things up for yourself to do that.

Later she adds, 'you'd like to do certain things sometimes that you can't do because of your family, your husband, whatever.'

Evaluating their Accommodations

When asked what they would change if they could redo their lives, many midlife women mention education saying, wistfully, that they wished they had either pursued further education or secured education prior to marriage and/or motherhood. Having given up a full-time teaching position in order to assist her husband in an unsuccessful business venture, a 60-year old immigrant woman— now divorced and working part-time—is angry with herself stating,

> I was independent but I didn't go all the way, you know, I didn't say 'Look, this teaching job will give me a pension' and it was never explained to me by the teachers either but . . . but that's no excuse. I should have known that myself.

Once again, frustration and anger is muffled by the ideology that women have a 'choice', should have known better and, ultimately, have only themselves to blame.

Aging brings women an increased sense of personal control. Even though many continue to care for grandchildren or aging parents, this work is viewed as more manageable and controllable than the obligations they faced with young children. Relieved to be finished with the emotional and physical complexity of young motherhood, women report feeling freer to speak their minds and set their own agendas. As one stay-at-home mother happily reports, 'I think I have a lot of control now. I think my life right now is pretty close to how I'd like to be. . .it is wonderful. I love being older . . . love, love, love it.'

However, too many midlife women seem vague about their economic futures. They frame retirement decisions tentatively, revealing an underlying fear and uncertainty. Unsure of whether she will have sufficient money to manage her retirement, one woman states that she supposes she can always 'sell the house'. Even well-to-do women describe their financial futures in contingent terms. Remaining economically secure presupposes being married. One 53-year old woman acknowledges her marital unhappiness, yet understands her financial dependence as binding her to marriage. The exceptions to this trend were the very few women who had their own money and property. One working-class woman who had been a stay-at-home mom for the past 37 years indicates that she has had significant control over family finances through years of paying the bills. Although she did not have an earned income, she had money of her own and property in her own name.

Conclusion: Facing the Future

Most Canadian women can anticipate a lifetime of paid employment. Most Canadian women enter into some caring relationship at some point in their lives—typically, with dependent children, aging parents or other relatives, and, less commonly, dependent or disabled siblings. Most of the work of these caring activities is undertaken by women (Chappell et al., 2003). For women who are single-parents, for disabled women, or for women who have multiple care-giving roles, care-giving burdens are attenuated.

When assessing their lifetimes of balancing paid and caring work, midlife women describe a 'winner–loser' scenario, especially when care giving responsibilities are at their most intense. This is a scenario in which most women, particularly those with few educational credentials, little in the way of financial resources, those who are disabled, who

are recent immigrants, and those from minority or socially marginalized populations are likely to be on the losing end. At the same time, there is a minority of women who have been able to reverse the winner–loser pattern and who have been able to rely on a partner to provide the lion's share of care giving work. While this allows some women to achieve educational, career, and economic success, it is often attached to a profound ambivalence about the sacrifices they have made in terms of personal relationships. What is missing are accounts in which balance is achieved, or even acknowledged, as a clearly articulated goal.

Individual strategies developed over a lifetime do not resolve the conflict women experience in trying to achieve a **work–family balance**. No woman describes her relationship as equitable and no woman expresses an expectation that the social structure should alter to accommodate dual-earning parents. Yet these very solutions which are now socially promoted to care giving women—part-time and marginal employment, periods of unemployment, employment in women's occupations, reliance on partner's economic contributions to the household, early retirement and so on—may imperil women's long-term, and often short-term, economic well-being. As the first wave of baby boomer women flood into retirement and widowhood, we can expect a dramatic increase in the numbers of Canadian women shouldering the negative outcomes of these earlier strategies. With estimates that baby boomers will constitute one-quarter, or approximately 10 million, of the population by the year 2041, it is imperative that we develop social policies to address the effects of these earlier caring and paid work decisions (Cheal, 2002).

References

Chappell, N., E. Gee, L. McDonald, and M. Stones. 2003. *Aging in Contemporary Canada*. Toronto: Prentice Hall.

Cheal, D., ed. 2002. *Aging and Demographic Change in Canadian Context*. Toronto: University of Toronto Press.

Connidis, I.A., and J.A. McMullin. 2002. 'Sociological Ambivalence and Family Ties: Critical Perspective', *Journal of Marriage and the Family* 64 (August): 558–67.

Duffy, A., and N. Pupo. 1989. *Part-time Paradox: Connecting Gender, Work and Family*. Toronto: McClelland and Stewart.

Luxton, M. 1987. 'Two Hands for the Clock: Changing Patterns in the Gendered Division of Labour in the Home', in *Gender Roles: Doing What Comes Naturally?*, E.D. Salamon and B.W. Robinson, eds. Toronto: Methuen.

Luxton, M., and J. Corman. 1997. *Getting By in Hard Times: Gendered about at Home and on the Job*. Toronto: University of Toronto Press.

Mandell, N., A. Duffy, and S. Wilson. 2006. *Canadian Women at Midlife*. Toronto: Oxford University Press.

McDaniel, S.A. 2002. 'Intergenerational Interlinkages: Public, Family and Work', in *Aging and Demographic Change in Canadian Context*, pp. 22–71, D. Cheal, ed. Toronto: University of Toronto Press.

Statistics Canada. 2000. *Women in Canada 2000*. Ottawa: Minister of Industry.

Vosko, L. 2000. *Temporary Work: The Gendered Rise of a Precarious Employment Relationship*. Toronto: University of Toronto Press.

Questions for Critical Thought

'THEY SHOULD MAKE IT MORE NORMAL': YOUNG PEOPLE'S CRITICAL STANDPOINTS AND THE SOCIAL ORGANIZATION OF SEXUALITY EDUCATION

1. What kinds of difficulties do young people face in seeking out resources and information about sexuality outside of school? What might some benefits be?
2. How do you interpret Audrey's statement of 'mak(ing) it normal'? What are some ways that 'normal' is made?
3. What does it mean to say that sex as a private act is always connected to the social? Do you agree? Why or why not? Give examples.
4. What does it mean to say that 'the facts of life' are a site of struggle? What are some examples of this?
5. What are the limitations of using rational choice explanations for sexual behaviour?

PRESERVING DOMESTICITY: READING TUPPERWARE IN WOMEN'S CHANGING DOMESTIC, SOCIAL, AND ECONOMIC ROLES

1. With regards to domestic, economic, and social roles, how would you describe women of then and now?
2. How can Canadian women and men achieve a dignified balance between their roles in life?
3. Would you classify Tupperware as exploiting women's natural skills or as a saviour for women?
4. What is Tupperware? How would you explain the convergence between women's domestic activities and Tupperware's business strategy?
5. Women's involvement in Tupperware demonstrates the elasticity of women's skills. How far do you agree with this statement?

ANALYZING WOMEN'S SITUATED KNOWLEDGE FOR MENOPAUSE CONSTRUCTION

1. How might the dominant biomedical representation of menopause as a disease limit women's situated knowledge about menopause?
2. Describe the ways that broader social relations and structures contribute to women's local menopause experiences.
3. What is the meaning of the statement 'biomedical knowledge about menopause can be seen as a form of power over women'?

4. White elite males have historically constructed biomedical knowledge about women's menopausal bodies. What implications does this have for women's menopause experiences today?
5. Describe the importance of considering women's different socio-economic and cultural locations for understanding women's menopause constructions.

BALANCING WORK AND CARING: MIDLIFE WOMEN ASSESS THEIR ACCOMMODATIONS

1. Was it possible for the average woman growing up in the 1960s to fashion a satisfying solution to the work–family conflict?
2. In what ways are disabled women, recent immigrants, or women from socially marginalized populations particularly disadvantaged in the struggle to balance home and work?
3. What kinds of issues are likely to face midlife women as they move into their senior years in the next two decades and what social policies might effectively address these concerns?
4. Contrast the decision patterns of contemporary young women to those of midlife women and consider the long-term implications in terms of both economic security and emotional satisfaction.
5. To what degree, if any, do contemporary young women construct their lives with a sense of 'inevitability' and 'ambivalence'? What role, if any, have educational advances amongst women impacted on these patterns?

Part XII · Immigration, Race, and Ethnicity

Racial and ethnic minority immigrants face a wide range of challenges in adapting to their new country. These challenges include, but are not limited to, barriers to essential services such as housing, health care, and education. The sociological study of immigrants, immigrant communities, and host populations provides a better understanding of problems that have arisen around immigration in Canadian society.

Prejudice and discriminatory attitudes can prevent minorities from fully participating within the host society. Richard Alba's article in this Part discusses boundaries between immigrants and the natives of a country, where assimilation involves crossing boundaries. Usually, these boundaries are invisible and behavioural, and Gillian Creese and Edith Ngene Kambere provide a strong example of behavioural boundaries as they show that speaking English with an African accent creates a boundary which African women are unable to cross. Their African accent is a marker for their race and immigrant status, excluding them from jobs and negatively hindering their sense of belonging in Canadian society. This has led to increased economic hardships experienced by newcomer families in Canada in recent decades. Paul Anisef and Kelli Phythian argue that this state of affair serves to compound the multiple risk factors confronting immigrant youth.

Another problem that racial minorities face is poverty, and one dimension of which is social exclusion. In a study of racialized minority girls and young women, Jo Anne Lee shows that the social exclusion these women experience is due to service providers who are unprepared to serve racial minorities. This reality is reflected in the women's feelings that they are not getting the support they need. Stereotypes are another source of exclusion, and often unfairly 'put down' racial minorities.

Despite all the challenges that minority immigrants face, there are some ways to help them cope with their new environment. Typically, immigrants are attracted to large cities for economic reasons, but they can live in rural areas and small towns too. Ho Hon Leung's paper describes Chinese immigrants who have settled in a small town. His findings show that families play a crucial role in helping immigrants to adjust, on the way to developing relations with the outside community. Another way that immigrants adapt to their host society is by keeping transnational ties with their native country.

In short, immigration has played and continues to play a crucial role in the diversity of Canada's communities. The following chapters give the reader an idea of the richness of sociological research into the experiences of immigrants and racial minorities.

CHAPTER 52

Immigrant–Native Boundaries in North America and Western Europe

Richard Alba

Introduction

Comparative research on immigration and on race and ethnicity has been hampered by a scarcity of concepts that can be applied in equivalent ways in societies that have very different histories and, to judge from the surface at least, different racial and ethnic landscapes. Thus, if we look across the societies of North America and Western Europe, the United States stands out for the seemingly unique, inflexible character of its racial division between whites and blacks, exemplified by the infamous one-drop rule.

I argue here that the boundary concept can be fashioned into a powerful tool for comparative research (Alba, 2005). By a boundary, I mean a social distinction that individuals make in their everyday lives that shapes their actions and mental orientations towards others

Assimilation and Boundaries

The virtues of the boundary concept for a comparative framework are several. First, one can differentiate between types of **boundaries** in a way that is relevant to the prospects of **assimilation** (i.e., access to the opportunities routinely available to the ethnic/racial/native majority) versus exclusion. Second, boundary differences can frequently be related to the institutions of societies and thereby to history; thus, the boundary concept offers a way to bring path dependency into the analysis, a need that is very apparent in the study of immigration and race/ethnicity. Third, by highlighting the ways in which boundaries are embedded in institutions, the concept also helps us to see some constraints on the powers of majorities.

Thus, it is common for native majorities to seek to impose disadvantages on immigrant minorities, or at a minimum to allow already existing barriers to stand. But in general they cannot manufacture boundaries *de novo* and are constrained by existing cultural, legal, and institutional materials, which therefore fundamentally determine the nature of assimilation and exclusion. Hence, the boundary concept helps us to account for the evident path-dependent character of immigrant–native relations in North America and Western Europe.

The boundary concept is also helpful in rethinking some established concepts in this field. Assimilation is a case in point. Assimilation has frequently been conceived as a one-way process: individuals and groups assimilate to 'something', becoming more like that entity. A more fruitful way of conceptualizing assimilation is in terms of boundaries; doing so makes apparent that an ethnic distinction can be affected by changes occurring on either or both sides of a boundary. Accordingly, Victor Nee and I (2003) define assimilation as the 'decline of an ethnic distinction and its corollary cultural and social differences'. 'Decline' in this context means that a distinction attenuates in salience, that the occurrences for which it is relevant diminish in number and contract to fewer and fewer domains of social life.

Boundaries are not all the same. A key distinction lies between bright and blurred boundaries. That is, some boundaries involve distinctions that are relatively unambiguous and individuals know at all times which side of the boundary they are on, as do others about them; such boundaries are 'bright'. Others involve zones of self-presentation and social representation that allow for ambiguous locations with respect to the boundary; they are 'blurry'. This could mean that individuals are seen simultaneously as belonging on both sides of the boundary or that sometimes they appear to be on one side and at other times on the other. Race in the United States is a bright boundary, whereas language in immigration societies typically involves a blurred boundary, especially for the second-generation children of immigrants who are reared in the society of reception.

This distinction, I argue, has a critical relationship to the possibilities for assimilation. When the boundary is bright, then assimilation usually takes the form of individuals singly crossing it in order to join the majority, and more privileged, group. Assimilation will generally be experienced by these individuals as something akin to a conversion (i.e., a departure from one group and a discarding of signs of membership in it), linked to an attempt to enter into another membership, with all of the social and psychic burdens a conversion process entails—growing distance from peers, feelings of disloyalty, and anxieties about acceptance. It is noteworthy that even when race marks the boundary, some assimilation occurs. In the US, some individuals born into the African American group have, because of their light skin tone and their European-like features, been able to 'pass'. The costs of passing for the individual have recently been described in an essay by Henry Louis Gates, analyzing the life of Anatole Broyard, the literary critic and essayist who lived his adult life as a white man, but was posthumously revealed to have been born black. His passing required that he cut himself off from his black relatives. His children, who did not know of his racial past, only met these family members at Broyard's funeral.

Bright boundaries are intimidating to the great majority of a minority group, unwilling to undertake the risks and pain assumed by Anatole Broyard. The prospects for assimilation are quite different in a blurred-boundary context. There, assimilation may be eased insofar as the individuals undergoing it do not sense a rupture between participation in mainstream institutions and familiar social and cultural practices and identities; and

they are not forced to choose between the mainstream and their group of origin.

Boundary concepts can help to identify analogues to the role of race in the US. These are analogues in a specific sense: that members of a minority are aware of belonging to a second-class population and of the difficulty and risk associated with an attempt to join the majority group, assuming that they even believe in the possibility of moving across the boundary. In this respect, we should consider the religious divide between Muslim immigrants and the mainstreams of the western European societies that receive them, such as France and Germany.

I pick France here because it is a more difficult case for my argument than, say, Germany, where the established versions of Christianity, Catholicism, and Lutheranism receive financial support through the tax system and are taught in religion classes in public schools by teachers employed by the state. In France, the institutionalization of Christianity is frequently subtle but nevertheless produces a bright boundary for Muslims. The state's role is not overt, since laïcité, or strict neutrality with respect to religion, is a fundamental principle of the French state. However, in a society where a single religion, Roman Catholicism, has been hegemonic for centuries, laïcité can work to confine outsider religions to a marginal position rather than to effect religious parity. Thus, the recognition of the major Christian holidays is taken for granted—in school and workplace schedules, for example (Zolberg and Long, 1999). There is no equivalent recognition for Muslim holidays.

In Europe, a widespread problem for Muslims is that of establishing suitable places of worship. Such buildings render the relationship between religion and society visible in material form. There is an inevitable contrast between the mainstream and Islam because of the centrality of numerous impressive Christian churches to national narratives—epitomized by Notre Dame, built on the location of Lutece, the original settlement around which Paris developed, and the site of subsequent important events (e.g., Napoleon's self-coronation).

By contrast, the places of worship of Muslims are often makeshift. As of 2000, the estimated 4–5 million Muslims had 1,558 prayer spaces in all of France, the vast majority of them quite small (Laurance, 2001). By contrast, there are some 40,000 Catholic buildings.

Moreover, the 1905 French law separating church and state has, in the current situation, the effect of subsidizing the mainstream religions while leaving stumbling blocks in the way of Islam. It placed previously existing Christian edifices in the hands of local and national authorities, thus obligating the state to maintain them, while barring it from contributing public money to the construction of new religious buildings. At the time of its passage, the Catholic Church strenuously resisted the law, but it now acts as an impediment to the construction of mosques without financial assistance from abroad (e.g., Saudi Arabia). In fairness, though, one must acknowledge that several mosques have been built with assistance from local or national authorities (Kepel, 1991).

Conclusion

Boundary concepts should prove useful in the comparative study of the incorporation of the second generation. It is especially critical to begin to identify the circumstances under which different incorporation patterns come into play, such as assimilation versus exclusion in which the latter is often described as 'downward' assimilation or assimilation into a racial or ethnic minority status (Portes and Zhou, 1993). Until we understand the varied situations faced by different immigrant groups, we will not be able to make much sense of the blooming variety in immigration societies.

References

Alba, R. 2005. 'Bright vs. Blurred Boundaries: Second-generation Assimilation and Exclusion in France, Germany, and the United States', *Ethnic and Racial Studies* 28 (January): 20–49.

Alba, R., and V. Nee. 2003. *Remaking the American Mainstream: Assimilation and the New Immigration*. Cambridge: Harvard University Press.

Gates, H.L. 1998. 'The Passing of Anatole Broyard', in *Thirteen Ways of Looking at a Black Man*. New York: Vintage.

Kepel, G. 1991. *Les Banlieues d'Islam: Naissance d'une Religion en France*. Paris: Editions du Seuil.

Laurence, J. 2001. 'Islam in France'. The Urban Institute. Available at http://www.brook.edu/dybdocroot/fp/cusf/analysis/islam.htm.

Portes, A., and M. Zhou. 1993. 'The New Second Generation: Segmented Assimilation and Its Variants', *The Annals* 530 (November): 74–96.

Zolberg, A., and L.L. Woon. 1999. 'Why Islam is like Spanish: Cultural Incorporation in Europe and the United States', *Politics & Society* 27: 5–38.

CHAPTER 53

What Colour Is Your English?

Gillian Creese and Edith Ngene Kambere

Introduction

The points system of immigrant selection rewards fluency in Canada's official languages, but perceptions of language fluency remain contested in everyday interactions. Drawing on preliminary research with **African immigrant women**, we highlight the need to explore the social construction of language fluency and the intersection between accents and processes of racialization.

Processes of immigration, like the projects of colonialism and nation-building in which they are embedded, are simultaneously racialized, gendered, sexualized, and classed (Anthias and Yuval-Davis, 1992; Stasiulis and Yuval-Davis, 1995; Strong-Boag, Grace, Eisenberg and Anderson, 1998; Bannerji, 2000; Calliste and Dei, 2000; Sharma, 2001). The 'imagined community' underlying the nation-building process (Anderson, 1991) is both a literal and figurative border that immigrants of colour negotiate.

This paper raises questions about one way the 'imagined nation' is discursively patrolled through accents. A 'foreign' **accent** is socially defined, such that British or Australian English accents do not seem to elicit the same treatment as described by the African immigrant women in our focus groups. Accents signify more than local/'Canadian' and extra-local/'immigrant'; accents, embodied by racialized subjects, also shape perceptions of language competency. Thus, accents may provide a rationale for (dis)entitlement in employment or full participation in civil society without troubling liberal discourses of equality.

Methodology

There is little research on African immigrants in Canada and even less on women who have migrated from Africa. Existing research documents show low socio-economic status, under-employment in the labour market, restricted access to suitable housing, and racial discrimination (Adjibolosoo and Mensah, 1998; Mensah and Adjibolosoo, 1998; Danso and Grant, 2000; Elabor-Idemudia, 2000). African immigrant women face additional demands negotiating paid work, family, and child rearing in an often unfriendly environment (Elabor-Idemudia, 2000).

Our research begins to explore issues affecting African immigrant women in Vancouver. Mindful of feminist debates on research for, rather than on, women (Smith, 1987; Wolf, 1996; DeVault, 1999; Smith, 1999; Razack, 2000), we put African women's experiences at the centre of our analysis. As exploratory research, with a limited budget, focus groups allowed us to talk to a larger group of women than individual interviews, and we were able to begin the process of mapping out key issues they identified.

The following discussion draws on two focus groups that were made up of Black women who are relatively recent migrants from Africa. They were conducted in Vancouver during the summer of 2002. The 12 focus group participants migrated from 6 African countries previously colonized by Britain (Nigeria, Sierra Leone, Sudan, Swaziland, Uganda, and Zambia), and one previously colonized by Belgium (Congo).

Almost all focus group participants defined themselves as fluent in English, and in two cases also fluent in French, before arriving in Canada.

Most had advanced post-secondary degrees undertaken at English-language institutions. One focus group was composed of professional women, five of whom had master's degrees that were completed in English (three of these from Canadian or American universities), and the sixth had a Canadian bachelor's degree. The second focus group was more diverse: one participant had a master's degree, two had post-secondary diplomas, and three had Grade 12 certificates. The length of residence in Canada varied from 2 to 13 years; 6 had been in Canada less than 5 years, and 5 had been here for more than 8 years. Our participants' comments about reaction to their 'African English' accents are all the more noteworthy given these high levels of education in English, and the length of time they had been in Canada.

Border Crossings: Localizing Language, Bordering Accents

'Canadian English' constitutes a border allowing only partial and provisional crossing for women in our focus groups. Language is performed and interpreted within a localized context and migration from English-speaking Africa to Canada might require initial translation of colloquial phrases, pace of speech, intonation, and syntax. However, the local vernacular is not only different, its difference implies [in]competence in the speaker. As the women in our focus groups made clear, perceptions that their 'African English' accents imply limited English skills persists well beyond an initial period of localizing within Canada.

The most common responses to 'African English' identified in our focus groups were being ignored when speaking, and being corrected rather than responding to the content of speech. Comments by Mapendo (all participants are referred to by pseudonyms) and Muhindo illustrate this point:

> It seems that somehow they put you in a spot where you become defensive. You have to defend how you talk (Mapendo).

> I feel the same way as you all do about accents. After finishing my [university degree] I feel I don't want to go and work in institutions where people will not listen to what I say, but only to correct my accent, which I have no control of (Muhindo).

Both Mapendo and Muhindo adopt strategies of resistance to assert their own identities. Mapendo asserts her right to pronounce words as she sees fit, and indeed to argue for equal validation of 'African' and 'Canadian' styles of English. Expressing her African accent celebrates her African identity and asserts a claim for respect and dignity.

The border around an 'African accent' has material and figurative consequences. Materially, an 'African accent' is frequently named as a rationale for not being hired in the labour market. Figuratively, daily accent policing makes it clear that African women do not really belong to the imaginary Canadian nation. Below, comments by Caroline exemplify the material consequences of accents bordering employment opportunities:

> English is a major barrier because it is the major language of communication. The accent which is part of the language, my accent is very heavy . . . when you don't have their own accent, they don't want to accept you in areas where you have to speak like receptionist, teacher of English, customer service. It is a big barrier (Caroline).

Caroline identifies particular types of occupations that are more difficult for her to enter. Since these jobs require speaking with the public, she suggests, 'Canadian English' may be seen as a job requirement. If it is the case that immigrants with a 'heavy accent' are typically barred from such employment, this poses a problem for large numbers of workers (who can't get jobs in the service sector) and customers (who can't be served by people like themselves).

African women are marked as 'Other' through the intonations of their voices and the colour of their skin; indeed, the former implies the latter. When women in our focus groups talked about the way their 'African accent' underscored their status as immigrants, they identified a form of boundary maintenance that prevents crossing from 'immigrant' to 'Canadian', regardless of formal citizenship processes.

The above examples of disparaging 'African English' recounted by participants in our focus groups are not occasional random acts—they are daily encounters. While each instance might seem minor, taken together, these examples point to systemic processes of marginalizing and 'Othering' African women.

Mabunda traces the systemic use of accent discrimination against African women to its roots in colonialism. Forms of English that emerged in one British colonial context are, perhaps ironically, rendered unacceptable in another former colony. As Mabunda argues: 'It is not that we don't know English. I think I know English. It is about Canadian or English accents.' She concludes that the accent barrier she encounters is systemic, a tool used 'to put us down'. It is not, after all, about communication. It is about power and exclusion, marginalization and 'Othering', racism, and discrimination. The problem, she suggests, is not mastery of the English language; the problem is being an African woman in Canada.

Conclusion

According to our focus groups, African immigrant women experience language as a problem in their daily lives not because they have difficulty with expression or comprehension, but because their 'African English' accents mark them as immigrant, African, Black, women perceived to have low English-language competency. As such, accents discursively patrol the borders within Canada. Although accent remains a site of community identity, resistance, and empowerment as African women assert their own identities, it is also a site through which racialized power relations are negotiated, and 'Others' are reproduced materially and figuratively within Canada.

References

Adjibolosoo, S., and J. Mensah. 1998. *The Provision of Settlement Services to African Immigrants in the Lower Mainland of B.C., Part 2.* Victoria, BC: Ministry Responsible for Multiculturalism and Immigration, Community Liaison Division.

Anderson, B. 1991. *Imagined Communities.* London: Verso.

Anthias, F., and N. Yuval-Davis. 1992. *Racialized Boundaries: Race, Nation, Gender, Colour and Class and the Anti-Racist Struggle.* London: Routledge.

Bannerji, H. 2000. *The Dark Side of the Nation: Essays on Multiculturalism, Nationalism and Gender.* Toronto: Canadian Scholars' Press.

Calliste, A., and G.S. Dei, eds. 2000. *Anti-Racist Feminism.* Halifax: Fernwood Publishing.

Danso, R., and M. Grant. 2000. 'Access to Housing as an Adaptive Strategy for Immigrant Groups: Africans in Calgary', *Canadian Ethnic Studies* 32, 3: 19–43.

DeVault, M. 1999. *Liberating Method: Feminism and Social Research.* Philadelphia: Temple University Press.

Elabor-Idemudia, E. 2000. 'Challenges Confronting African Immigrant Women in the Canadian workforce', in *Anti-Racist Feminism*, pp. 91–110, A. Calliste and G.S. Dei, eds. Halifax: Fernwood Publishing.

Mensah, J., and S. Adjibolosoo, 1998. *The Demographic Profile of African Immigrants in the Lower Mainland of B.C., Part 1.* Victoria: Ministry Responsible for Multiculturalism and Immigration, Community Liaison Division.

Razack, S. 2000. 'Your Place or Mine? Transnational Feminist Collaboration', in *Anti-Racist Feminism*, pp. 39–53, A. Calliste and G.S. Dei, eds. Halifax: Fernwood Publishing.

Sharma, N. 2001. 'On Being Not Canadian: The Social Organization of "Migrant Workers" in Canada', *Canadian Review of Sociology and Anthropology*, 38, 4: 415–39.

Smith, D. 1987. *The Everyday World as Problematic.* Toronto: University of Toronto Press.

Smith, L.T. 1999. *Decolonizing Methodologies: Research and Indigenous Peoples*. London: Zed Books.

Stasiulis, D., and N. Yuval-Davis. 1995. *Unsettling Settler Societies: Articulations of Gender, Race, Ethnicity and Class*. London: Sage.

Strong-Boag, V., S. Grace, A. Eisenberg, and J. Anderson, eds. 1998. *Painting the Maple: Essays on Race, Gender and the Construction of Canada*. Vancouver: UBC Press.

Wolf, D., ed. 1996. *Feminist Dilemmas in Fieldwork*. Boulder, CO: Westview Press.

CHAPTER 54

Rising Low-Income Rates and the Adaptation of Canadian Immigrant Youth

Paul Anisef and Kelli Phythian

Perhaps one of the most widely discussed concerns regarding **immigration** to Canada has been the decline in earnings among recent arrivals and the corresponding increase in the proportion of immigrants living in low-income conditions over the past thirty years (Picot, 2004). Research indicates that the at-entry earnings of immigrants arriving in the late 1990s were 47 per cent lower than for immigrants arriving in the late 1960s (Aydemir and Skuterud, 2003). Further, the low-income rate among **recent immigrants** has risen from 24.6 per cent in 1980 to 35.8 per cent in 2000 (Picot, 2004). Research on the decline in immigrant earnings has centered on the persistent barriers newcomers face in obtaining accreditation and jobs that are consistent with credentials acquired in their home countries (Alboim, Finnie, and Meng, 2005).

Less well documented is the impact of the earnings decline on immigrant children and youth. We argue that the increased economic difficulties experienced by newcomer families in recent decades will serve to compound the multiple **risk**-factors confronting immigrant youth.

When newcomer youth leave the familiar—schools, friends, family members, and cultural surroundings—they must find ways to cope with and adapt to life in a new and unfamiliar country.

These youth are confronted with a number of tensions that play themselves out in different spheres, including the school, family, friends, and the labour market. These tensions are a reflection of the processes all adolescents face as they mature from childhood to adulthood, but they may be especially challenging for newcomer youth trying to fit into a new **culture**. Furthermore, the difficulties associated with moving to a country whose language and behavioural norms are different from their own, and the potential for anxiety grows.

As a result, settlement and adaptation should be recognized as events of extraordinary intensity and stress. Immigrant youth are pulled in opposite directions, between seemingly irreconcilable cultural standards or value systems and a desire to fit in to their new surroundings. A number of recent studies of newcomer youth have revealed significant **integration** problems previously eclipsed by the **stereotype** that these youth are problem-free and have high rates of academic success. Adaptation to school life is often most difficult for those arriving at older ages. For older youth, firm friendships formed in their home countries are often severed, making the transition to a radically different school culture more difficult. Moreover, many of these young people come from countries where the official language is neither English nor French, adding to the stress of migration. The 2001 census indicates that 84 per cent of 15–24 year-old immigrants arriving in 2000–1 reported a mother-tongue that was neither English nor French. Despite these obstacles, many newcomer youth successfully negotiate life-course transitions. Yet, we suggest that a growing number face multiple risk-factors and that the intensity of the adversity they encounter is rising. If we were to construct a *recipe for risk*, we would include such factors as significant loss of family and friends in migration, family instability, English and/or French language deficiencies, arbitrary school grade placement, discrimination, minimal support networks, limited awareness of support services, and substance abuse (Siemiatycki, 2001).

A key correlate of risk that has negative implications for human development is poverty. Research documents that children reared in low-income conditions have poorer physical and mental health, perform more poorly in school, experience more punitive discipline styles and abuse, live in poorer neighbourhoods, and are more likely to be delinquent than are children raised in wealthier households. The Canadian Council on Social Development identified 27 elements important to child development, including family functioning, neighbourhood safety, aggression, health, math and vocabulary scores, and participation in sports or clubs. For 80 per cent of the elements examined, risks of negative child outcomes and poor living conditions were noticeably higher among children in families with annual incomes below $30,000 (Ross and Roberts, 1999).

To examine whether newcomer youth are facing increased likelihood of risk-exposure following migration, the low-income rates of immigrant and non-immigrant youth aged 14–19 were examined for Canada, its provinces, and major census metropolitan areas in 1991 and 2001. This age group was selected because these are important years of transition and development. Fourteen is the age at which most Canadian youth enter high school, and at 18 or 19, youth are typically entering post-

secondary educational institutions or the labour force. Results are presented in Table 54.1.

Findings indicate substantial differences between immigrants and native-born Canadians in terms of the proportion of youth belonging to economic families who live below the low-income cut-off (LICO). In 1991, recent immigrant youth were nearly three times as likely to live in low-income conditions as non-immigrant youth: 44 per cent of immigrant youth and 16 per cent of their Canadian-born counterparts lived below LICO. The situation worsened for later **cohorts** of newcomer youth. By 2001, about one-half of recent immigrants aged 14–19 were living in low-income families while the proportion of native-born youth living in such families remained constant. Thus, the rise in the low-income rate among immigrants aged 14–19 in recent decades cannot be attributed to a general rise in low-income rates across Canada. Newcomers are facing unique economic challenges that do not seem to be affecting the native-born.

Results for both 1991 and 2001 show that, in all provinces for which data are available, immigrant youth were more likely to live below LICO than non-immigrant youth. However, the magnitude of the difference varied substantially across provinces. Relatively speaking, British Columbia, Ontario, and Quebec stand out as having particularly high proportions of low-income immigrant youth in 2001. Compared with non-immigrants, newcomers in these provinces were nearly four times as likely to live in low-income families.

Turning to LICO trends between 1991 and 2001, findings indicate that the rise in low-income rates among immigrant youth in Canada is concentrated in the top three destination provinces: Ontario, British Columbia, and Quebec—the same provinces with the greatest proportion of immigrants living below LICO relative to non-immigrants. These provinces experienced substantial increases in their low-income rates among recent immigrant youth while the remaining provinces—Manitoba, Alberta, and Saskatchewan—saw a concomitant decline. Nonetheless, these latter provinces continued to

Table 54.1 Proportion of Recent Immigrant* and Non-Immigrant Youth Living in Low-Income Economic Families, 1991 and 2001.

| | 1991 Census | | | | | | 2001 Census | | | | | | Percent Change 1991–2001 | |
| | Recent Immigrants | | | Non-Immigrants | | | Recent Immigrants | | | Non-Immigrants | | | Recent Immigrants | Non-Immigrants |
	N	# living below LICO	%	N	# living below LICO	%	N	# living below LICO	%	N	# living below LICO	%		
Canada	71,266	31,533	44.2	2,000,698	311,933	15.6	95,166	46,539	48.9	2,144,605	323,710	15.1	10.6	–3.2
Provinces														
Newfoundland				63,033	12,233	19.4	112	75	67.0	47,852	10,858	22.7		17.0
Prince Edward Island				12,333	1,633	13.2				12,081	1,454	12.0		– 9.1
Nova Scotia				78,633	12,933	16.4	519	185	35.6	71,493	14,565	20.4		24.4
New Brunswick				65,800	11,433	17.4	222	74	33.3	59,942	11,253	18.8		8.0
Quebec	11,067	6,167	55.7	512,833	86,800	16.9	10,821	6,708	62.0	509,998	81,872	16.1	11.3	– 4.7
Ontario	38,233	14,900	39.0	691,833	84,100	12.2	54,217	24,344	44.9	759,703	93,407	12.3	15.1	0.8
Manitoba	2,000	1,067	53.4	86,200	16,733	19.4	2,023	915	45.2	87,212	17,829	20.4	–15.4	5.2
Saskatchewan	467	200	42.8	85,167	19,467	22.9	501	156	31.1	89,148	15,785	17.7	–27.3	–22.7
Alberta	6,500	3,733	57.4	188,300	33,300	17.7	5,855	2,541	43.4	244,246	35,919	14.7	–24.4	–16.9
British Columbia	13,000	5,467	42.1	216,566	33,300	15.4	20,895	11,540	55.2	262,928	40,766	15.5	31.1	0.6
CMAs														
Montreal	10,300	5,900	57.3	205,300	38,200	18.6	9,598	5,893	61.4	210,168	37,354	17.8	7.2	– 4.3
Toronto	28,434	11,167	39.3	215,966	24,633	11.4	42,288	18,860	44.6	247,637	28,807	11.6	13.5	1.8
Vancouver	11,434	4,867	42.6	90,467	13,267	14.7	18,593	10,650	57.3	105,407	14,477	13.7	34.5	– 6.8
Calgary	2,733	1,433	52.4	47,500	8,567	18.0	3,365	1,590	47.3	68,191	8,915	13.1	– 9.7	–27.2
Ottawa–Hull	2,266	1,033	45.6	66,400	8,433	12.7	2,749	1,671	60.8	71,038	9,177	12.9	33.3	1.6

*Recent immigrants are those who arrived in the 5 years preceding the census year.

Note: absolute values for 1991 are rounded to the nearest one-third, as specified by Statistics Canada user guidelines.

show sizeable gaps between immigrants and the native-born in terms of the proportion of youth living below LICO, since the number of Canadian-born youth living in low-income families decreased alongside that of immigrant youth.

Table 54.1 highlights the fact that the majority of immigrants settle in Canada's three largest cities. Of the roughly 95,000 recent immigrants aged 14–19 living in Canada in 2001, fully three-quarters were living in Toronto, Vancouver, and Montreal. One explanation for the rise in low-income rates among recent immigrant youth in Ontario, British Columbia, and Quebec, then, may be that high concentrations of immigrant families in major cities places strain on supporting infrastructures, thereby resulting in higher poverty levels. Policies designed to encourage settlement in Canada's smaller cities may, therefore, partially mitigate against rising low-income rates. Not only would pressure on resources be eased in the larger cities, immigrants might also fare better in smaller cities that have more room for population growth. Even so, Canada's major cities are likely to continue attracting the bulk of new immigrants for the foreseeable future and, as such, efforts to ensure successful integration of newcomer youth must be expanded and improved.

As mentioned at the outset, there has been much attention paid to the plight of skilled immigrants who arrive in Canada only to find that their qualifications are not well recognized. Failure to utilize the talents of immigrants is a national waste and policies have been introduced in order to create a more hospitable climate for **economic integration**. At the same time, we should not forget newcomer youth, particularly those that face multiple risks. This issue was emphasized recently in the *Report of the Standing Committee on Citizenship and Immigration*, which noted that:

> Although it is commonly believed that children can acclimatize to a new environment better than adults, witnesses appearing before the Commons indicated that more needs to be done to foster the development of young newcomers and that programs specifically geared to their needs should be augmented (House of Commons, 2003: 17).

Efforts to reach at-risk youth cannot remain passive. Rather, aggressive efforts are needed to deliver information and services that will enable newcomer youth to surmount the obstacles that exclude or marginalize them. One proposal that needs considering is the implementation of a national youth Host Program to address the multiple risk-factors facing newcomer children and youth (Anisef, 2005). The introduction of this program would need to build upon the findings presented here and on further research that explores regional variations in poverty and its consequences for newcomer youth.

References

Alboim, N., R. Finnie, and R. Meng. 2005. 'The Discounting of Immigrants' Skills in Canada: Evidence and Policy Recommendations', *IRPP Choices* 11, 2. Available at http://www.irpp.org.

Anisef, P. 2005. *A Study of Youth Host Models*. Report submitted to the Host program, Ottawa: Citizenship and Immigration Canada.

Aydemir A., and M. Skuterud. 2004. *Explaining the Deteriorating Entry Earnings of Canada's Immigrant Cohorts*. Analytical Studies Branch research papers, Catalogue No. 11F0019MIE No. 225. Ottawa: Statistics Canada.

House of Commons. 2003. 'Settlement and Integration: A Sense of Belonging, "Feeling at Home"', *A Report of the Standing Committee on Citizenship and Immigration*. Ottawa: Citizenship and Immigration Canada.

Picot, G. 2004. *The Deteriorating Economic Welfare of Immigrants and Possible Causes*. Analytical Studies Branch research papers, Catalogue No. 11F0019MIE No. 222. Ottawa: Statistics Canada.

Ross, D.P., and P. Roberts. 1999. *Income and Child Well-being: A New Perspective on the Poverty Debate*. Report No. 552. Ottawa: Canadian Council for Social Development.

Siemiatycki, M. 2001. 'Newcomer Youth at Risk: Group 2C—Youth Currently Out of School and Unemployed', in *To Build on Hope: Overcoming the Challenges Facing Newcomer Youth at Risk in Ontario*, Appendix F, pp. 1–36, M. Kilbride and P. Anisef, eds. Report submitted to Citizenship and Immigration Canada: OASIS.

CHAPTER 55

Poverty, Social Exclusion, and Racialized Girls and Young Women

Jo-Anne Lee

Introduction

Statistics Canada studies show that immigrants arriving in the last ten years from developing countries are having a more difficult time entering the labour market and in achieving parity with the non-immigrant population. Women from Aboriginal and other racial minority backgrounds are twice as likely as other Canadians to live in **poverty**. They are at higher risk of poor health, crime, incarceration, and unemployment. Some analysts call this trend the racialization and feminization of poverty.

Definitions of poverty have recently expanded to include **social exclusion** as one of many factors that must be considered as causal and consequential to poverty. The concept of social exclusion helps to incorporate many dimensions of poverty that have previously been ignored. This article examines the relationship between social exclusion and poverty and draws on research undertaken with individuals who are responsible for providing services to racialized minority girls in Victoria, British Columbia.

Social Exclusion and Poverty

Social exclusion not only refers to exclusion from labour markets and employment, but also to exclusion from social benefits of full citizenship. It includes those social benefits and entitlements that are funded or provided by governments that are supposedly available to and in some cases, required by all citizens, such as social welfare, health, and education. From this perspective, we can link poverty to regimes of governmentality (Foucault, 1991). Governmentality is the use of power by states to produce, in subjects, the willing consent to be governed; socially meaningful categories through which subjects can be observed, classified and regulated; and technologies through which governmentality is routinized and administered as normal and natural.

In white settler societies like Canada, governmentality takes on a particular logic. Three interlocking systems—racial formation, patriarchy, and capitalism—work together to produce normative ideas of Canadian governmentality. Omi and Winant's theory of the racial formation of the state identifies 'race' as a fundamental organizing principle of the state. After 500 years of colonialism, which can be understood as a system of knowledge about managing colonial societies, a naturalized regime of governmentality has been institutionalized into the administrative routines of daily life.

Having laid out a framework for understanding the intersectionality of race, class, and gender as meaningful for understanding social exclusion and poverty, the next part of this paper draws on research into racialized minority girls' and women's ability to access socially necessary and mandated health, education, leisure, and family support services, services that are government funded and supposedly universally available to all.

'Are They Being Served?'

Understanding poverty as social exclusion enables researchers to investigate poverty over the life course. In February 2001, our Victoria-based research team began meeting with over 70 girls and young women (ages 13 years to mid-20s) from diverse ethnic, religious, class, sexual orientation, and racial backgrounds. Over a period of 18 months, we asked racialized minority girls and young women, Canadian-born and immigrant, what it was like to grow up in Victoria, BC, and how they saw themselves within their families, schools, and the greater community. This research found that many racialized minority young women—both Canadian and foreign born—lived complex lives. Though many were well integrated and flourishing, there was a strong expression of isolation from others like themselves, marginalization from their 'white' classmates, and, for immigrant and refugee teens, few resources to support them in their adjustment. In the course of our research, several participants disclosed troubling physical, emotional, and mental health issues and reported that they had not sought help for their problems. Many participants reported that while school counselors, teachers, community workers, and other adults, including parents, were caring, supportive, and understanding, very few fully grasped the complexities of their lives. In other words, the girls spoke to feeling socially excluded.

Our main purpose for undertaking a survey of executive directors of organizations directed to women, families, and youth was to ascertain the present service delivery context for racialized girls and young women as one component in understanding how young racialized female teens grow up in Victoria, a mid-sized, predominantly white city. We also wished to deepen our understanding of why research participants feel isolated.

In the survey to executive directors, we investigated to what extent organizations who offer programs for youth and women are aware of racialized girls and women's specific needs, to what extent these organizations demonstrate a capacity to serve this population, and to what extent they have plans to begin offering programs and services. We also asked questions regarding service provisions for First Nations girls and young women.

We found a handful of organizations that are acting proactively to meet the needs of a changing, multicultural population. These organizations are mostly small and medium sized and are struggling to cope with their present load, and are mainly located in the health, leisure and recreation, and immigrant- and First Nations-serving sectors. These organizations demonstrate a high level of awareness of the needs and issues of racialized and First Nations female youth, but they are atypical in this regard.

More typical are providers of services for youth, women, and families in Victoria, BC, who are not well prepared to serve an increasingly diverse urban population. Funding cuts and uncertainties exacerbate an already barren environment and, alongside other justifications and rationales, have become an excuse for not acting more proactively to respond to the service needs of this population.

The research provides unequivocal evidence to support racialized minority girls' and young women's testimonies that they have no one [meaning responsible adults] who really understand the complexity of their lives, and who can provide the support they need. They are not imagining or inventing their stories of marginalization.

The findings support the call for developing multi-dimensional determinants of poverty and reveal empirical evidence of what Galabuzi (2002) identifies as the impacts of being excluded from the health, welfare, cultural, political, and economic systems that determine access to individual and community well-being.

I can only provide a glimpse of study findings here. We found several mutually reinforcing discourses that converged to hinder organizational change towards more diverse youth, gender, racial, and culturally sensitive programs and services in Victoria. These included the following:

- Lack of funding: Actual material effects of funding cuts and staff layoffs and limitations on expanding into new program and service areas as a result of neo-liberal shrinking of state responsibilities.
- Deferral of change until some distant future based on funding and numbers. These deferrals took the form of statements such as, 'Limited funding', 'When funding permits', 'If and when numbers warrant it', and 'Lack of demand'.
- The moral correctness of gender and race neutral/blind approaches. Race, gender, and class are seen as identificatory criteria, and asking questions or designing programs for any population based on such criteria is seen as discriminatory and exclusionary, while needs or demands are seen as universal and morally preferred. Conversely, gender, ethnicity, race, and class are perceived as particularistic criteria that restrict or exclude access and are morally incorrect.
- Universality and professionalism: From comments, it is clear that there is a perception that existing mainstream employees view themselves as professionals who possess skills that enable them to serve all clients equally because they are able to generalize from present training and experiences to all. Many executive directors do not see cultural knowledge and subjective experiences as job related skills and from that viewpoint, the professionalism of staff is not questioned.
- Reliance on referrals to agencies serving special populations: There is little need or desire for an organization to change to accommodate new needs and more diverse clients. Even where the needs of racialized minority and Aboriginal girls and young women are recognized or acknowledged, the idea that 'cultural' knowledge and expertise should be developed within the organization is seen as problematic. The problem is that the organization simply refers those who do not fit the normal client profile to another agency which is a band-aid approach that leaves core services unchanged in the mandated agency, and places an unfair burden on poorly funded non-profit organizations. In the end, **minority populations** receive second-class services.

Conclusion

The current situation for service provision in Victoria remains decidedly focused on and shaped by the needs of the dominant majority. Change will not come about in the near future without interventions at the policy and governance levels. If young girls are unable to access needed services, their vulnerability to poverty may be heightened. Poverty can only be addressed meaningfully within a framework that does not reduce poverty to a small number of economic indicators, but also includes an expanded understanding of social exclusion as an important dimension of poverty.

CHAPTER 56

The Sentiment of Settlement among Some Chinese Immigrants in Small Towns

Ho Hon Leung

Introduction

Most studies tend to focus on immigrants who reside in metropolitan cities. Although they have provided a good understanding of the lives of these immigrants and the **settlement** process, little is known about the immigrants who live in small towns and rural areas. Furthermore, when studies examine the process of settlement, the aspect of permanent settlement is often not included. Instead, the usual emphasis is on the initial settlement (George and Tsang, 2000) and the process of social and economic adaptation and assimilation (Portes and Zhou, 1993; Greene, 1997; Markovic and Manderson, 2000). This paper attempts to fill the gap in the literature by taking a more integrative approach, which examines a group of small-town **Chinese immigrants** in the whole process of settlement from the initial stage to permanent settlement. The Chinese notion of the family is used to analyze the qualitative data collected from 17 individuals from 11 families.

Conceptual Framework

Chain migration or network theory (Massey et al., 1993) explains how migrants are connected to former migrants and non-migrants in origin and destination areas through tie of kinship, friendship, and shared community origin. Furthermore, Booth et al. (1997) argues, the family plays an important economic and social role in immigrant adaptation. These immigrant families function as a unit that shares frustrations and develops support network to cope with these challenges. Thus, the role of family is an important component in the study of immigrants. Since Chinese culture always stresses the importance of family, family dynamics based on Serrie's 'familial to the familiar' model (1998: 214) will be used as a framework that guides the analysis of this study.

Methods

These Chinese immigrants lived in the Central New York State. The population of the county is 61,676 and there are 105 Chinese, which is about 0.2 per cent of the total population of the county (US Census Bureau, 2000). However, almost all the Chinese lived in a single small town, the population of which is 14,000 (US Census Bureau, 2000). A purposive snowball sampling was used to generate data from 17 persons who were part of 11 families.

Data for this study were taken from face-to-face, in-depth, and schedule-standardized interviews that took place in their homes at the time of their convenience, and in the language of their choice. The interviews were conducted in Cantonese, Mandarin, and English. The semi-structured interview schedule consisted of open-ended questions. This type of qualitative research instrument allowed the interviewees to elaborate their immigration experience in relation to the notion of family. Interviews were transcribed from tapes for analysis. The researcher identified themes and relationships among concepts by reading and re-reading the transcribed data until the themes and concepts became refined (see Taylor and Bogdan, 1984).

Findings and Discussion

INITIAL STAGE OF SETTLEMENT: REASONS TO COME TO SMALL TOWNS

Similar to other immigrants, Chinese immigrants have a wide range of reasons. All the Chinese immigrants in this study came to advance their education, seek better job opportunities, and look for a better life. They had lived in other cities and towns before moving to these small towns. What brought them there? Many interviewees indicated family-related reasons. Three Chinese immigrant women stayed in these towns because their husbands had been living in these towns for their careers. They had no choice, unless their husbands' future careers would change. Another case was that the husband of a couple, who were married in Taiwan, had a research opportunity offered in the United States. After he finished his research, he was looking for job opportunities. They chose the job in this town out of 20 other offers, for the simple reason that the wife's brother lived only four hours away and she would therefore be able to visit him often.

A restaurant owner decided to come to this town for a similar reason. He had worked in many different restaurants in different places. He said that he wanted to start his own restaurant and did not want to 'drift around'. He and his wife found this restaurant near where his parents lived. Recently, his brother's family and his sister all moved back to the parents. The wife described the feeling toward the decision on buying this business as 'family reunited'.

Unlike other interviewees, some Chinese restaurant workers in this study did not have any connection to anyone here. They were recruited by job advertisements. Due to their low education level and limited skills, they had to take whatever opportunities available to them; location is not their primary concern. However, the relationship between the employers and employees is based on origin and contract. Their working environment and employers are all Chinese. Yet, the development of this employer–employee relationship

during the adaptation process reflects the familial component in it. This will be discussed more in-depth in the next section.

ADAPTATION PROCESS: HELPING EACH OTHER OUT

Like many other immigrants, the Chinese interviewees faced a wide range of challenges when they first set their footsteps in the receiving society. Regardless what social, economic, and educational backgrounds they had, all interviewees expressed that language barrier and adaptation to the new environment were their very first challenges to face. These immigrants have received help both in the first city they landed in and the towns they reside in now. Depending on their social-economic and gender backgrounds, they rely on different levels of help from the familial-to-familiar.

Many interviewees expressed that their family members helped their adaptation in these small towns. The adaptation of the women, who married their husbands and settled in these small towns without any prior experiences living anywhere else in the US, relied almost exclusively on their husbands. In the beginning of the adaptation stage, most of their energy focused on the work in the families. After being more familiar with the social environment through their husbands, they started to integrate more into the communities.

Although the more educated professionals, who suffer far less language and cultural barriers, rely far less on this type of network, occasional use of such networks is very meaningful, comforting, and practical. Other than family members helping each other on the daily basis, professional Chinese immigrants also received different types of emotional and instrumental supports from other Chinese and from non-Chinese friends and/or colleagues.

New York's Chinatown provided many of the interviewees with rich resources where they were able to find work, housing, and a sense of belonging. This is particularly true of the restaurant workers who face serious language and cultural barriers. This study reveals that these immigrants described Chinatown as their 'base' or 'the second family'. Although they no longer lived in New

York's Chinatown, they still relied on the resources there to solve their everyday challenges, because small towns do not have strong community support to meet their needs.

PERMANENT SETTLEMENT: SETTLING OR SETTLED OR STRUGGLING?

The literature does not have a conclusive definition on settlement (see Leung, 2001), although most definitions agree on some operative conceptions that its processes advance in the following sequence: adjustment, adaptation, and integration (Leung, 2001). However, this study reveals a different dimension of settlement, which is subjectively perceived by the immigrants themselves. As discussed above, the interviewees had undergone the experience of adjustment, adaptation, and integration. But they only felt that they were settled permanently in these small towns if some conditions had been met. These conditions are definitely family-related. Many of these Chinese immigrants had worked and studied in different parts of the country and some of them indicated that they were tired of 'drifting from place to place'. If they could establish a business or a career in these small towns, they considered themselves settled. Furthermore, owning a house also strengthened their sense of permanent settlement. But carefully analyzing the data in the cultural context of the Chinese family, the notion of settlement takes extended family into consideration. This cultural practice is different from the American one. While the American concept of the family focuses on the nuclear family, the Chinese value their extended family, which is kinship-based.

Conclusion

The experiences of these Chinese in small towns indicate the notion that family network plays a very significant role in the process of settlement: the initial phase, adaptation, and permanent settlement. The effect of chain migration, which is facilitated by the family network, can be found not only at the international level, but also at the local level as this study indicates.

References

Booth, A., et al., eds. 1997. *Immigration and The Family: Research and Policy on U.S. Immigrants*. New Jersey: Lawrence Erlbaum Associates, Publishers.

George, U., and K.T. Tsang. 2000. 'Newcomers to Canada from Former Yugoslavia', *International Social Work* 43, 3: 381–93.

Leung, H.H. 2001. 'Settlement Service Policies and Settlement Issues Among Chinese Canadian in Toronto'. Toronto: Joint Center of Excellence for Research on Immigration and Settlement (CERIS). Available at http://ceris.metropolois.com.

Markovic, M., and L. Manderson. 2000. 'Nowhere is as at Home: Adjustment Strategies of Recent Immigrant Women from the Former Yugoslav Republics in Southeast Queensland', *Journal of Sociology* 36, 3: 315.

Massey, D.S., et al. 1993. 'Theories of International Migration: A Review and Appraisal', *Population and Development Review* 19, 3: 431–66.

Serrie, H. 1998. 'Chinese Around the World: The Familial and the Familiar', in *The Overseas Chinese: Ethnicity in National Context*, pp. 189–214, F.K.H. Hsu and H. Serrie. New York: University Press of America, Inc.

Taylor, S.J., and R. Bogdan. 1984. *Introduction to Qualitative Research Methods*, 2nd ed. New York: John Wiley.

US Census Bureau. 2000. Available at http://factfinder.census.gov.

Questions for Critical Thought

IMMIGRANT–NATIVE BOUNDARIES IN NORTH AMERICA AND WESTERN EUROPE

1. Explain concepts of boundaries, assimilation, and social exclusion.
2. What is the distinction between bright and blurred boundaries? How do these concepts manifest themselves in Canadian society?
3. How does the boundary conceptualization shape the character of immigrant–native relations in Canada?
4. Using the boundary conceptualization, how would you describe race in Canada?
5. Explain the importance of the concept of boundary in analyzing and understanding immigration issues in Canada.

WHAT COLOUR IS YOUR ENGLISH?

1. Would you agree with the assertion that African immigrant women are discriminated against in Canadian society?
2. A respondent concludes that the accent barrier she encounters is systemic, a tool used 'to put us down'. It is not, after all, about communication. It is about power and exclusion, marginalization and 'Othering', racism, and discrimination. Do you agree or disagree with this? Why?
3. How can immigrants be integrated and made more functional in Canadian society?
4. Accents provide a rationale for African immigrants to be disparaged and dispirited from participating fully in Canadian society. To what extent do you agree or disagree with this statement?
5. Full integration of African immigrants into Canadian society is an illusion. Is this statement true or false? Give reasons for your answer.

RISING LOW-INCOME RATES AND THE ADAPTATION OF CANADIAN IMMIGRANT YOUTH

1. In your opinion, what are some of the reasons that immigrants have difficulty integrating into the Canadian labour market? Why might immigrants arriving to Canada today have a more difficult time integrating than immigrants who arrived in the past?
2. As noted in this chapter, the majority of immigrants settle in Canada's three largest cities: Toronto, Vancouver, and Montreal. Furthermore, some areas—especially Atlantic Canada—receive very few immigrants. Why might immigrants choose these cities over others? Is this uneven distribution of immigrants a problem for Canada? If so, what steps could be taken to address this issue?
3. What are some of the problems that face immigrants, and immigrant youth in particular, when settling in a new society? Do you think recent immigrant youth will be able to overcome these problems?
4. In your opinion, what programs should the federal and provincial levels of government introduce to assist immigrant youth to more easily integrate into Canadian society?
5. What should be the role of Canadian immigrant youth in addressing the barriers that make it difficult for immigrants to participate fully in Canadian society?

POVERTY, SOCIAL EXCLUSION, AND RACIALIZED GIRLS AND YOUNG WOMEN

1. Identify and explain factors hindering organizational change towards more diverse youth, gender, racial, and culturally sensitive programs and services in Victoria, BC.
2. How does social exclusion manifest itself into poverty?
3. How can social exclusion and poverty experienced mainly by minority populations in Canada be addressed?
4. Social exclusion is a systemic problem. Discuss.
5. What interventions at the policy and governance levels should be put in place to address the problem of social exclusion in Canada?

THE SENTIMENT OF SETTLEMENT AMONG SOME CHINESE IMMIGRANTS IN SMALL TOWNS

1. According to the author, why is it important to include permanent settlement as a key component in the whole process of settlement?
2. How do immigrants who settle in metropolitan cities differ from those who settle in small towns?
3. Do other immigrants groups (e.g., Italians, Asian Indians, etc.) also use informal networks to help each other to settle in their host country like Chinese immigrants? What are the similarities and differences?
4. Inferring from the chapter, what does 'permanent settlement' mean to the Chinese immigrants who settle in small towns?
5. Does the settlement experience differ among immigrants from different social classes? If so, how do they differ?

Part XIII

Globalization

Globalization is criticized on the grounds that it entrenches increasing disparities in wealth both between countries and within countries. Many are currently looking for ways to address some of the negativities tied to globalization and sociologists have not been left out of this endeavour. The following chapters are sociologically informed on issues pertaining to how the excesses of globalization can be addressed both at the national and local, or community, levels.

Gordon Laxer admits being skeptical about globalization in its entirety. To unravel his skepticism, he questions the inevitability of globalization, how much of it is new, and whether it can fulfil basic human needs among others. In his paper, he recommends democratic social ownership of capital based on social solidarity as critical in offsetting some of the ills associated with globalization.

Ivanka Knezevic analyzes the nature of changes in post-socialist countries of Eastern Europe since the late eighties. The well held notion that these countries are experiencing unidirectional transition to free market capitalization is strongly challenged in the essay.

Craig Calhoun dilates on the skepticisms surrounding globalization further by providing an account of the construction of 'complex humanitarian emergencies' in terms of social imaginary, which shapes and direct the ways emergencies are produced and defined, and how interventions are structured to counter them. To Calhoun then, an end to social imagination rather than cosmetic interventions of emergencies is paramount in addressing the calamities, wars, and disasters currently being witnessed primarily in the developing world.

The adverse impacts of globalization manifest not only at the national, or macro, level, but also at the local, or micro, level. Justin Page and his colleagues, as well as Ralph Matthews and Nathan Young, in two separate papers, examine the impact of globalization at the grassroots level in British Columbia. In their paper on community resilience in the face of globalization, Page and his colleagues use the case of British Columbia coastal communities to examine the relative influence of social capital as a buffer to the vulnerability that comes along with globalization.

Matthews and Young use Lax Kw'Alaams, a rural community in British Columbia as a benchmark to establish that rural communities can develop under globalization, contrary to the general assertion that rural and marginalized communities become more underdeveloped under globalization. Lax Kw'Alaams's success story, therefore, becomes an example of hope for most rural communities currently experiencing the wrath of globalization.

The following essays provide valuable lessons that both nations and local communities within these nations can learn from globalization.

CHAPTER 57

Social Solidarity, Democracy, and Global Capitalism

Gordon Laxer

Introduction

'**Globalization**' has many connotations and is a short form for a cluster of related economic, political, technological, and cultural changes. The economic changes include such things as the internationalization of production, the harmonization of standards and of tastes, and the greatly increased mobility of capital and of transnational corporations. The ideological changes emphasize trade liberalization and deregulation in the marketplace and private enterprise. New information and communications technologies that shrink the globe and the economic shift from goods production to knowledge-based industries are part of the technological changes. Finally, cultural changes involve trends to a universal world culture and the erosion, or obsolescence, of nations.

Skepticism, however, remains a central feature of globalization. In this paper, my views about its assumptions are expressed by exploring the following questions: Can we accept the inevitability of it all? How much of 'globalization' is new? Will it lead to liberty, **democracy**, and an end to nationalisms? Will it fulfil basic human needs? Are there sources of **social solidarity** that form the bases for humanistic alternatives to globalization?

The Global Political Revolution

To understand the rise of the new right, we must examine the pre-existing situation. From the 1940s to the 1970s, corporations lost some of their freedom, especially in the advanced capitalist countries. Emerging from the cataclysmic shocks of the great depression and the World War against fascism, major political changes occurred.

In this context, the power of organized workers and citizens grew. Social democratic parties and democratic movements forced economic and political elites to abandon laissez-faire capitalism. A consensus, sometimes called the 'great compromise' between capital, labour, and the state, developed in the advanced countries. The compromise included governments committing themselves to maintaining full employment through Keynesian policies and to providing social services on the basis of citizenship rights. Corporations acknowledged the legitimacy of unions and agreed to grant workers a share in productivity gains (Bowles and Gintis, 1986). Seduced by these changes that resulted from a unique conjuncture of circumstances, the majority of Western socialists proclaimed old-style capitalism dead.

It usually went unnoticed that the great compromise was built on two foundations, both of which later collapsed: the politics of support for regulation and the embeddedness of corporations and capital in communities. By the 1980s neither condition held. The great compromise was, therefore, short-lived because corporations refused to accept reduced corporate manoeuvrability and profitability (Bowles et al., 1983). Governments had to scale back social citizenship rights and abandon a Keynesian-directive role. Further, the new right strategy involved freeing corporations from obligations to wage earners and citizens and reducing the autonomy of countries.

Democracy, the Neglected Aspect of Globalization

The ubiquitous term 'globalization' stands for much of the Western Enlightenment agenda of free markets and corporate property rights. But it does not stand for the best parts. Notably missing are the heart and soul of the Enlightenment—the goals of democracy, equality, and solidarity.

Robert Cox (1987) notes that the state used to act as a 'buffer between the external economic environment and the domestic economy' (254). In countries with representative government, the state was supposed to be accountable to its citizens, and its role was to defend domestic interests from external disturbances. With the recent technological and ideological revolutions, the role of the state became reversed. The primary task of elected leaders has become how to accommodate the structure of the domestic economy to the imperatives of a global economy driven by the 300 largest transnationals and the dominant supranational bodies such as the International Monetary Fund. Governments are praised by the IMF, the World Bank, and other agencies of international capital for being tough enough to impose harsh 'Structural Adjustment Programs' on their people. The content of these Adjustment Programs is the new right agenda and the effects are often devastating for the people (Adams, 1991).

Sovereignty and Democracy

To tame the democratic spirit, the international component of the new right strategy involved reducing the sovereignty of countries and using the threat of capital flight to discipline those deemed to be making excessive demands. Economic treaties called 'trade agreements' were negotiated in Europe, North and South America, Asia Pacific, and elsewhere to curb the power of effective political communities. These agreements were not mainly about trade in the traditional sense of moving goods across borders, rather, they were about removing 'non-tariff barriers' (Ostry, 1992: 17). Many of these were long-standing political arrangements worked out in each country in areas such as the environment, safety, or domestic ownership that inadvertently hindered transnational

corporations from treating the world as one homogeneous market, played by the same rules.

The globalization strategy is about facilitating corporate mobility. This is done by granting citizenship-like status to transnational corporations through international agreements. In the language of the European Community, 'nationals of a member state will have "the freedom of establishment"' (Burrows, 1987: 180). This appears to treat foreign citizens generously. But 'nationals' mean only corporations.

Foreign-owned corporations act differently than domestically-owned ones. The former have a high propensity to engage in intracorporate transfers, from one branch of the transnational in one country to another branch of the same company in another country. They rely less on local producers and instead import from other branches of the transnational abroad (Dunning, 1993).

Prospects for Social Solidarity in the Global Economy

Are there alternatives to new right globalization? Should we believe the inevitabilities of the neo-liberal, Western Enlightenment project? Has history in Hegel's sense of a dialectical struggle between opposing ideas, really ended? Should we settle into a post-modernist despair that the future is not what it used to be?

What is new about globalization is that socialist alternatives to capitalism are, for the first time in over a century, not credible. That is not to say that new versions of democratic socialism cannot become credible as the bases for powerful movements. What we need are new language and concepts that are more inclusive than that of class and that place less emphasis on unity as uniformity and more on respect for differences. I am not the first to suggest resurrecting the language of democracy, and of citizens' rights in the campaign for radical changes (Laclau and Mouffe, 1985; Bowles and Gintis, 1986). I would add that popular democratic-inclusive nationalisms are also crucial to develop the necessary solidarities of purpose.

The heart of the socialist vision—an end to exploitation, social solidarities, the development of human capacities and democratic control—are as relevant as ever (Harrington, 1990).

Because environmentalists, feminists, economic nationalists, and others are all threatened by new right globalization, they can develop coalitions for common purposes. I use the word 'can' rather than 'must' because there is nothing inevitable about this. Transnational globalization may encourage each group to look beyond its issues and ways of doing politics and seek allies amongst other groups that oppose the new right's attempt to commodify everything and to dispose of politics.

Ownership and Location Commitment

There are many things that must be done to develop democratic alternatives, so that there can be sufficient investment to create full employment and fulfil human needs. The one I will briefly discuss has to do with democratic social ownership by wage earners and communities that have 'location commitment' to immobile labour and to territorially-confined communities. These alternatives cover a wide range: worker co-ops and worker-owned enterprises, community-controlled development funds, worker controlled pension funds, and labour-movement controlled investment funds.

Ravaged by two severe recessions since 1981 and massive flights of capital, the Canadian labour movement has become increasingly aware of the inadequacies of capitalism's willingness to invest sufficient capital in Canada to create employment for all who want it. More and more trade unionists have become drawn to the importance of wage-earner capital funds, first pioneered by the Swedish unions in the 1970s and adopted and adapted by the Quebec Federation of Labour in its Solidarity Fund (1984). In the 1990s, several provincial labour investment-funds have been established, among them Manitoba's Crocus Fund, which was set up in 1991 explicitly to counter the flight of capital and jobs from Manitoba (Quarter, forthcoming). These labour funds are well on their way to becoming the dominant form of venture capital in Canada. As such, they have the leverage power to promote social ends such as work place democracy, human rights, and environmental protection.

A strategy of displacement rather than nationalization of corporate capital has pitfalls and advantages. Depending on how they are set up and the culture surrounding them, worker controlled capital funds can lead to the popularization of capitalism. If, in a worker-owned enterprise for example, individual workers can sell their shares to anyone, the workers as a collectivity could gradually lose democratic control and the enterprise could revert to a traditional capitalist model. If on the other hand, the workers retain control as in the cooperative model, the potential is there to develop democratic communities with goals other than profit maximization (Mygind and Rock, 1993). But worker and community ownerships operating within market confines have difficulty overcoming the unjustly unequal rewards of the market system and the motivation of greed (Cohen, 1991: 18). However, a major advantage of social capital funds is that they circumvent international 'trade' agreements that prevent expropriation of transnationals by governments.

To pose alternatives to the transnationals, coalitions of labour and other social movements would have to be massive and on an international level. How to build a democratic internationalism from below to counter globalization from above is a subject for another day. But if popular democratic control is to be enhanced, there remains a major role for democratic states with sufficient sovereignty to represent immobile labour and territorially-based communities.

Conclusion

With the fall of communism in Eastern Europe and the scaling back of the great compromise, the new right is talking the language of triumph, of inevitability. History has led to convergence, so they say. We have heard this kind of talk before. It is rooted in the capitalist version of the Western

Enlightenment project. Earlier predictions were proven wrong. As before, history is unlikely to move totally in the direction they want.

One element of relative continuity, though, is that the values and aspirations of democratic-egalitarian social movements have remained similar. People want a sense of belonging, security, equality, respect, personal development, and freedom. These can be fulfilled best in socially supportive, democratic, and egalitarian communities. The globalization vision of the transnationals is not indifferent to these needs and aspirations. It is hostile to them.

References

Adams, P. 1991. *Odious Debts. Loose Lending, Corruption, and the Third World's Environmental Legacy*. Toronto: Earthscan.

Bowles, S., and H. Gintis. 1986. *Democracy and Capitalism: Property, Community and the Contradictions of Modern Social Thought*. New York: Basic Books.

Bowles, S., D. Gordon, and T. Weisskopf. 1983. *Beyond the Waste Land. A Democratic Alternative to Economic Decline*. Garden City, NY: Anchor Press.

Burrows, F. 1987. *Free Movement in European Community Law*. Oxford: Clarendon Press.

Cohen, G.A. 1991. 'The Future of a Disillusion', *New Left Review* 190.

Cox, R. 1987. *Production, Power, and World Order*. New York: Columbia University Press.

Dunning, J.H. 1983. 'Changes in the Level and Structure of International Production: The Last One Hundred Years', in *The Growth of International Business*, M. Casson, ed. London: George Allen and Unwin.

Harrington, M. 1990. *Socialism: Past and Future*. New York: Penguin Books.

Laclau, E., and C. Mouffe. 1985. *Hegemony and Socialist Strategy: Towards a Radical Democratic Politics*. London: Verso.

Mygind, N., and C.P. Rock. 1993 'Financial Participation and the Democratization of Work', *Economic and Industrial Democracy* 14, 2 (May): 163–78.

Ostry, S. 1992. 'The Domestic Domain: The New International Policy Arena', *Transnational Corporations* 1, 1.

Quarter, J. Forthcoming. *Crossing the Line, Unionized Employee Ownership and Investment Funds*. Unpublished manuscript.

CHAPTER 58

Post-Socialist Transition and Globalization: Academic Debates in Political Surroundings

Ivanka Knezevic

The purpose of this paper is to analyze some aspects of the academic discussion about the nature of changes in post-socialist countries of Eastern Europe since 1989. It is generally agreed that the main characteristics of these societies are persistence of state-socialist patterns of inequality, fragmented and uneven change as a result of the introduction of political reforms, and presence of some elements of capitalist economy. Because of such complexity, explanations that suppose that these countries are undergoing a unidirectional **transition** to free-market capitalism do not correspond well to reality. Yet, these explanations dominate English-speaking sociological discussions of Eastern Europe.

We believe that their dominance in the debate is caused by political, extra-academic factors, and that the situation thus parallels the second stage of the 'great globalization debate' (Giddens, 1999).

Post-Socialism: Transition or Transformation?

Concepts of 'transition' and '**transitology**' have assumed new meanings in the recent debate about post-socialist societies. They are distinct from the established meaning of transitology in political science, where it refers to the study of transitions from autocratic to democratic political regimes. In discussions of post-socialism by politicians, social scientists, and policy advisors, the term is used to denote all the economic, social, and political changes that are supposed to lead these societies along a one-way path to the inevitable 'free-market democracy'.

Economic reform is assumed to lead spontaneously and nearly simultaneously to a stable, responsive, and capable politico-legal system. This view, that democracy is a nearly inevitable result of progress in other realms, is very similar to the 1970s modernization theory that assumed the industrialization of undeveloped countries would lead to rapid improvement in education, which, in turn, would lead to rapid democratization.

The 'orthodox approach to transition' is usually referred to as the 'Washington consensus', (Lavigne, 2000). It shares many elements with structural-adjustment programs devised for developing countries. It proscribes 'liberalize as much as you can, privatize as fast as you can' as a recipe for economic growth (Bunce, 1999).

'**Transformation**' theorists provide the opposite side of the debate. They see changes in post-socialist societies as multifaceted, multi-directional, and not necessarily coordinated (Bunce, 1995; Melich, 2000). Positive social outcomes are not an automatic result of changes in economic systems. Furthermore, the outcome of transformative change may be different in different countries, as empirical evidence from these countries shows (for

details, see Bunce, 1999). Ten years after the beginning of post-socialist changes, Eastern European countries were more varied politically and economically than they used to be. For example, the GDP ratio between the poorest and the richest of them has grown from 1:3 to 1:7 (Bunce, 1995).

This diversity is not captured by the prevailing practice to divide the countries of this region into two groups: European Union applicants, which have more or less achieved macro-economic stabilization, have resumed economic growth, and are considered to be on road to democratization; and the rest of the region, where stabilization has not been completed, growth remains uncertain, the market is underdeveloped, and prospects for democracy remain murky. This division is not only simplistic, but fundamentally flawed: economic stabilization and democratization often do not go hand in hand. It also has tremendous consequences on the lives of people in these countries: the EU imposes very low trade quotas on countries that are not considered to be EU candidates, thus perpetuating their economic decline and instability. This is done with the declared goal of punishing them for their insufficient democratization. However, since general poverty and extreme inequality have never been good predictors of democracy, one wonders what outcome this policy might achieve.

Bunce (1995) has noted a peculiar way in which transitologists deal with the problem of diversity in Eastern Europe. Many have been including and excluding various post-socialist countries from their analyses without specified reasons, but in ways that supported their general theses about the direction in which the region is going. There are also problems of interpretation of empirical data. It is seldom clear what makes a post-socialist country a democracy, what makes a democracy 'superficial' or 'genuine', and so on.

Overall, we believe that the transformation approach is useful as a corrective to underlying teleological notions of transitology. Since 'transformation' allows for uncertain outcomes, it enables us to evaluate changes in relationship to the initial situation in a country, instead of some goal in the future. How has society changed? What are consequences of that change for various groups? Do the changes seem to lead to any societal goal that we would like to consider, such as uncontrolled market economy, welfare state, or anything in between? This is crucial if we want to consider Eastern Europeans' support for these changes. They compare themselves to their way of life fifteen years earlier, measuring both the costs and the improvements. English-speaking analysts often bemoan the low level of popular support for policies of change, discounting the fact that the population sees first-hand the costs of building capitalism and multi-party parliamentarism, costs that have been spread over 250 years in the West so that they have become nearly invisible.

'Transformationism' has an apparent policy handicap. Its emphasis on open-ended changes makes it seem unsuitable as an alternative to the monumental assurance of neo-liberal transitology. However, 'transformationists' had been the first to focus their research on institutions in post-socialist countries, and a significant number of transitologists have thought sufficiently well of the idea to adopt it. Johnson (2001), for instance, writes about the importance of concrete policy choices and policy sequencing for achievement of democratic and capitalist goals, instead of just automatically blaming any setback on socialist institutional legacy and corruption.

Western Political Influence, Western Models, and the East

Surprisingly, transitologists do not have much to say about the real political influence of foreign decision-making, although the obvious influence of foreign models of development is acknowledged. Bunce (1995) criticizes transitologists for failing to appreciate the extreme uncertainty of an international environment in which post-socialist countries find themselves, brought on by the failure of military and trade alliances in the former Soviet bloc. It left Eastern European states

extremely open (or vulnerable) to Western political influences. One of the reasons why **laissez-faire** economic models have not produced much growth in Eastern European countries is that those countries are now competing with well established, technologically advanced Western countries (Melich, 2000).

Two Debates: Eastern European Transition and Globalization

We find interesting parallels in the development of these two debates in English-speaking sociology in the last 15 years. In both fields, the debate proceeds in two distinct phases. The first one is concerned with large theoretical issues. Post-socialist scholars were trying to decide between teleological and contingent, multidimensional models of change. Meanwhile, globalization scholars were trying to decide if the current process was indeed qualitatively different from older processes of internationalization and imperialism.

In both cases, the second phase of the debate is conducted at a lower level of generality and is contained within *one* of the positions of the initial debate. 'Free-market democracy' is considered inevitable, and globalization is viewed as the master process of our time, rather than its master project.

An academic with a comfortable belief in the cumulative nature of science might expect this to happen *if* one side has won the initial debate by proving its superior explanatory power. This, however, has not happened. Transitologists have been unable to prove transformationists wrong, and second-wave globalization theorists have found themselves obliged to acknowledge that the agency of nation states remains significant. Fundamental questions of initial debates have not been resolved, but merely supplanted by more specific ones.

We contend that the dominance of transitology in discussion about post-socialist societies in English-speaking sociology is due not to its superior explanatory power, but to its compatibility with neo-liberal views on economy and policy.

Steinmetz (2005) points out that American political science in the 1950s and 1960s was understood as a useful weapon of the Cold War and was integrated into the prestigious area of foreign policy. This is an important consideration for the eventual development of transitology. Its tenets make sense within a mindset of the Cold War. From this perspective, the complete destruction of the early post-socialist state appears as an undoubted benefit. No thought is given to the question of an agency that would then regulate the extremely complex and unstable post-socialist economies.

Conclusion

What, then, are we to do with transitology? It is, of course, preposterous to paraphrase Cohn-Bendit (1968) and exclaim: 'Tuez les transitologues!'

We could look at it critically, with a view of advancing an academic debate and broadening available policy options. In order to do this, we should ask two kinds of questions. The first kind is well known to the sociology of science: are there any non-academic reasons for the popularity of this academic trend? The other kind of question is simply: does this theory fit the 'realit[y] that [it] purport[s] to analyze' (Steinmetz and Chae, 2002)?

This would lead us to a synthesis of post-socialist research thus far, which should include significant elements of transformationist thinking. At least two possible frameworks occur.

One framework is to regard post-socialist changes not as a transition, but as a *revolution*. Bunce (1999) has noted that this would enable researchers to consider economic, political, and social dimensions of the transformations together. Moreover, it emphasizes the role of conflict and instability—prominent features in those post-socialist societies most in need of policy intervention, if high social costs of their transformations are to be controlled.

Another viable framework of analysis would focus on the changing place of post-socialist states in the international system. Janos (2001), for example, has argued that the central change for this region during the 1990s has not been one from **state socialism** to democracy and capitalism, but from submission to the international state-socialist regime led by the Soviet Union to submission to the new hegemonic international regime of the West. There is already a wealth of literature analyzing globalization as such a regime (for instance, Chossudovsky 1997; Kim et al. 2000). Theoretical insights gained through it should be examined for applicability to post-socialist changes. There is thus no need to 'tuer les transitologues'. We have tried to offer some answer to the question: 'Why are there transitologists?' The time is now to ground them in new research that would better reflect the reality of post-socialist societies and their global environment.

References

Bunce, V. 1995. 'Should Transitologists Be Grounded?', *Slavic Review* 54, 1: 111–27.

———. 1999. 'Political Economy of Postsocialism', *Slavic Review* 58, 4: 756–93.

Chossudovsky, M. 1997. *The Globalization of Poverty: Impacts of IMF and World Bank Reforms*. London: Zed Books.

Cohn-Bendit, D., and G. Cohn-Bendit. 1968. *Le Gauchisme: Remède à la Maladie Sénile du Communisme*. Paris: Nanterre.

Giddens, A. 1999. *The Runaway World: How Globalization Is Reshaping Our Lives*. London: Verso.

Janos, A.C. 2001. 'From Eastern Empire to Western Hegemony: East Central Europe under Two International Regimes', *East European Politics and Society* 15, 2: 230–59.

Johnson, J. 2001. 'Path Contingency in Post-communist Transformations', *Comparative Politics* 33, 3: 253.

Kim, J.Y., J.V. Millen, A. Irwin, and J. Gershman, eds. 2000. *Dying for Growth: Global Inequality and the*

Health of the Poor. Monroe, ME: Common Courage Press.

Lavigne, M. 2000. 'Ten Years of Transition: A Review Article', *Communist and Post-Communist Studies* 33: 475–83.

Lipset, S.M., and G. Bynce. 1994. 'Anticipation of the Failure of Communism', *Theory and Society* 23, 2: 169–210.

Melich, J.S. 2000. 'The Relationship between the Political and the Economic in the Transformations in Eastern Europe: Continuity and Discontinuity and the Problem of Models', *East European Quarterly* 34, 2: 131–57.

Steinmetz, G., ed. 2005. *Politics of Method in the Social Sciences: Positivism and Its Epistemological Others* Durham, NC: Duke University Press.

Steinmetz, G., and O. Chae. 2002. 'Sociology in an Era of Fragmentation: From the Sociology of Knowledge to the Philosophy of Science, and Back Again', *The Sociological Quarterly* 43, 1: 111–37.

CHAPTER 59

A World of Emergencies: Fear, Interventions, and the Limits of Cosmopolitan Order

Craig Calhoun

Introduction

In the midst of the Second World War, Pitirim Sorokin (1968) wrote one of the first important sociological studies of 'emergencies', *Man and Society in Calamity: The Effects of War, Revolution, Famine, Pestilence upon Human Mind, Behavior, Social Organization and Cultural Life*. Predictably, Sorokin was concerned to situate the immediate situation in relation to long-term social and cultural dynamics. How did different sorts of cultures take hold of calamities, he asked, and how did calamities change social and cultural organization? With these questions, Sorokin sought to do his part to encourage more 'creative altruism' and he worried that sociology in general was not doing its part. But he also wondered whether the world would recognize the importance of altruism only when shocked by unprecedented 'tragedy, suffering and crucifixion'.

Impressive altruism has indeed shaped responses to the world's tragedies in recent years. Since the Second World War, and especially since 1989, there has been an extraordinary growth in the number of **non-governmental organizations** devoted to providing humanitarian assistance to those suffering the effects of wars, famines, and diseases.

But the social sciences have still not paid as much attention to calamities as they might. There has not been enough attention given to calamities, emergencies, and disasters in the context of sociological accounts of globalization, and it is to this task that I would like to contribute. I want to outline the way in which I think the emergency—for this, rather than 'calamity', has become the standard term—has been woven into a social imaginary, a way of seeing the world that fundamentally shapes action in it.

The Emergency Imaginary

Emergency is a category that shapes the way in which we understand and respond to specific events, and the limits to what we think are possible actions and implications. Think for a moment of Rwanda and Congo, Liberia and Sierra Leone, Colombia and Peru, Israel and Palestine, the former Yugoslavia, and, of course, September 11th, the resulting crises in Afghanistan, and now Iraq. Each of these is commonly spoken of as an 'emergency'. But why, and with what distortions?

This notion of 'emergency' is produced and reproduced in social imagination, at a level that Charles Taylor (2002) has described as between explicit doctrine and the embodied knowledge of habitus. It is more than simply an easily definable concept because it is part of a complex package of terms through which the social world is simultaneously grasped and constructed, and produced and reproduced, together with others in the social imaginary. Emergency is, in this vocabulary, partially analogous to nation, corporation, market, or public. Each of these is produced as a basic structuring image and gives shape to how we understand the world, ourselves, and the nature and potential of social action. While many factors, both material and social, go into the production of specific emergencies, we need to inquire into the cultural processes of the social imaginary to grasp why they are understood through this category and what the implications are.

A 'Wave' of Emergencies

At the moment, one international NGO lists 25 emergencies of pressing humanitarian concern; 23 of the 25 are conflict-related (Relief Web, 2004). It is primarily these conflict-related emergencies that led the United Nations University and World Institute for Development Economics Research to speak at the end of the 1990s of 'the wave of **emergencies** of the last decade' (Klugman, 1999). The various factors are summed up by the United Nations, which says that countries face 'complex emergencies' when they confront 'armed conflicts affecting large civilian populations through direct violence, forced displacement and food scarcity, resulting in malnutrition, high morbidity and mortality' (Relief Web, 2001). 'Complex' here is mostly a polite way of saying that there are multiple sides in a conflict, not merely victims, and that they are often still fighting. Of course, there is much the definition does not convey, including

the fact that this suffering is inflicted mainly on the less developed world particularly Africa and Asia, though it also poses huge risks for the more developed world.

The idea of a wave of emergencies reflects the notion that the global system somehow worked less well during the 1990s. Perhaps, in some ways, this was true, due to the adjustment to the end of the Cold War. Its problems have only multiplied in the current decade. But notice that the imagery of a 'wave' suggests not friction within the system, but surges from outside. The other common image is of a need for early warning, as though the issue were the increasing failure rate of established cybernetic feedback mechanisms. What this obscures is that the wave of emergencies arises precisely as globalization is extended and intensified, not as it deteriorates.

Complex emergencies—and for that matter financial, ecological and other sorts of emergencies—affect all human beings. But the idea of managing them is a concern and orientation that figures especially prominently in those countries, such as the United States, Japan, Canada, and the members of the EU, that are large-scale international donors and senders of relief workers. These countries, and a few others, also have special concerns because their relative peace and prosperity depend in considerable part on how well they and their agents do in reducing both the human cost of emergencies and the social, economic, and political violence and instability of which they are a part and which they make worse. The US invasion and occupation of Iraq, for instance, has made the production of emergencies and the need to address them one of the rationales for global power.

Bad Things Happen

The rise of the new rhetoric of emergencies marks, among other things, a shift from accepting chance or fate as an adequate account of many problems. Disasters are always with us. We have not even escaped some of the oldest kinds of collective disasters: crop failures, earthquakes, fires, and floods.

These continue, and indeed many recur with new severity, because changing patterns of human settlement and economic production make us more vulnerable.

We commonly speak of fires, floods, earthquakes, and famines as 'natural disasters'. We distinguish them thus from the divine or diabolical visitations of the Book of Revelations and attribute them to the order of a non-human world working of its own inner impetus. Yet, in important senses it is misleading to speak of 'natural disasters'. Disasters often occur precisely because we have meddled with nature and they kill and injure on a large scale because of risks we take in relation to nature. As the saying goes, 'God makes droughts, but people make famines.'

In any case, natural disasters—or, as the International Red Cross terms them, 'Un/natural disasters'—have in fact increased in recent years. The Red Cross reports an official total of 280,000 deaths from famine in the 1990s. Yet this may be as little as a fifth of the true total. Observers estimate that between 800,000 and 1.5 million famine deaths occurred in the Democratic People's Republic of Korea between 1995 and 1998; they simply were never officially reported. The North Korean famine also exemplifies how nature and human activities are increasingly intertwined in the production of disaster. Concentration of population also matters: during the last decade, 83 per cent of those who died in ostensibly 'natural' disasters were Asians (International Federation of Red Cross and Red Crescent Societies, 2001).

Consider HIV/AIDS, which now appears as less an emergency to most North Americans in the wake of antiretroviral drugs. This may be foolish complacency in Canada or the US, but when we speak of the AIDS emergency now we speak most immediately of Africa. Indeed, an 'emergency' is precisely what President Bush evoked in his 2003 State of the Union address promising increased US action on AIDS. The implications of the pandemic are quite staggering, though distanced for most of us by the location of the emergency on that continent. The so-called emergency is, in fact, a basic

social transformation in many African societies and, potentially, elsewhere.

Though the term dates from the 1980s, complex emergencies are of course much older. They have come in the wake of wars, for example, including not least the Second World War, and in cases of chronic conflict like that in Palestine. Civil wars, ethnic conflicts, and, even more centrally, refugees and population displacement make emergencies complex—even when the origins of a crisis are partly 'natural'. Thus, the Sahel drought of the 1980s was a natural disaster, made worse by bad social policies. It contributed to a flow of refugees across borders, and added complexity came from the refusal of certain states (notably Ethiopia) to aid those it considered politically rebellious, and from the involvement of various liberation fronts in humanitarian aid, as well as independence struggles. Consider Sudan as well.

Sudan has been torn by civil war for all but 11 of the nearly 50 years of its independent existence. Race, religion, language, and ethnicity have all been factors in the Civil War between Northern and Southern Sudanese, even though none of them explains it. There were also many international factors. Some of these involved neighbouring countries, like the destabilizing effect of wars in Ethiopia and Uganda, which both pushed hundreds of thousands of refugees into Sudan and provided ready access to military training and arms. Others connected Sudanese events to richer and more distant countries, most importantly the discovery of large supplies of oil in Southern Sudan, which dramatically increased the North's interest in hanging on to that region and which by now provides more than $1 million a day to sustain the government's arms purchases and other military expenses. And of course, the oil goes mainly to the world's richer countries, reminding us of one of the reasons why chaos in the poorer ones is a constant concern.

This is not simply a historical reminiscence. The same issues remain current in complex humanitarian emergencies around the world. State failure is one of the most important causes of these emergencies, but the way emergencies are handled commonly contributes to further state failure and thus to recurrence of crises, rather than development out of that cycle. And while the work of donors is evidence of global humanitarian concern, it is astonishingly chaotic in its own organization. As Arthur Helton (2002a; 2002b) commented on aid to Afghanistan and central Asia (shortly before his death in the bombing of the UN mission in Iraq): 'How coordinated can the effort be when donors will give money through both multilateral and bilateral channels, international organizations and NGOs will jockey for roles and money, and relief work will run up against recovery and development plans?' Too little emergency relief will be organized through international NGOs that maintain a long-term, rather than episodic, presence in crisis-prone regions. Much too little will build local capacity of either government or civil society.

Interventions into complex emergencies are therefore not 'solutions', because emergencies themselves are not autonomous problems in themselves but the symptoms of other, underlying problems (Terry, 2002). At the same time, it would be a mistake to think that humanitarian response should, or could, simply be abandoned in favour of working directly on the underlying problems. Assistance in dire circumstances is important, not least because the underlying problems usually admit no ready solutions.

However, to ignore the limits of emergency assistance is to divert attention from those problems and also to forfeit opportunities to make responses more effective. We need to grasp more clearly why emergencies are 'normal'—however paradoxical that may sound—not only in order to study something else, but also to improve how we deal with emergencies. And we need to make this the starting point for building better institutions and plans for dealing with emergencies and their underlying problems.

Private charities and other NGOs are also a central part of the story. The prominence of the idea of complex emergencies reflects not only new kinds of crisis in the world but, and perhaps more importantly, a new willingness to intervene. This willingness is shaped by several factors. The importance of global news coverage cannot be underestimated. While this may have helped to create awareness and sympathy, it does not, in itself, produce the sense that 'something must be done'. Equally important are three other factors pertaining to the spread of human rights idea, the interest in public health, and the sense of potential effectiveness of interventions.

Conclusion

In conclusion, I want to note a few other features of the emergency imaginary. The emergency imaginary is, first off, a secular view. Emergencies are identified with regard to these worldly causes and effects, even if they mobilize people committed to more transcendent notions of the good. And emergencies may also reflect a notion of purity that Taylor has analyzed in connection with monotheism and the idea of purging evil from the terrain of an ideally pure good. As a result, the 'bracketing' of politics and economics has effects on how emergencies are produced and reproduced. Further, emergencies are perceived as a humanitarian responsibility rather than a socially located responsibility. Accounts of emergencies often bring cultural factors—notably ethnicity—into consideration on an *ad hoc* basis to explain violence and conflict, while implying that the stable functioning of the global order is more or less independent of culture. Emergencies are also often approached as though what they do is simply take away the supports of 'normal' life. This leads even those who work in them, let alone others who consider emergencies at more of a distance, to imagine them as involving 'regressions'. Finally, it is important to note that the emergency imaginary serves an important function as a mirror in which we, the developed world, are able to affirm our own shaky normality. Approaching conflicts as emergencies is perhaps the least unpalatable way of accepting their ubiquity, but it feeds unfocused fear even as it reassures, and it encourages responses that may do good, but usually not deeply.

References

Helton, A.C. 2002a. 'Rescuing the Refugees', *Foreign Affairs* 81, 2: 72.

———. 2002b. *The Price of Indifference*. Oxford: Oxford University Press.

International Federation of Red Cross and Red Crescent Societies. 2001. *World Disasters Report*. Geneva: Oxford Press.

Klugman, J. 1999. *Social and Economic Policies to Prevent Complex Humanitarian Emergencies: Lessons from Experience*. Helsinki: United Nations University, World Institute for Development Economics Research.

Relief Web. 2001. '2001 UN appeals'. Available at http://www.reliefweb.int/appeals/01appeals.html (accessed 26 March 2004).

———. 2004. 'Complex Emergencies'. Available at http://www.ReliefWeb.int/w/rwb.nsf/WCE?OpenForm (accessed 26 March 2004).

Sorokin, P. 1968. *Man and Society in Calamity: The Effects of War, Revolution, Famine, Pestilence upon Human Mind, Behavior, Social Organization and Cultural Life*, Rep. ed. New York: Greenwood Press.

Taylor, C. 2002. 'Modern Social Imaginaries', *Public Culture* 14, 1: 91–123.

Terry, F. 2002. *Condemned to Repeat? The Paradox of Humanitarian Action*. Ithaca, NY: Cornell University Press.

CHAPTER 60

Should I Stay or Should I Go? Investigating Resilience in British Columbia's Coastal Communities

Justin Page, Sandra Enns, Todd E. Malinick, and Ralph Matthews

Introduction

Many of British Columbia's rural, coastal communities are facing an 'economic shock' due to changing demands for their resources. This paper examines the extent to which a set of key social factors—conceptualized here as **social capital**—contribute to a community's resilience in the face of such an economic decline.

In this context, we define **community resilience** as the capacity to respond to ongoing economic and social changes in positive and constructive ways. While some of the resilience of a community rests in its ability to provide local residents with economic well-being, we also see resilience as related to the underlying social processes and organization of the community. Social capital can be understood as a way of theorizing the social benefits that living in such communities may provide. This includes co-operation for mutual gain and social cohesion. Social capital can also be understood as the benefits associated with social networks of interaction, including trust, network ties, civic engagement, political access, collective efficacy, and institutional performance.

In the following analysis, we examine the relative influence of these social capital factors versus economic factors as the 'independent variables' associated with whether or not social capital is able to buffer the vulnerability created by a declining economy. For our analysis, we assume that the ultimate test of the power of these variables is whether or not they influence the decision to leave the community. A community's social resilience, in the final analysis, rests on whether its inhabitants chose to remain even in the face of economic hardship and potential economic benefits elsewhere. Thus, resilience is operationally defined as agreement or disagreement with the statement, 'I would move away from this community if a good job came up somewhere else.'

Levels of Analysis

We consider both economic and social characteristics in our analysis of willingness to leave, at both individual and community levels. This approach provides a typology, yielding four analytic models that may be associated with the dependent variable.

INDIVIDUAL-LEVEL ECONOMIC CHARACTERISTICS AND SOCIO-DEMOGRAPHICS

Those who remain after the first wave of economically-motivated exodus continue to feel pressure to leave related to employment and income levels. We expect, then, that employment status and income levels are negatively associated with willingness to leave.

Beyond individual-level **economic characteristics**, socio-demographic variables are likely to come into play. We expect age, gender, marital status, presence of children in the household, length of time in the community, and level of education to be associated with willingness to leave.

INDIVIDUAL-LEVEL SOCIAL CHARACTERISTICS

Trust is an important individual-level social characteristic that takes two forms: institutional and generalized. We created an 'institutional trust scale' from several questions asking about trust in police and different types of community leaders. We also asked respondents about their more generalized trust of community members.

In addition to trust, we expect that people who are actively involved in their communities are also committed to them, and are thus less willing to leave. We measure *civic engagement* in two ways.

First, we examine whether people are engaged in the local political process, indicated by interest in local politics and voting in local elections. Second, we examine civic engagement at a sub-political level, measured by volunteering behaviour.

Lastly, we suggest that people who have *ties* to individuals inside the community are less willing to leave, since they can draw on their resources in times of need. In contrast, we suggest that individuals who have ties to people outside their communities would be more predisposed to leave, since access to embedded resources outside of the community can help them adjust to a new community.

COMMUNITY-LEVEL ECONOMIC CHARACTERISTICS

At the community level, *isolation* impacts both cost of living and business viability due to transportation costs, and therefore willingness to leave. We have included an 'isolation scale' to measure degree of isolation. Furthermore, we include two measures of *economic opportunity* and assess their association with willingness to leave. The first is an evaluation of the creation of economic opportunities by local business leaders; the second is an evaluation of employment opportunities.

COMMUNITY-LEVEL SOCIAL CHARACTERISTICS

In terms of community-level social characteristics, we suggest that *social cohesion* enables both material and affective resilience to economic shock. We measure this concept in two ways: first, we consider respondents' sense of community; second, we ask respondents to evaluate community inclusiveness in terms of how difficult it is to make close friends.

Beyond social cohesion, we expect that a community's sense of its ability to direct its own affairs— or *collective efficacy*—is related to the dependent variable. We measure this concept with a question about sense of the community's control over the future. Furthermore, *political environment* is likely related to willingness to leave. Here, we consider political representation, and political access.

Lastly, we expect that evaluations of *institutional functioning* are associated with willingness to leave.

Table 60.1 Multiple Linear Regression on Willingness to Leave

		Coefficient
Demographics	Age	−.028****
	Gender	−.228****
	Married/with partner	−.152*
Individual-level Social Characteristics	Institutional trust	−.177***
	Trust in community members	−.282****
	Volunteering	−.209***
	Interest in local politics	−.097*
	Ties to relatives: out	.080***
Community-Level Economic Characteristics	Business leaders creating economic opportunities	−.179****
	Good/Poor employment opportunities	−.138****
	Isolated/Not Isolated	.092****
Community-Level Social Characteristics	People have weak sense of community	.186****
	Hard to make close friends	.133****
	Future depends on outside	.126****
	Political leaders represent the powerful few	.091**
	Safe/Dangerous	−.231****

N = 1814
Sig.: *.05, **.01, ***.005, ****.0001

The institutions that we consider are health-care, crime, and safety, and education.

Research Instrument

We mailed 4,800 questionnaires to a random sample of households in 24 communities. Multiple mailed reminders produced a 60 per cent response rate. Our analysis here is based on a subset of the sample aged 19–59, resulting in an N of 1,814.

Results

WILLINGNESS TO LEAVE AND DEMOGRAPHICS/INDIVIDUAL-LEVEL ECONOMIC CHARACTERISTICS

A multivariate linear regression was conducted on the demographic variables' association with willingness to leave. Age, gender, and marital status are each significantly negatively associated with willingness to leave. However, when we add individual-level economic characteristics (e.g., personal income and employment status) to the regression, neither variable shows a significant association with willingness to leave. This finding indicates that, at the individual level, social considerations may be more important than economic considerations with respect to decisions to leave a community.

WILLINGNESS TO LEAVE AND INDIVIDUAL-LEVEL SOCIAL CHARACTERISTICS

Both forms of trust—trust of institutions and trust of community members—are negatively associated with willingness to leave (sig. < .01, sig. < .001, respectively). Thus, more trusting people are less willing to leave.

Civic engagement is also negatively associated with willingness to leave. People who volunteer and people who are interested in local politics are less willing to leave (sig. < .01, sig. < .05, respectively).

Finally, ties to individuals in positions that are rich with resources demonstrate a pattern of association with willingness to leave. Ties to relatives *outside* the community show a positive association (sig. = .005). These findings suggest that, at the individual level, social capital that is directed toward the collectivity, but not to the individual, contributes to community resilience.

WILLINGNESS TO LEAVE AND COMMUNITY-LEVEL ECONOMIC CHARACTERISTICS

Individuals who said that business leaders are creating economic opportunities in their community are less willing to leave (sig. < .001). The same pattern exists for evaluations of employment opportunities. Those who evaluate their community as having good employment opportunities are less willing to leave (sig. < .001). In addition, individuals who rate their community as more isolated are more willing to leave (sig. < .001).

These findings point to the continuing need for economic development projects. However, when this result is combined with our finding of a lack of association between full-time employment and willingness to leave, it suggests that economic development should focus on diverse, bottom-up development (that is, driven by local business leaders) that creates many employment opportunities.

WILLINGNESS TO LEAVE AND COMMUNITY-LEVEL SOCIAL CHARACTERISTICS

Individuals who say that their communities are *not* socially cohesive, as measured by a sense of community and inclusiveness, are more willing to leave (sig. < .001 for both variables). Along the same lines, people who say that their communities are *not* in control of their own futures are more willing to leave (sig. < .001).

Evaluations of a community's political environment are also significantly associated with willingness to leave. People who say that their community's political leaders 'generally represent the interests of a few powerful groups' are more willing to leave (sig. = .005).

Finally, evaluations of institutional functioning are not associated with willingness to leave, save for evaluations of safety. These findings support a key argument in the social capital literature, namely that the social characteristics of communities influence whether or not their populace stays put in the face of an economic shock. They establish that the social character of communities is important in terms of whether or not people want to continue to live there.

Conclusion

The broader implications of these findings, we feel, point to the need for capacity-building at the community level. Community resilience depends on social factors (in addition to economic ones) including trust, civic engagement, a sense of community, social cohesion, community efficacy, and political representation. That is, *community members* themselves are key to their communities' resilience: they volunteer, join associations, and work to better their communities in a context of trust, civic spirit, and local political representation. But communities do not always have the skills and funding necessary to protect their communities from economic shocks. Initiatives from outside agencies in *support* of community-led initiatives and activities may well be of critical importance to the ability of a community to withstand and recover from economic downturn.

CHAPTER 61

Globalization and 'Repositioning' in Coastal British Columbia

Ralph Matthews and Nathan Young

Introduction

Globalization is variously described as a fundamental transformation of the relationship between economy, state and society (Castells, 2002), and conversely, as a process in collapse (Saul, 2005). Support for either alternative comes primarily from 'grand' analyses of worldwide institutional changes, often with little regard to the processes through which globalization occurs at a local (regional or community) level. In this paper, we consider how globalization may be understood in the context of one such rural area, namely coastal British Columbia. We also provide a case example from that region of how globalizing processes are being utilized by one community to 'reposition' itself within the flows of globalization itself.

Locality, Glocalization, and Repositioning

Globalization is seen as a process whereby nation states engage in strategies to position subnational spaces within supernational spheres of economic activity (Scott, 2001; Brenner, 2003). Such works demonstrate that globalization has a territorial component in that, within nation states, some subnational centres are deliberately privileged while other areas are left out. These works, however, generally depict local areas *as acted upon rather than as actors*.

In contrast, recent work by Shepherd sets out a framework to examine 'how different entities are positioned with respect to one another in space/time' (2002: 313). This 'positionality' perspective focuses on the patterns of connection between places and, in doing so, focuses on how local places continually challenge and attempt to change pre-existing configurations, even sometimes in opposition to state globalizations policies deliberately constructed to favour other locations.

From such a perspective, even peripheral places can become *actors within globalization* by developing direct economic ties with distant places that are centrally located within globalization. Shepherd uses the metaphor of 'wormholes', borrowed from relativity theory, to describe how such relationships work. In Shepherd's use of the term, wormholes are relational links that open between positionally advantaged and positionally disadvantaged locations. Often such links are not possible due to local cultural differences, strong state opposition, and environmental factors that may hamper the ability of the disadvantaged location to take advantage of such opportunities. Some communities, however, may actively search out such relational links as a way of overcoming their peripheral position within the flows of global processes. When this happens, we suggest that it is possible for even the most marginalized of places to actually *use* globalization as a means of overcoming prior dependencies. The following description of the community of Lax Kw'Alaams is one such example.

The 'Repositioning' of Lax Kw'Alaams

Few communities in Canada are as marginalized as Lax Kw'Alaams. Marginalized by geography, Lax Kw'Alaams is located at the very north end of the British Columbia coast, just below the Alaska panhandle, and without a road link. Lax Kw'Alaams is also economically marginalized, as its economy is based on the resources of forestry and fishing, both in sharp decline. Furthermore, Lax Kw'Alaams is marginalized by being a First Nation 'reserve' community in a society where First Nation peoples are half as likely to attend high school and four times more likely to be unemployed than the population as a whole (CCJS, 2001). Other than direct social assistance from government sources, the Lax Kw'Alaams Band received much of its meager income from granting multinational firms the right to clear-cut old growth forests in their traditional territory. Even so, by 2001 the Band was severely in debt.

Today, in stark contrast, Lax Kw'Alaams is out of debt, roads in the community have recently been paved and have sidewalks; construction has nearly finished on a new 25-metre indoor swimming pool with a huge waterslide and adjoining elders' centre, as well as a refurbished recreation centre and gymnasium, among other improvements. Thus, from being an isolated coastal village on the open Pacific, Lax Kw'Alaams has become transformed into an easily accessible adjunct of the nearby City of Prince Rupert. However, the most striking improvement in Lax Kw'Alaams has been its economic transformation. Band officials now indicate that less than five per cent of the able-bodied labour force is unemployed, despite the fact that the community has grown as residents who had left have now returned to take advantage of local opportunities.

Lax Kw'Alaams' renaissance began with the Band reclaiming control of its logging from outside forces and their development using a sustainable cutting model rather than a clear cutting model. This is being done under the leadership of a new Band Manager with unique managerial experience as a Certified Registered Forester. Faced with the need to market this timber, the Manager hired consultants to locate outlets in Asia, thus bypassing the traditional ties of dependency with economic interests in Vancouver and the United States. After visiting the area, Japanese investors signed long-term contracts with the Lax Kw'Alaams Band for their timber. Notably, another nearby Band, seeing the impact of this arrangement, then signed a contract with the Lax Kw'Alaams Band for it to market their wood in Japan.

What we have just described fits the description of 'repositioning' under globalization. Lax Kw'Alaams' success stems from its ability to sever its long-standing ties of economic dependency with urban Canada, and negotiate a new arrangement with overseas interests. It might be argued that this is simply trading one dependency for another. Yet that position does not take into account that Lax Kw'Alaams has been able to regain management of its forestry resources, develop a different harvesting model, and negotiate a deal directly on its own terms. Still, as long as Lax Kw'Alaams remained dependent on only one 'wormhole', its future remained vulnerable to the viscidities of one partnership.

It is in this context that Lax Kw'Alaams most recent economic activities take on particular analytic significance. Over the past 20 years, while Lax Kw'Alaams remained an economic backwater, the British Columbia government invested heavily in a pulp mill in Prince Rupert, following closely the pattern of glocalization that sees the state support the transition into globalization of some localities while ignoring others. Despite continuing state support and bailout efforts, the mill went into final bankruptcy proceedings. In December 2004, flushed with cash from its existing logging operations and new bank lines of credit, the Lax Kw'Alaams Band made a surprise offer of $4.3 million to purchase the timber license holdings of the defunct mill. Their offer was accepted. The Band now has the license to cut in excess of over 800,000 cubic metres per year, making it one of the larger British Columbia forest holding firms.

Without any remaining timber rights, the Prince Rupert mill appeared to have no future. This was confirmed by news reports that investors from China would purchase the mill's equipment, disassemble it, and move it to China. However, the Lax Kw'Alaams Band asked government representatives to arrange a direct face-to-face meeting with these Chinese interests. As the Lax Kw'Alaams Band Manager put it, 'We pointed out to the Chinese that, when they moved the equipment to China, they would still not have a wood supply.

But, if they purchased the mill and ran it in Canada, we could guarantee them a supply of all the wood they might need' (personal communication). Lax Kw'Alaams and the Chinese investors are now in the process of negotiating such a deal.

However, Lax Kw'Alaams has also begun to diversify under globalization in the fisheries resource sector. The Band has invested in refurbishing its long-closed fish processing plant in conjunction with a recently signed agreement with Japanese interests to buy virtually all of the fish that it can produce as well as, potentially, also buying the fish caught by other nearby communities that are processed in the Lax Kw'Alaams plant. These Japanese and yet other Chinese investors are also negotiating with the Lax Kw'Alaams Band to build a fishmeal production plant in Lax Kw'Alaams to produce meal from fish by-products obtained throughout northern British Columbia and Alaska. The intention is to ship these to markets in Japan, China, Taiwan, and other parts of Asia where they are in high demand both by aquaculture and animal producers.

Conclusion

In this paper we have examined how globalization effects marginalized regions and communities, notably those that are resource based and isolated. However, whereas the primary dynamics of globalization in metropolitan regions may be those connected with knowledge innovation, the primary dynamics of globalization in hinterland regions centre on the transformation of social and economic relationships. Furthermore, as our case example of Lax Kw'Alaams demonstrates, contrary to much assertion that, under globalization, marginalized areas become even further victimized, it is possible for globalization to also be a liberating influence.

References

Brenner, N. 2003. '"Glocalization" as a State Spatial Strategy: Urban Entrepreneurialism and the New Politics of Uneven Development in Western Europe', in *Remaking the Global Economy: Economic-Geographical Perspectives*, pp. 197–215, J. Peck and H. Yeung, eds. Thousand Oaks, CA: Sage.

Castells, M. 2002. *The Rise of the Network Society*, 2nd ed. Oxford: Blackwell Publishers.

CCJS (Canadian Centre for Justice Statistics). 2001. *Report on Aboriginal Peoples in Canada. Canadian Centre for Justice Statistics Profile Series*. Ottawa: Minister of Industry.

Saul, J.R. 2005. *The Collapse of Globalization and the Reinvention of the World*. Toronto: Viking Canada.

Scott, A. 2001. 'Globalization and the Rise of City Regions', *European Planning Studies* 9, 7: 813–27.

Sheppard, E. 2002. 'The Spaces and Times of Globalization: Place, Scale, Networks, and Positionality', *Economic Geography* 78, 3: 307–30.

Questions for Critical Thought

Social Solidarity, Democracy, and Global Capitalism

1. What are the prospects of social solidarity in global economy?
2. The sovereignty of nation states has been usurped by globalization. Discuss.
3. Democracy is a neglected aspect of globalization. How far do you agree with the statement?
4. Discuss how democratic alternatives can be developed to ensure sufficient investment to create full employment and fulfill human needs.
5. What is democratic social ownership? How can the excesses tied to globalization be addressed by democratic social ownership?

Post-Socialist Transition and Globalization: Academic Debates in Political Surroundings

1. Some 'transformation' theorists study the dependence of post-socialist countries on powerful Western countries, such as the United States or members of the European Union. What forms does this dependence take?
2. What similarity does the author see between the globalization debate and the sociological debate about the future of post socialist-countries? Does she attribute this similarity to scientific or political reasons?
3. How can the concept of 'revolution' be useful in explaining changes in post-socialist countries?
4. Transitologists believe that a 'free market' economy inevitably leads to true democracy, while transformationists do not share this belief. What do you think? Explain your position.
5. One of the main requirements of the 'Washington consensus' is absence of government involvement in the economy. Do you support or oppose this idea? Why or why not? What changes would you see in Canadian society if your views were implemented in Canada?

A World of Emergencies: Fear, Interventions, and the Limits of Cosmopolitan Order

1. What are some of the global factors leading to the current increasing wave of emergencies in the world?
2. Why are emergencies more prevalent in the developing world than anywhere else?
3. What do you think should be done to minimize the high incidence of emergencies in the developing world?
4. Explain the following concepts as used in the text; emergencies, social imaginary, and emergency imaginary.
5. With examples, explain how emergencies change social and cultural organizations?

Should I Stay or Should I Go? Investigating Resilience in British Columbia's Coastal Communities

1. Explain the following terms: social capital, community resilience, social cohesion, capacity building, and collective efficacy.
2. How does social capital influence individuals' decisions to stay or move out of a community?
3. Community resilience correlates positively with social capital. Discuss.
4. Discuss four social factors critical in ensuring community resilience.
5. How does social cohesion translate into material and affective resilience to counteract economic downturns?

Globalization and 'Repositioning' in Coastal British Columbia

1. What is globalization? How can local communities benefit from the dynamics of globalization?
2. What lessons are there to be learnt from the metaphor 'wormholes' by marginalized local communities?
3. What factors accounted for the renaissance of the Lax Kw'Alaams community?
4. How do social and economic relationships affect the primary dynamic of globalization in rural regions?
5. Globalization as an economic approach has a double edge. Explain this statement in the light of the experience of Lax Kw'Alaams.

Part XIV   States and Government

Different modes of discourse carry different effects. Because of this, individuals, institutions, and groups use various means of discourse to bridge the gap between the state and the civil society. The chapters in Part XIV emphasize the significance of the visual news media, the use of information technologies, and feminist representation in making political inputs to the state.

Erin E. Armi Kaipanen presents a host of instances where human rights movements in Argentina have used graffiti in the struggle against social amnesia. He argues that the use of graffiti is a powerful medium of protecting the heritage of the people of Argentina.

Erin Kruger identifies the redefinition of the 'enemy', the creation of inter-agency collaborations, and de-territorialization as ways information technologies are used by Canadian political and legal actors in conducting security initiatives, particularly in the wake of the 9/11 attacks.

Jacinthe Michaud discusses how feminist interpretations of women's needs are formed through social interactions. She uses the case of women on welfare in francophone communities in Ontario to assess the efficacy, as well as the deficiencies, associated with feminist group activities in understanding and representing the needs of marginalized women in society.

John R. Parkins believes that interpersonal and institutional relationships thrive on trust. Based on this notion, he reviews the concepts of trust and distrust in contemporary democratic society by applying them to the case of public advisory committees in the forest sector of Alberta, Canada.

Another form of visual news discourse is the use of political cartoons. From the perspectives of interactionist theorists Goffman and Mead, Josh Greenberg underscores the importance of political cartoons in capturing, classifying, and interpreting experiences about the world. He draws on two political cartoons that appeared in Canadian newspapers to demonstrate how political cartoons easily make impressions on the minds of their audience.

Issues discussed in this Part, particularly the use of visual news discourse, are under-explored in sociological research. Because of this, these chapters are likely to generate interest, further debates on the issues, and additional research in the future.

CHAPTER 62

Thirty Thousand Calls for Justice: The Human Rights Movement, Political Graffiti, and the Struggles over Collective Memory in Argentina

Erin E. Armi Kaipainen

Introduction

Thursday, 24 March 2005 marked the 29th anniversary of the 1976 military coup in Argentina. Free elections have been held since 1983, and yet, text and images in the streets continue to remind the public of the crimes of this ominous period, and the lack of 'adequate' closure to the disappearance and torture of some 30,000 people. Most of these public reminders are ephemeral. Few are permanent. None are uncontested. They come in a number of forms, among them graffiti. Very little work has focused on Latin American **political graffiti**—or social graffiti—despite its relationship to other protest strategies, and its involvement in human rights issues and the deep rooted-ness of graffiti in Argentina.

Tim Cresswell (1996) emphasizes the importance of space and the placement of graffiti, suggesting graffiti is a transgressive act and is tied up in the contestation of space. The placement of graffiti then, is often specific and related to the places it defaces. Political street art interrupts the present. In the way that it permits the past to break into the present, people remain less able to forget the military dictatorship and the partiality of institutional treatment of human rights violations in Argentina. In this sense, graffiti as well as the other street politics of the movement function as what Alexander Wilde calls the 'irruptions of memory' (1999).

In what follows, I present a number of instances where graffiti has been used by the **human rights movement** in Argentina in the struggles against social amnesia.

Human Rights Movement, Graffiti Use, and Social Amnesia

Jelin suggests that the human rights movement is concerned not with the individual forgetting of victims and victims' families, but with 'collective forgetting' (1994: 49). As such, the tactics and strategies of this movement can be seen as efforts to combat oblivion.

The struggle against forgetting has in large part included the struggle over contested spaces, most notably former detention centres in Buenos Aires including El Olímpo, El Club Atlético, and the Escuela Mecánica de la Armada (the Navy Mechanics School or the ESMA). All three of these former detention centres have been the site of graffiti and other forms of political street art. As a former detention centre, El Olímpo housed, until very recently, an automobile registration office for the Federal Police (Jelin and Kaufman, 1998). Following the dictatorship, the building continued to operate as a police facility. In 1996, human rights groups submitted a proposal to city council, motioning for the detention centre to be turned into a museum of memory. Symbolically, the motion for the museum was revisited only days before the 20th anniversary of the military coup. Two days before the anniversary, human rights groups attempted to claim the building by painting a mural on its exterior. Council did not pass the motion, the chief of police resisted the idea of the museum, and police prevented the painting of the mural. The demonstrators succeeded only in painting the words 'Museo de la memoria NUNCA MÁS'—Museum of Memory, Never Again (Jelin and Kaufman, 1998). Drawing on Cresswell's ideas of

'Twenty-seven years of false justice. Thirty thousand calls for vengeance.' Graffiti in downtown Buenos Aires, July 2003. *Photo: E. Kaipainen*

the contestation of space (1996), in all likelihood, it was not the 'defacement' of the building's exterior that sparked concern, but rather the anti-military, pro-memory message that the mural was to contain. Such a message would be considered a threat to stability, the social order, and the dominant historical narrative. Jelin and Kaufman (1998) outline that in this particular case, the initiative by the human rights groups was defeated because the Museum of Memory had not received 'official' permission granted through the 'official' channel of the city council. Here, human rights movements sought to attribute new meaning to a space with a particular history, but the city and the police were not about to allow the meaning of that place to change.

In 2001, 2003, and then twice in 2005, I documented Argentine graffiti in Rosario and Buenos

Aires. The graffiti addressing economic issues was overwhelming, but amongst all of this, I was surprised to find messages that made reference to the military dictatorship. These messages emphasize a culture of impunity. They also seem to repeat over and over again the same facts and phrases along the lines of 'enough impunity' and 'we continue the fight'. The figure of 30,000, the number of people who disappeared, is often mentioned in these messages. This figure, used by the human rights movement in Argentina and put forth by the Mothers of the Plaza de Mayo (Feitlowitz, 1998) contests much more conservative estimates. This consistent repetition of the same figure says a great deal about presence of the past in Argentina today. The human rights movement must insist on this figure; it must articulate it over and over, register it in the streets so that it will become part of history, so that it will make the official register instead of a figure put forth by the 'winners'. The steady presence of human rights graffiti more than 20 years after the transition back to democracy signals that history of this period remains contentious and that disagreement remains over how to deal with the past and how to remember the past in the present. The presence of graffiti, monuments, murals, and other forms of political street art that refer to the dictatorship indicates that the possibility of collective amnesia remains a very real threat in Argentina.

Aside from being part of the political process in Argentina, graffiti is a cost effective, non-monopolistic, and democratic form of communication (Chaffee, 1993), but I suggest that graffiti and street art are more than just bulletin boards of information because of the way they challenge the 'official story' and attempt to rearticulate and transmit **collective memory**. In its challenges to the 'official story', graffiti also works to increase participation in debates over contentious issues. In this sense, instead of being only a form of mass communication, graffiti writing is an open form of communication that increases political participation and citizenship, and broadens democracy. The Argentine human rights movement has often used graffiti in its protests since the return to democracy in 1983. Graffiti makes the existence of a counter-narrative evident to the public, the government, and the military. The continued persistence of the human rights movement in Argentina has challenged the discourse of reconciliation articulated by many, including former president Carlos Menem, who in a national address stated, 'Argentina will not be possible if we continue tearing apart the old wounds, if we keep fomenting hatred among conationals on the basis of false grounds of discord' (cited in Roniger and Sznajder, 1998: 148). And in the 22 years since the return to democracy, and despite countless obstacles, this persistence has resulted in minor victories for the movement including the Argentine National Commission on the Disappeared (CONADEP), the prosecution of kidnapping cases for children born in detention centres, and the recent sentencing of (Retired) Navy Captain Adolfo Scilingo in Spain to 640 years for his participation in the notorious 'death flights'.

Also, in Buenos Aires, there is a chance that the nearly complete lack of institutionally commissioned commemorative sites may soon change. On 24 March 2004, President Néstor Kirchner announced, in the presence of many from the human rights movement, that the most notorious detention centre—the Navy Mechanics School—would be turned into a Museum of Memory. More recently, in May 2005, the president announced that El Olímpo would cease to operate as a police building and would be turned over to a number of human rights groups in Buenos Aires to be used as a 'space for memory'.

Conclusion

These new developments outlined above in the area of traumatic and collective memory in Argentina raise new issues that need to be explored by those involved with 'memory work'. Struggles over memory since the end of the dictatorship have debated over what should be remembered. New debates are emerging now over how to remember the past in Argentina, particularly in spaces and museums of memory, such as at the Navy Mechanics School and El Olímpo.

It will be interesting to note any changes to the graffiti following this, and particularly, if the ESMA will remain such a hotly contested space when the museum is complete. Elsewhere, the graffiti and memory struggles will continue as multiple interpretations of the past continue to compete with each other, and with the threat of total silence.

References

Bosco, F.J. 2001. 'Place, Space, Networks, and the Sustainability of Collective Action: the Madres de Plaza de Mayo', *Global Networks* 1, 4: 307–29.

Chaffee, L. 1993. *Political Protest and Street Art: Popular Tools for Democratization in Hispanic Countries.* Westport, CT: Greenwood Press.

Cresswell, T. 1996. 'Heretical Geography 1: The Crucial "Where" of Graffiti', in *In Place/Out of Place: Geography, Ideology, and Transgression*, pp. 31–61. Minneapolis: University of Minnesota Press.

Feitlowitz, M. 1998. *A Lexicon of Terror: Argentina and the Legacies of Torture.* New York: Oxford University Press.

Gready, P. 2003. 'Introduction', in 'Commemorations in a Comparative Perspective', in *Political Transition: Politics and Culture*, pp. 1–26, Paul Gready, ed. London: Pluto Press.

Halbwachs, M. 1992. *On Collective Memory*, Lewis A. Coser, ed., trans. Chicago: University of Chicago Press.

Jelin, E. 1994. 'The Politics of Memory: The Human Rights Movement and the Construction of Democracy in Argentina', *Latin American Perspectives* 21, 2: 38–58.

————. 1998. 'The Minefields of Memory', *NACLA Report on the Americas* 32, 2: 23–30.

————. 2003. 'Contested Memories of Repression in the Southern Cone: Commemorations in a Comparative Perspective', in *Political Transition: Politics and Culture*, pp. 53–69, Paul Gready, ed. London: Pluto Press.

Jelin, E., and S.G. Kaufman. 1998. 'Layers of Memory: Twenty Years After in Argentina'. Conference Paper.

Manco, T. 2004. *Stencil Graffiti.* New York: Thames and Hudson.

Roniger, L., and M. Sznajder. 1998. 'Politics of Memory and Oblivion in Redemocratized Argentina and Uruguay', *History and Memory* 10, 1: 133–69.

ThinkSpain. 2005. 'Scilingo Sentenced to 640 Years for Genocide and Torture', 19 April 2005. Available at http://www.thinkspain.com/news-spain/8614.

Wilde, A. 1999. 'Irruptions of Memory: Expressive Politics in Chile's Transition to Democracy', *Journal of Latin American Studies* 31, 2: 473–500.

CHAPTER 63

The Emerging Role of Information in Canada's Security Environment

Erin Kruger

Relocating Conflict: Information as the 'New Security'

Emerging security strategies in Canada depend on information systems and technologies to facilitate communications between a variety of political and legal agencies on a national and global level. Especially under global security initiatives designed to eradicate 'terrorism', communication technologies are increasingly transforming the nature of deterrence by transferring information through computers systems (see Guisnel, 1997; Sassen, 2004). The impact of emerging security measures are that they alter political strategies to 'protect the nation' by increasing the speed and sophistication of information technologies. Instead of fighting against a specific geo-political 'enemy'—such as the United States and the Soviet Union during the Cold War—now deterring the enemy means analyzing and amalgamating information. Information as the means to define, deter, and respond to the 'enemy' thus signals a transformation of the idea and practice of 'warfare' from that of nuclear weapons to a 'digital' way of war (see Virilio, 1997; Dillon, 2003).

Although there are many issues at hand in discussions of 'information warfare' (such as computer break-ins and sabotage, espionage, intelligence operations, telecommunications and fraud, and perception management), this chapter focuses on three ways Canadian political and legal actors use information technologies to conduct security initiatives, particularly in the wake of the 9/11 attacks. These include redefining the 'enemy', creating inter-agency collaborations, and de-territorializing.

Redefining the 'Enemy'

In Canada, one of the strongest motivations to use information as a security practice is because of its assumed ability to more clearly define the 'enemy'. In the case of 'terrorism', there is uncertainty about exactly who, or what, the 'enemy' is. Particularly since 9/11, definitions are increasingly vague. One way this confusion manifests is in the blurring of conceptual boundaries between entities such as organized crime, terrorism, and immigration (see Shelley, 2002). Law enforcement in Canada identifies perceived similarities between organized crime and terrorism based on their 'emerging and consolidating' crime trends. The idea of a 'matrix model' of criminal activity between the two entities is presumed in some cases, particularly in the area of drug trafficking or 'narco-terrorism'. As well, organized crime was perceived to have benefited from the global focus on terrorism after the 9/11 attacks (RCMP, 2002, 2003).

Similar confusions exist between ideas of terrorism and immigration, implicating Canada's immigration department—Citizenship and Immigration Canada (CIC)—as a necessary source of information to govern terrorism. For instance, overlapping notions of the 'foreign national' and the 'terrorist' imply that the 'terrorist threat' is an imported problem, and encourages security initiatives dedicated to preventing and deterring outsiders from entering Canada. The new agency—Public Safety and Emergency Preparedness Canada

(PSEPC)—reinforces this mentality by stating: 'The best way to stop terrorists from entering Canada is to stop them before they get here,' and that 'many of the real and direct threats to Canada originate from far beyond our borders' (PSEPC, 2004). Although many policies are in place to ensure the safety and security of foreign nationals and immigrants in Canada, such a statement implies foreign nationals want to enter Canada for terrorist purposes while indirectly creating the 'outsider' as a target.

The above examples indicate how defining the 'enemy' depends on a potentially very wide range of information sources. The focus on information takes **national security** outside of law enforcement domains to multiple other agencies, on the premise of anticipating and predicting future harms. Paradoxically, however, as the number of participants contributing information multiplies and diversifies, so do the techno-scientific measures designed to handle it.

Inter-agency Collaboration

Part of the process required to define the 'enemy' includes the involvement of agencies deemed 'bearers' of important security information, particularly under the rubric of 'national security,' that inter-agency collaborations foster through information sharing as the best strategy to 'protect the nation'. Immediately after the 9/11 attacks, for instance, the Government of Canada announced:

> funding [is] for 17 specific national security programs in an effort to meet four objectives: further enhance integrated investigative/enforcement agencies; improve technology; increase protection services, and; enhance information sharing with other governmental departments and international and domestic law enforcement agencies (RCMP, 2001).

The greatest distinction between pre- and post-9/11 security strategies, however, is the active participation of traditionally non-security agencies in security strategies. As discussed previously, the presumption that terrorism emanates from outside Canadian borders, for instance, has CIC playing a major role in recent security initiatives. In 2003, they released a statement claiming,

> The events of September 11 made all countries aware of the importance of intelligence information. While our department had an intelligence department prior to 9/11, CIC has formalized this function within the Intelligence Branch to provide a focal point for intelligence gathering, analysis and our sharing of information on immigration cases and migration trends with our partners inside and outside of Canada. Information sharing and collaboration between Canadian and US intelligence services are critical in stopping terrorism, giving the activities of the branch increasing importance in the current environment (CIC, 2003: 2).

Sharing information between agencies is thus condoned as the most beneficial and efficient means to govern terrorism. CIC's participation is indicative of a larger governmental trend that depends on the fundamental premise that security threats exist and the possibilities for harm are multi-faceted. By redistributing authority to CIC and other agencies hitherto uninvolved in security practices, the breadth of agencies participating in regulatory control has increased exponentially. In Canada, this includes upgrading for intelligence systems within law enforcement and intelligence agencies, government departments involved in immigration, transportation, as well as agencies responsible for points of entry such as borders, marine, and airports. Globally, Canadian police and intelligence agencies have coordinated information systems with international counterparts, such as the United Nations and the Organization of American States. 'National' security is no longer confined to one nation and through the integration of information systems, Canadian security practices are moving onto the world stage.

De-territorialization

Perhaps the greatest attraction to intelligence and communication systems is the ability to deregulate distance by transferring information instantly. Advances in security technology to increase speed and enables information technologies to process and transfer intelligence between agencies in **real-time**, regardless of the physical placement of each agency in the world. Faster technologies enable security and related institutions to co-ordinate their information and interactions within the same virtual universe of knowledge, thus removing the barriers from the rest of the world that geographical distance used to provide (Gaddis, 1992). Levy (1997) contends that this transition from territorial to de-territorial spaces and communications is not only a matter of modelling the conventional physical environment into cyberspace, but of enabling delocalized territories to interact. Events, decisions, actions, and individuals are now situated along 'dynamic maps' in cyberspace, leading to the continual transformation of the virtual universe in which they assume meaning.

For security practices both in Canada and globally, the appeal of technology is that it leaves very little information out of reach. Communications and digital intelligence in the late twentieth century render political, military, intellectual, industrial, or commercial information instantly available for security purposes. Although the physical environment continues to be monitored with technologies such as improved satellite and aerial techniques, the emphasis on speed and real-time intelligence changes perceptions of territory into the instantaneous, allowing for much faster planning and decision-making for governments and law enforcement alike.

Further Discussion

Information is not war. It is the perceived use of information to define and respond to 'enemies' and 'threats' to national security, which constitutes information as a replacement to traditional war strategies such as weapons and combat. This raises some interesting implications for future thought and practice pertaining to security initiatives in Canada. First, if information and technology are viewed as the new weapons to 'defeat the enemy,' it simultaneously implies that information and communication technologies are also the new target to be conquered. Although they are seen as the best 'solution' in contemporary political and security discourses, in the case of a breakdown or attack, what will be the solution to information technologies?

Secondly, the increased privilege granted to technology displaces other forms of intervention. While there is still a 'combat' dimension to war— such as armies of men and casualties—it is often 'on the ground' rather than 'behind the scenes'. That is, intelligence technologies are playing increasing roles in decision-making processes of Western governments as they pertain to national security issues. The role of the 'human being' is no longer to think, but to fight, while political decision-making results from the mechanical and computerized analysis and dissemination of information between agencies.

Although there are obvious benefits to information technologies, the emphasis on only information as a solution dismisses possible disadvantages to these technologies that have not been acknowledged with the same fervour as their assumed benefits. For instance, increasingly centralized information systems invoke vulnerability to security and law enforcement networks due to the susceptibility to information system breakdowns and attacks (Boyne, 2000). The trend towards amalgamating information systems may also produce all-encompassing systems of scrutiny, where 'threats' are defined and understood in the same way across the world. What may be the most harmful consequence of these dismissals is that it leaves little room for dissent and differing opinions, and little space for consideration of what alternative options might be possible.

References

Boyne, R. 2000. 'Post-panopticism', *Economy and Society* 29, 2: 285–307.

CIC. 2003. *Citizenship and Immigration: CIC's Role in Public Safety*. Ottawa: Public Works and Government Services. Available at http://www.cic.gc.ca/english/pub/sept11.htm (accessed 25 May 2004).

Dillon, M. 2003. 'Intelligence Incarnate: Martial Corporeality in the Digital Age', *Body & Society* 9, 4: 123–47.

Gaddis, J.L. 1992. *The United States and the End of the Cold War: Implications, Reconsiderations, Provocations*. Oxford: Oxford University Press.

Levy, J. 1997. *Collective Intelligence: Mankind's Emerging World in Cyberspace*. New York: Plenum Trade.

PSPEC. 2004. *Securing Canada: Laying the Groundwork for Canada's First National Security Policy*. Ottawa: Public Works and Government Services. Available at http://www.psepc-sppcc.gc.ca/media/sp/2004/sp20040325-en.asp (accessed 26 May 2004).

RCMP. 2001. 'Canadian Police Recognized as an International Role Model', *Gazette* 63, 3: 1–56.

———. 2002. 'Narcoterrorism and Canada'. Available at http://www.rcmp-grc.gc.ca/crim_int/narcoterror_e.htm.

———. 2003. *RCMP Environmental Scan*. Ottawa: Royal Canadian Mounted Police.

Sassen, S. 2004. 'Local Actors in Global Politics', *Current Sociology* 52, 4: 649–70.

Shelley, L. 2002. 'The Nexus of Organized Crime, International Criminals and Terrorism', *International Annals of Criminology* 40, 1/2: 85–92.

Virilio, P. 1997. *Pure War*. New York: Semiotext(e).

CHAPTER 64

Feminist Representations of Women Living on Welfare: The Case of Workfare and the Erosion of Volunteer Time

Jacinthe Michaud

Introduction

The neo-liberal state's restructuring of major public policies has impacted strongly on the relationship between the state and civil society. This picture becomes much more complicated when one takes into account how the meaning of the work performed within community groups and women's groups has shifted during the last decade due to the introduction of public policies such as **workfare**. By requesting that these groups absorb significant numbers of workfare placements, the Ontario government is implicitly acknowledging some segments of the community sector. This chapter illustrates how these new features, as introduced through the Ontario workfare policy, characterize the community sector.

Methodologies

For this research, I conducted two series of interviews between the spring of 1998 and the summer of 1999, for a total of 36 interviews. During the first series, I met with 19 francophone women on **welfare** who live in Ontario. Most of them—but not all—had been recruited through contacts with women's groups and community groups. Qualitative methods similar to the 'life narrative' method was used for the study.

The second series of interviews focused entirely on community organizations; most of these interviews—but not all—were held with women's groups. I met with representatives of 17 community organizations during the summer of 1999. These groups were located in the same Ontario regions as the interviews. All representatives, with the exception of one, were women. The 17 organizations had been selected on the basis of their work with women who were dealing with situations of social and economic hardship.

Women Living on Welfare: Caught between Volunteer Work and Workfare

Doing volunteer work for community services becomes very problematic when the welfare system tries to transform volunteer time into a compulsory requirement of workfare. All those women on welfare who were already doing volunteer work and who had integrated community services into their lives reported that workfare transformed a relation of choice into a relation of coercion. This said, whatever position they may have on the issue of compulsory work in exchange for their welfare allowance has to be placed in relationship with the simple fact that they have no choice.

Being on welfare itself is a daily struggle. There are bills to pay and children to feed. None of the women I interviewed expected to stay on welfare long, but in consideration of their circumstances, they needed time to transition out of the system. Women on welfare, mainly those who are single mothers, are in constant contact with professionals from all kinds of organizations—welfare agents, school administrators, bankers, and health-care professionals, as well as community organizers and representatives from women's groups. They can testify to the kind of images many people have of them and how they are stereotyped. Any situation women find themselves in can be the subject of harsh criticism.

Generally speaking, however, women on welfare have good relationships with their community organizations and with local women's groups. However, the interactions between women's groups and women living on welfare are not interactions between equals. On the one hand, we have an organization that has its structures, political orientation, administrative rules, and human and financial resources. On the other hand, we have women on welfare who receive only what they cannot afford to lose: their welfare allowance. Nevertheless, simply because women are living on public assistance, with little or no resources, does not mean that they cannot decide for themselves what is best for them. The presence of these women within an organization has some influence on the way in which the organization forms its feminist discourse and practices about poverty. Indeed, a woman on welfare may occupy a 'marginal' position in the organization, but her position of marginality does not deprive her of any dialogical interactions with its members.

Group Interpretations of Women's Needs

The dominant position within the community sector seems to reject workfare placements (Morrison, 1998). At times, despite the large consensus within the community sector, some local groups adopted a very different strategy than their provincial network. Their decision was based less on a lack of solidarity with the network than on the specific relationship their organization maintained with women living on welfare. The crucial moment of decision would come when a woman already volunteering for an organization was forced to find a place where she could fulfill her workfare requirement. If she was already volunteering for an organization, she could more easily make her request of that organization. Some group representatives suggested that women who replaced their volunteer time with workfare were not doing 'compulsory labour', since they were already working for the organization. The representative made

this statement after she had made it clear to the interviewer that the group disliked workfare, but that an exception was necessary for the woman who came from within the organization's own ranks, the 'insider' whose situation was known and who faced the unbearable prospect of being cut off from her welfare benefits.

Once it is known within the community that an organization is accepting workfare placements, other welfare recipients who are not necessarily users of the group's services and are not volunteer workers can also request a placement. The situation becomes complicated when a group publicly rejects any form of workfare placement but does not refuse a welfare recipient who attempts to transform her volunteer time into workfare. Furthermore, the difficult lived realities of women on welfare become the reason some groups accept workfare placements. Sometimes, it is the needs of an entire community that determine that such a strategy is required, as in the case of immigrant communities whose members are collectively subjected to racism and whose individual academic backgrounds and expertise are completely unrecognized.

Even if women's groups are not affected by the same level of prejudice and do not practice discrimination, it is not at all certain that these groups—even those that do oppose workfare policy—will recognize a woman's autonomy and allow her to actively participate in the decision-making process. Images of the 'oppressed' circulating within women's groups determine how women's needs are interpreted. The image of a woman on welfare as a victim of a system that increases her vulnerability and threatens her security and that of her children will not necessarily eliminate negative images that women's groups have of welfare recipients.

Discussion

The community sector, perhaps the most hybridized sector of the economy, joins segments of the private and public sector, especially in the areas of health and social services. Among the many categories of community practitioners within this sector, volunteer workers are especially coveted. Furthermore, in the eyes of policy makers and managers of the welfare system, the community sector represents a site for the confinement of the poor. The notion of 'volunteering' that goes with such a vision is fast becoming a ragbag that makes us forget the social and economic status of those who are volunteer workers and, among them, those who are subjected to the workfare policy. 'Volunteering' is the new scale by which the poor are valued and judged. In such a context, women's groups have to counter some of the most pervasive effects of the workfare policy. In order to do so, some of the issues women's groups need to revisit include taking another look at the conflicting tasks that women on welfare often have to perform in order to resist workfare; the complex and multifaceted situations these women face daily; and the ongoing characterization of women on welfare as victims whose 'contradictory' actions require representation by community organizations.

Indeed, there are multiple ways of representing the needs, desires, and lived experiences of individuals and communities. As well, there are different ways that groups and other collective forces can express their demands. The 1990s saw a shift in government relations with the community sector. At the same time that the Ontario government devoted its best efforts to severing channels of communication between the state's institutions and some segments of civil society, it also re-engineered the community sector. The workfare policy, for instance, did more than simply put welfare recipients to work in exchange for their meager welfare benefits. Its implementation attempted to control the work performed within community groups and gave rise to a new economy of authoritarian working conditions within the community sector in which so many women are involved. Still, for people living on welfare, as well as for many social categories of women and men, community groups remain the best channels for being heard and being visible within the political/public sphere.

Conclusion

For the most part, community practitioners/professionals—acting as women's supporters, translators, and judicial representatives—are aware of the danger, contempt, and prejudices that affect women living on welfare. They also believe that their presence will increase the chances of obtaining a favourable decision on these women's behalf. However, feminist discourses—in part shaped by women living on welfare who volunteer within these organizations—are neither uniform nor exempt from the ambiguities produced through the reduction of lived experiences. In the short term, the representation of women as victims of a welfare system, which increases their vulnerability and places them and their children in situations of danger, may provide some relief from the risk of losing their one and only source of income. In the long term, however, the impact of such an approach runs the risk of reinforcing negative pathological images, as well as subjecting women to constant institutional control that intends to 'cure' them through coercive measures.

References

Morrison, I. 1998. 'Ontario Works: A Preliminary Assessment', *Journal of Law and Social Policy* 13 (Spring): 1–46.

CHAPTER 65

The Distrustful Citizen: Theories and Observations from Small-group Settings

John R. Parkins

Introduction

This chapter briefly reviews the concepts of trust and distrust in contemporary democratic society and then applies these concepts to the case of public advisory committees in the forest sector. Evidence from this case study suggests that public oversight of forest management and planning activities—a key mandate for these committees—is compromised when levels of **interpersonal trust** between committee members and the sponsoring agency is high. Conversely, with high levels of **institutional trust** (i.e. trust in group processes), coupled with a level of public skepticism, such committees can resume some of their intended role as a critical and constructive domain of public inquiry and oversight.

Theories of Trust

The concept of trust is thoroughly embedded in modern sociological thinking. Within traditional societies, trust was understood as a kind of social glue that held together social and economic relations through interpersonal ties and family bonds. In modern societies, however, trust is thought to hinge on a radical extension of these personal relationships to a more faceless trust in the experts who manage our complex technological systems (such as water and energy resources) and the politicians who set public policy and manage public resources (Luhmann, 1979; Giddens, 1990). Scholars argue that with this trusting relationship between citizen and expert, societies can become more economically efficient and more prosperous (Fukuyama, 1995; Helliwell and Putnam, 1995). These efficiencies are realized, for instance, when societies are able to dispense with legal and contractual arrangements and can rely on more informal and interpersonal relations. Societies can also rely on what Putnam (2000) calls social capital (social networks, norms of reciprocity, and trustworthiness) as another type of asset that can support the mobilization of economic and human resources. This line of scholarly inquiry leads to a high degree of compatibility between notions of trust, trustworthiness, and the prosperity of society.

Somewhat consistent with this line of scholarly inquiry, literature that examines the practical ways in which small groups interact and achieve common goals also defines a clear connection between group success and the existence of trust (Beierle and Konisky, 2000; Wondolleck and Yaffee, 2000; Lachapelle et al., 2003). These authors work in the field of natural resource management where diverse public interests are thought to be most constructively taken into consideration within a local collaborative context. Authors in this field find a trusting relationship between government officials, industry officials, and civil society to be an important factor in the success of collaborative efforts (Shindler and Neburka, 1997; McCool and Guthrie, 2001). Among other means, trust is fostered through fair and equitable procedures and through a constructive dialogue that is respectful of all ideas and interests (Smith and McDonough, 2001).

The role of trust in this literature focuses attention on the quality of interpersonal and institutional relationships and how these close social relations create possibilities for constructive dialogue and decision-making. In most instances, these definitions of trust are grounded in the everyday realities of political life: 'I trust you, therefore, I am willing to work with you, to understand your perspective, and to live with decisions that are jointly derived.'

Theories of Distrust

In contrast to this theoretical and **applied sociology** that identifies a very prominent role for trust in the functioning of modern democratic society, a group of authors are beginning to discuss the relationship between trust and prosperity, or trust and successful group outcomes, as not entirely beneficial. Fearing that societies are beginning to lose a critical edge that fuels the political system, some scholars are attempting to re-invigorate the idea of dissent in modern society (Warren, 1999; Sunstein, 2003). These writers are attempting to focus attention on institutional, rather than interpersonal, forms of trust as a critical feature of democratic society. This emphasis acknowledges that institutions play an important role in the social co-ordination of complex modern societies, but that face-to-face forms of trust (to the extent that such interactions tend to limit critical thinking and de-politicize the democratic process) may represent a debilitating aspect of public life.

For instance, where high levels of interpersonal trust builds up over months or years of interaction, a high-trust context may create awkward group dynamics where challenging the status quo and established ways of thinking may be required to explore the complexity or uncertainty of an issue. In these small-group settings, trust can serve to facilitate the smooth functioning of group processes, but it can also diminish the critical nature of discussion and debate and serve to de-politicize group proceedings altogether. In contrast, Trettin and Musham contend that distrust can offer a 'healthy skepticism, critical thinking, and the ability to question whether the rules of the game are operating as they should' (2000: 423).

This literature is also closely connected to several other important theoretical traditions—including a general trend toward small group processes in environmental management (Van Tatenhove and Leroy, 2003), the important role of sub-politics in

theories of risk society (Holzer and Sørensen, 2003), and the emerging interest in small groups as a foundational element in civil society (Fine and Harington, 2004). These connected themes provide an even more pressing reason to investigate real-world settings where government interests, corporate interests, and the interests of civil society merge and where decisions are being made about the management of public resources.

Empirical Approach

Using observational and interview data from forest sector public advisory committees in Alberta, I investigated the differential outcomes emerging from multi-layered notions of trust within small-group settings. There are approximately 14 such committees in Alberta that are sponsored by large-scale forest companies. These companies act as stewards of forestlands under license from the provincial government. Membership in these committees commonly includes 10 to 15 local citizens from diverse backgrounds (labour unions, recreation user groups, business community, educational institutions, clergy) along with several representatives from government and the sponsoring forest company. Most committees meet on a monthly basis to receive information from industry and non-industry sources about forest management issues in the region, to provide input into a discussion of these issues, and to exert influence over company plans and activities.

Earlier work suggests that these advisory committees meet some basic criteria for democratic legitimacy, in terms of inclusiveness and opportunities for public debate (Parkins, 2002). However, this research deals with the unique challenges associated with long-standing public advisory committees, where interpersonal as well as institutional forms of trust tend to build up (or sometimes decay into debilitating social relations) over years of collective activity. In one small-group setting, high levels of interpersonal trust between public members and company officials involved the development of a shared history and a sense of shared values and common objectives. The outcome of these group dynamics resulted in a highly anemic public oversight of company plans and activities. Conversely, high levels of trust in committee rules and procedures marked another small group, but a level of skepticism about company plans and activities that resulted in critical reflection and robust public oversight. These contrasting outcomes point to the functional role that distrust tends to play in some small group settings.

Practical Insights

As a policy recommendation, it is difficult to envision a call for more distrustful small group relations in order to achieve some level of functional public oversight in the forest sector. Fortunately, some recent work by Poortinga and Piegeon (2003) provides a constructive alternative by proposing a role for what they define as **critical trust** in these small-group settings. Critical trust involves a high level of general trust coupled with a high level of skepticism. For instance, citizens may be comfortable with the general trustworthiness of actors and processes, but they may also maintain a high degree of skepticism about the direction of industrial forestry and seek change by actively engaging company and government officials within a deliberative setting. Based on the case study research with forest sector advisory committees in Alberta, committees who maintained this critical trust

profile (where trust was directed at the institutional level), enjoyed vast improvements in the quality of committee deliberations. In contrast to the small groups that were characterized by high levels of interpersonal trust, these groups were politicized and engaged in debates across multiple points of public interest.

Public advisory committees in Alberta provide a window into the increasingly important role that small groups play in the management of public forests. These settings operate below the radar screen of most Canadians, yet they provide an important legitimating tool for state and corporate interests. They are often characterized by high levels of interpersonal trust between company officials and committee members—the kind of trust that tends to build up over years of face-to-face contact and personal interaction. In contrast to theory and practice that espouses a role for interpersonal trust in the production of positive group outcomes, this empirical exploration represents a point of caution. Not all forms of trust are conducive to robust democratic outcomes. Rather, a critical trust (that is more skeptical and questioning and focused on the institutional integrity under which deliberation takes place) may be more important in these small-group settings. By re-invigorating and re-politicizing these committees, they may assume the kind of public oversight that is crucial to the effective management of public resources.

References

Beierle, T.C., and D.M. Konisky. 2000. 'Values, Conflict, and Trust in Participatory Environmental Planning', *Journal of Policy Analysis and Management* 19, 4: 587–602.

Fine, G.A., and B. Harrington. 2004. 'Tiny Publics: Small Groups and Civil Society', *Sociological Theory* 22, 3: 341–56.

Fukuyama, F. 1995. *Trust: The Social Virtues and the Creation of Prosperity*. Toronto: Penguin Books.

Giddens, A. 1990. *The Consequences of Modernity*. Cambridge: Polity Press.

Helliwell, J.F., and R.D. Putnam. 1995. 'Economic Growth and Social Capital in Italy', *Eastern Economic Journal* 21: 295–307.

Holzer, B. and M. Sørensen. 2003. 'Rethinking Subpolitics: Beyond the "iron cage" of Modern Politics?', *Theory, Culture & Society* 20, 2: 79–102.

Lachapelle, P.R., S.F. McCool, and M.E. Patterson. 2003. 'Barriers to Effective Natural Resource Planning in a "Messy" World', *Society and Natural Resources* 16: 473–90.

Luhmann, N. 1979. *Trust and Power: Two Works by Niklas Luhmann*. London: John Wiley and Sons.

McCool, S.F., and K. Guthrie. 2001.'Mapping the Dimensions of Successful Public Participation in Messy Natural Resources Management Situations', *Society and Natural Resources* 14: 309–23.

Parkins, J. 2002. 'Forest Management and Advisory Groups in Alberta: An Empirical Critique of an Emergent Public Sphere', *Canadian Journal of Sociology* 27, 2: 163–84.

Poortinga, W., and N.F. Pidgeon. 2003. 'Exploring the Dimensionality of Trust in Risk Regulation', *Risk Analysis* 23, 5: 961–72.

Putnam, R.D. 2000. *Bowling Alone: The Collapse and Revival of American Community*. Toronto: Touchstone.

Shindler, B., and J. Neburka. 1997. 'Public Participation in Forest Planning: 8 Attributes of Success', *Journal of Forestry* 95, 1: 17–19.

Smith, P.D., and M.H. McDonough. 2001. 'Beyond Public Participation: Fairness in Natural Resource Decision Making', *Society and Natural Resources* 14: 239–41.

Sunstein, C.R. 2003. *Why Societies Need Dissent*. Cambridge, MA: Harvard.

Trettin, L., and C. Musham. 2000. 'Is Trust a Realistic Goal of Environmental Risk Communication?', *Environment and Behavior* 32, 3: 410–26.

Van Tatenhove, J.P.M., and P. Leroy. 2003. 'Environment and Participation in a Context of Political Modernization', *Environmental Values* 12: 155–74.

Warren, M.E., ed. 1999. *Democracy and Trust*. Cambridge: Cambridge University Press.

Wondolleck, J.M., and S.L. Yaffee. 2000. *Making Collaboration Work: Lessons from Innovation in Natural Resource Management*. Washington, DC: Island.

CHAPTER 66

Framing and Temporality in Political Cartoons: A Critical Analysis of Visual News Discourse

Josh Greenberg

Introduction

That the news media can be seen as a forum within which institutions, groups, and individuals struggle over the definition and construction of social reality is now something of a sociological truism. In focusing upon the discursive accomplishment of social problems, we find a distinction routinely made by scholars between verbal or written claims and visual claims. Scholars who examine the role that news media play in the construction of social problems argue that different modes of discourse are likely to register different kinds of attitudinal or behavioural effects.

While scholarly attention has centred mostly on the examination of written or verbal discourse, visual news discourse has remained relatively unexamined. This study examines **political cartoons**, a form of satirical journalism and a type of visual opinion news discourse, and theorizes on the role of cartoons in the construction of social problems.

Theoretical Framework: Framing and Temporality in Visual News Discourse

In what is now a classic treatise, Goffman (1974) argues that human beings organize or 'frame' everyday life in order to comprehend and respond to social phenomena. When applied to studies of news, 'media frames' allow readers to 'locate, perceive, identify, and label' (21) the multiple happenings of the social world in a way that will be meaningful to them.

Despite offering a rather useful framework for examining the selectivity, partiality, and inclusion or exclusion of particular claims, the **framing** metaphor is theoretically limited in terms of being able to properly capture the temporal or unfolding character of social reality (Knight, 2001). To account for the shifting and temporal character of the social world, and our understanding of it and how political cartoons capture this process, Mead's theory of **temporality** (1929, 1932, 1938; Maines et al., 1983) may be useful as a complementary framework in conceptualizing contemporary 'social problems' from the standpoint of the new problems of today (Schwartz, 1991).

Methodological Considerations

In making a case for the sociological import of political cartoons, this study draws upon the methodological schema developed by Morris's sociology of visual rhetoric (1989, 1991, 1992a, 1992b, 1993, 1995). Morris (1993) argues that four rhetorical devices will affect the contents, intended meanings and negotiated meanings of political cartoons. First, condensation involves the compression of disconnected events to a common, singular frame. Second, combination involves the construction and organization of various ideas from different domains with numerous and perhaps conflicting meanings. Third, opposition is a process whereby the complexity of a problem is reduced to a binary struggle. And fourth, domestication (see also Goffman, 1979) occurs when distant events remote from the everyday experiences of the reader are translated into concrete happenings that can be experienced as close and familiar.

To enrich Morris's schema, I propose an additional analytic device: the notion of 'transference'. The notion of 'transference' fits neatly within the rhetorical framework of opinion discourse in that it not only evaluates social phenomena and social process, but it also explains these events in ways

that have first and foremost to do with the allocation of blame and attribution of responsibility (Greenberg, 2000).

Context: The Putative 'Problem' of Illegal Immigration to Canada

Crucial to the analysis of discourse is an awareness of the broader context within which a 'social problem' is constructed. During the summer of 1999, four unmarked boats in near-abysmal condition arrived at the coast of British Columbia, Canada, transporting 599 undocumented, would-be refugees from China's Fujian province. From the arrival of the first boat, tension mounted among media observers and the general public concerning Canada's commitment to provide humanitarian aid to those in need without appearing, at the same time, too lenient to unqualified, would-be refugees. News coverage of these events suggested that these Chinese migrants were posing a unique and significant threat to law and order and national security.

Analysis: Two Illustrative Examples

The two cartoons shown below illustrate some of the theoretical imperatives and methodological processes discussed above. To varying degrees these cartoons illustrate the rhetorical processes of condensation, opposition, combination, domestication, and transference in accounting for some of the responses and reactions to the migrants' arrivals by political, media, and lay audiences alike.

The first cartoon, 'Farmers and Immigrants' (6 September 1999), was published in the Vancouver Sun—a middlebrow family newspaper catering to a socio-economically diverse readership—and shows four farmers devising a strategy for gaining financial assistance from the state.

Having established the farmers as comical characters, the artist then attributes to one of them a common-sense utterance suggesting that the first responsibility of the state should be to take care of its own citizens before attending to the wants of others. While mocking the absurdity of the farmers'

Figure 66.1

"Farmers and Immigrants" *(Published 6 Sept. 1999, Vancouver Sun, A14).* Cam Cardow/*Ottawa Citizen*

Figure 66.2

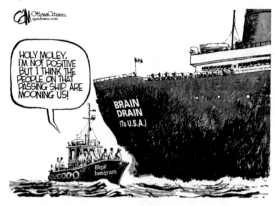

"Brain Drain" *(Published 7 Sept. 1999, National Post, A9).* Cam Cardow/*Ottawa Citizen*

plan, the artist indicates no disagreement with their general viewpoint. The prescription of action is implicit in the causal connection that changing the refugee determination process will mean that farmers can now receive help from the state.

The absurdity of the farmers' scheme is also transferred implicitly to the absurdity of the migrants' arrivals. In this sense, transference operates as a mechanism of meaning construction that, on the one hand, travels along an articulatory chain of referents while, on the other, making this articulatory travel possible. The artist condenses the entire refugee process to a rather simple scheme, showing that if refugees can have it this easy, so too should farmers. Rather than working to change the government's stance in terms of restoring previously cut expenditures on farmer income, the characters seem convinced that a loophole in the refugee law is the surest and only means of obtaining their goal. The clearest indication that the cartoon employs the process of combination is the linkage of increased transnational population movements with decreased government funding to Canadian farmers, insofar as the image blends into a single and complete frame, containing both the crisis in immigration and the crisis in farmer income. The reader is invited by the cartoon characters to see the immigration and

refugee system as the 'cause' of (and solution to) the problems facing farmers.

In the second cartoon (7 September 1999), a massive ship carrying Canadian citizens is shown to be sailing to the United States. The Canadian passengers are gesturing rudely at the small tugboat of illegal immigrants who, we are to assume given the direction of the boat, are on their way to 'freedom' in Canada. In framing this issue, the cartoonist suggests that the negative effects of immigration policies are compounding the negative effects of taxation policies. The relationship of these two issues may be interpreted in three ways: first, that problem A (immigration) has a direct and causal relationship to problem B (brain drain); second, the relationship between these problems is ridiculous, and the cartoon is intended to be ironic; and third, while the public is becoming so upset over a small number of migrants whose wish is to come to Canada, no one is bothered by those citizens who, trained and educated by Canadian tax dollars, wish only to leave the country.

Discussion

It is instructive at this point to recall the usefulness of Mead's notion of temporality for investigating how news discourse conceptualizes contemporary 'social problems' in terms of past events, situated presents, and future goals. Mead argued that the social construction of the past is of sociological concern because of the political, ideological and material implications it poses. The image of the destitute farmer, coupled with the implicit proposition that migrants and refugees 'have it easy', connotes the gradual collapse of what were previously shared perceptions about basic certainties, that is, old modes of capital accumulation and relations among citizens are being supplanted by something new and unknown. Such depictions situate 'readers qua subjects' within specific discursive contexts (Hall, 1977). For example, the interpellation of the 'law-abiding citizen' brings into play a certain configuration of discourses which are presupposed to motivate such subjects to celebrate 'hard work' and 'respect for the law', and which set up the possibility of opposition to 'rule breakers' and others who eschew these normative standards. When public debate is inflected with normative linguistic terminologies, such as referring to refugees as 'illegals', 'queue-jumpers' or 'aliens', this attribution precludes analysis of the concrete ideological, political, and economic conditions refuge-seekers might experience in their homelands (c.f., van Dijk, 1998). The extent to which graphic depictions of 'migrant waves' will resonate with readers and precipitate attitudinal change are empirical questions that require a methodological schema different from that employed here. Whether we are referring to visual or verbal/written journalistic texts, discourse 'provides a vehicle for thought, communication and action' (Purvis and Hunt, 1993: 485). That is, visual news discourse has both an ideational and material quality that confronts readers and poses possibilities for changes in consciousness and calls to action.

Conclusion

So far it has been established that cartoonists draw on timely topics that have already been established in the mainstream media as worthy of public attention. Though they speak of the world in hyper figurative terms, political cartoons are but one mode of opinion news discourse that enables the public to actively classify, organize, and interpret what they see and experience in meaningful ways.

References

Goffman, E. 1974. *Frame Analysis: An Essay on the Organization of Experience*. New York: Harper and Row.

———. 1979. *Gender Advertisements*. Cambridge: Harvard University Press.

Greenberg, J. 2000. 'Opinion Discourse and Canadian Newspapers: The Case of the Chinese "Boat People"', *Canadian Journal of Communication* 25, 4: 517–38.

Hall, S. 1977. 'Culture, the Media and the "ideological effect"', in *Mass Communications and Society*, pp. 315–48, J. Curran, et al., eds. London: Edward Arnold.

Knight, G. 2001. 'Prospective News: Press Pre-framing of the 1996 Ontario Public Service Strike', *Journalism Studies* 2, 1: 73–91.

Maines, D., N. Sugrue, and M. Katovich. 1983. 'The Sociological Import of G.H. Mead's Theory of the Past', *American Sociological Review* 48: 161–73.

Mead, G.H. 1929. 'The Nature of the Past', in *Essays in Honor of John Dewey*, pp. 235–42, J. Coss, ed. New York: Henry Holt and Company.

———. 1932. *The Philosophy of the Present*. LaSalle, IL: Open Court.

———. 1938. *The Philosophy of the Act*. Chicago: University of Chicago Press.

Morris, R. 1989. *Behind the Jester's Mask*. Toronto: University of Toronto Press.

———. 1991. 'Cultural Analysis through Semiotics: Len Norris' Cartoons on Official Bilingualism', *Canadian Review of Sociology and Anthropology* 28, 2: 225–54.

———. 1992a. 'Cartoons and the Political System: Canada, Quebec, Wales and England', *Canadian Journal of Communication* 17, 2: 253–8.

———. 1992b. 'Editorial Cartoons and the Reproduction of Capitalist Order', in *Critical Studies of*

Canadian Mass Media, pp. 145–54, M. Grenier, ed. Toronto: Butterworths.

———. 1993. 'Visual Rhetoric in Political Cartoons: A Structuralist Approach', *Metaphor and Symbolic Activity* 8, 3: 195–210.

———. 1995. *The Carnivalization of Politics: Quebec Cartoons on Relations with Canada, England and France, 1960–1979*. Montreal and Kingston: McGill-Queen's University Press.

Purvis, T., and A. Hunt. 1993. 'Discourse, Ideology, Discourse, Ideology, Discourse, Ideology . . .', *British Journal of Sociology* 44, 3: 473–99.

Schwartz, B. 1991. 'Social Change and Collective Memory: The Democratization of George Washington', *American Sociological Review* 56: 221–36.

Van Dijk, T. 1998. 'Opinions and Ideologies in the Press', in *Approaches to Media Discourse*, pp. 21–63, A. Bell and P. Garrett, eds. Oxford: Blackwell.

Questions for Critical Thought

Thirty Thousand Calls for Justice: The Human Rights Movement, Political Graffiti, and the Struggles over Collective Memory in Argentina

1. The use of graffiti in Argentina for social and political causes is much more accepted by, and ingrained in, society. How do you think street art might be effective in North American social struggles?
2. Why do you think graffiti is an important tactic in social struggle? Can you think of other examples in which graffiti is used elsewhere by various groups and movements? What might make graffiti a useful tool for these movements?
3. What sort of things could sociologists learn about the world through studying graffiti? How might you design such studies?
4. With reference to Argentina or other places, discuss why the past can be contentious.
5. Use an example in Canadian society to outline how the past has continued to 'irrupt' in the present through the use of signs, graffiti, posters, monuments, and anniversary coverage in the media.

The Emerging Role of Information in Canada's Security Environment

1. Other than technological advancements related to information processing, what other factors play a role in a 'non-traditional' war?
2. Does technology indicate a new form of warfare, or is it a traditional war with new players, 'enemies', weapons, and so forth?
3. What is 'peace' if 'war' is defined through information and information technologies?
4. What is the difference between 'national security' and 'warfare'?
5. Who are the targets of war, if they are only known and responded to through information technologies and information profiles?

Feminist Representations of Women Living on Welfare: The Case of Workfare and the Erosion of Volunteer Time

1. Distinguish between welfare and workfare. What is the significance of welfare policy in overall social planning of Canada?
2. All welfare recipients should volunteer some form of services to the state. How far do you agree with that statement?
3. How effective are feminist groups in representing the concerns of marginalized minority women in Ontario?

4. Assess, from the feminist perspective, the effectiveness of the welfare system in Canadian society?
5. What alternative programs would you recommend in addressing the problems confronting women on welfare in Canada?

THE DISTRUSTFUL CITIZEN: THEORIES AND OBSERVATIONS FROM SMALL-GROUP SETTINGS

1. How does social capital support the mobilization of economic and human resources, and contribute to the prosperity of society?
2. Although the idea of social capital is linked to the prosperity of society, why is this concept a potentially corrosive element within democratic processes?
3. Given that some analysts fear the political system is losing its critical edge, what does it mean to re-politicize the political process and what are the potential consequences of this action?
4. Is it possible for small groups to function without some level of interpersonal trust between participants?
5. How do advisory groups act as a tool for legitimating state and corporate interests?

FRAMING AND TEMPORALITY IN POLITICAL CARTOONS: A CRITICAL ANALYSIS OF VISUAL NEWS DISCOURSE

1. How effective are political cartoons as news discourse in Canada?
2. What is your candid assessment of the two political cartons presented in this paper?
3. Discuss the role of cartoons in constructing social problems in Canada.
4. Discuss the four rhetorical devices capable of affecting the contents, intended meanings, and negotiated meanings of political cartoons.
5. Assess the usefulness of Mead's notion of temporality in investigating how news discourse conceptualizes social problems.

Part XV

Environment

The environment is currently subjected to abuse from a host of human activities. Many, unfortunately, are meting out most of these activities unconsciously. The responsibility of addressing the mishaps to the environment is being placed at the doorposts of both the state and the civil society. The following chapters recommend ways of mitigating the excesses of human activities on the environment.

The over-reliance on automobility and its disastrous impacts on the environment is articulated by Arlene Tigar McLaren. She argues that neoliberalism has made it difficult for the state to live up to its responsibility by addressing comprehensively the social problems of traffic safety. Tackling automobile dominance in Canadian society, to McLaren, should be the task and concern of the government, rather than civil society.

S. Harris Ali recognizes the importance of the state in tackling environmental concerns in society. However, he changes the discourse slightly by recommending civil society's involvement in tackling environmental problems. With the fire outburst at the Hamilton recycling factory as reference, Ali argues that an overly intense focus on technical rationality at the expense of cultural rationality in managing risk is detrimental in providing a complete description of environmental problems confronting society.

Justin Page also examines the environmental reflexivity of identity by exploring the ways in which environmentally destructive identities become socialized and normalized in society, and the chances for resisting and transforming such identity.

Miriam Padolsky further highlights the role of civil society in ensuring sustainable environment. The example of a sustainable consumption movement in Australia is used as the benchmark in establishing how the collective identity of an environmentally conscious group at the micro level influences the general lifestyle of the larger population in Australia.

The urgent need for all hands to be on deck in ensuring the sustainable use of the environment is accentuated in Part XV.

CHAPTER 67

Automobilization and Traffic Safety

Arlene Tigar McLaren

Introduction

Automobile traffic is a major feature of urban and suburban life in Canada and elsewhere. Automobiles accomplish many things, including getting people to their jobs, to leisure activities, to shopping, and to school. Yet automobiles are also a primary source of traffic congestion, injuries, and fatalities as well as many other social ills such as inequities and environmental degradation. Why then have sociologists shown little interest in how the automobile organizes social institutions, social spaces, mobilities, and everyday practices? And why, more particularly, have sociologists and others in society failed to address **traffic safety** and injury as a serious social problem? To begin to answer this question, it is necessary to explore the **automobilization** of society, which refers to the process by which the automobile as a mass-consumption commodity has profoundly altered many aspects of social existence for all strata of society (Sweezy, 2000).

As a case in point, the paper briefly examines British Columbia legislation on drunk driving to illustrate how traffic safety promotion individualizes **social responsibility** and risk. The paper also shows, on the other hand, that other forms of traffic safety promotion can be found in local and global struggles to counter the denial and normalization of traffic risk. Such initiatives illustrate that people do not necessarily accept the 'inevitability' of automobilization, but seek to turn traffic safety into a serious and visible social issue.

Traffic Safety Promotion

Traffic safety is a major yet curiously invisible social problem in Canada and elsewhere. Numerous statistics tell us that traffic collisions result in high rates of fatalities and injuries in the developed world and even more so in developing countries. In its 2004 Report, the World Health Organization estimated that, on average each year, 1.2 million people are killed and as many as 50 million are injured worldwide in accidents involving automobiles (World Health Organization and World Bank, 2004). In 2002, almost 3,000 people died and over 220,000 were injured as a result of motor vehicle collisions in Canada (Transport Canada, 2004).

According to Urry (2004), the automobile has a specific character of domination that is more systemic and awesome in its consequences than other world-shaping technologies such as the cinema, television, or computer. He identifies six components of automobility that constitute the dominance of the automobile in contemporary life: as a leading industrial sector; a sector deeply connected to other powerful industries; a major item of consumption after housing; a dominant form of mobility that subordinates other forms; a potent symbol of the good life; and the single most important cause of environmental resource use. Urry argues that country after country is developing an 'automobility culture'.

In exploring automobility and safety, Beckmann (2004: 94) claims that automobility works '*because its accidents are denied*' (emphasis in original). The 'civil society of automobility' has invented a response to the risks of driving that constructs the illusion of safety. That is:

Accident-workers cleanse the road, repair the car, heal the victims and lock up irresponsible drivers—suggesting that afterwards driving has become safe. With such treatment, the accident is not just subject to a particular kind of denial, but also removed to another region in the auto network (Beckmann 2004: 95).

In managing accidents, a variety of organizations and sites (e.g. the road, courthouse, hospital, laboratory, newspaper) reinforce the idea that vehicle traffic and collisions are a normal, inescapable, and ordinary part of modern life. Though safety-expert knowledge and practices play a central role in ruling accident discourses, they are, nevertheless, coming under increased scrutiny (Beckmann 2004). The 2004 WHO Report, for example, critically assesses the traditional view of road safety, still widely held today, that individual road users are solely responsible and must adopt 'error-free' behaviour. The Report suggests that, as road safety experts increasingly define traffic deaths and casualties as a public health issue, they shift the responsibility away from the individual to the 'system' (Featherstone, 2004).

I briefly turn to government discourse on impaired driving as an example of traditional traffic safety promotion that denies the severity of car collisions as a social problem, that focuses on the individual driver as responsible for dangerous driving rather than the larger system, and that fails to consider alternatives to automobility and traffic growth.

BC Legislation on Drunk Driving

In October 2004, the British Columbia government passed new impaired driving laws (British Columbia, 2004). This legislation followed the very public scandal of Premier Gordon Campbell's conviction of drunk driving during a Hawaiian holiday the preceding year.

While Premier Campbell was not forced to resign, his government had to introduce impaired driving legislation to show that it took drunk driving seriously. Ironically, however, not only was the government able to ride out the political storm, it used the legislation to incorporate its governing philosophy of neoliberalism into the amendments it added to the Motor Vehicle Act on impaired driving.

According to the Solicitor General, Rich Coleman, the BC government's new impaired driving laws would send 'a strong message that we will not tolerate drinking and driving in British Columbia' (Rid Roads of Impaired Drivers, 2005). Despite the government's claim that the laws send a strong message, some commentators (e.g., Rid Roads of Impaired Drivers [RRID] and Mothers Against Drunk Drivers [MADD], see Beatty, 2004) are concerned that they are not tough enough. While the legislation may not satisfy groups who want stronger laws, it is important to examine what the law—and the government's Discussion Paper (British Columbia, 2003) preceding it—accomplish in constructing a particular view of drinking and driving.

In particular, the government's legislation adopts such strategies as a user-pay ignition interlock program, a user-pay rehabilitation program, and the management of the opportunity to drink and drive by establishments that serve alcohol. These strategies reinforce the prevalent notion in traffic safety promotion that individuals (including employees of private drinking establishments) are responsible for drinking and driving and that only their behaviour need be modified (Gusfield, 1981; Reinarman, 1988). For example, recent task force recommendations adopted by Canada's *Road Safety Vision 2010* involve a re-categorizing of 'hard-core drinking drivers' as 'high risk drivers', which displays continued focus on behaviour change and technological fixes for traffic safety:

> The targeted product is behaviour. Behaviour change can be obtained through promotional, legislative and enforcement means. However, current technology offers the possibility of systematically controlling some high-risk behaviours. For instance, alcohol ignition interlock devices should be used as extensively as possible (Canadian Council of Motor Transport Administrators, 2001).

In addition, by adopting 'user-pay' systems to modify individual behaviour, the BC government draws upon neoliberal ideas and practices that intend to download government responsibility onto individuals and markets.

Automobilization and Alternatives

Some, as Adams (2005) notes, believe that traffic growth is inevitable and that the death of the car is unlikely. Some consider its replacement by public transport to be the forlorn dream of some environmentalists (Featherstone, 2004). Featherstone suggests, 'it is hard to imagine car crashes becoming a public health issue commanding the necessary governmental resources' (17) to implement comprehensive alternatives to current automobile and road designs. Others are not so willing to forego imagining and struggling for alternatives. Many argue that substitutes for the car are affordable (e.g., MacGregor, 2002; Litman, 2004; Adams, 2005) and that automobile dependency is not a foregone conclusion.

Groups such as environmentalists, communities, and neighbourhoods continue to mobilize against car domination and in favour of mobility alternatives. In East Vancouver, for example, groups recently countered the BC government's proposal to expand a major highway by organizing a street hockey protest that took over a section of one of the major thoroughfares (Crawford, 2004). In another protest, this time directly against a pedestrian's death, residents posted signs on the street where a 73-year-old woman was struck by an SUV. As a resident stated: 'Five people have been killed or injured in a month (in the same area). If that's not a priority, what is?' (O'Connor, 2004). The steadily rising cost of petroleum in the face of escalating Middle-East crises and dwindling supply (Kunstler, 2005) provides still more effective pressure in favour of alternatives to the automobility system.

Conclusion

In its practices and ideology, automobility makes itself invisible, while it makes other issues, such as the drunk driver, the visible culprit. It does not address the broader social, economic, and political features of society shaped so deeply by its presence. Further, as an approach to governance, neoliberalism disables society's ability to address comprehensively social problems such as traffic safety. Without tackling car dependency at a societal level, traffic safety efforts will continue to fall tragically short.

References

Adams, J. 2005. 'Hypermobility: A Challenge to Governance', in *New Modes of Governance: Developing an Integrated Policy Approach to Science, Technology, Risk and the Environment*, C. Cyall and J. Tait, eds. Aldershot: Ashgate.

Beatty, J. 2004. 'New Law Aims to Force Drunks off the Road', *The Vancouver Sun*, 19 October.

Beckmann, J. 2004. 'Mobility and Safety', *Theory, Culture & Society* 21: 81–100.

British Columbia. 2003. *Drinking and Driving Issues and Strategies in British Columbia: Discussion Paper*. Victoria, BC.

———. 2004. *Bill 66 Motor Vehicle Amendment Act—Key Amendments*. Available at http://www.2news.gov.bc.ca/nrm_news_releases/2004PSSG0024-000818-Attachment1.htm (accessed 15 March 2005).

Canadian Council of Motor Transport Administrators (CCMTA). 2001. *Strategy to Deal with the High Risk Driver*. Ottawa: CCMTA's Standing Committee on Road Safety Research and Policies.

Crawford, T. 2004. 'Street-hockey Players Protest Expansion of Highways', *The Vancouver Sun*, 8 March.

Featherstone, M. 2004. 'Automobilities', *Theory, Culture & Society* 21: 1–24.

Gusfield, J. 1981. *The Culture of Public Problems*. Chicago: University of Chicago Press.

Kunstler, J.H. 2005. *The Long Emergency*. Berkeley, CA: Grove/Atlantic, Inc.

Litman, T. 2004. *Evaluating Public Transit Benefits and Costs*. Victoria: Victoria Transport Policy Institute.

MacGregor, D. 2002. 'Sugar Bear in the Hot Zone', in *Driving Lessons: Exploring Systems that Make Traffic*

Safer, pp. 125–42, P. Rothe, ed. Edmonton: University of Alberta Press.

O'Connor, N. 2004. 'Victoria Drive Neighbours React to Elderly Woman's Death', *The Vancouver Courier*, 17 November: 27.

Reinarman, C. 1988. 'The Social Construction of an Alcohol Problem: The Case of Mothers Against Drunk Drivers and Social Control in the 1980s', *Theory and Society* 17, 1: 91–120.

Rid Roads of Impaired Drivers—Vancouver Island. 2005. *New Year—New Laws*. Available at http://www.rrid.org/comment.htm (accessed 17 January 2005).

Sweezy, P.M. 2000. 'Cars and Cities', *Monthly Review* 51, 11: 19–34.

Transport Canada. 2004. *Canadian Motor Vehicle Traffic Collision Statistics: 2002*. Ottawa: Transport Canada.

Urry, J. 2004. 'The "System" of Automobility', *Theory, Culture & Society* 21: 25–39.

World Health Organization and World Bank. 2004. *World Report on Road Traffic Injury Prevention*. Geneva: World Health Organization.

CHAPTER 68

Dealing with Toxicity in the Risk Society: The Case of the Hamilton, Ontario Plastic Recycling Fire

S. Harris Ali

Introduction

On the evening of 9 July 1997 a large fire erupted at the Plastimet plastics recycling facility that was situated in the mixed residential/industrial North End area of the city of Hamilton, Ontario (population of 337,000). The conflagration lasted for four days and was fuelled by such materials as polyvinyl chloride and polyurethane foam from dashboards, interior door panels, and other soft components of automobiles. As the plastic materials burned, a huge dense plume of black smoke drifted across the city, leaving a thin film of black ash in its wake. Of concern was the fact that this smoke and ash contained a toxic mix of chemicals including, among others, dioxin, furan, benzene, hydrogen chloride, and heavy metals. Due to the potential for exposure to these airborne and deposited chemicals, nearly 600 residents were forced to evacuate the area.

This study uses the Plastimet case as an empirical referent to illustrate how risk was treated within the **social context** that emerged in the aftermath of a technological disaster. This paper focuses on environmental risks such as radiation, toxins in foodstuffs, pollution, genetically modified organisms, and, for the present study, chemical contamination.

Methods and Data

Several days after the North End residents returned to their homes, a series of Ministry of Environment and Energy (MOEE)-sponsored community meetings were held to deal with the management of the risks stemming from the fire. The overall data collection orientation adopted during these meetings was aimed at gathering information about the substantive claims that were being made about the environmental and health risk issues associated with the toxic fire from the period shortly after the fire to about two years subsequent (i.e., September 1997 to June 1999). Aside from data gained through the observational component of the study, other documents on the disaster were consulted.

Characterizing the Post-disaster Setting

According to the risk society thesis (Beck, 1992), Western societies presently find themselves in situations where they must urgently confront the unanticipated side effects and by-products of industrialization that take the form of large-scale environmental risks and technological disasters. The experience of these risks is made even more frightening in light of the fact that the negative impacts of these insidious threats to the body may not manifest themselves until some unknown time in the future.

It is exactly these types of concerns that have led Kroll-Smith, Couch, and Marshall (1997) to characterize the post-disaster setting as an 'extreme environment' in which victims are significantly burdened by a pervasive and long-lasting sense of inescapable peril or dread, as well as other anxiety-driven, psychosocial impacts (see for example, Edelstein, 1988; Eyles et al., 1993). Kroll-Smith et al. note that extreme environments provide important opportunities to conduct sociological research because these situations 'reveal and magnify aspects of social systems and processes that are typically obscured by the routinization of everyday life' (1997: 2). In this light, the analytical emphasis of the social constructionist approach on claimsmaking is particularly well-suited to the study of extreme environments characterized by a socially disruptive backdrop referred to as a 'corrosive community' by William Freudenberg (1997).

Emergency Response and the Development of the Corrosive Community

Identification of the risk object was particularly critical during the early stages of the Plastimet fire because information concerning the risk object was needed not only to effectively combat the blaze, but also to come to a decision about the evacuation of residents. For some time after the onset of the fire, the contaminants that arose failed to be recognized as risk objects by the firefighters and government officials present at the emergency scene. As a consequence, the fire was not classified as a hazardous chemical fire and, for a certain duration, firefighters were not wearing the appropriate protective gear and crowds of onlookers were permitted to stand by and watch the spectacular blaze. The failure to identify and recognize the risk object was soon brought to public attention by the chief toxicologist of the environmental group Greenpeace, who had flown in from England to take dioxin measurements from the site.

A second issue that was brought to public attention by Greenpeace dealt with the limitations of the technological methods used by government officials to determine the environmental health risks during the emergency period. In the absence of the more sophisticated monitoring technologies housed in the mobile Trace Atmospheric Gas Analyzers (known as TAGA units), early air quality tests were conducted by MOEE officials through the use of hand-held Gastec colorimetric tubes. It was noted by Greenpeace, however, that these devices could only give a crude indication of airborne contamination as their range of accuracy falls within plus or minus 30 per cent (Greenpeace press conference, 27 August 1997). An added complication arose from the fact that these colorimetric tubes had a specific shelf life and the ones used during the Plastimet fire had exceeded their expiry date. Based on the information from Greenpeace, many residents were dissatisfied with the official assessment.

Claims about Risk in the Corrosive Community

In the days and weeks that followed, the chemical dioxin was firmly established as the risk object of concern and was the topic of discussion for many community meetings. The awareness of dioxin risk was further heightened as a city-wide directive warned residents not to consume any of the produce they had grown in their gardens. They were also told not to allow their children to play on lawns and sandboxes in the area, and were advised to thoroughly wash all outdoor items before use. Several weeks after the fire, the regional health department declared that no harmful long-term health effects would result from exposure to the fire ash and soot and that home-grown produce could be eaten if carefully washed. However, suspicions about the validity of these government claims and advice surfaced when the MOEE claimed that the laboratory analysis of the dioxin samples from the Plastimet site would take several weeks (despite the fact that they had earlier been able to obtain laboratory results in a few days). Such claims appeared to support Greenpeace's claim that the MOEE was trying to conceal the seriousness of the situation from the public for as long as possible (Greenpeace press conference, 27 August 1997).

Discussion: Risk Communication and Cultural Rationality in the Corrosive Community

The field of risk communication was initiated around 1984 to deal with the differences between the evaluation of risks made by technical experts on the one hand, and members of the lay public on the other (Powell and Leiss, 1997). With this focus, earlier research efforts in risk communication were based on the premise that lay individuals would be convinced of the acceptability of the findings and recommendations of the risk assessors if they were to simply become better educated and informed on technical matters (Fischer, 2000: 106). With time, such efforts were found to be ineffective and the current work in risk communication has moved away from a unilateral view of risk information dissemination to a model based on a two-way exchange of information between technical experts and lay individuals. Evidence from the Plastimet case, however, reveals that a two-way exchange of risk information did not occur.

Plough and Krimsky (1987) define technical rationality as a mindset that is based on the scientific method and relies exclusively on the judgments of technical experts. Cultural rationality, on the other hand, relies on personal and familiar experiences rather than the depersonalized technical calculations involved in formal risk assessment. Since cultural rationality tends to focus on case-specific contextual information, it also influences lay people's decisions about whom they can trust and under what circumstances (Fischer, 2000: 138; see also Wynne, 1996) and, as we have seen in the Plastimet case, such decisions are especially problematic under the extreme conditions of a corrosive community.

The negative lay reactions to the technical work of the government officials in the Plastimet case can therefore be understood as a culturally rational response to specific context factors related to the government's handling of earlier controversies (i.e., the late evacuation call, the slow dispatch of the TAGA units, and the questionable detection methods used to identify the risk objects-all deficiencies which the government did not acknowledge).

Conclusion

The risk society conceptualization—on a theoretical level—and the risk communication perspective, on a more practical level, appear to neglect not only the cultural dimensions of risk conflicts (Lash, 1994; Wynne, 1996), but the political-economic aspects of risk management as well. A corrective to this may be found in importing the broadened focus of a critical social constructionist approach that will not only consider the cultural rationality that is brought into the risk conflict, but will also focus attention on the question of how the claims-making process is informed by the larger structural issues related to social class, power, environmental inequality and environmental justice, and the political economy of place.

References

Beck, U. 1992. *Risk Society: Towards a New Modernity*, Mark Ritter, trans. London: Sage.

Edelstein, M.R. 1988. *Contaminated Communities: The Social and Psychological Impacts of Residential Toxic Exposure*. Boulder, CO: Westview Press.

Eyles, J.S., M. Taylor, J. Baxter, D. Sider, and D. Willms. 1993. 'The Social Construction of Risk in a Rural Community: Responses of Local Residents to the 1990 Hagersville (Ontario) Tire Fire', *Risk Analysis* 13, 3: 281–9.

Fischer, F. 2000. *Citizens, Experts, and the Environment: The Politics of Local Knowledge*. Durham: Duke University Press.

Freudenberg, W. 1997. 'Contamination, Corrosion and the Social Order: An Overview', *Current Sociology* 45, 3: 19–39.

Kroll-Smith, S., S.R. Couch, and B.K. Marshall. 1997. 'Sociology, Extreme Environments and Social Change', *Current Sociology* 45, 3: 1–18.

Lash, S. 1994. 'Reflexivity and Its Doubles: Structure, Aesthetics, Community', in *Reflexive Modernization: Politics, Tradition and Aesthetics in the Modern Social Order*, pp. 110–73, U. Beck, A. Giddens, and S. Lash, eds. Stanford, CA: Stanford University Press.

Plough, A., and S. Krimsky. 1987. 'The Emergence of Risk Communication Studies: Social and Political Context', *Science, Technology, and Human Values* 12, 3/4: 4–10.

Powell, D., and W. Leiss. 1997. *Mad Cows and Mother's Milk: The Perils of Poor Risk Communication*. Montreal and Kingston: McGill-Queen's University Press.

Wynne, B. 1996. 'May the Sheep Safely Graze? A Reflexive View of the Expert–Lay Knowledge Divide', in *Risk, Environment and Modernity. Towards a New Ecology*, pp. 44–83, S. Lash, B. Szerszynski, and B. Wynne, eds. London: Sage.

CHAPTER 69

Constructing Environmental Identity: The Constraints of Power and Common Sense

Justin Page

Modern forms of life are characterized by an increasing awareness of their own constitutive elements, and by how this knowledge is fed back into social practices in order to transform them (Giddens, 1990). One of the most transformative consequences of the increasing reflexivity of modernity is the relation between society and nature.

Science has played a central role in this newly developing environmental consciousness. However, while most contemporary environmental conflicts are fought through science (even while fighting against science; see Beck, 1992), a movement within contemporary environmentalism takes a philosophical and speculative, rather than technocratic and managerial approach. This latter approach is described by its proponents as 'deep' as opposed to 'shallow', 'radical' as opposed to 'reformist', and as concerned with the 'roots' of the 'ecological crisis'—which it generally locates in the structures of identity (Zimmerman, 1994).

In this paper, I explore the environmental reflexivity of identity. As a social scientific contribution to this reflexivity, I draw on the work of social theorists to elaborate the main features of this form of modern environmental reflexivity. Working through Althusser and Bourdieu, I consider the ways in which (environmentally destructive) identities become socialized and normalized, and the chances for resisting and transforming identity.

Environmental Reflexivity of Identity

Radical environmentalists argue that the problematic modern human relation to nature is irrevocably tied to historically constituted cultural beliefs and values, or **worldview**. In particular, they focus on the negative consequences of the belief that the human and the natural orders are different in kind and the belief that the realms are hierarchically ordered (Plumwood, 1993).

The interesting feature of the radical environmentalist analysis is that it locates the anti-environmental western worldview in identity, and, in light of information about the effects of this form of subjectivity (environmental destruction, human alienation), seeks to transform identity in order to transform the human relation to nature (see, for example, Naess, 1989; Plumwood, 1993; Fox, 1995; Roszak et al., 1995).

Ideology, Identity, and Perception

This transformation flows, first of all, from an alteration of ideology. Radical ecologists espouse a 'green ideology' wherein humanity is regarded as essentially interrelated and interdependent with the 'rest of' nature, nature is regarded as 'alive' in the sense of being imbued with subjecthood and meaning, and nature is recognized as possessing intrinsic value. The concomitant identity is the 'ecological self'. The ecological self recognizes its earthly embeddedness, its relations with human and non-human others, the subjecthood of non-humans, and the intrinsic value of all of nature (Plumwood, 1993).

Yet, green identity entails more than an intellectual grasping of green ideology. It is to be lived: the ecological self must *feel* itself to be a part of nature, and nature a part of itself; it must perceive other earthly lifeforms as intrinsically valuable subjects. Thus, the development of ecological self-

hood entails the alteration of perception, both of one's self and one's world. As one radical ecologist writes, 'the ecological crisis may be the result of a recent and collective *perceptual disorder* in our species, a unique form of myopia which it now forces us to correct' (Abram, 1995: 57; emphasis added). However, perceptual transformations are not easy to achieve.

Altering Identity: the Constraints of Power and Commonsense

The first reason why it may be difficult to assume the 'ecological self' is that individuals are (always) already produced as subjects by and through—or at least in relation to—the dominant ideology. In the West, the dominant ideology is capitalist, sustainable development, and it, like all dominant ideologies (Althusser, 1971), envelops individuals even before they are born, providing the horizon within which their understanding of themselves and their world develops. As such, the dominant ideology constructs the identities of those within its purview; it institutes identity at such a deep level that it is not easily shed, even if one comes to challenge its primary beliefs and values.

Louis Althusser's (1971) discussion of ideology suggests that the strength of the ideological production of identity derives from the fact that ideology forms a key dimension of dominant material and social relations of power. The function of ideology, in Althusser's analysis, is to reproduce the relations of production and the relations that derive from them.

Similarly, Bourdieu (1990) argues that submission to the given social order derives from relations of power, which are instituted in material and social conditions of existence. The structures characterizing the conditions of existence, he argues, produce, through the actions of the state (Bourdieu, 1998), corresponding cognitive structures that are instituted in individuals. 'Through the framing it imposes on practices,' Bourdieu writes, 'the state establishes and inculcates common forms and categories of perception and appreciation, social frameworks of perceptions, of understanding or of memory' (1998: 54). This is the deep level at which identity—Bourdieu refers to it as *habitus*—is instituted: cognitive structures taking the form of largely unconscious bodily dispositions that order perception and action. Even when radical environmentalists challenge the dominant ideology, therefore, they find that their very perception of reality continues to be subjected to the pre-reflexive categories of perception that have been instituted within them: they thus remain, at this level, beholden to the dominant ideology. These pre-reflexive bodily dispositions respond to the 'calls to order' of the social world or, as Althusser says, to the 'hailing' of ideology.

Althusser claims 'ideology interpellates individuals as subjects' (1971: 170). Interpellation—the 'hailing' of individuals—is an act of subjection: it produces an individual as a 'free subjectivity, a centre of initiatives, author of and responsible for its action' (1971: 182); it also produces 'a subjected being, who submits to a higher authority, and is therefore stripped of all freedom except that of freely accepting his [or her] submission' (1971: 182). Thus, before they begin to work on themselves as free subjects who reject the dominant ideology, radical environmentalists have already been produced as subjects by the social order they reject, and their freedom is defined by subjection to that order. This is not to deny that subjects are 'free' to transcend the conditions of their constitution; it only entails that the means to do so are provided by, and constrained by, those conditions.

A second reason why it is difficult to develop new forms of subjectivity has to do with the 'obviousness' with which the structures of identity and the structures of the 'objective' world are endowed. Althusser and Bourdieu both attribute this feature of experience to the manner in which identity and world reflect one another. Althusser argues that the process of 'interpellation' has a 'speculary, i.e. a mirror-structure' (1971: 180). That is, subjects are produced as the mirror image of a centred ideology: subjects and the dominant ideology reflect one another in a duplication of beliefs and values. As a result, subjects, produced in and through the dominant ideology, see themselves reflected in it, and this provides the 'absolute guarantee that everything really is so' (1971: 181).

Similarly, Bourdieu argues that 'when the embodied structures and the objective structures are in agreement, when perception is constructed according to the structures of what is perceived, everything seems obvious and goes without saying' (1998: 81). That is, an 'ontological complicity' obtains between objective and subjective structures, rendering a seemingly 'natural', or commonsense, world.

The commonsense world deriving from the 'ontological complicity' between objective and subjective structures, in Bourdieu's sense, or from the ontological 'guarantee' provided by the speculary structure of interpellation, in Althusser's sense, is not easily shaken. One may break with the beliefs and values of the dominant ideology, but find that one's ways of seeing the world remain the same, since they flow out of a subjectivity that reflects the structures of the dominant ideology out of which it was produced. Ideology does not exist as ideas, but as practices (Althusser, 1971). The practices of the media representation of nature (animals used and disparaged in entertainment), of industrial agriculture (removing animals from experience and remaking them into packaged food products), of the suppression of wildness in the city (controlling and removing weeds and 'pests'), of the exploitation of resources (cut blocks and hydro-electric dams), and so on, reflect the interpellated consumer self and suggest that 'everything really is so'.

Conclusion

Radical environmentalists, if they are to develop the 'ecological self', must go beyond a 'mere' shift in ideology. They need to become conscious of their largely unconscious embodied structures, and they must make the pre-reflexive agreement between subjective and objective structures reflexive: this is the heart of the environmental reflexivity of identity. And since ideology exists as practices, interpellating individuals as subjects who embody belief, other practices need to be engaged in, transformative practices designed to embody green ideology at the level of perception and feeling, of *habitus*. The environmental reflexivity of identity thus consists in

awareness of one's habitual forms of perception and how they are related to objective structures and practices; also, it consists in practices designed to replace socialized cognitive structures with structures in line with green ideology.

References

Abram, D. 1995. 'Merleau-Ponty and the Voice of the Earth', in *Postmodern Environmental Ethics*, pp. 57–78, M. Oelschlaeger, ed. Albany, NY: SUNY Press.

Althusser, L. 1971. 'Ideology and Ideological State Apparatuses', in *Lenin and Philosophy and Other Essays*, pp. 127–86, B. Brewster, trans. New York and London: Monthly Review Press.

Beck, U. 1992. *Risk Society: Towards a New Modernity*. Thousand Oaks, CA: Sage.

Bourdieu, P. 1998. *Practical Reason: On the Theory of Action*. Stanford, CA: Stanford University Press.

———. 1990. *The Logic of Practice*. Stanford, CA: Stanford University Press.

Giddens, A. 1990. *The Consequences of Modernity*. Stanford, CA: Stanford University Press.

Naess, A. 1989. *Ecology, Community, And Lifestyle: Outline Of An Ecosophy*. Cambridge: Cambridge University Press.

Plumwood, V. 1993. *Feminism and the Mastery of Nature*. New York: Routledge.

Roszak, T., M. Gomez, and A. Kanner. 1995. *Ecopsychology: Restoring the Earth, Healing the Mind*. San Francisco, CA: Sierra Club Books.

Zimmerman, M. 1994. *Contesting Earth's Future: Radical Ecology and Postmodernity*. Berkeley, CA: University of California Press.

CHAPTER 70

Collective Identity in the Sustainable Consumption Movement: The Case of Cool Communities

Miriam Padolsky

Introduction

Adherents of the **sustainable consumption** movement seek to imbue their purchasing decisions with social and **environmental consciousness**. Sustainable consumption activists, however, do not seek only to reform their own lifestyles; the goal of the movement is to inspire a cultural shift in which all individuals will choose to consume in environmentally and socially responsible ways. *Cool Communities* was a sustainable consumption campaign funded by the Australian government and executed

by a coalition of Australian Environment Organizations (AEOs). AEO campaigners used their collective identity as sustainable consumers to set themselves apart from their government partners. At the same time, the AEO staff actively encouraged others, including their government patrons, to mimic their consumption choices. The **collective identity** of the campaign thus pulled the AEOs in different directions, both distinguishing them from others and broadening their identity to as many individuals as possible.

About *Cool Communities*

Cool Communities ran throughout Australia from 2001–4. Its stated purpose was to work with community groups to reduce their greenhouse gas emissions. The participants were encouraged to take simple actions in their daily lives, such as installing energy-saving light bulbs or walking instead of driving. In total, 38 communities participated in the program, including municipal governments, a church parish, a low-income apartment building, and a credit union. The program was funded by the Australian Greenhouse Office (AGO), an agency of the federal government, and delivered by a coalition of AGO staff, AEOs from each state and territory, and community groups. For many of them, especially from the AEOs, this campaign was not just about reducing emissions, but was more significantly a step towards the long term goal of sustainable consumption. This movement 'suggests that all social actors should optimize their efficient use of available resources by "doing more with less"', and that everyone should adopt a '"sustainable lifestyle", wherein considerations of the environmental impacts of personal consumption become part of day-to-day practices and decisions' (Hobson, 2003: 95–6).

Collective Identity

The social movements literature has numerous definitions of collective identity, but there is a general agreement that 'its essence resides in a shared sense of "one-ness" or "we-ness" among those individuals who compose the collectivity' (Snow and McAdam, 2000: 42). Throughout this literature, collective identity is also described as relational; that is, it draws a boundary between the group and outsiders (Lamont and Molnar, 2002). Taylor and Whittier argued that 'the creation of boundaries' and 'the valorization of a group's "essential differences"' (1992: 122) are two of the key factors that contribute to the formation of collective identity. For Melucci, collective identity consists in part of 'the delimitation of this subject with respect to

others' (1996: 71). Finally, for McAdam, Tarrow, and Tilly, identities 'in general consist of social relations and their representations' (2001: 131). These social relations involve the formation of categories of actors, based in part on the invention and borrowing of boundaries (Lamont and Molnar, 2002). In the case of *Cool Communities*, however, the AEOs' collective identity was not only one that distinguished them from their government patrons. The AEOs also sought to broaden their identity to society as a whole. This is not just a form of recruitment, in which a social movement organization seeks members to share their distinctive identity. For this movement to succeed, its collective identity would be broadened to all individuals, including those in government. Unlike many other social movement campaigns, then, there is no common enemy that their identity is defined against. The distinguishing and broadening aspects of their collective identity may thus be seen as pulls or flows in different directions.

Distinguishing

Despite the frequently cited opposition of social movements to the state (e.g. McAdam et al., 2001), we cannot take for granted that the AEOs would automatically distinguish themselves from the government. They have, after all, been working together on the same project for three years. Yet, there was a major distinction between the AEOs and the AGO, and it revolved around the AEOs' collective identity as sustainable consumers. One of the primary responsibilities of the AEO staff working on *Cool Communities* was to distribute energy-saving products—such as compact fluorescent bulbs, low-flow showerheads, and draught-stoppers—to communities. Yet the staff also enthusiastically embraced these products for themselves. For example, one person distributed low-flow showerheads to all her co-workers. In the office, there were extensive discussions around installing the showerheads, how they worked, and which kinds were the best. In workshops with the public, the presenter would report in detail on the feedback from her colleagues. Some of the recommended products were also an important part of the working environment in the office.

Another major consumption difference can be captured with the word 'feral'. In Australia, this word does not only refer to domesticated animals that have gone wild, such as feral cats. It is also used to refer to people, often environmentalists, who are 'undomesticated'. The head of one AEO office constantly referred to himself and everyone at the AEOs as feral. What does this mean in practice? At times the AEO staff fetishized old products, even ones that led to worse environmental outcomes. This head staff member, for example, drove an old car that produced large amounts of greenhouse gas emissions. At a *Cool Communities* dinner, the AEO staff favourably compared this car to the more posh (newer, less polluting) AGO cars. Many of the AEO staff also favoured older, and more unconventional clothing. This is only partly attributable to their relatively low salaries. As one AEO staff member explained, their clothes epitomized the differences between them and the AGO: 'If I had a meeting with them I would think more of what I would wear that day.' Their consumption choices, then, are a major way of distinguishing their collective identity from their AGO partners.

Broadening

The collective identity is not only one that distinguishes the AEOs from others. There is also a broadening aspect of this identity, one that would extend it to include their government partners and all of society. This broadening pull was on display at a major event organized by one of the AEOs. The event consisted of a public shower in a local mall. A temporary stage was set up in the food court, and a portable shower was mounted on a pedestal with its door tied open. The AEO staff invited local politicians, athletes, and media personalities to participate. Their role was to compete against each other to see who could take the shortest shower using an energy-saving showerhead. The event modelled the sustainable lifestyle and invited the

audience to take up that lifestyle as their own. In other words, it attempted to extend the AEOs' collective identity to the audience. To the extent that the AEOs succeed in precipitating a cultural shift, however, their collective identity would no longer be unique to them. Shoppers, people watching the evening news, and the AGO staff would all become sustainable consumers too.

This collective identity, then, can be distinguishing and broadening with regards to the same group. At the public shower, the government employees in attendance were a key audience for the sustainable consumption message. Indeed, various AEO staff members commented that the shower was bringing the government people into the real world, into the community. On another occasion, the same AEO staff member mentioned earlier, who described the essential differences between the government and their AEO as epitomized by differences in their dress, expressed a strong identification with the government's involvement in *Cool Communities*. She said, 'When people say things to me, and this is in a non-work context, about the dire state of the environment and the government's position on the issues, it's just really nice to be able to talk about something positive.' To the extent that her movement succeeds in promoting sustainable consumption, this collective identity would be broadened not just to the government, but to all of us.

Conclusion

The AEOs of *Cool Communities* shared a collective identity with the other members of their group; they strove to be sustainable consumers, considering the environmental and social consequences of their consumption choices. As the social movements literature would lead us to expect, this collective identity involved distinguishing their group from others. For the AEOs, the distinguishing features of their identity involved embracing 'sustainable' products such as low-flow showerheads and looking like 'ferals'. These elements distinguished them from their government partners, but this did not mean that their identity was defined against a common enemy. Rather, the AEOs' modelling of sustainable consumption behaviours, such as the public shower, invited their government partners and all of us to join them in the sustainable lifestyle. This sustainable consumption campaign, then, held a collective identity that simultaneously constructed boundaries and expanded them in order to embrace as much of society as possible.

References

Hobson, K. 2003. 'Thinking Habits into Action: The Role of Knowledge and Process in Questioning Household Consumption Practices', *Local Environment* 8, 1: 95–112.

Lamont, M., and V. Molnar. 2002. 'The Study of Boundaries in the Social Sciences', *Annual Review of Sociology* 28: 167–95.

McAdam, D., S. Tarrow, and C. Tilly. 2001. *Dynamics of Contention*. Cambridge: Cambridge University Press.

Melucci, A. 1996. *Challenging Codes: Collective Action in the Information Age*. Cambridge: Cambridge University Press.

Putnam, R.D. 2000. *Bowling Alone: The Collapse and Revival of American Community*. New York: Simon & Schuster.

Snow, D.A., and D. McAdam. 2000. 'Identity Work Processes in the Context of Social Movements: Clarifying the Identity/Movement Nexus', *Self, Identity, and Social Movements*, S. Stryker, T.J. Owens, and R.W. White, eds. Minneapolis: University of Minnesota Press.

Taylor, V., and N.E. Whittier. 1992. 'Collective Identity in Social Movement Communities: Lesbian Feminist Mobilization', *Frontiers in Social Movement Theory*, A.D. Morris and C. McClurg Mueller, eds. New Haven: Yale University Press.

Questions for Critical Thought

Automobilization and Traffic Safety

1. Define automobility. How does neoliberalism support automobilization?
2. Describe the problems associated with current traffic safety promotion. How do these problems highlight changing individual behaviours rather than systems.
3. In what ways are groups challenging the automobilization of society (look, for example, at various websites)? How successful do you think they might be?
4. How does automobility privilege the rights of motorists over other road users?
5. As an approach to governance, neoliberalism disables society's ability to address comprehensively social problems such as traffic safety. How far do you agree or disagree with this statement?

Dealing with Toxicity in the Risk Society: The Case of the Hamilton, Ontario Plastic Recycling Fire

1. Technical rationality should be the only criterion in determining risk. How far do you agree with the statement?
2. What is the difference between technical rationality and cultural rationality?
3. A comprehensive understanding of risk in society depends on the social constructionist approach. Discuss.

4. Explain the following concepts as used in understanding risk in society: cultural rationality, technical rationality, risk communication, and risk society conceptualization.

5. How true is the statement that risk society conceptualization and the risk communication perspective downplay both the cultural dimensions of risk conflict as well as the political-economic aspects of risk management?

Constructing Environmental Identity: The Constraints of Power and Common Sense

1. How have social institutions, including those associated with the economy, science and technology, and politics changed in response to increasing environmental awareness?

2. In what sense can it be said that today we live in a risk society?

3. Does **sustainable development** represent a fundamental alteration of the relationship between society and nature? Explain.

4. What is the radical environmentalist critique of sustainable development? What do they propose as an alternative?

5. What impediments exist to the development of environmentally reflexive beliefs, values, perceptions, and identity?

Collective Identity in the Sustainable Consumption Movement: The Case of Cool Communities

1. What is sustainable consumption? How did the environmentalists practice sustainable consumption in their own lives? How did they encourage others to become sustainable consumers?

2. Were the environmental organizations' distinguishing and broadening identities contradictory, complementary, or both?

3. What kinds of social movements have both distinguishing and broadening collective identities? What kinds of social movements do not?

4. With reference to the Australian Environment Organizations (AEOs), assess the effectiveness of sustainable consumption movements towards environmental consciousness.

5. Environmental movements render a critical role in developing and sustaining environmental consciousness. Evaluate this statement in the light of an environmental movement in Canada.

Glossary

Aboriginal Canadians: Indigenous people recognized in the Canadian Constitution Act, 1982, section 25 and 35, respectively as Indians (First Nations), Métis, and Inuit.

Accent: A manner of pronunciation.

African immigrant women: Refers to women who have migrated from African countries to Canada. There are various categories of these women; some are currently Canadian citizens, permanent residents, temporary immigrants, and refugees.

Ageism: Refers to a set of ideas, attitudes, and practices based on a negative view of older people. Prejudice and discrimination against the old is common in highly developed societies such as Canada and the United States.

Ageless self: A sense of self without a sense of age; more of a focus on the idea of continuity.

Applied sociology: The branch of sociology that deals with the application of sociological knowledge and research methods to various areas of inquiry such as policy studies, evaluation research, social statistics, democratic processes, or human-environment interaction.

Assimilation: Refers to the 'decline of an ethnic distinction and its corollary cultural and social differences'. 'Decline' in this context means that a distinction attenuates in salience, that the occurrences for which it is relevant diminish in number and contract to fewer and fewer domains of social life.

Authority: Power that people accept as legitimate rather than coercive.

Automobilization: A process by which the automobile as a mass-consumption commodity has profoundly altered many aspects of social existence for all strata of society

Bad mother: Refers to a mother who for some reason(s) fails to keep to the motherhood myth of being a 'perfect mother'. She is perceived as not being devoted to her children and to the traditional roles associated with femininity such as nurturing, softness, and intimacy.

Basic instrumental activities of daily living (ADL): Activities of personal care performed by an individual on a daily basis, including bathing, mobility, and eating.

Biomedical knowledge: Expertise in the application of the principles of the natural sciences—especially biology and physiology—to clinical medicine.

Black community: A place in a town or city where black people predominate.

Boomerang kid: Young adult (typically aged 19–35) who returns to live in the parental home for four or more months after an initial departure of four or more months.

Boundaries: Constitute social distinctions that individuals make in their everyday lives that shape their actions and mental orientations towards others.

Boundary-spanning communication: Communication with one or more persons who are located outside of the primary group of interest.

Building Hope Coalition: An attempt geared towards community-centred sustainable responses to the crisis that have engulfed the black community of Toronto, Canada. The objective is to seek community specific alternatives to mainstream institutional responses to the violence characterizing the community.

Canadian Charter of Rights and Freedoms: Seeks to protect individual rights and freedoms. The Charter expresses fundamental laws that help build the kind of community Canadians would like to enjoy.

Capitalist mode of production: An economic system based on private legal ownership of major means of production and primary use of hired workers to make and sell commodities in competitive markets to generate profits for owners.

Cartesian mind/body duality/dualism: An idea of philosopher/mathematician Rene Descartes in which he defined the mind as independent of the body and physical laws.

Caste: Hereditary social status in society, which is often linked with ideas of spiritual purity and socioeconomic stratification. In Hindu Indian society, movement and marriage between castes are not acceptable.

Chicago School: A tradition of sociology associated with the University of Chicago for the first four decades of the twentieth century. The tradition emphasized the direct observation of experience and the analysis of urban social processes. Chicago sociology was committed to direct fieldwork and empirical study in contrast to some of the more abstract, systematizing and theoretical tendencies of many early North American sociologists.

Chinese immigrants: Individuals who have migrated from China to Canada; most are currently Canadian citizens or permanent residents.

Chronic pain treatment: Medical therapy aimed at addressing pain associated with actual or potential tissue damage that continues for three months or longer.

Class: The relative location of a person or group within a larger society, based on wealth, power, prestige, or other valued resources.

Closed labour market: A labour market in which jobs are tightly linked to qualifications. Jobs are filled primarily by people who have specific and narrowly defined education, credentials or job experience that prepare them specifically or particularly for these occupations.

Coefficient: A number used to indicate the strength of a relationship between two variables.

Cohort: A group of people that share a common starting point, for example, people who were born in the same decade, started school at the same time, or who migrated in the same year. The baby boom cohort, for example, is composed of people who were born in the twenty years following the Second World War.

Collaborative or more egalitarian model: Both partners do the same amount of unpaid work.

Collective identity: The sense of self that is held by a group in which individuals bond together and separate themselves from others through shared values and ideologies.

Collective memory: Refers to narratives that are shared, supported, articulated, and rearticulated by social groups.

Colonial theory: Adds to social-construction approaches by accounting for social conceptualizations of race based on historical relations among different racial and ethnic groups.

Community resilience: The capacity to respond to ongoing economic and social changes in positive and constructive ways.

Complementary and alternative medicine: A group of diverse medical and health care practices that are yet to be accredited as conventional medicine.

Complex emergencies: Ways of differentiating situations where armed conflicts and political instability are the principal causes of humanitarian needs from those where natural hazards are the principal causes of such needs.

Computer mediated communication (CMC): Any form of communication between two or more people via the Internet or a network connection.

Counterculture: A cultural group whose norms, values, and lifestyle are contrary to that of the social mainstream.

Criminal activity: An act committed in violation of a law and for which possible penalties could be meted out to the culprit.

Criminology: Sub-field of sociology that studies crimes, criminal behaviour, and law enforcement.

Critical trust: Involves a high level of general trust coupled with a high level of scepticism.

Cross-sectional survey: A study where a large group (or groups) of individuals is collected into a single sample and studied at the same point in time.

Cultural capital: Skills, knowledge, and education that lead to higher status in society.

Cultural tourism: Tourism motivated by a desire to experience the history, folklore, social, or artistic culture of another region.

Culture: The sum total of the human-produced environment (the objects, artifacts, ideas, beliefs, and values that make up the symbolic and learned aspects of human society) as separate from the natural environment. More often, the term refers to the norms, values, beliefs, ideas, and meanings of a society.

Democracy: A form of government in which the citizens have a vote or voice in shaping policy.

Dependency: One partner relies upon the other economically.

Deviance: Behaviour that is at odds with social norms.

Diaspora: A dispersion of people throughout the world.

Disability: Refers to the social effects of physical, emotional, or mental impairment. This definition, known as the 'social model' of disability, makes a clear distinction between the impairment itself (such as a medical condition that makes a person unable to walk or unable to sit) and the disabling effects of society in relation to that impairment.

Disaster management: A discipline that involves avoiding risk, and also preparing, supporting, and rebuilding society in the wake of natural or unnatural disasters.

Discourse: The study of language, its structure, functions, and patterns in use through conversations, texts, and other audiovisual representations.

Discourse of motherhood: Social discussions on the roles of mothers in contemporary society.

Double burden model: One partner does the same amount (or even more) paid work, and more unpaid work.

Double day/second shift: Working in the marketplace while retaining responsibility for work done in the home.

Dowry: Marriage or property provided by a bride's family upon her marriage to help obtain a suitable husband and to be used by her in case of divorce or widowhood.

Duality: The quality or character of being two-sided.

Ecological fallacy: Refers to instances where it is falsely assumed that conclusions drawn from large group data are equally applicable to individuals. Furlong and Cartmel (1997) use this concept to suggest that while we think that inequality has been individualized, social structure (or structural determinants) continue to affect people's life paths.

Economic characteristics: Indicators used in measuring changing economic conditions.

Economic integration: The ability of an immigrant or immigrant group to attain occupational, educational, and income equality relative to the native-born population.

Education: The social institution responsible for the systematic transmission of knowledge, skills, and cultural values within a formally organized structure.

Empirical studies: Research that uses verifiable evidence from observation, not just theory.

Endogamy is the practice of marrying someone belonging to one's own social group or ethnic community.

Environmental consciousness: An awareness of the impact of humans on the environment, at both an individual and a corporate level.

Epidemic: A disease that appears as new cases in a given human population, during a given period, at a rate that substantially exceeds what is 'expected'.

Epistemology: The study of how we understand and perceive knowledge.

Essential self: The constant core of the identity over time, even though the body and mind might change.

Ethnocentric beliefs: Beliefs about the world from the perspective of one's ethnic group.

Ethnographic approach: The study of a way of life of a group of people. The primary methodologies are observation, participant observation, and extended open-ended interviewing.

Family ties: The relationship existing among a group of people based on kinship.

Feminist/feminism: Theoretical paradigm that focuses on the social construction and consequences of gender inequality.

Feminist scholar: An academic of Feminism, a theoretical paradigm that focuses on social constructions of gender and inequality between the sexes.

Financial compensation: Money given or received as payment for a service or loss or injury.

Focus groups: A qualitative method of data collection that involves interactive discussion among a small number of people.

Framing: The interpretation human beings offer to everyday life in order to comprehend and respond to social phenomena.

Gender: Socially determined set of qualities and behaviours expected from males and females.

Gender domesticity: The interrelationship between men and women in the context of their home life activities.

Gender identity: The gender an individual identifies with, or that which others ascribe to an individual.

Gender role: The expression of an individual's gender identity by attitude or behaviour.

General Theory: Based on the idea that crime is committed by people who have low self-control who do not consider long-term consequences.

Generalizable: The ability to assume or infer something about a population based on specific observations found in the sample (the ability to make judgments about a larger group based on observations of a smaller one). The ability to do this is limited, depending upon how a sample is selected.

Generic social processes (GSPs): Activity-related concepts (e.g., developing identities, managing relationships) that have transsituational or trans-contextual relevance. These processes enable comparisons across different substantive contexts (e.g., consider the generic features of relationships among dating couples, doctors and patients, parents and children, etc.).

Globalization: A complex series of economic, social, technological, cultural, and political changes associated with the increasing interdependence, integration, and interaction between people and companies in disparate locations.

Glocalization: A strategy that empowers local communities by linking them to global resources and knowledge while facilitating initiatives for peace and development. It provides opportunities for the local communities to direct positive social change in the areas that most directly affect them, and to shape an innovative and more equitable international system.

Good mother: Refers to the mother who adheres to the motherhood myth of being a 'perfect mother'. She must be completely devoted not just to her children, but also to her role and she must embody all the qualities traditionally associated with femininity such as nurturing, softness, and intimacy.

Governance of health: The deployment of agents of governance to regulate the social space of individuals regarding health decisions/choices through the creation of public health campaigns and ensuring their actualization.

Health care system: A variety of organizations and structures delivering health care, encompassing health sector categorization and linkages based on the core functions (financing, provision of inputs, and service delivery/coverage), main actors (government and consumers), and outcomes (health, fairness in financing, and responsiveness).

Health discourse: Refers to an ordering system, or system of representation, that organizes how health issues and concerns can be meaningfully discussed and articulated.

Hegemonic ideology (hegemony): The phenomenon where a social class, state, or nation exerts dominance or power over other levels of government through the control of ideological and material production.

Hierarchy: Categorization of groups of people according to ability or to economic, social, or professional standing.

Human capital: The economic value that is derived from the actual application of knowledge, collaboration, and process-management.

Human rights movements: Functions to protect the rights considered to be justifiably belonging to people.

Hyperconnectivity: Very frequent communication among two or more individuals due to their constant availability anywhere, anytime using a wide range of media.

Identity: The way in which the individual views him- or herself, or the ways in which others view the individual.

Ideology: The way in which a group views and makes sense out of the world that serves to justify the existence of the group and its accompanying values and beliefs.

Image-oriented policing: Policing and security that is driven by the logic of maintaining images through the regulation of signs of disorder; usually tied to the policing of particular locations, such a business districts or quasi-public spaces such as malls or hotels.

Immigration: People moving into a country over a give period of time

Individualization theory: A position that argues that the late twentieth century has seen a shift towards individual life paths, risks, and responsibilities with the dismantling of community ties and rigid gender and economic expectations. Young people must no longer directly follow in the footsteps of their parents, for instance. Individualization theorists argue that people's experiences of risk, including inequality, have also been individualized: we experience our lives as fraught with potential dangers and we hold ourselves individually responsible for avoiding or dealing with them.

Institutional Ethnography: A method of inquiry that allows people to explore the social relations that structure their every day lives by emphasizing connections among the sites and situations of everyday life, professional practice, and policy making.

Institutional racism: Discrimination that is formally sanctioned by the state.

Institutional Theory: Attends to the deeper and more resilient aspects of social structure and considers the processes by which structures, rules, norms, and routines, become established as authoritative guidelines for social behaviour.

Institutional trust: Trust is formed through formal procedural and legal arrangements. Within small group settings, these arrangements may involve specific 'rules of the game' that allow individuals to feel safe and to voice their views in spite of distrustful relations between certain individuals.

Instrumental activities of daily living (IADL): More complex activities important for independent living, including housework, shopping, and managing personal finances.

Integration: A process by which an immigrant, or immigrant group, takes on the customs, values, and social attributes of his or her host society while simultaneously maintaining a distinct ethnic identity.

Intergenerational relations: Family relationships and patterns of support that exist among the generations, such as between midlife parents and their young adult children.

Interpersonal trust: Trust is formed on the basis of familiarity and direct contact with other individuals.

Knowledge management: A recently emergent organizational practice and field of study focussing on the identification, control, and retention of 'intellectual capital', strategic knowledge held by employees.

Knowledge production: How information is produced and controlled in society; research is almost always influenced by the politics of funding and the politics of the organization.

Knowledge worker: Term used broadly, and often ambiguously, to denote highly credentialed employees who possess economically useful, theoretical knowledge in scientific, technical, and/or professional fields. Some have restricted the definition to emerging technologically sophisticated sectors; many theorists are expanding the definition to include highly educated workers in all sectors.

Laissez-faire: An economic doctrine that opposes governmental intervention in the economy and advocates a free market where prices are determined by unregulated competition among producers for customers.

Life course: Socially structured by transitions and processes of age-grading, such as when to leave home and marry, and varies across time and location in response to changing demographic, cultural, socioeconomic, and political environments.

Life stage: Examination of the life course in the social sciences by focusing on the successive stages that people pass through from birth to death, with each stage framed in terms of associated physiological, psychological and/or social patterns. Scholars may also examine transitions from one stage to the next, such as leaving school or starting a job.

Linked lives: Relates to the fact that lives are not lived in isolation, but are experienced interdependently such that our actions are shaped by, and shape the actions of, those to whom we are closely connected.

Local communities: Geographically defined communities with groups of people living close to each other.

Malaria: Life-threatening parasitic disease transmitted by mosquitoes.

Managerial perspective: Promotes, in universities, cost-efficiency and applied knowledge in place of a scholarly pursuit of truth guided by universal values.

Mandatory retirement: A rule governing workplace relations that provides for the forced removal of employees at a predetermined age, usually age 65; also called institutionalized ageism.

Marxism: The political and social theory based on the works of Karl Marx and Friedrich Engels. Marxism stresses the exploitative effects, such as inequality of wealth, produced by the capitalistic economic system.

Mask of aging: The changes imposed by aging on the physical body, which are often seen as being separate from the self.

Master narratives: An ideological system that asserts it has all the answers.

Mean: A measure of the central value of a frequency or distribution. The mean is calculated by summing all the values and dividing by the number of values, in order to obtain the average.

Mega-events: High profile, one-time events of a limited duration hosted by a city that receives global media attention. Mega-events typically circulate amongst host cities rather than recurring at the same city multiple times. The Calgary Stampede, for example, is not a mega-event. The frequency of a mega-event is often determined by a fixed schedule, such as the four-year cycle of the Winter and Summer Olympic Games.

Mega-security: Security systems at short-term, high-profile urban mega-events where the intensive security needs generated by the event far outstrips that which can be provided locally and which thus require additional security resources drawn from outside and often specialized resources.

Menopause: The end of a woman's menstruation and menstrual cycles.

Minority population: A group that does not belong to the dominant population of a given society. A sociological minority is not necessarily a numerical minority—it may include any group that is disadvantaged with respect to a dominant group in terms of social status, education, employment, wealth, and political power.

Modernization theory: Theory emphasizing that positive change in social conditions is related to the modernization of attitudes and beliefs.

Moral panic: An overreaction of the community, mass media, and government to a disturbance which is, in reality, much more minor than how it is portrayed.

Multivariate analysis: Considers the simultaneous effects of many independent variables together on a dependent variable.

Narrative: Another word for 'story'. A narrative usually follows a sequence of events from initial calm through ensuing conflict to eventual climax, conclusion and (once more) calm.

National Occupational Classification (NOC): A standardized framework for organizing the world of work in a manageable, understandable, and coherent system. It is produced by the Department of Human Resources and Skills Development and is based on extensive occupational research, analysis, and consultation conducted across the country, reflecting the changes in the Canadian labour market.

National security: Canadian national security deals with threats that have the potential to undermine the security of the state or society; it is closely linked to both personal and international security.

Neo-traditionalism: A revival of traditional styles and customs.

Network: Individuals (or more rarely, collectivities and roles) who are linked together by one or more social relationships (e.g., friendship and kinship).

Non-Aboriginal Canadians: Refers to Canadians who are not of Aboriginal ancestry.

Non-Governmental Organizations (NGOs): Private or non-profit organizations that are not affiliated with a governmental body or institution.

Non-probability sample: A self-selected sample that does not ensure that each element in the population has an equal probability of being included. A probability sample, also referred to as a random sample, ensures that each element in the population has an equal probability of being included.

Norm: Shared expectation of behaviour that reflects what is considered culturally desirable and appropriate. Norms are similar to rules or regulations because they are prescriptive, but they lack the formal status of rules.

Normativity: Activity consistent with socially constructed norms.

Occupational prestige: Socioeconomic stratification system; the social esteem attributed to a certain occupation that influences an individual's social status.

One-drop rule: Needs more explanation than is provided on the first page and a marginal definition would help provide the necessary explanation.

Open labour market: A labour market in which jobs and qualifications are loosely linked. Jobs are filled by people who come from a broad variety of backgrounds and whose education, credentials, and previous experience prepare them for a broad variety of occupations.

Open-ended interviews: Interview that allows the subject to direct the path of the discussion through questions without a set of specific answers.

Outcomes: Results or visible effects of an intervention or a programme.

Out-marriage: The practice of marrying someone not belonging to one's own social group or ethnic community. This is also referred to as exogamy.

Panopticon: Architectural design proposed by Jeremy Bentham as a means to reform the eighteenth century English prison system. Inmates could be watched constantly (or not) by prison guards standing behind semi-closed blinds on a centralized observation deck surrounded by a circular housing of cells. That prisoners did not know if they were being gazed upon induced in them a state of conscious and permanent visibility that assured the automatic functioning of power.

Partial regression coefficient (ß): Represents the independent effect of an independent variable on the dependent variable, controlling for (that is, removing the linear effect of) the other independent variables.

Participant observation: A research method that involves acquiring observational data by directly participating in the real-life settings of the group being studied. By interacting with group members and participating in aspects of their everyday lives, the researcher seeks to acquire an intimate understanding of how the subjects define their life-worlds. The researcher's goal is to offer a fine-grained description and analysis of the experiences, behaviours, and perspectives of those being observed.

Patrilocal multigenerational family: After marriage, the wife lives in her husband's household, near or with the husband's kin and extended family.

People with disability: The phrase 'people with disabilities' has been in circulation since at least the 1970s, but until the 1990s such phraseology was one of a number of ways to make reference to disabled people (see, for example, Canada, 1981). Since sometime after the 1983 International Year of the Disabled, these various expressions of disability have been supplanted almost entirely by 'people-first' phraseology (see, for example, Human Resources Development Canada, 1995; Canada, 1996; 1998).

People-first language: A new way of thinking about people with disabilities. People-first language puts the person before the disability, and it describes what a person has, not who a person is. If people with disabilities are to be included in all aspects of society, language that sets them apart and devalues them should never be used.

Pilot study: A small-scale study used to test preliminary versions of a measure, explore new ground, and prepare for future research in an area.

Political cartoons: A form of satirical journalism and a type of visual opinion news discourse

Political graffiti: Drawings or scribbles on a flat surface for political purposes.

Population statistics: Related to demography; statistics are used to analyze population changes or trends.

Post-industrialism: An understanding of the economic and political context of North American and Western European countries in the late twentieth century (largely from the 1970s onwards) that points to the declining reliance of society upon industrial production and the increasing reliance upon knowledge- and service-based forms of production as indicative of a new era of capitalism.

Poverty: The state of being poor; want of the necessities (basic needs) of life.

Power-control theory: Based on the idea that parental occupations affect patriarchal attitudes in the home, and thus the level of control placed on girls versus boys. The level of control determines the chance of children taking risks and being deviant.

Primary sector: The sector of the economy (including agriculture, fishing, mining, and lumber) concerned with the production and extraction of raw materials.

Problematization: The making of claims to harm or danger associated with certain behaviours, presented in forms that constitute those behaviours as 'social problems' and render them objects for regulation.

Professionalization process: The social process by which any trade or occupation transforms itself into a true profession; tends to involve establishing acceptable qualifications, a professional body or association to oversee the conduct of members of the profession, and some degree of demarcation of the qualified from unqualified individuals.

Punishment: An action designed to deprive a person of things of value (including liberty) because of some offence the person is thought to have committed.

Qualitative interviews: A research technique that allows the researcher to pursue issues in depth and gives the respondent freedom to direct the flow of the conversation.

Questionnaire: A quantitative method of data collection that employs a set of questions posed to a large number of people.

Real-time: A term used to refer to numerous computer features that operate immediately and that can respond to information immediately. Real time operating systems, for instance, respond to information input immediately. Real-time can also refer to events simulated by a computer at the same speed that they would occur in real life.

Recent immigrant: Defined in this chapter as one who migrated to Canada in the five years preceding the census.

Reflexive sociology: A sociological theory that aims for a study of the sociologist himself or herself. It is based on the idea that knowledge is filtered through the researcher's own concepts of the world.

Reflexivity: Tendency of a thing, whether an individual or an institution, to be directed back to itself in a manner that influences how it exists.

Regression analysis: Statistical calculation to determine relationship trends between two variables.

Responsibilization: Refers to a recent neo-liberal strategy of government, where there are attempts to broaden state agencies by linking them to agencies in the private sector and in the community, thereby extending the control of the state and increasing cost-efficiency.

Rise of the primary individual: Refers to the increasing tendency for individuals (e.g., widows, non-married) to live alone as heads of households or in households containing non-relatives.

Risk: Choices with respect to economic ends (such as investment and profit) are always uncertain because knowledge of the situation is imperfect.

Risk society: A society in which perception of risk is extremely important. This perception causes insecurity among citizens and propels them to seek strategies of reducing the perceived risk.

Roles: Characteristics and expected social behaviours associated with professions, gender, etc.

Sample: The cases studied from the population.

Satisfice: Satisfaction is possible in both the home and workplace with the sacrifice of some initial goals or hopes in these parts of their lives; professional occupations often allow women to do this.

Scientific management: An approach to the management of industrial production that attempted to centralize production knowledge, thereby allowing owners/managers to increase productivity and reduce labour costs.

Second-generation migrants: Individuals who were born in Canada, or migrated to Canada during their elementary school years, and who have one or more foreign-born parent(s).

Self: A state in which the body and the conscious mind function together to create a constantly changing sense of identity.

Self-employment: The self-employed individual is not an employee of another person or organization; he or she runs his or her own business to generate income.

Service sector: The sector of the economy that provides personal or business services. It is also known as the tertiary sector.

Settlement: Sociologists do not have a consensus definition for settlement. It could refer to the initial settlement of immigrants who just arrived in their new host countries. Some refer it to a process of social and economic adaptation and assimilation. This process could also include the concept of permanent settlement in which immigrants make their host countries as their homes.

Sex: Conventionally, it refers to biological characteristics of a person that indicate whether one is female or male. However, in some cases it refers to the act of sexual intercourse.

Sexual dysfunction: Persistent or recurrent inability to react emotionally or physically to sexual stimulation in a way expected of the average healthy person or according to one's own standards of acceptable sexual response.

Sexual health: A state of physical, emotional, mental, and social well-being related to sexuality; it is not merely the absence of disease, dysfunction or infirmity. Sexual health requires a positive and respectful approach to sexuality and sexual relationships, as well as the possibility of having pleasurable and safe sexual experiences, free of coercion, discrimination, and violence.

Sexuality education: A lifelong process of acquiring information and forming attitudes, beliefs, and values about identity, relationships, and intimacy; it is more than teaching young people about anatomy and the physiology of reproduction. It encompasses sexual development, reproductive health, interpersonal relationships, affection, intimacy, body image, and gender roles. Parents, peers, schools, religion, the media, friends, and partners all influence the way people learn about sexuality.

Situated knowledge: What an individual knows about a topic gathered from ideas within the local setting as embedded within the globalized world.

Snowball sample: A non-probability sampling method often employed in field research whereby each person interviewed may be asked to suggest additional people for interviewing. The sample size grows as the study progresses, like a snowball rolling down a hill.

Social capital: Resources potentially accessible to an individual because of that individual's connections to others.

Social cohesion: How connected, united, cooperative, and trustful people are of each other.

Social construction theory: Individuals define themselves according to the ideas and beliefs of the group to which they claim membership.

Social context: The situation surrounding individuals' or groups' actions and behaviours; determines how an act or behaviour is viewed.

Social control: Social mechanisms that regulate individual and group behaviour, in terms of greater sanctions and rewards. Informal social control is exercised by a society without explicitly stating these rules.

Social disorganization theory: When a community is unable to conform to common values and to solve the problems of its residents, delinquency may arise.

Social exclusion: Refers to exclusion from labour markets and employment, and to the exclusion from social benefits of full citizenship. It includes those social benefits and entitlements that are funded or provided by governments that are supposedly available to, and in some cases required of, all citizens, such as social welfare, health and education.

Social network: A social structure between actors, mostly individuals or organizations, who are linked together by one or more types of interdependencies.

Social responsibility: Claim that an entity whether it is state, government, corporation, organization, or individual has an obligation to society. This obligation can be 'negative,' in that it is an obligation to refrain from acting, or it can be 'positive,' meaning an obligation to act.

Social solidarity: Integration, and degree or type of integration, manifested by a society or group.

Socialization: Process by which individuals internalize and adapt to norms of their societies. This is a two-stage process that includes primary socialization and secondary socialization.

Socioeconomic status (SES): Social status or prestige based on various factors, including education, income, and occupation.

Staged authenticity: Performances in which history and culture are represented and sold for profit.

State socialism: A socio-economic system prevalent in Eastern Europe and the Soviet Union until 1989, characterized by state ownership over the means of production, significant governmental control of the market, and significant status/income inequalities.

Stereotype: Assumptions of what people are like, based on previous associations with them or with people who have similar characteristics, whether true or false.

Street youth: Youth who seek their livelihood from engaging mainly in illicit businesses on the street.

Structural contradictions: The ways in which societal structures may exert pressures in opposing directions; for example, increasingly women are expected to contribute to their families in terms of earned income but the very process of earning income undermines their abilities to fulfil other family responsibilities.

Structured ambivalence: Describes the uneasy compromises that are embedded in our societal arrangements; for example, the compromises between caring and paid work, which are created by contemporary societal structures underlying employment and family life.

Subculture: As defined by Prus (1997) a subculture is 'a set of interactionally linked people characterized by some sense of distinctiveness (outsider and insider definitions) within the broader community' (41).

Succession question: Refers to the process of replacing an older generation of university teachers with younger scholars. This change may create conflict as new entrants challenge the principles and practices of experienced scholars and attempt to take their place in the university power structure.

Supreme Court of Canada: Provides the ultimate interpretation of individual rights protected under the Charter of Rights and Freedoms.

Surplus population: Related to Marx's 'reserve army of labour'; a characteristic of capitalistic demography made up of the temporarily unemployed, the sector of society that has not yet been integrated into production, and the people who cannot or will not pursue legal labour.

Sustainable consumption: A movement to inspire a cultural shift in which all individuals will choose to consume in environmentally and socially responsible ways.

Sustainable development: Development that meets the needs of the present and maintains a balanced social, economic, and environmental system, without compromising the ability of future generations to meet their own needs.

Symbolic interactionist: A sociological approach to the study of human group life that emphasizes the centrality of activity, language, and human interchange. This perspective builds on the pragmatist philosophy with an emphasis on community, self, and reflective activity and it relies on ethnographic research.

Synchronous communication: Communication that is occurring instantaneously, without time delay.

Synopticon: The idea that, through forms of mass media communication, the traditionally-conceived surveillance relationship between 'the watcher' and 'the watched' is reversed, so that there is now an increased monitoring of elites and their extravagance but also a greater mediatization of crime, inflating the perceived need to implement surveillance.

Systems theory: Also known as systemics, this theory studies both unified whole and self-organizing systems. The relationships in a system, or community, are interdependent and interactional. A society is more than the sum of all its members.

Temporality: Condition of being bounded in time.

Toxicity: The degree to which something is toxic or poisonous.

Traditional or complementary role model: One partner does more paid work and the other more unpaid work.

Traffic safety: Refers to measures institutionalized to reduce the harm (deaths, injuries, and property damage) resulting from crashes of road vehicles traveling on public roads.

Transformation: A significant change of a society. Various aspects of change (e.g. economic, political, and cultural) may not be coordinated, and the end result of the transformation cannot be predicted with certainty.

Transition: A unidirectional, irreversible, and predictable change from one known social form to another.

Transnational identities: The construction of self developed through a series of material and symbolic flows across national borders.

Transnational social field: The border-spanning arena that is formed by the relationships that tie individuals to one another across national borders and which allow individuals the option to remain actively involved in both nation-states.

Transnational ties: A network of relationships and interactions linking people or institutions across national borders.

Tupperware: In North America it consists of two types of products: kitchenware and toys for children. The kitchenware usually serves to store food or to serve it, and often does both. The toys comprise a much smaller range of goods. A glance at the catalogue indicates that there has been significant change in Tupperware's offerings since the 1950s to keep up with advances in kitchen technology, but that the scope of the product has remained dedicated to kitchen and children.

Two-worlds thesis: The idea that immigrants are caught between two worlds: their homeland and their host country.

Unemployment: State of not working. Generally, individuals in this state are willing to work at a prevailing wage rate yet they are unable to find a paying job.

Violence: Use of aggressive physical force.

Vocabulary of motive: Rationalizations and accounts used to explain or justify one's situation or actions.

Welfare: System whereby the state undertakes to protect the health and well-being of its citizens—especially those in financial need—by means of grants, pensions, etc.

Women's inequality: Structural discrimination of women as individuals or social group.

Women's roles: Socially constructed activities expected of women.

Work–family balance: Refers to the efforts by women and men in contemporary Canadian society to find a manageable combination of paid work obligations and time devoted to family responsibilities.

Workfare: A welfare system that requires some work or training from those receiving benefits.

Workplace: Refers to a place at which a person works, such as an office, factory, etc.

Workplace accommodation: Steps put in place to take care of the interests of all individuals at a workplace irrespective of one's situation.

World system: An account of the transnational development of capitalism and a theory of the global structure of inequality among nations.

Worldview: The structure of beliefs, attitudes, and values through which individuals and groups understand and interpret the world around them.

Xiao: Filial piety, a Confucian concept encompassing a broad range of beliefs and behaviours including children's respect, obedience, loyalty, material provision, and physical care to parents.

Young people: Individuals not far advanced in life.

Acknowledgements

Richard Alba, 'Immigrant–Native Boundaries in North America and Western Europe'. Excerpted and reprinted by permission of the author.

Patrizia Albanese, 'Quebec's $7/day Childcare: Some Preliminary Findings'. Extracted and reprinted by permission of the author. This project has been funded by the Ryerson New Faculty SRC Development Fund (2004–2006). It appears in a longer version in the CRSA (May 2006).

Libby Alexander, ' "They should make it more normal": Young People's Critical Standpoints and the Social Organization of Sexuality Education'. Excerpted and reprinted by permission of the author.

S. Harris Ali, 'Dealing with Toxicity in the Risk Society: The Case of the Hamilton, Ontario Plastic Recycling Fire', Canadian Review of Sociology and Anthropology 39, 1 (2001): 29–49. This paper has been both edited to suit the purpose of this publication and reprinted with permission from the CRSA.

Paul Anisef and Kelli Phythian, 'Rising Low-Income Rates and the Adaptation of Canadian Immigrant Youth'. Excerpted and reprinted by permission of the authors.

A. Bruce Arai, 'Self-Employment as a Response to the Double-Day for Women and Men in Canada', Canadian Review of Sociology and Anthropology 3, 2 (2000): 125–42. This paper has been both edited to suit the purpose of this publication and reprinted with permission from the CRSA.

Michael Atkinson, 'Tattooing and Civilizing Processes: Body Modification as Self-control', Canadian Review of Sociology and Anthropology 41, 2 (2004): 125–46. This paper has been both edited to suit the purpose of this publication and reprinted with permission from the CRSA.

Janice Aurini, 'Crafting Legitimation Projects: An Institutional Analysis of Private Education Businesses'. Excerpted and reprinted by permission of the author. Janice Aurini's project was generously supported by a Social Science and Humanities Doctoral Fellowship.

Stephen Baron, 'Street Youth Labour Market Experiences and Crime', Canadian Review of Sociology and Anthropology 38, 2 (2001): 189–216. This paper has been both edited to suit the purpose of this publication and reprinted with permission from the CRSA.

Christie Barron and Dany Lacombe, 'Moral Panic and the Nasty Girl', Canadian Review of Sociology and Anthropology 42, 1 (2005): 51–69. This paper has been both edited to suit the purpose of this publication and reprinted with permission from the CRSA.

Brenda L. Beagan, ' "Even if I don't know what I'm doing, I can make it look like I know what I'm doing': Becoming a Doctor in the 1990s'.

Roderic Beaujot, 'Earning and Caring', excerpted from the Porter Lecture on Families. Excerpted and reprinted by permission of the author.

Philip Boyle, 'Mega-security: Concepts and Context for Olympic-sized Security Networks'. Excerpted and reprinted by permission of the author.

Craig Calhoun, 'A World of Emergencies: Fear, Intervention, and the Limits of Cosmopolitan Order', Canadian Review of Sociology and Anthropology 41, 4 (2004): 373–93. This paper has been both edited to suit the purpose of this publication and reprinted with permission from the CRSA.

Tara Carnochan, 'Short-Changed: Media Representations of Squeegeeing and Panhandling'. Excerpted and reprinted by permission of the author.

Neena L. Chappell, 'Aging among Chinese Canadian Immigrants—Reflections'. Excerpted and reprinted by permission of the author.

Laura Hurd Clarke, 'Older Women's Bodies and the Self: The Construction of Identity in Later Life', Canadian Review of Sociology and Anthropology 38, 4 (2001): 441–64. This paper has been both edited to suit the purpose of this publication and reprinted with permission from the CRSA.

Gillian Creese and Edith Ngene Kambere, 'What Colour is Your English?', Canadian Review of Sociology and Anthropology 40, 5 (2003): 565–73. This paper has been both edited to suit the purpose of this publication and reprinted with permission from the CRSA.

Bruce Curtis, 'Reading Reflexively'. Excerpted and reprinted by permission of Blackwell Publishing.

Seigrid Deutschlander and Leslie J. Miller, 'Politicizing Aboriginal Cultural Tourism: The Discourse of Primitivism in the Tourist Encounter', Canadian Review of Sociology and Anthropology 40, 1 (2003): 27–44. This paper has been both edited to suit the purpose of this publication and reprinted with permission from the CRSA.

J.L. Deveau, 'Workplace Accommodation for the Disabled in the Federal Public Service: An Institutional Ethnography'. Excerpted and reprinted by permission of the author.

Ann Duffy, Nancy Mandell, Sue Wilson, 'Balancing Work and Caring: Midlife Women Assess their Accommodations'. Excerpted and reprinted by permission of the authors.

Margrit Eichler and Ann Matthews, 'What is Work? Looking at All Work through the Lens of Unpaid Housework'. Excerpted and reprinted by permission of the authors.

Kimberly-Anne Ford, 'Citizenship and Health: The Governance of "Imported Malaria" and the Safety of Anti-Malarial Drugs'. Excerpted and reprinted by permission of the author. Kimberly-Anne Ford, PhD, Carleton University.

Grace-Edward Galabuzi, 'Building Hope: Confronting Social Exclusion and Violence in Toronto's Black Community, 2001'. Extracted and reprinted by permission of the author.

Amber Gazso, 'Women's Inequality in the Workplace as Framed in News Discourse: Refracting from Gender Ideology'. Excerpted and reprinted by permission of the author.

John Goyder, Corinne Carter, Jaime Robinson, and Marina Korotkikh, 'What Can I Do With a Sociology Degree?' Society/Société November (2005): 83–91. This paper has been both edited to suit the purpose of this publication and reprinted with permission from the CRSA.

Josh Greenberg, 'Framing and Temporality in Political Cartoons: A Critical Analysis of Visual News Discourse', Canadian Review of Sociology and Anthropology 39, 2 (2002): 181–99. This paper has been both edited to suit the purpose of this publication and reprinted with permission from the CRSA.

Joanna C. Jacob, 'Gender, Crime, and Community: An Ecological Analysis of Youth Crime in Canada'. Excerpted and reprinted by permission of the author. I am grateful for the very helpful comments on earlier drafts provided by Peter Carrington, Jim Curtis, Augie Fleras, Jennifer Schulenberg, Jane Sprott, and Keith Warriner. Custom tabulations for the Concordance of Census Subdivisions and UCR Respondents for 1996, and for Youth Population by Gender for 1996-Annual Demographic Statistics, 2001 were created by the Canadian Centre for Justice Statistics (CCJS). I am also grateful to Lucie Ogrodnik and Gayatri Shankarraman for the interpretation of CCJS files. This research was supported by funding from the Social Sciences and Humanities Research Council (SSHRC) Fellowship No. 752-2004-1273, and by SSHRC Standard Grants Nos. 410-2000-0361 and 410-2004-2136.

Erin E. Armi Kaipainen, 'Thirty Thousand Calls for Justice: The Human Rights Movement, Political Graffiti, and the Struggles over Collective Memory in Argentina'. Excerpted and reprinted by permission of the author.

Nedim Karakayali, 'Duality and Diversity in the Lives of Immigrant Children: Rethinking the "Problem of the Second Generation" in Light of Immigrant Autobiographies', Canadian Review of Sociology and Anthropology 42, 3 (2005): 325–44. This paper has been both edited to suit the purpose of this publication and reprinted with permission from the CRSA.

Steven Kleinknecht, 'The Hacker Spirit: An Interactionist Analysis of the Hacker Ideology'. Excerpted and reprinted by permission of the author. The author would like to thank William Shaffir, Dorothy Pawluch, and Charlene Miall for their advice and guidance, as well as the participants who graciously shared their time talking about their passion, computer hacking.

Ivanka Knezevic, 'Post-Socialist Transition and Globalization: Academic Debates in Political Surroundings'. Excerpted and reprinted by permission of the author.

Erin Kruger, 'The Emerging Role of Information in Canada's Security Environment'. Excerpted and reprinted by permission of the author.

Gordon Laxer, 'Social Solidarity, Democracy, and Global Capitalism'. Extracted and reprinted by permission of the author.

Jo-Anne Lee, 'Poverty, Social Exclusion, and Racialized Girls and Young Women'. Excerpted and reprinted by permission of the author. Jo-Anne Lee is an associate professor in the department of Women's Studies at the University of Victoria.

Ho Hon Leung, 'The Sentiment of Settlement Experience among Some Chinese Immigrants in Small Towns'. Excerpted and reprinted by permission of the author. This paper is a result of a project funded by the Research Foundation of State University of New York. 1005795-25385

David Lewis, Kevin Brazil, and Paul Krueger, 'The Impact of Financial Compensation on Treatment Outcomes for Chronic Pain: A Test of the "Money Matters" Thesis'. Excerpted and reprinted by permission of the authors. Kevin Brazil is an Associate Professor in the Department of Clinical Epidermiology & Biostatistics at McMaster University. Paul Krueger, PhD, is a Senior Research Associate for St. Joseph's Health System Research Network, and an Assistant Professor in the Department of Clinical Epidemiology and Biostatistics, at McMaster University. David Lewis, PhD, Depts of Medicine and Family Medicine, McMaster University & Regional Geriatrics Program Central.

David MacGregor and Thomas R. Klassen, 'The Great Purge: Forced Retirement and the "Succession Question" in Canadian Sociology'. Excerpted and reprinted by permission of the authors. David MacGregor is a professor of Sociology, King's University College at the University of Western Ontario. Thomas R. Klassen is an associate professor in the Department of Political Science at York University.

Arlene Tigar McLaren, 'Automobilization and Traffic Safety'. Excerpted and reprinted by permission of the author.

Janet McLellan, 'Buddhism in the Multicultural Context of Toronto, Canada: Local Communities, Global Networks', excerpted from the Porter Lecutre on Buddhism in Canada. Excerpted and reprinted by permission of the author.

John F. Manzo and Monetta M. Bailey, 'On the Assimilation of Racial Stereotypes among Black Canadian Young Offenders', *Canadian Review of Sociology and Anthropology* 42, 3 (2005): 283–300. This paper has been both edited to suit the purpose of this publication and reprinted with permission from the CRSA.

Alexandra Marin, 'How Job Information Enters and Flows through Social Networks: The Role of Labour Market Characteristics and Tie Strength'. Excerpted and reprinted by permission of the author.

Barbara L. Marshall, 'An Epidemic in Search of a Disease: The Construction of Sexual Dysfunction as a Social Problem'. Excerpted and reprinted by permission of the author. Barbara L. Marshall, Department of Sociology, Trent University.

Ralph Matthews and Nathan Young, 'Globalization and "Repositioning" in Coastal British Columbia'. Excerpted and reprinted by permission of the authors.

Paul S. Maxim, Jerry P. White, Dan Beavon, and Paul C. Whitehead, 'Dispersion and Polarization of Income among Aboriginal and Non-Aboriginal Canadians', *Canadian Review of Sociology and Anthropology* 38, 4 (2001): 465–76. This paper has been both edited to suit the purpose of this publication and reprinted with permission from the CRSA.

Jacinthe Michaud, 'Feminist Representations of Women Living on Welfare: The Case of Workfare and the Erosion of Volunteer Time'. Excerpted and reprinted by permission of the author. Jacinthe Michaud, School of Women's Studies, York University.

Barbara A. Mitchell, 'The Pendulum of Family Change: Comparative Life Course Transitions of Young Adults'. Excerpted and reprinted by permission of the author. An earlier version of this paper was presented at the annual Canadian Sociology and Anthropology Association meeting at the University of Western Ontario, London, Ontario, on 1 June 2005.

M. Reza Nakhaie, Robert A Silverman, and Teresa C. LaGrange, 'Resistance to Education: Self-Control and Resistance to School', *Canadian Review of Sociology and Anthropology* 37, 4 (2000): 433–60. This paper has been both edited to suit the purpose of this publication and reprinted with permission from the CRSA.

Nancy S. Netting, 'Love- and Arranged-Marriage in India Today: Negotiating Adulthood'. Excerpted and reprinted by permission of the author.

Miriam Padolsky, 'Collective Identity in the Sustainable Consumption Movement: The Case of *Cool Communities*'. Excerpted and reprinted by permission of the author. This research was made possible by a grant from the University of California Pacific Rim Research Program.

Justin Page, 'Constructing Environmental Identity: The Constraints of Power and Common Sense'. Excerpted and reprinted by permission of the author.

Justin Page, Sandra Enns, Todd E. Malinick, and Ralph Matthews, 'Should I Stay or Should I Go? Investigating Resilience in British Columbia's Coastal Communities'. Excerpted and reprinted by permission of the authors.

John R. Parkins, 'The Distrustful Citizen: Theories and Observations from Small-group Settings'. Excerpted and reprinted by permission of the author.

Mary Patton, 'Analyzing Women's Situated Knowledge for Menopause Construction'. Excerpted and reprinted by permission of the author.

Robert Prus, 'Activities and Interdependencies in the Educational Process: An Interactionist Approach to

Student Ventures in Learning'. Excerpted and reprinted by permission of the author.

Anabel Quan-Haase, 'The Use of Communication Media: A Case Study of a High-Tech Organization'. Excerpted and reprinted by permission of the author. This paper was first presented at the Canadian Sociology and Anthropology Association in 2005 and is based on a paper published in: Quan-Haase, A., & Wellman, B. (2006). Hyperconnected net work. In C. Heckscher & P. Adler (Eds.), *Collaborative community in business and society*. London: Oxford University Press. Assistance was provided from the Alumni Research Awards Program, Faculty of Social Science, The University of Western Ontario.

Rebecca Raby, 'Polite, Well-dressed, and On Time: Secondary School Conduct Codes and the Production of Docile Citizens', *Canadian Review of Sociology and Anthropology* 42, 1 (2005): 71–92. This paper has been both edited to suit the purpose of this publication and reprinted with permission from the CRSA.

Rebecca Raby, 'Searching, Working, and Shopping: Is This Prolonged Youth?'. Excerpted and reprinted by permission of the author.

Marilee Reimer and Adele Mueller, 'University Restructuring and the Female Liberal Arts Undergraduate: Does She Get "Value for the Money" at Corporate U?', Excerpted and reprinted by permission of Marilee Reimer. Drs Marilee Reimer and Adele Mueller are in Sociology and Women's Studies at St. Thomas University in Fredericton, New Brunswick.

Stephen Harold Riggins, 'The Value of Anecdotal Evidence'. Excerpted and reprinted by permission of the author.

Krista Robson, ' "Canada's Most Notorious Bad Mother": The Newspaper Coverage of the Jordan Heikamp Inquest', *Canadian Review of Sociology and Anthropology* 42, 2 (2005): 217–231. This paper has been both edited to suit the purpose of this publication and reprinted with permission from the CRSA.

Arnaud Sales, Réjean Drolet, and Isabelle Bonneau, 'Academic Paths, Aging, and the Living Conditions of Students in the Late Twentieth Century', *Canadian Review of Sociology and Anthropology* 38, 2 (2001): 167–88. This paper has been both edited to suit the purpose of this publication and reprinted with permission from the CRSA.

Randal F. Schnoor and Morton Weinfeld, 'Balancing Ethnicity and Sexuality: Gay Jewish Men Seek the Same'. Excerpted and reprinted by permission of the authors. Randal F. Schnoor is in the Department of Sociology at York University. Morton Weinfeld is a professor of Sociology and holds the Chair in Canadian Ethnic Studies at McGill University.

Antonie Scholtz and David W. Livingstone, ' "Knowledge Workers" and the "New Economy": A Critical Assessment'. Excerpted and reprinted by permission of the authors.

Kara Somerville, 'Life Cycle Events and the Creation of Transnational Ties among Second Generation South Indians'. Excerpted and reprinted by permission of the author. An earlier draft of this chapter was presented at the CSAA Conference, University of Western Ontario, 31 May–3 June 2005. Direct correspondence to Kara Somerville, Department of Sociology, University of Toronto, 725 Spadina Ave, Toronto, ON, M5S 2J4. k.somerville@utoronto.ca.

Tanya Titchkosky, 'Disability: A Rose By Any Other Name? "People-first" Language in Canadian Society', *Canadian Review of Sociology and Anthropology* 38, 2 (2001): 125–40. This paper has been both edited to suit the purpose of this publication and reprinted with permission from the CRSA.

Susan Vincent, 'Preserving Domesticity: Reading Tupperware in Women's Changing Domestic, Social, and Economic Roles', *Canadian Review of Sociology and Anthropology* 40, 2 (2003): 171–196. This paper has been both edited to suit the purpose of this publication and reprinted with permission from the CRSA.

Kevin Walby, 'Keeping an Eye on Crime Control Culture: The Rise of Open-street Closed-circuit Television Surveillance in Canada'. Excerpted and reprinted by permission of the author. Kevin Walby is a PhD candidate at Carleton University, kwaly@connect.carleton.ca.

Sandy Welsh, Heather Boon, Merrijoy Kelner, and Beverley Wellman, 'Where Will the Jurisdiction Fall? The Possible Regulation of Traditional Chinese Medicine/Acupuncturists in Ontario'. Excerpted and reprinted by permission of the authors. Sandy Welsh, associate professor, Department of Sociology, University of Toronto. Heather Boon, BScPhm, PhD, Leslie Dan Faculty of Pharmacy, University of Toronto. Merrijoy Kelner, professor emeritus, Faculty of Medicine, University of Toronto. Beverley Wellman, Institute for Human Development, Life Course and Aging, University of Toronto.